HEIST

HEIST

The True Story of the World's
Biggest Cash Robbery

HOWARD SOUNES

SIMON &
SCHUSTER

London · New York · Sydney · Toronto

A CBS COMPANY

First published in Great Britain by Simon & Schuster UK Ltd, 2009
A CBS COMPANY

3 5 7 9 10 8 6 4 2

Simon & Schuster UK Ltd
1st Floor
222 Gray's Inn Road
London WC1X 8HB

www.simonandschuster.co.uk

Simon & Schuster Australia
Sydney

A CIP catalogue record for this book is available
from the British Library.

ISBN: 978-1-84739-055-4

Typeset by M Rules
Printed by CPI Cox & Wyman, Reading, Berkshire RG1 8EX

For Geoff Garvey

CONTENTS

'The story has, I believe, been told more than once in the newspapers, but, like all such narratives, its effect is much less striking when set forth *en bloc* in a single half-column of print than when the facts slowly evolve before your own eyes and the mystery clears gradually away as each new discovery furnishes a step which leads on to the complete truth.'

Dr Watson's introduction to *The Engineer's Thumb*
by Sir Arthur Conan Doyle

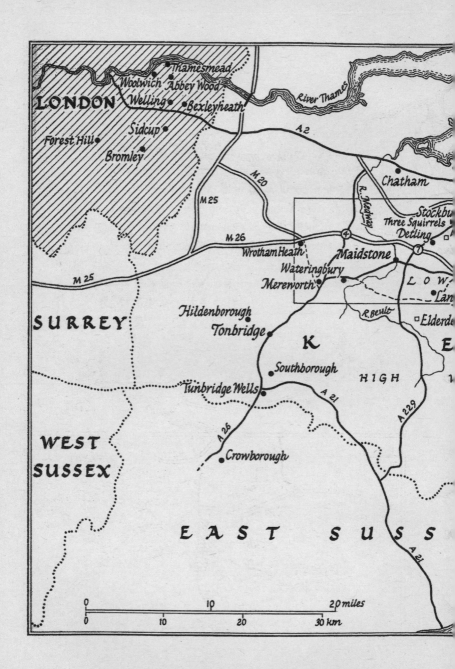

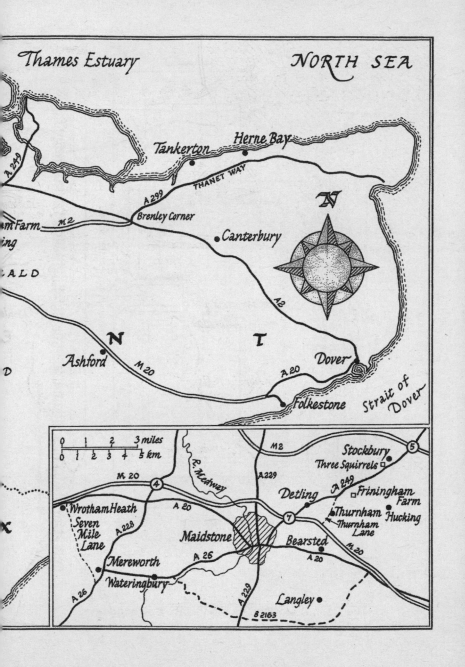

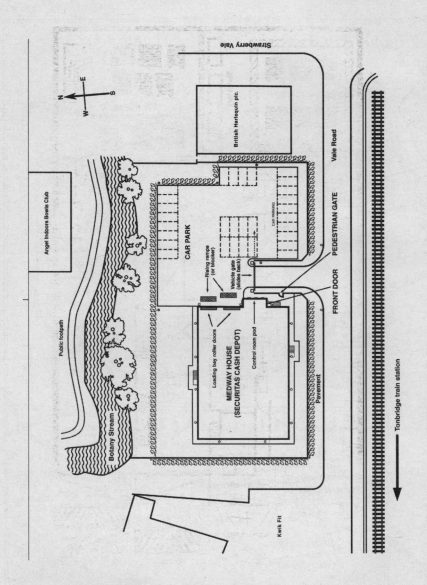

The Cash Depot and its Immediate Surroundings

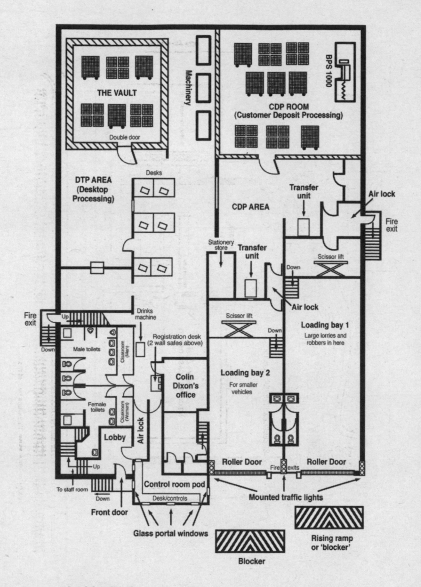

Inside the Cash Depot at the Time of the Robbery

Introduction

ONE IN 53 MILLION

This is the true story of a robbery, the biggest cash robbery in peacetime history anywhere in the world. It happened in Tonbridge, Kent, in February 2006, when an armed gang kidnapped the manager of a high-security cash warehouse, run by the firm Securitas, and coerced him into helping them ransack the depot. The robbers made off with a lorry-load of money, approximately £53 million. A large gang was involved, and the principal members had numerous associates. There are many characters in this book. But one man dominates the story, despite the fact that he hasn't been tried for the crime.

'Lightning' Lee Murray, also known as Lee Lamrani-Murray, is a young tough guy from south-east London who first made a name for himself in the sport of cage-fighting. Detectives investigating the Tonbridge heist believe that Murray was one of the main men behind the robbery, if not the ringleader. His name came up repeatedly during their investigation, and he was identified in evidence during two recent court cases at the Old Bailey as a gangster and a drug dealer, who planned the heist and took a leading part in the kidnapping and robbery on the night. The world's press have reported this much. There have been television documentaries in the United States identifying have the balls to be me. And, two, why the fuck would I want to come home to face an indeterminate* sentence? OK, I am in 24–hour solitary confinement in a fuckin' dungeon in Morocco, with rats and cockroaches the size of mice, and a[n] English prison is like a Hilton Hotel compared to this fuckin' place, but it's still four walls and a door. What was you thinking I was coming home to, beers and fuckin' buffets with fireworks in the yard, surrounded by beautiful girls with fat arses? Listen, my friend, a prison is a fuckin' prison. Who gives a shit where it is.'

Lee is married, with two children by his wife, a third child with his mistress. He was missing the kids. 'My main concern is to get out of jail as soon as possible for my three children, and if [that] means I have to ride it out, and hang fuckin' tough in Morocco, then so be it.' He went on: 'I'm a guy that always keeps faith, and I know, if I stay here in Morocco, I will at least get a release date. In England, I would never know if I would ever be released from prison again. Someone like me don't get released from indeterminate sentences. And what chance do I have of getting a "not guilty"? They have already made it sound like I committed the robbery . . .'

Lee acknowledged that, outside the UK, he had been named repeatedly in the media as the man behind the Tonbridge heist. 'I read in several newspapers and magazines that I am the mastermind, a gang leader, a Mr fuckin' Big, a Mafia member, and a notorious drug dealer that robs his rivals. I read this in magazines and newspapers all around the world . . . Where do they get their bullshit from? They missed something out. I blow fireballs from my arse and fly across London wearing a cape, and I have

---

*Judges tend to give indeterminate or open-ended sentences, with release subject to review at a later date, when dealing with the most serious offenders. A fixed tariff of, say, ten years is preferable from the prisoner's point of view, because they have a firm release date to look forward to.

a fuckin' 'S'* on my chest. I thought it was innocent until proven guilty, not the other way around.'

Murray declined to go into the details of the Tonbridge case, either to deny or accept any guilt, but he was enjoying the attention he received as the supposed mastermind of the heist: 'I know who I am and what I'm about and I don't regret one thing that's happened in my life, because that's what makes me who I am. How many tough kids on the street will grow up and get to where I got to? And I don't mean a prison cell. Probably one in a million. Or should I say one in 53 million?' he asked, unable to resist making a joke of the amount stolen in the robbery. 'I had it all. I had style. I was street smart. I could fight like a dog. I was a great fuckin' earner, with balls the size of coconuts, and I was a big hit with the fuckin' ladies as well. Some people might say I was flash, cocky and full of myself and, yeah, I did drive flashy cars, and like nice things, and wherever I went I threw money about like it was nothing. So what? . . . I was [a] confident guy with some big fuckin' dreams and, being a Scorpio, I did everything to the extreme.'

He acknowledged that some people disliked him. 'Them same people would probably say I was a bully, too, but a bully to me is someone that goes for easy targets and people who can't fight back. Me, I went for all targets. I didn't give a fuck who you were, or who you knew. My attitude was "you wanna dance? Then let's dance, motherfucker."'

Dismissing his critics as 'fuckin' nobodys' Murray blustered: 'I was the most talked about guy in London before the robbery and I'm still the most talked about guy in London now, and I'm sitting 3,000 fuckin' miles away in a dungeon. That takes ability, to be able to leave that kind of mark behind . . .

---

*S for Superman, presumably.

'My biggest problem was I got too big too quick, at a young age, and that's why the police were gunning for me so fuckin' bad. Not because I'm the suspected mastermind. But not to worry, I can accept that. If you want to be a big shot, then you gotta be prepared to take the shit that comes with it, like everyone fuckin' gunning for you, more than anyone else, and being put in solitary confinement, away from the rest of the prison, but I expected that, too. I'm a dangerous motherfucker.

'But I will be back, my friend, just you wait and see. Lee Murray always bounces back, even from the biggest of falls. Only tough guys can get back up and brush themselves off and I'm [the] last of the fuckin' tough guys!'

Be that as it may, this book is not all about Lee Murray. There were many members of the heist gang, several of whom have been convicted in the British courts, including a cage-fighting friend of Murray's named Lea Rusha. We start with his story.

Chapter One

NO HOLDS BARRED

1

As he warmed up in the ring at the Circus Tavern Nite Club, Lea Rusha harboured a secret. He was planning the world's biggest robbery. But first he had this fight to win. The Master of Ceremonies, Phil 'Boo' Walker, introduced Lea and his opponent, 'the warriors' as he called them, for the final fight of the evening. As he did so, MC Walker urged the audience to make some noise. 'If you are ready for the fight let me hear you go BOO!' the MC encouraged the crowd, mostly family and friends of the fighters.

'BOO!' they boomed back from tables around the ring, positioned close enough to the ropes to be showered with spittle, sweat and blood during the battle. It was a male audience primarily, a few wives and girlfriends perched on their partners' knees, drink glittering in their eyes at this late stage in the evening. Almost everybody had a pint in hand, and a fag on the go. Chicken and chip dinners, at £3 a head, had been consumed, the paper plates used as ashtrays. The carpet underfoot was sticky with spilt drinks.

The Circus Tavern, located on a dismal stretch of road approaching the northern entrance to the Dartford Tunnel, in

Essex, has long been a cheap and cheerful fun house for the working class of east London. It boasts of being 'the home of world darts since 1973', and regular host to 'American-style lap dancing with the lucious [sic] ladies from *Sunday Sport*'. On this Sunday evening in March 2005, the club was entertaining its low-paid, heavily tattooed patrons with a 'Slugfest', in which amateur fighters knocked seven bells out of each other in a free-form mixed martial arts (MMA) contest.

MC Walker made the introductions: 'Out of the blue corner from Canvey Island bringing to the ring a fighting record of three fights and three victories, welcome DAR–REN GUISHA!' Fair and short with a muscular physique, Guisha wore the customary long shorts and fingerless gloves of MMA fighters, nothing on his feet. Kicking and stomping with bare feet is part of mixed martial arts, also known as No Holds Barred fighting.

'In the red corner from Kent . . . LEA RUSHA!'

With short, dark-brown hair and a grim expression, Rusha was similarly diminutive, only five foot six, but overweight. As he raised his arms to acknowledge a cheer, Lea's little body quivered. His legs appeared comically short and stout. Still he got a good reception from the crowd, having brought plenty of mates along, including his best friend, Jetmir, who was screaming encouragement ringside. Jet was in on Lea's big secret. Together they were planning to steal Bank of England money stored in a warehouse in Lea's home town of Tonbridge, forty miles south of London in the county of Kent.

2

Lea was born five miles up the road from Tonbridge in Royal Tunbridge Wells which has always been considered superior to its neighbour, the residents typified as 'Disgusted of Tunbridge Wells', upper-class correspondents of the *Daily Telegraph*. Lea's parents were living over a shop near the Pantiles in the genteel heart of the town when Lea was born in 1972. His teenage dad, Robin Rusha, gave his occupation on Lea's birth certificate as 'professional footballer', but within a couple of years he was working as a tiler. Robin broke up with his wife, Tina, who took Lea to live in Sherwood Park, a scruffy estate on the outskirts of the spa town.

Although some streets are pleasant, many of the council flats in Sherwood Park resemble barrack blocks. A sign in the post-office window informs would-be robbers that, on advice from the police, no cash is kept on the premises. Prior to the smoking ban, the local Robin Hood pub smelt like an ashtray. A photo montage on the wall displayed the pinched faces and bare arses of its regulars. Lea's divorced parents moved around the estate with their respective partners over the years, living in a succession of council houses, often in areas the council put its difficult tenants. One such address was a terrace in Wiltshire Way, an unkempt place where angry dogs snarl and harassed mothers scream 'Shaddup!' at their kids.

Little Lea, as he became known, for he was never tall, left school at fifteen to work as a labourer, later a roofer, and he was in trouble with the police from an early age. When he was seventeen he broke into a house and punched the owner in the face for good measure, breaking his teeth. Lea gained a conviction for Grievous Bodily Harm (GBH), and was sentenced to 180 hours' community service later revoked in favour of four months in a Young Offenders Institution. Convictions for shoplifting, stealing and fraudulent use of a tax disc followed. Four days after his eighteenth birthday Lea became a father for the first time, but parental responsibility didn't calm him down. An argument in a pub led to Lea threatening a man with a knife, then bashing him over the head with an ashtray, for which he received his second GBH conviction, in 1991, and two years in prison. Shortly after he got out, Lea acquired a conviction for assault.

It was around this time that Lea met Lee Banda, a local man who'd learned the martial art of Jeet Kune Do (JKD) from followers of Bruce Lee in San Francisco, then returned home to open a JKD gym in Tonbridge, styling himself 'Guru' Lee Banda. Tearaway Rusha became one of Guru Lee's students and, for a short time, the relationship seems to have given structure and discipline to a wild boy who, as Banda says, could barely sit still for a haircut in his youth without telling the barber to 'fucking hurry up'.

In 1994 the friends travelled to the Philippines to compete in an MMA championship, with Lea winning a silver medal. 'I kept him out of trouble,' claims Banda, and indeed his protégé lived an apparently law-abiding life for seven years, until a drink-driving conviction in 2000, after which he slid back into his old ways.

Lea had a new girlfriend, Karen Backley, who bore him two children. They moved into a semi-detached house, at 12 Lambersart Close, Southborough, a housing association property on a new estate between Tonbridge and Tunbridge Wells. Neighbours gained the erroneous impression that Lea was a big shot in martial arts. The rumour was that, when he was away from home, Lea was prize-fighting. In fact he was most often travelling the country erecting industrial roofing, with his half-brother, Ollie, and cousin, Jason. All three worked for the Essex roofing firm, SD Samuels. Like many of the people in this story, there was something of the Walter Mitty about Lea who, despite his ordinary occupation, liked to show off and present himself as being special.

'He's renowned for being a bit of a thug,' says Robert Neve, a mechanic who lived next door in Lambersart Close. Robert would often hear Lea yelling at Karen and the kids and there were constant stories of fights in town. Rusha was banned from Da Vinci's nightclub in Tunbridge Wells as 'an unsavoury character', and banned from the Imperial Hotel in Southborough. In January 2004 he was convicted of affray after getting involved in a pub brawl in which a man suffered a serious stab wound. Lea served 12 months in HMP Elmley. Lea and Karen had broken up by now and he was dating Katie Philp, a pretty brunette, born in 1983, who sold cosmetics at Fenwick's in the Royal Victoria Place Shopping Centre in Tunbridge Wells. Lea's mate, Jetmir, worked in the mall as a security guard.

3

Back at the Circus Tavern, Round 1 of the fight between Lea Rusha and Darren Guisha got under way. There would be a maximum of three, five-minute rounds, the bout decided by knock-out (KO), submission or referee's decision.

When the bell rang, the boozed-up audience yelled loud and often obscene encouragement. Lea quickly got Darren in a neck hold, but the Essex boy freed himself, and punched, then kneed Lea.

'Come on, Darren!' yelled his mates.

'Fuck him up!'

'RUSHA! RUSHA! RUSHA!' chanted Jetmir in reply.

Jetmir was born in 1981, in Albania, the small, impoverished nation on the Adriatic Sea, opposite the boot heel of Italy. Jet and his brother were the only children of a Muslim couple named Alush and Hajrie Bucpapa, the family name pronounced 'Butch-papa'. Alush worked as a construction engineer, Hajrie was a school teacher. As a young boy, during the era of communist rule, Jet marched in formation at Asim Vokshi School in Bajram Curri dressed in a white shirt and a communist-red tie. He grew into a tall lad, well over six foot; he played basketball at school, and learned to speak English with a curious accent that made him sound South African.

Albania is one of the poorest nations in Europe and Jet wanted to move to the United Kingdom. He thought naïvely that if he got to the UK he might complete his education at Oxford University. But it was almost impossible for somebody such as himself to work legally in Britain. So, shortly after leaving school in 1998, aged eighteen, Jet paid to be smuggled across the Adriatic by speedboat – the favourite method for people traffickers using that stretch of coastline – then travelled north through Italy and France to the English Channel. Typically, at that time, migrants were smuggled into the UK in the backs of lorries, travelling by ferry from Calais or Boulogne, presenting themselves to the British authorities on the other side of the Channel as Kosovan refugees of the Balkans war. Migrants are usually granted the right to stay temporarily.

While the British authorities investigated Jet's background, he moved to London and rented a flat, probably with benefit money, in Deptford High Street, SE8, and attended college in nearby Lewisham. Jet wasn't permitted to take up permanent employment, so he had a series of part-time jobs. His search for work took him far afield, to Tunbridge Wells in fact, where he got a job as a nightclub bouncer and thereby met Rebecca Tapper.

Jet was not particularly handsome. He had an angular, even cruel face, his complexion troubled by acne. But he was tall and well-built, with a flirtatious manner, and Rebecca was one of several women to fall for him. 'We got chatting in a queue for a club one night. The first thing that struck me was how fit and muscular he was.' Rebecca lived in town with her mum, Carol, and stepfather David Conquest, both strict Baptists. They liked

Jet, too. Many people did. Rebecca: 'He was known locally as the Big Friendly Giant, because he got on so well with everybody.'

The couple married in December 2001, when they were both twenty. Jetmir gave false information on the marriage certificate, stating that his father was deceased. This may have been a story he was telling the authorities in order to remain in the UK; illegal immigrants sometimes pose as orphans to bolster their claim. After they married, the Bucpapas rented a ground floor flat at 34 Hadlow Road, Tonbridge, the last house of an Edwardian terrace near the town centre. Rebecca made a cosy home for them both. The kitchen was kept well-stocked and clean. She stretched a piece of diaphanous fabric over their double bed. There were flowers in vases, framed photos of the couple on the side and little notes on the kitchen message board. One from Rebecca to her husband read typically: 'Love U J.'

Jet was not an ideal husband, however. Although he didn't drink, he gambled, and he was a womanizer. In 2005, he struck up a friendship with a schoolgirl named Rebecca Weale, whose father worked for a salvage yard that Jet frequented. 'He told me he was married, but separated,' says Miss Weale, who saw Jet regularly in the months leading up to the robbery, though she insists they didn't become lovers. There were other girls, too, at least one of whom did become his mistress.

Rebecca Bucpapa had a steady job with an Alfa Romeo dealership in Tonbridge. Jet did all sorts of jobs. He drove a van for the *Daily Mail*. He worked for the BBC, and dabbled in buying cars that were insurance write-offs. Rebeccas's stepdad gained the impression that Jet was most at home in the black economy, as well as being disgruntled by low-paid agency work. 'He was working for various agencies doing security work, but it appears he wasn't happy not being his own boss, which is why he chose to work in other ways. His ambition appears to have been to own his own business – possibly running a car wash,' says David Conquest. 'Jetmir comes from a totally different culture than ours in England. Over the years I have begun to understand a little of how he sees things as an outsider in our British society [and] I would also say that his background from a troubled country probably coloured the way he operated . . . It is quite likely that operating in the black economy meant working close to legal limits or maybe beyond them.'

Lea Rusha later told the Old Bailey he met Jet when his girlfriend, Katie Philp, was managing a restaurant. Lea came to pick Kate up and the Albanian chefs introduced him to their mate, Jet. The boys began training together, including taking a martial-arts class Lee Banda held at the Angel Centre in Tonbridge, next to Sainsbury's, and just across the road from an anonymous building which Lea and Jet discovered was a counting house for the Bank of England. How they found this out is not clear. One of them may have known somebody who worked there, or perhaps they simply overheard staff talking about the depot in local pubs, clubs or gyms. Either scenario would be plausible. Lea and Jet were local, outgoing lads who knew a lot of people in what is a small town.

Lea and Jet couldn't rob the cash depot on their own, however. That would be beyond their experience. Little Lea was a thug, a bar brawler and thief, but not a bank robber. Bucpapa was an illegal immigrant and scallywag, not a heavy-duty villain. The lads needed help from somebody with more criminal knowledge than they possessed, or simply more chutzpah, or *balls*, as they would say.

In all probability, it was Lea Rusha who broached the subject of a robbery with Lee Murray, a south London tough guy who boasts of having 'balls the size of coconuts'. The young men were both involved in MMA fighting. Both trained at a gym in London called London Shootfighters. Murray was by far the more accomplished fighter. In recent years he had become a star of a hybrid form of MMA known as cage-fighting, winning a major event in Las Vegas in 2004. The Old Bailey would later hear that Murray was also a seasoned gangster who dealt drugs.

Rusha had wanted Lee Murray in his corner at the Circus Tavern for the Guisha fight, but Guru Lee, whom he asked first, objected to working with a second corner man. 'Because I don't know what techniques he knows and what strategy he will try.' In the event, Murray didn't show up at the Slugfest in March, 2005, but many of Murray's mates were ringside on the night, joining in the chanting of 'RUSHA! RUSHA! RUSHA!'

'Fuck him up, Lea!'

4

Round Two. Lea Rusha tried to kick Darren Guisha, but was too weary from the exertions of the first round to lift his fat legs. So he took the fight to the floor, smothering the Essex boy. For several seconds Guisha wriggled helplessly under Rusha's flab. Both men were breathing hard now, their faces red and streaming sweat, neck veins standing proud.

'Get his leg up!' ordered members of the audience, impatient for more dynamic action. Ringside, Jet was shouting himself hoarse.

'Punch him!'

Rusha started slugging his opponent wearily in the side.

'Come on, Darren!' yelled his supporters and, suddenly, Guisha was free. He got on top of Rusha, and began punishing the Man of Kent with his fists. The ref inspected the damage and, 3 minutes and 37 seconds into the second round, he stopped the fight.

The medal went to DAR-REN GUISHA! 'And don't forget an awesome opponent who came here to fight tonight,' MC Walker reminded the thinning crowd, 'LEA RUSH-A!'

Jet and the handful of mates who hadn't already headed for the car park gave Lea a half-hearted cheer. Lea shrugged. Fuck it, he'd show them. When he and Jet and Lee Murray pulled off the Tonbridge job, they would be rich enough to buy and sell the lot of them. He'd have a fucking big house, flashy cars, girls, drugs, everything. They were going to become multi-millionaires.

Chapter Two

LIGHTNING LEE

1

On his Mum's side, Lee Murray's family are from Bermondsey, a densely populated part of south London, between Tower Bridge and the Old Kent Road, which has traditionally been a breeding ground for professional criminals, especially armed robbers. Granddad Patrick Murray was an Irish-born docker, who married Gladys Wigley, with whom he had three children: the eldest, Barbara, being Lee's mother. After the war, the Murrays were among thousands of working-class families moved out of bomb-damaged, inner London to new council estates on the outskirts of the capital, the Murrays relocating to Abbey Wood, between Shooters Hill – so-named because it was once notorious for high-way robbery – and the River Thames, in the south-east corner of Greater London. The Murrays moved into 6 Godstow Road. Glad took a cleaning job at the new comprehensive round the corner. Barbara went to work as a hairdresser, then a telephonist.

Barbara was on her holidays in Gran Canaria when she met Lee's father, Brahim Lamrani, a Moroccan kitchen hand. Brahim was from the fishing port of Sidi Ifni, in the south of Morocco, where he says his father was an important man. 'My father is sharif! SHARIF!' Brahim roared at me when I met him, half-drunk in a Woolwich off-licence in 2007. Sharif is a title given to people with religious authority in Morocco, while the sur-name Lamrani is a notable one because many Moroccans believe it to be the name of descendants of the Prophet Mohammed. In recognition of this, Lamrani men are entitled to the appellation Moulay, which translates as Majesty. Neither Brahim nor his son would live up to such a grand moniker.

Brahim and Barbara's first child, Lee Brahim Lamrani-Murray, better known as Lee Murray, was born in St Nicholas Hospital, Plumstead, on 12 November 1977. Barbara brought the boy up on her own initially, as Brahim continued to live in the Canary Islands. Eventually he came to the UK, marrying Barbara in London in 1984. The following year she gave birth to a daugh-ter, Rkia, completing the family.

They were living a couple of miles from Abbey Wood now, at 11 Buttmarsh Close, Plumstead, the name Buttmarsh deriving from the fact that this was originally marshland beside the Thames. Lee attended Foxfield Primary School, where he met his wife-to-be, Siobhan Rowlings, three years his junior. But his closest associations at this age were with the boys on Buttmarsh and the surrounding estates.

The Buttmarsh Boys, as Lee and his mates styled themselves, included the Coutts brothers, Edward, Nicky and Roger, whose parents were Indian. Roger, known to Lee as Gurb, became a lifelong friend, and a member of the heist gang. 'We were happy kids. We used to play like normal kids on the estate,' recalls Mark Hollands who lived next door to Lee. Their games often had a violent side to them, however, with such evocative names as Torture Run Outs. The boys fought to establish a pecking order, and believed they had a duty to 'look after' Buttmarsh, which meant fighting boys from neighbouring estates. A skinny lad, Lee's favourite form of attack was to run into battle wind-milling his arms around his head with a manic expression on his face that, together with his sticky-out ears, earned him the nickname of the Alien, which he hated.

Dad, Brahim Lamrani, became a well-known local character. In fact, he was a figure of fun in the Plumstead area. Residents who couldn't be bothered to pronounce his Moroccan name called him Brian. When he wore his traditional *djellaba*, people laughed and said Brian was wearing his 'dress'. The Moroccan made himself a target for mockery. He had a curious manic manner, speaking quickly and excitedly in a mixture of French, Arabic and English gangster slang. When drunk, as he often was, he was virtually incomprehensible, and he could be a frightening, violent man.

There was a lot of trouble at the Lamrani household, with Lee having a difficult relationship with his volatile and domineering father, who had been largely absent from his life until he was seven. Now that he was living with the family in England, Brahim demanded respect and obedience from his son. He says that Lee was a 'bad boy'. So he chastised him, so much so that the police cautioned Brahim for mistreating the lad. Eventually Lee hit back. 'One day Brian actually went and hit Lee and Lee snapped, just turned round and knocked his dad clean out,' recalls Mark Hollands. 'Once he realized he could take down a big man like that I think that's what changed Lee into the man he is now — a thug.'

Brahim says he decided that if he stayed at home he would end up killing his son, or Lee would kill him. Either way it was an impossible situation and so Brahim left home. He remained married to Barbara, but from now on she brought up the children largely on her own, moving back to the Abbey Wood Estate with the kids, getting a council house in Grovebury Road around the corner from Mum and Dad. Lee made important new friends here, including Gary Armitage, whose Dad was an alcoholic, always in and out of prison. Some of the time Gary and his sister Kelly stayed with their grandma, some of the time with Mum. 'What start you get is what makes you, i'n't?' says Kelly. 'Gary's had no one there for him.'

Lee and Gary formed the nucleus of a group of tough lads who attended Eaglesfield Boys School which is where Lee met his boon companion and partner in crime. Paul Allen was a year younger than Lee, born in 1978 in Woolwich to Theresa Allen and a father whose name doesn't appear on the birth certificate, and seems to have been almost entirely absent from his life. He was a black man, of African descent, and Paul is of mixed race. Other friends the boys made around this time included the Basar brothers – Hussein, Kozan and Mustafa – sons of a Turkish Cypriot named Taner Basar and his English wife Doreen. When the Basars' marriage broke up, the boys moved unsupervised into a council flat in Shooters Hill, where they caused a huge amount of aggravation. Tenants called the police time and again, and eventually the council had the Basars evicted. It was the same story repeated: broken relationships leading to kids going off the rails, getting involved in crime and ultimately prison. It happened to Lee Murray, Paul Allen, Gary Armitage and Mus Basar. Lea Rusha's story was much the same down in Kent.

Lee Murray didn't achieve much at school and grew into an inarticulate young man who sounds less than intelligent when he speaks. But he is not as stupid as he appears. He enjoys reading, and puzzles, and writes a good letter, as I discovered when we corresponded after the robbery. Indeed he claims in his letters to be a very clever fellow indeed. 'I am a smart guy with an exceptional IQ,' he told me, adding: 'I'm in the process of writing my own IQ puzzle book. It will be called *Mastermind Book of Puzzles*.' At school, the only talent he showed was for playing soccer and he wasn't especially good at that; he failed to make the school team. Teachers at Eaglesfield found they couldn't do anything with him. So they expelled Lee, along with several of his uncontrollable mates, sending the bothersome boys over to Woolwich Polytechnic to complete their statutory years of education.

In truth, Lee's life was now on the streets, where thieving and drug dealing was an everyday activity. Boys typically broke into cars to steal the radio. Then there was a spate of burglaries at schools and council offices whereby boys broke in to steal computer memory cards which could be sold to computer shops. The tearaways spent their earnings on green (marijuana) and solid (cannabis). Some of the Buttmarsh boys progressed to Charlie (cocaine). Crack was also increasingly used, and dealt. Drug use brought the boys into daily contact with the Nigerian dealers who operated at Plumstead train station. When these dealers started 'jacking' their young customers, stealing their mobile phones and wallets, the Buttmarsh Boys went into battle. 'I remember literally everyone we knew has gone down there and kicked off with all these Nigerian boys, and they never come back to the area again,' says Mark Hollands. In winning this turf fight the lads inherited the local drug trade, and became professional dealers. 'It got to the point where our boys got into selling drugs, and the area just lost the plot. They didn't care about the area then. They just wanted to get as much money as they could.'

In adult life Lee Murray would be convicted of possession of cocaine and marijuana, and named in the Old Bailey as a notorious London drug dealer who employed Paul Allen as his right-hand man, and a network of drug runners including

Hussein Basar. One of Lee's best friends from this time was a local tough guy named Mark Epstein, a slightly older man who, like Lee, later became a cage fighter, using the ring name of 'the Beast'. Mark 'the Beast' Epstein says he earned his living as a crack dealer on the estates before he became a professional fighter, and he says Lee was a crack dealer, too. 'He made a lot of money from that.'

Drug dealing and violence go together, dealers using muscle to control their territory and make sure their customers pay. All his life Lee has been a violent man and a bully. He knows people say as much. 'Some people would probably say I was a bully,' as he told me, 'but a bully to me is someone that goes for easy targets and people who can't fight back. Me, I went for all targets.' The truth is that, as a lad, he was a thoroughly nasty piece of work who took pleasure in dealing out punishment often to people who couldn't fight back. He would punch people almost randomly in the street, for fun; and harass the man who ran the corner shop.

One day Lee Murray and Gary Armitage were caught by police in possession of a stolen TV, soon after which Gary got mixed up in an attempt to steal from a post office, for which he was sent to the Feltham Young Offenders Institution. Lee was soon sent there, too, the first of several custodial sentences for relatively minor offences – essentially punching people and nicking things. Mark Epstein recalls visiting Lee in at least three different institutions: at Feltham, Dover and Norwich.

The youth who emerged from Feltham Young Offenders was six foot three and slender as a beanpole. To beef himself up Lee started attending the gym, lifting weights and drinking food supplements. Paul Allen, six foot two and similarly skinny, became Lee's gym buddy. Before long, two lanky lads had transformed themselves into He-Men pumped-up on steroids. Paul had a black panther tattooed on his upper right arm and went by the nickname The Enforcer, presumably because he was enforcing Lee's control over drug dealing in their patch of south-east London.

The money they earned was spent on cars. Lee's first motor was a second-hand, red Vauxhall Astra, which he customized. Bigger, flashier cars followed. Of an evening he and his mates would congregate at Buttmarsh. As many mates as possible would pile into Lee's car and tour local pubs and clubs. The police stopped Lee regularly. They suspected that he was dealing drugs and tried to put an informer in his group, but failed to get sufficient evidence to prosecute. Lee was contemptuous of the police, and bold enough to mock and intimidate them on the streets. Officers who took an interest in Lee's affairs looked in their rear-view mirror to find him following their car. They got the impression it wouldn't be healthy for them if Lee found out where they lived. Some officers at Plumstead Police Station were scared of Lee, and there is a rumour within the station that certain policemen preferred not to confront the boy. 'I'm not going to disclose what I know about him [because] to be totally honest with you, he's a very dangerous man, do you know what I mean?' a detective constable who knew Lee as a youngster told me nervously. 'He's a very dangerous man.'

Another, braver detective says that, when he was a young constable, he had reason to stop Lee several times and recalls an occasion when he was showered with obscene, threatening invective by the teenager as a result. Lee told the constable that he would: 'Fuck your wife, I will fuck your sister, and I will fuck your mother . . .'

The police officer decided to get his own back. He glanced coolly at the pale girl in the back of the car. 'Is that your girlfriend, Lee?'

'Yeah.'

'Bit of a dog, isn't she?' Murray went berserk.

The girl was Siobhan Rowlings. On Christmas Eve, 1998, she gave birth to Lee's first child, Lilly Jane. Lee was 21. Siobhan was still a teenager. A few weeks later, in January 1999, Lee was caught up in a turf war between rival drug dealers that culminated in Mark Epstein and more than a dozen others being arrested, many ultimately jailed. But Murray got clean away. 'He was the only one that slipped through the net,' says Epstein, with admiration and wonder. 'I mean, lucky boy! But he's always been lucky . . . I went to prison for three years.'

2

It was around this time that Lee was introduced to mixed martial arts, a form of combat that combines boxing, wrestling and judo-type holds, first pioneered in Brazil, then popularized in the USA. To stop the fighters rolling out of the ring into the audience, American promoters enclosed the ring with an octagonal mesh cage. This also gave the impression that the men were so dangerous they had to fight in a cage, and they would stay in the cage until one man was declared the victor. Cage-fighting, as it became known, played well on pay-per-view TV in the States.

In the UK, things were much more low-key at first. The sport was run by enthusiasts at club level, with amateur contests staged in sports halls and nightclubs such as the Circus Tavern in Essex. Unlike traditional British wrestling, the fights were for real, and they were mostly clean and fair. Shortly before Christmas 1999 Lee Murray competed in his first amateur contest, the so-called Millennium Brawl at the Hemel Hempstead Pavilion. When Lee knocked his opponent out in the first round he earned himself a new nickname. 'He was so quick they called him Lightning Lee Murray,' explains fight promoter Andy Jardine.

Lee began to train seriously. He pounded the block around the Abbey Wood Estate, with his hood up, like Rocky, and attended two gyms on a regular basis. He went up west to London Shootfighters in White City to work on his wrestling techniques. Then he crossed to Peacock's Gym, in Canning Town, east London, to work on his boxing. 'He was a very nice boy, conducted himself well,' says Martin Bowers, who ran Peacock's with his brothers Tony and Paul. Martin Bowers saw Lee in the mould of countless young men who had been through the gym over the years, lads from difficult backgrounds, often with criminal histories, whose lives were given structure by sport. 'You've got sport, you've got a direction. You've got something. You've got somewhere you belong. Because even if you've got a broken home you can come here, and you meet people who you talk to and who are interested in what you do, interested in your well-being, they're interested in what you're doing of a night, what time you go a-bed, what time you eat. Once you've got a trainer, you've got someone like that. So even if you haven't got that at home you've got it in this environment . . . When you walk in, people know ya, go "Hallo, Lee, how are ya? When you out, when you fighting? How's your training going?"'

Peacock's was popular with local people and professional fighters. It was a boon to the community. But behind the scenes the three Bowers brothers were steeped in criminality, earning themselves a mention in Kate Kray's book *Hard Bastards*, as being among the 'hardest men in Britain'. At the time Lee was training at Peacock's, the Bowers were planning a series of robberies, the biggest being an audacious raid on a high-security warehouse at Gatwick Airport. The brothers' idea was to disguise themselves as security men, drive a fake Brink's-Mat van into the depot, and steal £1 million in foreign currency. Scotland Yard's Flying Squad found out about the would-be heist, bugged the Bowers' conversations at the gym, and arrested them as they attempted the crime in 2003, for which Tony, Paul and Martin Bowers were jailed the following year. Murray would have known about this, if only from the press coverage, and the case may have given him ideas for the not-dissimilar Tonbridge heist. But for the time being, most of Lee's energy went into developing as a cage fighter.

He had four professional fights in 2000, two of which he won, and though he was paid small money at first he started to see mixed martial arts as a career, especially if he could fight abroad where there was better prize money. When Lee married Siobhan on 24 November, 2000, he described himself on their wedding certificate as a 'professional fighter'. He even had the words 'BORN TO FIGHT' tattooed in Gothic letters across his back. Lee travelled to the US and Holland to train with well-known MMA coaches. And when he entered a contest these days a claque of supporters came to cheer him on. The self-styled Woolwich Massive was a vociferous and unruly mob. 'I kept them under control as best I could, [but] they just got ridiculous after a while,' says promoter Andy Jardine. 'I told Lee loads of times, I said, "You need to keep your lot under control."'

One of the friends who attended Lee's fights was Dave Courtney, south London gangster turned crime author who lived near Murray. Dodgy Dave revels in his tough-guy reputation. He claims in his books to have killed people. But he showed respect to Murray. 'For a sport, he gets in the ring and tries to get killed, right, *for sport*. Right? That's his chosen past-time, getting punched and kicked in the fuckin' face by a load of people, that's his chosen past-time. And don't mind 'aving it done to him in front of thousands of people.' Which is why Courtney describes Murray admiringly as a 'scary cunt'.

When he wasn't fighting, Lee liked to go clubbing in London, and these evenings often ended in a street fight. His Dutch coach and friend Remco Pardoel was walking with Lee near Leicester Square one evening in February 2002 when somebody opened a car door hitting Lee accidentally on the leg. Lee asked the guy what he thought he was doing and the men began brawling. Lee's opponent was with a group of friends who came to his aid, outnumbering Murray. Remco had to persuade him to run for it.

Five months later, Lee got into another rumble outside a fashionable Soho nightclub. The American cage-fighting organization Ultimate Fighting Championship had just staged UFC 38: Brawl at the Hall at the Albert Hall, showing how popular the sport was becoming in the UK. The party afterwards was at China White, the club in Air Street, London W1. Paul Allen got into an altercation with a pal of the American fighter Tito Ortiz, the so-called Huntingdon Beach Bad Boy. 'Paul got into a fight and punched the guy, then Paul got punched so I punched him,' Murray later gave an account of the fight. 'Then Tito came right at me, he hit me right on my ear, we clinched, I punched him two straight ones, two uppercuts and then he went down and I kicked him in the face. He didn't really KO . . . but he did go down.' Murray's US coach, Pat Miletich, who was present, says that Murray kicked Tito twice in the head. This unsportsmanlike behaviour attracted attention in the cage-fighting world, building Lee up in the eyes of some British MMA fans, while others thought he had behaved like a lout. Either way, it was typical of Murray to get into street fights. 'It is the story of his life. He is attracted to these kind of things,' observes Remco Pardoel. 'Those things never happen to me, but with Lee it just happens. It's bad.'

Murray claims that he soon got rich from cage-fighting, and allied business ventures. 'I was a fuckin' millionaire a long time before that robbery,' he told me. This is nonsense. Despite his

growing notoriety as a cage fighter, Lee wasn't earning even a
basic living from MMA. Nor did he have a job or legitimate business that brought in a steady income. He has hardly held down
a regular job in his life. He worked as a labourer for a while after
leaving school, but he hadn't done building work for years. Like
many burly young men of his background he dabbled in the
security industry, which is to say he worked as a bouncer occasionally. In 2003 Lee went into partnership with a mate in a firm
called Top One Security, hiring out bouncers to clubs. There
were fights with rival teams over territory. Lee was 'a little 'eavy
'anded,' according to Dave Courtney, who was in the same game.
The business didn't make him rich, though. Lee resigned from
the company within the year.

Despite this failed business venture Lee and Siobhan somehow
had the wherewithal to buy a £285,000 house in the suburbs,
which is to say an average-priced family home in outer London
in 2003. Not a mansion. Like many working-class people from
the mean streets of south-east London, when Lee made a bit of
money – from drug dealing, presumably – he chose to move out
to the nearby London Borough of Bexley, which includes the
suburbs of Welling, Bexleyheath and Sidcup, twelve miles or so
from central London. These were village communities surrounded by fields and orchards until the 1920s, when the railways
were extended from London and speculative builders smothered
the landscape with small, cheaply built semi-detached houses.
Most were bought on a mortgage by people of modest income
who hitherto would have rented or lived in council property.
Today the suburbs form a seamless extension of Greater London,
respectable, dull and increasingly tatty. Moving to this area was,
however, a step up in the world for Lee and Siobhan, who, in
August 2003, bought 32 Onslow Drive, Sidcup, a typical, three-
bedroom semi-detached property. Their new neighbours

included retired civil servants and a police officer. The lady across the road had won several Bexley in Bloom certificates for the excellence of her front garden, the awards displayed proudly in her porch. Like so many younger residents, the Lamrani-Murrays had little time for gardening and paved over their front lawn to make a double parking bay. They also added an extension to the property to give them a garage, an extra bedroom and a home gym for Lee. Money was apparently flowing from somewhere, because Lee was also driving a £50,000 Range Rover Vogue. He was in this car on Christmas Day, 2003, when he got involved in a very nasty incident.

Shortly after lunch Lee was driving his family to Mum's house in Abbey Wood. In the car were Siobhan, who was pregnant, and their daughter Lilly. Lee was driving through Bexleyheath when he found himself behind a slow-moving Volkswagen Bora. The VW was driven by David Meyer, a 38-year-old lorry driver, returning home from his mother Dorothy's house with his family: son David, 17, and daughter Julia, 14. Meyer slowed further as he descended Knee Hill, a narrow road which slopes down to Thamesmead. At the bottom of the hill, a frustrated Lee Murray found space to overtake, 'weaved in front and [then] slammed on his brakes,' as David Meyer Junior recalls. Dad drove around the silver Range Rover, giving Murray abuse, then the two vehicles proceeded onto the Harrow Manor Way flyover, where the Meyers claim the Range Rover started nudging their car. David told his kids to write down the registration number. As they searched for a pen, Murray got ahead of them.

David Meyer followed the Range Rover into Grovebury Road, Lee Murray driving to his mum's house at the end of the street. Meyer stopped further back, near the junction of Godstow Road. His kids were still looking for a pen. David Meyer then saw the Range Rover's reverse lights come on. Sensing trouble,

he turned right into Godstow Road, intending to drive through
the estate and away, but it appeared to be a dead end. So he
reversed into Grovebury Road, colliding with Murray's reversing
car.

David's son leapt out and began shouting at Murray. David
Meyer Jr was a big lad of six foot two, but he was no match for
the cage fighter who laid the boy out cold with one punch. Julia
Meyer shrieked. Dad reversed towards his son, hitting the Range
Rover a second time. Siobhan Murray, who had been getting out
of the car, was struck by the passenger door. Murray went for
Meyer. 'He got in the car and started attacking my Dad,' recalls
Julia, who saw Murray reach into their car to take the keys out
of the ignition, at which point her father bit Murray's arm.
Murray threw the keys out of the car, and the two men spilled
into the road brawling. Julia says Murray punched and kicked her
father. Residents came out of their houses and yelled at Lee to
leave the older man alone. Roy and Maureen Price brought the
children inside for safety, and allowed them to call their grand-
mother. Another resident, who says she saw Lee kicking the man
on the ground, called the police. 'I thought he'd killed him.'

Officers arrived to find Murray in the road, stripped to the
waist, using his shirt to staunch the flow of blood from his arm
where David Meyer had bit him. Meyer himself was flat out in
a coma. He was choppered by air ambulance to the London
Hospital where his injuries included a collapsed lung, and frac-
tures to his jaw and skull. Murray was questioned and released on
police bail. The police had to wait until New Year's Eve before
David Meyer regained consciousness, and when he came to he
couldn't remember anything about the fight; his son also suffered
amnesia. Julia Meyer told police it was Murray's fault, but a witness said the VW rammed the Range Rover deliberately, and the
ensuing fight was 'six of one and half a dozen of the other'.

Murray admitted hitting Meyer and son in self-defence, and maintained he hadn't kicked anybody. It then emerged that David Meyer Sr had a conviction for criminal damage from a previous road-rage incident. The case was far from clear cut. But the police took the allegations against Murray seriously.

The worry of this incident was not all that Lee had on his mind in the first weeks of 2004. On 25 January, his wife gave birth to a son, whom they named Lee Brahim. What Siobhan Lamrani-Murray didn't know was that Lee was celebrating another happy event almost simultaneously. Two weeks earlier his mistress, Nicola Barnes, a girl from Dartford, had borne him another son named Lenie Brahim. As if that wasn't enough to think about, the young dad was about to fly to the United States to take part in the biggest professional fight of his life.

3

Ever since he got into mixed martial arts Lee Murray had aspired to compete in America's glitzy Ultimate Fighting Championship, and he had managed to get himself on the bill at the 46th UFC, held on 31 January 2004 at the Mandalay Bay Resort in Las Vegas. The sell-out fight was being televised on pay-per-view TV, with ringside tickets costing $350.

The headline bout featured UFC Heavyweight Champion Randy 'the Natural' Couture, who was being paid $120,000 with an $80,000 win bonus. In the exaggerated world of mixed martial arts it is these sort of figures that are given as examples of how big the sport has become, but the reality is that most fighters on the bill were paid less than $5,000 to appear, topped up with a small win bonus. Murray was virtually unknown in the USA and his fee was correspondingly modest at $3,000 (£1,613), out of which he had to pay tax and expenses. If he won, Lee would double his money, but tonight wasn't going to make him a millionaire. Neither was it a title fight. It was a minor middleweight bout to fill out the card. Still it was his big break.

Cage-fighting in the USA is pure showbiz with fighters having gimmicky names and wearing costumes, not unlike old-style British wrestlers. For his walk to the ring Lightning Lee wore a convict's orange boiler suit and Hannibal Lecter mask. He had this bizarre outfit on backstage as his boxing coach Terry Coulter, a baggy-faced old bruiser from London, gave him a pep talk. Paul Allen was also present. 'Lee!' barked Terry, to get his fighter's attention. 'Nice and sharp – boom! Alright?' Lee nodded. His fists were his best weapon, and he hoped to punch his opponent out. To toughen himself for the blows that would come the other way, Lee started smacking himself in the head, gritting his teeth as he took the impact. 'This is your dream, man. Alright?' Terry continued, sounding like a butch Michael Barrymore. 'Your dream. Don't let no one take it away from you. What are we gonna do?'

'Fuck him up,' muttered Murray, focused on the dream.

'Fuck him up!'

Alwight?

Alwight.

The putative victim of this fucking up was Jorge 'El Conquistador' Rivera, a 34-year-old construction worker. When he reached the ring, Murray, introduced to the crowd as 'the battling Brit', stripped off his prison costume and stood nervously in shorts as skimpy as swimming trunks, muscles twitching, padding from foot to foot on the blue mat emblazoned with an advertisement for Miller beer. The lights were bright for the TV cameras and Lee's old enemy Tito Ortiz was ringside. Words were exchanged.

Round One. Aware of Murray's prowess as a puncher, Rivera moved swiftly to unbalance his rangy rival and soon both men were on the mat, where a more compact fighter has the advantage. Sure enough Rivera got on top, but Murray managed to put the American's left arm in a lock and, 1 minute and 45 seconds into round 1, Rivera submitted.

Murray had won! Ecstatic, he leapt on to the cage wall and raised his arms. *Yes!* He could hardly believe it. He had won his debut American fight, at the UFC, the victory beamed around the world, and the UFC wanted him back to fight again. This time he would get better money.

4

Back in London, police investigating the Christmas Day road-rage incident charged Murray with GBH and dangerous driving. As a result, the American authorities refused to grant him a visa to fight in UFC 48. The UFC was angry with Murray for not telling them he was facing criminal charges when he fought Rivera. Murray was unrepentant. 'What it was, when I fought [in] UFC 46, I was on trial for charges for attempted murder,' he told a journalist. (He was never on trial for attempted murder, but may have feared that was a possibility, or wanted to pose as a more dangerous individual.) 'I didn't tell them that I had charges outstanding when I went to America. When I come back and reapplied, they went crazy. They said, you didn't tell us you were on trial for murder and attempted murder . . . I said, so what? I didn't get charged for it. I got brought to a police station and questioned about it. I said, why have I got to tell you that for? It ain't something that I've been convicted for.' Murray contested the decision, but the authorities wouldn't relent,* and the UFC announced that Murray wouldn't fight again for them until he resolved his visa issues. Murray was left kicking his heels in Sidcup, the dream of becoming a cage-fighting star in America slipping away.

One night a friend of Lee's came to see David Meyer at home in Thamesmead. 'He said, "I understand you got in a bit of bother with someone recently . . . He's a very good friend of mine, and we'll give you £10,000 to not give any evidence, not [to] take it to court." I said, "It's a police case" [and] he sort of said, "It wouldn't be good for your children to give evidence . . ." It was a threat, but it wasn't a threat.' Meyer declined the bribe, and reported the matter to police. Around this same time, one of the witnesses from the Abbey Wood Estate received a visit from men representing Murray asking what she planned to say in court. She too made a complaint.

As he waited for his case to come to court, Murray signed a deal with British fight promoters Andy Geer and Dave O'Donnell to star in their Cage Rage contest at Wembley Conference Centre in September 2004. Although much smaller than the UFC, Cage Rage was the biggest event of its type in the UK at the time, televised on Sky Sports. Lee was the favourite on the night against Brazilian Anderson Silva, but Silva beat him. 'He was very, very disappointed,' says Andy Geer, who consoled Murray by talking about him maybe fighting in Cage Rage 10. But that wasn't until February 2005.

Two months after his surprise defeat at Wembley Lee appeared at Woolwich Crown Court to plead not guilty to dangerous driving and GBH. After a ten-day trial he was acquitted of dangerous

---

*It later emerged in court, in 2008, that the Metropolitan Police had passed intelligence to US Immigration about Murray's criminal activities.

driving, with the jury unable to reach a decision on GBH. A retrial was scheduled, but the Crown Prosecution Service decided not to proceed and Murray was acquitted. It was the first bit of good news he'd had for a long time. Still the Americans wouldn't give him a visa. His cage-fighting career was therefore effectively stalled when his friend from Kent, the even less successful MMA fighter Lea Rusha, had the idea of robbing a local cash depot.

Criminal conspiracies are by their nature secret, and nobody outside the heist gang knows for certain who first had the idea to commit what turned out to be the biggest cash robbery in history. But in all likelihood it started with the Tonbridge roofer Lea Rusha, or his Albanian mate Jetmir Bucpapa, picking up local information about the cash warehouse in town. It is probable that Rusha then shared their knowledge with the toughest guy he knew, Lee Murray, who now drove down to Kent to take a look at the job.

Chapter Three

THE CASH DEPOT AND THE GANG

1

Lee Murray may have come to Tonbridge to take a look at the cash depot prior to July 2005, but he was certainly there on 28 July, because he behaved so suspiciously in the town that day that he attracted the attention of the police: something that would happen time and again to the heist gang before and after the robbery. They were men who seemingly walked around with signs on their heads saying: 'Arrest me.'

Around 11.00 p.m. that Thursday two Kent Police officers in a patrol car spotted a silver Range Rover Vogue parked in Strawberry Vale, a lane that ends in a dead end near the Tonbridge Securitas depot. The lane overlooks the depot car park. There were three men with the car. 'We thought this looked suspicious,' says PC Stephanie Kirkin, who approached the men with her colleague, PC Ross Shearing. Lee Murray gave the officers his name and confirmed that he owned the Range Rover. The other men didn't identify themselves. They may well have been Lea Rusha and Jetmir Bucpapa. PC Kirkin asked Murray for his driver's licence, MOT and insurance. He didn't have the documents with him, so Kirkin told Murray she was reporting him. He had seven days to produce the paperwork at a police station. The constable issued Murray with a written notice and then drove off with her colleague. Murray may have driven off soon afterwards. But the gang evidently returned to Tonbridge to watch the depot more closely.

The cash depot, properly known as Medway House, was in the middle of Tonbridge. The high street was only a few yards away, flanked by the Angel Walk Shopping Centre and Sports Centre, where Rusha and Bucpapa sometimes trained. The buildings were adjacent to a large Sainsbury's. Just to the east, on Vale Road, alongside a parallel train line, was an area of industrial buildings. The first business on Vale Road was Kwik Fit, and next to this was Medway House. The nature of the work done inside the building was not widely known in town. At the same time it wasn't a complete secret. Medway House was a deliberately anonymous building: a large, two-storey, flat-roofed shed, built of blockwork, and clad in brown, corrugated metal. It could have been used by almost any type of business, except for the exceptional security in place.

On the front façade there was a steel door, reached by a flight of concrete steps. Next to this door was a pod, jutting out from the main building. Inset into the pod were the building's only windows: five portals fitted with toughened glass, so thick it was hard to see in. On the other side of the security pod, furthest away from Vale Road, were two double-height roller doors, painted green, in front of which were twin retractable steel risers, or blockers, striped black and yellow like wasps. The building itself was within a secure compound, surrounded by a high steel palisade fence, spiked and entwined with razor wire. It was under CCTV surveillance, and floodlit at night. A discreet plaque on one wall stated that the building was owned by

Securitas Cash Management Ltd, whose logo was three red circles in a black rectangle.*

Murray may have tried to watch this building from Vale Road when he first drove down from London. But this wasn't practical. Double yellow lines meant it was illegal to park outside the building. Also anybody loitering by the turning was under watch by staff, as well as CCTV. The closest Murray could park legally and still see the depot was from Strawberry Vale, next to British Harlequin plc, a company which made dance equipment. Murray could see across, through the palisade fence, into the car park of Medway House. But it seems the gang soon found an even better vantage point.

The cash centre was next to a public footpath. Following the path, the boys crossed a small bridge, over Botany Stream, which ran behind the depot, just outside its fence. The path brought them to the Angel Indoors Bowls Club, from where they had a fine view of the comings and goings of staff and delivery vehicles at Medway House. Bowling-club members later told the police they had seen men in the car park watching the depot. Depot staff also sometimes ate their lunch in the club, and it is possible the gang picked up information about the depot casually from such workers, or from depot staff they bumped into at the gym or met in pubs and clubs in town. It is the way such things are done. '[Criminals] hang around in pubs, and they listen, they target the face: *Oh that guy works in a cash depot. Oh right, OK,*' says cash-in-transit expert Jim Easton, who visited the Tonbridge depot. 'It's a long game for them, you know, you buy the guy a beer, you generally find out is he happy, is he not happy.' One

---

*Since the robbery the company has rebranded itself as Loomis, with a new logo, and the company no longer operates Medway House.

way or another the boys discovered the basic story of what Medway House did. Eventually they would get their own man inside the building to tell them all its secrets.

2

The Tonbridge depot is part of a cash distribution chain, linked directly to the Bank of England. All bank notes are issued by the Bank of England, whose headquarters is famously in Threadneedle Street, in the City of London. The paper money the bank issues is printed under licence by the company De La Rue at its high-security factory at Debden, Essex. Some of this new money stays in store at Debden, in a part of the building owned and staffed by the Bank of England. A proportion is trucked up to the Bank of England's depository in Leeds, to supply Wales and the North of England (Scotland has a separate system). A relatively small amount is taken into London for storage at Threadneedle Street. At the time of the heist the wider, national distribution of new bank notes was handled by five organizations that belong to what the Bank of England terms the Note Circulation Scheme (NCS). They were the Post Office, Royal Bank of Scotland, Halifax Bank of Scotland (HBOS), Group 4 Securicor and Securitas. These last two acted as cash carriers and counting houses for many large UK businesses, including supermarkets and high-street banks.

Prior to 2001, Barclays was one of those high-street banks that stored and counted its own cash. It was Barclays that built Medway House in 1980. The bank situated its new cash depot on Vale Road, Tonbridge, because it was within a triangle of three 24-hour police stations at Sevenoaks, Royal Tunbridge Wells and Tonbridge itself, the latter station only 300 yards away. In support of the original planning application, Kent Police assured the council that a cash depot on Vale Road would be 'easily policed at all times of the day and night'.

There are 28 cash centres like Medway House dotted around England and Wales, with additional depots handling coins. The Bank of England distributes the nation's money regionally in this way to avoid the danger of a single calamitous incident at one building destroying its stock of bank notes. This is important because, despite cheques and plastic, the public still uses a vast amount of cash. Approximately £37 billion is fluttering around the national economy daily in paper money. This money is checked, counted and stored by regional cash depots like Medway House.

In 2001 Barclays and HSBC outsourced the dull but risky work of counting and storing ready cash to a newly formed private company, Securitas Cash Management, in which they retained a share-holding. Securitas Cash Management is essentially a subsidiary of the Swedish firm Securitas, one of the biggest security organizations in the world. Securitas cash depots had been targeted by thieves before. In 1995–96, the company lost in excess of £2 million during ram–raids in Liverpool and Manchester, whereby criminals simply drove into the buildings, knocking down the walls, and grabbed what they could before running away. Such robberies became rarer as cash centres were more heavily fortified, with concrete blocks positioned in front of them. Inside jobs were rarer still but, when successful, such robberies can yield richer hauls. In 1983, a gang working with inside information stole £6 million from a cash depot in Curtain Road, east London, run by Security Express, a company later taken over by Securitas. That same year saw the £26 million gold-bullion robbery on a Brink's-Mat warehouse near Heathrow Airport. Again the gang had inside help. By and large, though, professional criminals consider high-security depots too difficult. 'Most robbers don't have the desire [to rob cash centres],' a senior Bank of England official explained to me. 'They look more to rob a van. It requires less planning.'

While this is true, there is anecdotal evidence within the security industry that cash centres became easier to rob after high-street banks such as Barclays passed their old counting houses into the care of private contractors like Securitas, because these companies had to turn a profit on small margins and they cut costs to do so.

The evidence is that Medway House was generally not as well-run as it might have been in the five years preceding the robbery, based on information supplied by former staff and security experts who visited the depot, evidence that emerged later in court, and the plain fact that the company massively upgraded security at the depot after the robbery, rectifying problems that perhaps should have been addressed earlier. Securitas didn't invest in the best security devices, and sloppy practices crept in. Also, the overworked, low-paid staff were not always vetted properly. In the blunt assessment of the company's own former Security Inspector, Steve Morris, security at Medway House was 'rubbish'.

3

As the gang would have seen by watching the depot, the working week at Medway House started on Sunday evening when four staff members opened up the building. Prior to 2001, the depot operated during office hours only, but after Securitas took over a night shift was instigated to boost productivity. The depot was operational 24 hours a day prior to the heist, with approximately eighty workers split between three shifts: 10.00 p.m. to

6.00 a.m.; 6.00 a.m. to 2.00 p.m.; and 2.00 p.m. to 10.00 p.m.
No money was processed on Saturday, which was used to clean
up the depot in preparation for the following week.

The basic business done inside the building was sorting and
storing bank notes. As the gang could observe from the car park
of the bowling club, money came and went throughout the day
in armoured vans, which turned left off Vale Road to the steel
vehicle gate. These vans are the sort seen every day in the high
street picking up money from supermarkets and banks. One of the
most important jobs Securitas did was the restocking of hole-in-
the-wall cash machines, or Automated Teller Machines (ATMs)
as they are known in the industry. Approximately 60 per cent of
the bank notes in circulation are drawn from cash machines, inside
which are five cassettes, three loaded with twenty-pound notes
and two with tenners, which is why the £20 is the most common
bank note in circulation.

Van staff also collected takings from customers, which they
placed in sealed plastic cases, booby-trapped to extrude coloured
dye if they were tampered with. Nevertheless 'across the pavement' robberies of van staff by armed robbers are commonplace,
with 1,033 attacks on security industry staff in the UK in 2006
alone. These robberies are invariably committed by masked,
armed men who simply run up to the unarmed van staff on the
pavement, grab the box, then run off. It's an easy way to steal a
few grand. So long as they don't get robbed in this way, van staff
place the plastic money cases in a revolving hatch in the back of
their vehicle, which rotates, depositing the case in an onboard
safe, which is emptied by cash-centre staff at the depot.

Staff working in counting houses like Medway House count
and credit deliveries to customer accounts, storing the money in
cages. The Bank of England also sends deliveries of new bank
notes to these centres to replace damaged or counterfeit notes,

which are returned to the bank to be destroyed. To ensure that there is always enough cash to hand, the bank insists that a substantial stock of money is kept in depots like Medway House. This stock of money is held in what the Bank of England refers to as its 'bond', and the sums involved are huge.

Anybody working in Medway House could have told the gangsters that the depot handled vast amounts of cash. This was self-evident to staff who saw money being routinely batched up into 'bricks', wrapped in colour-coordinated plastic to indicate the denomination of the notes. These bricks were all clearly labelled with a value. A standard brick of £5 notes wrapped in green plastic was worth £2,500; tenners were made up into £5,000 bricks wrapped in blue plastic; twenties into £5,000 red plastic bricks; and fifties into yellow £12,500 bricks. These money bricks were then loaded into cash cages of a standard size. A Bank of England cage filled with yellow bricks of £50 notes was worth £7.5 million, for example, and the vault at Medway House was stacked high with such cages. The precise amount held in bond at Medway House could only be estimated by anybody other than the most senior staff, but there were obviously tens of millions, maybe hundreds of millions, of pounds in the vault.

The question for the gang was how to steal some of it.

4

While the boys pondered this fundamental problem, the heist gang grew. It seems that Lea Rusha was responsible for recruiting at least some of the new people. Shortly after his defeat at the Circus Tavern, Rusha had stopped attending Lee Banda's martial-arts class, apparently having given up MMA, and almost simultaneously he threw in his roofing job with SD Samuels. 'He came in here one day, having finished the project he was on, and he said, "Look, I've got an involvement in a nightclub. I'd like to leave the company,"' recalls his boss, Fred Mills. Lea had invested in a pub in Hastings. He was also driving expensive cars. It was a mystery where he was getting his money. Lee Banda asked Jetmir Bucpapa what Rusha was mixed up in, and as a result the coach was confronted by an angry Rusha. 'He said, "Why are you asking questions about me?" I was shocked really. I said, "Because I care for you, Lea. How come you are driving around in a different car every week?"'

One answer was that Lea and Jet were doing driving jobs for a car-dealer mate of theirs who became a key member of the heist gang. Indeed, he may have been party to the original idea to rob the depot because, like Lea and Jet, he was a local man who could have picked up information about Medway House. His name was Stuart Royle and he operated a small used-car lot, which traded under a succession of names, but was known mostly as Wateringbury Car Sales. This tuppenny-ha'penny business occupied part of a Shell forecourt at 115 Tonbridge Road in Wateringbury, a village near Tonbridge. The space was just large enough to accommodate a sales cabin and twenty runarounds, advertised boldly as 'Quality Pre-owned Vehicles'.

Warranties Available . . . Finance Turned Down? . . . Try Us!

Most days Stuart Royle was sitting in the sales cabin under this sign. A portly, middle-aged bloke, with a gold bracelet on his wrist, and a fag on the go, Stuart turned 47 in the year of the heist, but he looked older. He was red in the face from drink, smoking and tension, flushing crimson when angry. Stuart had a weak, receding chin, grizzled with white stubble. His hair was snow-white, high and long, also receding and thinning. Stuart wore glasses; he was going deaf; he suffered

with an ulcer; and had a bad back, that meant he walked with
a waddle. All in all he was a sorry physical specimen. And he
had evidently not prospered in life. In fact, he was perpetually
broke. Still, he was a cocky bloke, with a high opinion of himself.

Stuart was the younger of two brothers, the sons of Cynthia
and Brian Royle, from South Yorkshire. Brian Royle's work as an
engineer brought the family to Maidstone, in Kent, where Stuart
grew up, swimming competitively as a teenager. His mum recalls
her son as being an exceptionally talented swimmer, thus introducing a theme to Stuart's life story: everything was
exaggerated. When he left school, Stuart went to work in the
naval dockyard in Chatham, giving rise to the legend that he did
important and possibly secret naval work, maybe in the Special
Boat Service. '[Stuart] was something special with the boats,' says
Mum. 'He had a special connection and special duties.' Stuart
never served in the Royal Navy. He was an apprentice ship-
wright. That was his occupation when he married the daughter
of a police inspector in 1979. When the marriage failed, Stuart
took up with a divorcee named Diane Sedge, who recalls being
swept off her feet by a young man, still slim, his hair not yet
white. 'If you met him, you'd think he was charming.' They set
up home in Derbyshire, where Stuart sold photocopiers. Diane
gave birth to twin girls in 1984, Chrissy and Vicky, after which
they moved back to Kent.

Stuart was hopeless with money, forever borrowing and
seldom paying back what he owed. Part of the reason he moved
frequently was to avoid his creditors. Diane discovered that her
husband was associated with criminals, and was light-fingered.
The police came knocking at their door several times, but Stuart
managed to avoid serious trouble. At the time of the heist, his
criminal history amounted to very little indeed: a conviction for

drink-driving and a spent conviction for theft. He was a lousy husband, though. He cheated on Diane, fathering a son by a girl-friend during their marriage. He then returned to Diane who bore him another son, James, also known as Jimmy. The family moved into Stuart's parents' home in Maidstone. Brian and Cynthia Royle were divorcing, and Stuart took over the family house, which is where the marriage reached its nadir.

One afternoon the neighbours saw Stuart give Diane a clip round the ear outside the house. Worse went on inside. Vicky Royle says her father punched her repeatedly and attacked her mother. 'I was in bed and Mum and Dad were in their room, which was next door to ours, and I heard them shouting and arguing so I got up and went in their bedroom, and Dad told me to go out, and I said no. Mum was up against the wall, and he sort of had her round the neck with his fist in her face, about to punch her, and he told me to go and I said, "I'm not going any-where," and I stood in front of Mum and I said, "If you want to hit her, then hit me first," and he wouldn't, [but] then he threw her out . . . Then he spat in her eye.'

Stuart and Diane divorced, with Stuart retaining custody of the children, though Vicky wanted to live with Mum. Dad said she could do as she liked when she was sixteen. In the meantime, they moved into a rented house at 88 Union Street, Maidstone, with Stuart's girlfriend, Kim Shackelton, a Chatham hairdresser nine years his junior. Kim is short and buxom, with a prominent gold tooth and a fondness for heavy gold jewellery and flam-boyant outfits. There is a piratical look about her. The couple opened a hairdressing salon at the bottom of Union Street, over a newsagent which Stuart also ran. He got his mum to work in the shop, even though Mrs Royle was in her seventies and the shop wasn't heated. Upstairs, in A Cut Above, Kim styled the hair of little old ladies, children and travellers, with whom Stuart had links. Kim's customers appreciated her low prices and grew fond of her little boy, who was deaf. It was a busy salon, but business never ran smoothly when Royle was involved. He got into a dispute with the salon up the road over poaching staff, and failed to pay his bills. One day the bailiffs came and closed the salon and newsagent. Among other creditors, Stuart hadn't paid the Kent Messenger Group for the local paper. Shortly afterwards, A Cut Above reopened in new premises directly opposite, and Royle was causing more aggravation. He got into the habit of putting hair in the bin of the charity shop next door, which led to arguments.

All was not well at home either. When Vicky reached her sixteenth birthday, in 2000, she decided to remind Dad of his promise that she could now go and live with Mum. Vicky found her father next door in the Style and Winch. Royle appeared to give his daughter his consent. Vicky went home to pack. As she did so, her father returned from the boozer 'all guns blazing', and demanded: 'Why did you tell the whole pub you don't love me?' Vicky was nonplussed; she had spoken to him in a quiet corner. 'Well, for all that, you can get out,' he said, 'and he literally picked up my suitcase and bags, everything, and chucked the stuff out the front door.'

Not long after this Stuart did a flit from Union Street, leaving unpaid rent of £5,000, and went to live on the outskirts of Maidstone, renting 1 Cudham Close with a gang of mates who treated the house as a boys' club: drinking hard and playing their music at all hours. The neighbours complained. Stuart, who always had fingers in different pies, was working as a warehouseman at the time. One day he opened up his garage to show his neighbour what he had apparently stolen from work, including clothes, keep-fit equipment, and booze. 'If I want something, I'll go and buy it,' his neighbour replied, declining an offer to help himself. Soon afterwards the neighbour heard that Royle had been sacked from his job. Then he vanished from Cudham Close, leaving more unpaid bills.

5

Throughout these misadventures Stuart Royle kept his car yard at Wateringbury. He traded cars under a series of names, and sometimes used the alias David Lawrence. But the business remained essentially the same, selling cheap, used motors, many of which were supplied by a friend named John Fowler, another man who features prominently in this story.

John was slightly older than Stuart, having been born in 1945, to lorry driver Harry Fowler and his wife Nell. The family were from Langley, a village south-east of Maidstone. The Fowlers separated when John was a boy and he and his sister were brought up by Nell in a council maisonette. Money was short and Mum had to go out to work in a laundry. 'Nell was ever so poor,' remembers neighbour June Underdown.

After he gave up haulage Harry sold second-hand motors, and John went to work for his dad. A small, quick-witted lad, always ready with a smile, John was a very good salesman. 'He was a wheeler dealer. He would buy and sell anything, mostly cars,' says Dave Payne, who worked for John at one time. '[He] always had the gift of the gab.' Fowler claimed to have made his first million by the age of twenty-five. He opened a Saab dealership at Linton, and bought a substantial country house, Elderden Farm, in a picturesque part of the Low Weald between Maidstone and Staplehurst. The property had been a hop farm, broken up and sold off in parcels when the old farmer retired. John bought the main house – a handsome, half-timbered, L-shaped building of uncertain age – and approximately three acres of land. He built a tennis court and swimming pool, and converted the barn into offices which he leased to a software company.

John lived here with a good-looking blonde named Linda Horne, a former synchronized swimmer, whom he married on holiday abroad. The couple had three children – Amy, Harriet and Jack – losing a fourth to a cot death. Aside from this tragedy, theirs was a good life. 'It was a great match,' says Linda's father, Derek Horne. 'They're what I call soul mates.' John was adept at making money, and Linda liked spending it. She enjoyed nice clothes, foreign holidays and fancy cars. The couple bought flats and houses around Kent as investment properties, and had sufficient income to keep a Porsche in the garage, a boat on the Medway and a holiday home in Thailand. 'We have a nice lifestyle,' Linda says. 'He worked very hard. He worked *very* hard. He was from a very working-class background. If you work hard you get rewards.'

John had not always made his money honestly, however. In April 1992 he was convicted, at Snaresbrook Crown Court, of conspiracy to obtain property by deception (passing fake credit cards through his Saab dealership), for which he was sentenced to nine months in jail. He served four. 'He lost his whole business through that. Up until that time he was a very, very well-respected businessman, and through that he lost so much,' says Linda, who claims John 'took the rap' for somebody else. 'And it completely and utterly ruined all his credibility.'

Fowler's bank accounts were closed; he had difficulty borrowing money and lost his Saab franchise. The Fowlers still received income from their portfolio of properties, and John continued his interest in the car trade by buying and selling vehicles from home. He employed two men at the farm, mechanic Norman Underdown and driver Mick Tasker, working out of a quadrangle of outbuildings adjacent to the main house: there was a small brick house which they called the 'Bungalow', a prefabricated double garage used as a workshop, another garage, an old stable and a shed, which had a lean-to roof. There were facilities to re-spray cars, and a steam-cleaning machine for valeting cars. John's sprightly father-in-law, Derek, sometimes lent them a hand. Vehicles were bought cheaply, spruced up and sold onto private buyers and local dealers, such as Stuart Royle, known to Tasker and Underdown as 'Slippery' because of his deceitful and unreliable ways.

John Fowler had been associated with Slippery Royle since the 1990s, when Royle took over Wateringbury Car Sales from a dealer Fowler traded with. Fowler continued to do business with the lot, which didn't prosper under Royle's ownership. Unlike John, Stuart was a poor salesman. Royle began to owe Fowler money, as much as £80,000 by the time of the heist. This large and growing debt irritated John, but it enraged his wife. 'Stuart Royle I hated, absolutely hated,' says Linda Fowler, 'because he owed my husband a lot of money . . . He's a conman, Stuart Royle, absolute conman. He has used my husband in all of this.' In an attempt to recoup his money, Fowler effectively took over Royle's car yard, which began trading under a new name, Monarch Retail Ltd, Fowler being the sole director. Linda explains: 'Stuart Royle ended up owing my husband a lot of money and my husband set Monarch Retail up so that Mr Royle could sell cars. Money would go into Monarch Retail, in theory, to pay my husband back.' But Royle didn't sell many cars and the debt grew.

A court would later hear that the Tonbridge gang used Elderden Farm as a headquarters before and after the robbery. John Fowler admits he was duped by Slippery Royle into doing certain things in connection with the heist, as he was duped time and again by Slippery in business, but he says that if his property was used by the gang in the way the police believe he didn't know anything about it.

It is true that Royle had a history of conning and using people. He was not above taking advantage of family members, even the disabled. Royle employed a car washer, Martin Bloe, a man with learning difficulties, who lived in sheltered accommodation opposite the Wateringbury garage. Royle discovered he could get away with hiring Martin on a low 'therapeutic wage' which he did. Then he made him do more than wash cars. Martin manned the yard when Royle wasn't there, and often had to deal with angry customers. One day men came to the yard looking for Royle armed with a shotgun. Martin's carer, Sue Broughton, watched his relationship with Royle with concern. Although Martin had what she calls 'subtle' problems, he was prone to fitting when put under stress, and his supposedly therapeutic car-washing job was very stressful. Apart from the angry customers and extra duties, Martin complained that Stuart didn't always pay him properly. But Sue was reluctant to intervene because Martin also made it plain that he wanted to keep this job, which made him feel like a normal member of society.

Martin's other aspiration was to move out of sheltered accommodation into a flat of his own. Because of his disability, his landlord could receive rent money direct from the local authority. Royle suggested that Martin might come and live in the flat over his new barber shop in Maidstone, even though he may not have had the right to sublet the space. Sue Broughton remembers the agreement Royle drew up, asking the council for an inflated rent for the small, shabby flat over A Cut Above. 'I wrote to Martin's care manager with my doubts,' she says. 'I knew Stuart Royle and didn't like him. I didn't trust him with somebody who was as vulnerable as Martin . . . Stuart Royle is not the sort of

man to have genuine consideration, and be thoughtful to somebody like Martin. He hasn't got it in his bones.'

Although Royle was scrabbling around for rent money from
his car washer, he had expectations of coming into a large sum of
money. In fact he was boasting to friends he was going to get rich
because of a robbery. 'He told us about it [in 2005]. Everybody
knew [that] something big was going to happen, and he was
going to make his millions,' says Tony Gaskin, a Maidstone wheel
clamper who bought cars from Royle. 'He liked to tell you he
was a gangster. He bragged that he was a gangster.' But in Gaskin's
opinion, Royle was usually 'waffling'.

The boastful car dealer was effectively homeless when another
wheel clamper mate, a lad who went by the name Clamper
Craig, told him about a cottage in Langley where Stuart might be
able to stay. Redpits, as the property was known, was not one
house, but a cluster of buildings on a small plot of land off the
main road. There was an old barn, a summer house, a swimming
pool and a tumble-down cottage, where Clamper Craig had been
living with his stripper girlfriend, and a mate called Fat Pete. The
trio were moving on, so Craig suggested Stuart rent the cottage
with Kim. The landlord was a local businessman named Geoff
Crabtree, who was also developing a new property on the site, a
large detached house next to the cottage.

Stuart and Kim moved into Redpits Cottage with her son, and
almost immediately they started talking about buying the house and
its outbuildings from Crabtree. The asking price was £450,000.
Stuart put in an offer, indicating that he planned to buy Redpits in
conjunction with his son Jimmy and daughter Chrissy. Lea Rusha
was also involved. On 1 February 2005, Royle drew up an agreement with Kim and Lea which stated that, upon purchase of
Redpits, Rusha was to buy the barn for £250,000, apparently in
order to turn this into a home for himself and his girlfriend.

Stuart Royle's business affairs had always been tangled, and in the months preceding the robbery they became labyrinthine. What he did during this time doesn't always make sense, and one should remember that he was essentially a conman. He routinely dealt in half-truths and outright lies. But some of the schemes he got involved in have a bearing on the heist. Around the time he started to try and buy Redpits, Royle apparently lent £10,000 to a car dealer named Terry Lynch. This is odd, as Royle was usually broke. Nevertheless, Lynch says Royle lent him the money. Soon afterwards Lynch introduced Royle to a Swiss real-estate investment, described in the Old Bailey as a 'classic advance fee fraud'. In the months leading up to the robbery Lynch, Royle and several associates of Royle were all suckered into this scam.

While Royle was lending money to Lynch, and pondering putting money into real estate in Switzerland, he was struggling to raise the relatively modest £45,000 deposit which would be the first step on the road to buying Redpits. Stuart went to his mother for the deposit. Cynthia Royle was now 77. She lived in a small, two-bedroom bungalow at 33 Shaftesbury Drive, Maidstone, with her poodle, Scamp. Cynthia was happy here. She had good neighbours, being especially friendly with Ray and Ann Berry next door. Her two sons were local. Andrew, an entirely respectable man, quite a contrast to his brother, lived in a nice big house on the outskirts of Chatham. Stuart was a problem, of course. All the neighbours knew it. He had borrowed a lot of money from Mum over the years. Cynthia referred to these loans as 'subs', though some ran into thousands, and on one occasion a neighbour had been asked to witness a loan from mother to son, giving the impression that Mrs Royle was concerned Stuart might not pay her back. Still, she wouldn't say a bad word about Stuart.

This time Stuart wanted more than Mum had in her savings

account. He persuaded the old lady to sign paperwork that enabled him to raise a loan on her property which he could use as a deposit for Redpits. Mrs Royle is vague on the details. 'I wouldn't say he conned me. He just said he was taking a mortgage for it and he said, "Can I use your name?" And I said, "Yes.". . . . Not so much I said yes, he told me he was *doing* it,' explains the old lady, who told the Berrys that Stuart came to her with a piece of paper and ordered her to sign it, without explaining what it all meant.

Shortly afterwards, on 11 April 2005, Stuart and Kim Shackelton, together with Chrissy Royle, put down a deposit on Redpits. Geoff Crabtree allowed them all to live in the house rent free on the understanding they would complete by 10 June. Meanwhile, Mrs Royle continued to live in her bungalow, but with less peace of mind. If Stuart failed to make the repayments on the loan he was taking out, she risked losing her home.

Stuart was confident that he would soon have enough to pay off the loan, purchase Redpits and much more. He told the estate agent handling the sale of Redpits that he also wanted to buy the new, five-bedroom house being built next door to his cottage. It was being marketed at £600,000. This meant that Royle was looking to spend £1 million on property – an extraordinary sum for a man who, until recently, hadn't been able to pay his rent. The vendors received letters from obscure African banks assuring them that Royle was good for the money. He told his new neighbours that he had £2 million coming from an 'offshore account'.

Stuart and Kim failed to meet the June 2005 deadline to complete the purchase of Redpits, which meant they faced losing their deposit. Royle blamed his mortgage broker and insisted the couple still wanted to buy the house, in Kim's name only. (No mortgage company would have loaned money to Royle.) A compromise was reached. Shackelton and Royle lost half the original deposit, the remaining half being used as a new deposit. They had to come up with the full purchase price by 19 August. Royle ran around trying to raise the money.

The car dealer asked Terry Lynch for his £10,000 back. Lynch says Royle sounded 'desperate'. He gave him the money. Still, that wasn't enough. Tony Gaskin says Royle asked for his help in scamming his insurance company. Stuart wanted Gaskin and another man to back up a story that he had fallen down a man-hole at Redpits. 'There was a manhole cover that was damaged,' recalls Gaskin. 'The council hadn't fixed it, and he was going to say that he fell down it, and hurt his back, and he wanted us to say, yeah, we were there, we [saw it].' Nothing came of this plan and soon enough it was August. Royle and Shackelton failed to meet the payment deadline and forfeited the rest of their deposit. They were under notice to vacate Redpits now, and were warned they would be charged rent for every additional week they stayed there. But they didn't move. They threw a party.

Chrissy Royle had recently given birth to a baby boy, and Stuart decided to have the child christened at Redpits, with a party in the garden. He chose to hold this party on the day the estate agency Page & Wells were showing prospective purchasers the new house next door, the one Royle wanted to buy. Apart from the desire to see his grandson christened, it seems that Royle threw the garden party to disrupt the open day. He arranged speakers around the swimming pool, and turned the volume up very loud. The neigh-bours had become used to Royle's anti-social ways in the short time he'd lived at Redpits. There had been a huge, noxious bonfire, and he'd erected signs warning of a 'Neighbourhood Dispute'. But the volume of the music was beyond the pale, and it was of course very off-putting to anybody coming to view the house next door.

The principal guest at this raucous garden party was Chrissy and her son. Also attending was Chrissy's twin, Vicky, who had been estranged from Dad until recently. In fact she hated him so much at one stage she'd changed her surname. Stuart responded with a text message. 'You are completely disinherited and disowned,' he informed his daughter, blind to the fact that he had neither money nor property to pass on. 'You are not a Royle. You are nothing.' Since then there had been a thaw in relations. When Chrissy and Vicky turned 21, Stuart arranged for the twins to take a limousine to Brighton. Now Vicky was invited to her nephew's christening. It was more like a booze-up, according to Vicky.

Along with family members, such as Grandma Royle, there were also unusual guests at this christening. 'This is Lee Murray,' said Dad, presenting the cage fighter to Vicky. Lea Rusha and other people associated with the heist were also present. In fact, the christening party seems to have been used as a cover for a gang meeting, a low-rent equivalent of the wedding scene in *The Godfather*. As the family celebrated outside in the sunshine, Stuart led his criminal associates into the stygian recesses of Redpits Cottage to talk darkly of business. Vicky had reason to go in and found her dad talking conspiratorially with Rusha, Murray and others in the kitchen. 'Dad told me to go out. Quite sharpish. But I still had time to hear what was said: they were going to use "these cars" or "those cars", those were their exact words. . . And then they were just talking about money. They didn't say how much, or where it was coming from, they just kept mentioning money.' She later deduced they had been discussing the robbery. After half an hour, the men emerged all smiles and rejoined the party.

6

Stuart Royle apparently expected the robbery to happen earlier than it did, and he was already banking on his share of the loot. As time passed and the heist didn't happen, he seems to have tried another way of making a few quid. Royle borrowed money from up to thirty friends, including Lee Murray and Lea Rusha, then invested the cash in the real-estate scheme his friend Terry Lynch introduced him to. The story Lynch told Royle was that a big retail and business development, called Gottéron Village, was being built near Fribourg in Switzerland. An investor had pulled out at the last minute, jeopardizing the venture. Anybody who stepped in to plug the financial gap was promised very high returns on their money. Gottéron Village existed on paper only. But Lynch and Royle were foolish enough to fall for the scam, and having taken a whip-round from his mates that summer, Royle transferred $36,000 to bank accounts in Florida.

Soon afterwards Royle came to Lynch saying he needed all this money back, plus a huge amount in interest. In fact he expected to be repaid £500,000. When Lynch demurred, Royle told him that he had received death threats over the money, but Lynch 'would be the first to get it'. Royle then sent a mate named Sean Lupton – a burly, cross-eyed builder, who had apparently been one of those idiots who loaned money to Royle – to impress upon Lynch the need to pay.

Sean Lupton becomes an important secondary character in the heist. Aged 47, Sean was from the seaside town of Herne Bay, on the north coast of Kent, but now lived in a house he had built in neighbouring Whitstable. He was married to Therese and they had two teenage children. Lupton boxed as a young man and looked like a bruiser, with his pugnacious features and boss eyes. Sean was still involved in fighting as a hobby. He ran a boxing club for kids in a hall next to Herne Bay Train Station. Sean also had a criminal past. He was convicted in 1994 of conspiracy to rob a petrol station, for which he served 15 months. In 2007 he was named in the Old Bailey as someone who dealt cannabis with

Lee Murray and Jetmir Bucpapa, and may have played a support role in the heist.

Sean Lupton was certainly thick as thieves with Stuart Royle in the months leading up to the Tonbridge robbery, often meeting the car dealer in a fish and chip shop in Whitstable. Sean and Stuart may have been talking about getting their money back from Terry Lynch over their fish and chips, but more likely they were discussing the robbery. 'I thought [Royle] sounded dodgy. I confronted Sean about it many times, but he brushed it aside,' says Therese Lupton. Sean didn't always tell her what he was up to, and he had been particularly close with his affairs since his time in prison. Therese told her husband straight that she wouldn't forgive a second 'mistake' like the one that landed him inside in 1994, but she thought him 'too dim' to be involved in proper, organized crime. She does note, though, that Sean watched the heist movie *Ocean's Eleven* repeatedly in the run-up to the Tonbridge job. As we shall see, there are several similarities between the George Clooney movie, in which a misfit gang of crooks raid a cash vault in Las Vegas, and the Securitas robbery.

The whole business of Terry Lynch and the Swiss real-estate scam is hard to understand. It baffled detectives who looked into it after the robbery. One of the mysteries is where Royle's mates got the money to invest, unless it was drug money. Rusha later claimed in court to make a fair amount dealing marijuana with Bucpapa and Murray. His only other source of income at this time was doing little driving jobs for Royle, which brought in beer money at best. In fact, Rusha got himself arrested around this time driving a Mercedes Benz, from Stuart's garage, which police believed was stolen. Where Lee Murray got his money from had always been mysterious. He hadn't climbed into the ring to fight professionally since he was beaten at Wembley the previous September. Nevertheless he apparently had thousands to invest in the Swiss deal, and spare cash to go on holiday to Barbados with his wife and kids in the summer of 2005. Accompanying the family on this Caribbean jaunt was Lee's childhood mate, Roger Coutts, his partner, Fiona Neary, and their son.

Roger was probably Lee's oldest friend. He had picked up a number of criminal convictions since they were boys together on the Buttmarsh Estate, including stealing a car, theft and disorderly behaviour. Like Lee, Roger was a ladies' man, conducting an affair prior to the heist with a barmaid at the Duchess of Edinburgh pub in Welling. Fiona's nickname for Roger was Valentino. He resembled the movie star slightly, being slim and dark. In contrast to Lee Murray, however, Roger Coutts had made a legitimate career for himself. He ran a garage named Northfleet Transit that serviced and repaired Ford Transit vans, and had a sideline buying and selling cars with a mate named Nigel Reeve who ran ENR Cars in Welling. Roger's brother, Nicholas, worked for him at Northfleet Transit, as did Hussein Basar, one of the boys Lee and Roger had grown up with. Roger's other brother, Edward, hanged himself in 2005, around the time their father died. The Barbados holiday was an attempt to get over these deaths.

From Lee's point of view, the holiday was an opportunity to repair damage to his marriage. Siobhan had just discovered that Lee's mistress Nicky had given birth to his son, and was none too pleased about it. Lee's Dutch trainer Remco Pardoel says that Siobhan found out when she took her son round to see Grandma Lamrani in Abbey Wood and virtually bumped into Nicola Barnes and her baby on the garden path.

While they were in Barbados, Lee and Roger talked of other matters. Like Lee, Roger had moved out of the council estates of south-east London into the suburbs, buying a maisonette in

Bexleyheath. Now he and Fiona wanted something bigger. Murray suggested they buy his house in Sidcup. It may well be that during the holiday the boys also first discussed the robbery, with Lee recruiting Roger into the heist gang. Certainly Roger became a central member of the conspiracy shortly thereafter.

It seems the boys hoped to commit the Tonbridge robbery quite soon. When he got back from the Caribbean, Murray went up to London to have an electronic tracking device repaired. Electronic surveillance would be a key part of their plan to rob Medway House. Then everything was thrown into disarray when Lee almost got himself killed.

Chapter Four

STABBED IN THE HEART

1

Of an evening, Lee Murray liked to go gambling and night-clubbing in London, usually accompanied by Paul Allen. One of their haunts was the Funky Buddha in Mayfair: a pricey disco popular with footballers and Page Three girls. Leaving the club one night in September 2005 Murray got into a street fight during which he was stabbed twice, with the bizarre result that one of his nipples was almost sliced off. 'Every time I get into a fight on the street, it's usually when I go out to night-clubs,' Murray told sports journalist Jeff Cain. 'The way I see it, the only way street fighting for me is going to stop is I'm going to have to stop going out to night-clubs.'

Murray got into more scraps in a year than most men do in a lifetime, but this time he may have been targeted. With the likes of Stuart Royle boasting about getting rich from a heist, the fact that a gang was planning a large job had become common knowledge in the underworld. Established London criminals were already of the opinion that Murray was getting above himself. Rumours were going about that he was double-crossing associates in the drugs trade, and it was said he was now refusing requests from fellow crooks to join in the robbery being planned in Kent. In short, Murray had made enemies within the criminal community. Dave Courtney comments: 'He thinks he's got all the friends in the world, but he's not a well-liked man.' Courtney points out, for example, that Murray was definitely off Freddie Foreman's Christmas-card list. Freddie 'the Undertaker' Foreman, a former hit man for the Krays, was elderly, but well-connected. There is no suggestion Foreman was behind the attack on Murray, or had anything to do with the heist, but it is possible that a younger London gangster of his ilk wanted to pay Murray a lesson when he was stabbed for the first time outside Funky Buddha.

A week later, on the evening of Tuesday, 27 September, Lee visited a casino in the West End before going back to Funky Buddha. Common sense might have told Murray to stay clear of the club where he had so recently been attacked. His mum almost had a fit when she heard her son had returned to *that place*. But a glamour model named Lauren Pope was celebrating her birthday at the club and Lee fancied hanging out with Page Three girls. They wore fancy dress for the evening. Lauren came as Superwoman, her girlfriends in the garb of Barbie Doll, nurse and Playboy bunny among other male-fantasy figures. The party went on until 3.00 a.m. on Wednesday, 28 September, when the bar finally shut. A few minutes later Lauren's guests tottered out into Berkeley Street to hail taxi cabs to take them home. Watching from across the road, their backs to the Mayfair Hotel, were a group of grim-faced young thugs.

What happened next appears to have started as yet another Murray street brawl. As he tells the story: 'Did a bit of partying. Come out of the club and there was a big fight that broke out outside the club between a group of guys and some guy that was with a friend of mine. One of my friends got involved in the fight. I tried to help him, because about six or seven guys was on one of my friends.'

As Murray went to his friend's aid, he was stabbed by one of the youths who had been lurking outside the Mayfair Hotel. 'I got stabbed in the head first. I thought it was a punch. When I felt the blood coming down my face, I just wiped the blood and just continued to fight. Next, I looked down at my chest and blood was literally shooting out of my chest. I looked down, and I knew I had been stabbed in the heart by the way the flow of the blood was coming out of my chest. It was literally flying out of my chest like a yard in front of me.'

Although Murray was obviously the target, a general mêlée broke out. Men were fighting on the pavement and in the road, blocking traffic. Bodies slammed against cars, and into metal barriers. A motor scooter was knocked over. In the midst of this brawl, Murray was stabbed again and again in his head and upper body.

The clubbers who weren't fighting stood back and watched the violence, some with their hands to their faces. Others took refuge inside the lobby of the Mayfair Hotel. One man was on the ground outside the glass doors to the hotel bar being kicked. Murray was slumped on the ground outside the front entrance, on Stratton Street, surrounded by assailants who were kicking him viciously.

Then the police showed up. The would-be assassins fled immediately, some on foot towards Piccadilly; others jumping into a BMW that sped away, against the traffic, down one-way side streets. Murray also headed away from the police, staggering down Stratton Street, past Langan's Brasserie, smearing parked cars with his blood as he did so. He emerged into Piccadilly, which was virtually deserted at a quarter past three in the morning, and tried to flag down a taxi. The driver refused to stop. Lee crossed to Green Park Tube Station and peeled off his shirt to stem the flow of blood from the wound in his chest. He asked two girls in a car to help.

'Take me to the hospital,' he pleaded. 'I've been stabbed in the heart.'

The women, casino workers who had just finished their shift, helped Murray into the back of their car. 'I lay down in the back seat and the blood was squirting up to the roof with such force that it was streaming back down on to me,' he says. 'I remember thinking, "This is it, you are dying."'

The girls drove towards Hyde Park Corner, but soon realized that they didn't know the way to the nearest hospital. So they pulled over and called the ambulance service who sent a team to meet them. 'I lost so much blood that I was out,' Murray continues the story. 'Then I remember waking up in the ambulance with [a] mask on my face, and I tried to rip the mask off. I didn't know what was going on.' Murray blacked out again on the journey to St Mary's Hospital. 'I woke back up in the hospital on the operating table. One of my friends come charging through and they were shouting at him to get out because [of] the danger of getting an infection.'

West End Central police picked up two more wounded men from the fight: an 18-year-old youth in Hay Hill; and a 25-year-old at Piccadilly Circus. Both were taken to hospital where their condition was classified as stable. CID began their investigation, questioning club staff, and appealing to the public for information. They wanted to know particularly about a dark-coloured BMW X5 which had apparently transported the would-be assassins to the scene.

Murray underwent seven hours of surgery that night, primarily in an attempt to patch his heart and punctured left lung. He received thirty pints of blood by transfusion. His family was warned that, even if he did pull through, Lee might be brain-damaged.

Two days later Murray opened his eyes to find himself in a hospital bed, hooked up to machines, his head and upper body covered in bandages. 'They said to me, if it was the average person they'd be dead. They would have never survived it. They said because you're an athlete, and all the training you put your body through, that's what saved your life.' The experience caused Murray to turn philosopher. 'I think it's made me stronger mentally. I think it's made me stronger as a person [and] I think my day is already written for when I'm going to die and that's that. I don't think I can change the way I am. That's me. If I wasn't like that I wouldn't be the fighter I am, and I wouldn't be who I am.'

The police investigation made no progress and ten days later Murray discharged himself from hospital. But it would be a long time before he regained full health. His head and upper body were now criss-crossed with scars: he had a gash over his right eye, a slash across his forehead; a scar ran vertically down his chest where surgeons had cut him open like a chicken to access his heart. He had been stabbed in the heart from his left side, evidently by a right-handed man. There was a gaping wound under his armpit where the knife had also gone in. He had been stabbed in the left lung, leaving a puncture wound in the pectoral muscle; while a knife had scythed through his abdominals leaving another long, curving scar. Murray concluded: 'I look like Frankenstein.'

Some might say that Lee had always been a monster. Now he was a weakened one. Before the stabbing, Lee weighed 190 lb. Now he was 20 lb lighter. Yet when he came home to Sidcup he spent much of the time on the telephone regaling MMA journalists with accounts of his adventure, boasting that he 'died three times' in hospital, and was going to get back into training as soon as possible. 'I never put one hundred per cent in my training [before]. If I had a fight coming up, I'd train eight to ten weeks before the fight, and after the fight I'd go out partying for two months and I wouldn't train,' he told Jeff Cain. 'I think, now, once I'm recovered, and I can train properly, I'm going to put one hundred per cent into my training.' Andy Jardine advised Lee to put the cage-fighting on hold and concentrate on boxing, 'because boxing's ninety per cent head shots and not so much punching to the body, whereas UFC is a lot of wrestling, twisting, and stuff like that and I don't think his body would have been ready for that, not with all the internal scars, you know. That scar tissue takes years to heal.' Murray seemed unconvinced.

A reporter from the Ferrari Press Agency came to the house. The agency has been feeding stories from south-east London and Kent to the national newspapers since 1945. I started my career here. The reporter asked Lee if he would be interested in doing an interview about the fight, and his injuries. Negotiations were opened with the *News of the World*. Murray asked for £15,000. A more modest fee was agreed and he stripped to show the photographer his injuries. The pictures were dramatic, but the newspaper chose not to run them. Lee Murray wasn't yet a big enough name to warrant a feature in the *News of the World*.

A month after the stabbing Murray went back into training at London Shootfighters. His first session was videoed and made into a little film that was posted on his website, www.teammurray.co.uk. Murray was revelling in the fact he had survived the knife attack. The film featured ragouts of national-newspaper articles about the incident, followed by footage of Lee working on pads at the gym, the sequence concluding with the words: 'Heroes are remembered, but legends never die.' Lee vowed he'd be back in the cage by July 2006.

In reality, it was doubtful that any doctor would clear Murray to fight professionally in the foreseeable future. Fellow fighters were wary of sparring with him, much less fighting for real, in case they reopened Lee's wounds. His career as a cage fighter had been dubious for some time. He hadn't been able to obtain a visa to return to the USA, and was defeated in his one and only Cage Rage event in the UK. Promoter Andy Geer had been trying to fix Murray up with another UK bout, but hadn't been able to organize one. 'Then [the] incident at the Funky Buddha happened, and then it was all over. His career was finished by then.'

When he reviewed his options, Lee didn't have many choices left as to ways to make money. He had been trying to sell his Sidcup house to Roger Coutts for £340,000, which would have given him a £55,000 profit. But the sale fell through when Roger discovered that Lee hadn't obtained planning permission for his extension. Perhaps it was time to have a go at the robbery the boys had been talking about all these months.

2

Possibly it was vanity, or maybe it was a test for the plan he had in mind for the heist, but shortly after the stabbing Lee Murray began to experiment with changing his appearance. One of Lee's friends was a barber named Michael Demetris, a 29-year-old of Cypriot origin who had grown up in Lambeth, then moved to Bromley, not far from Lee's house. Lee and Michael were close, so much so that they spent time together on holiday in 2005.

A swarthy man with a scar on the bridge of his nose and a diamond set in his teeth, Michael ran a busy hair salon in Forest Hill with the gimmicky name Hair Hectik, the *k* expressed back to front. He had several stylists working for him including his sister, Barbara, and cousins Mike and Maria. Michael's mother had run the salon, which was essentially a family business, before him. Also employed at the salon was a man named Vasos Kestar, and three girls named Eva, Nina and Maggie. Michael cut hair for the Channel 4 TV show *Streets Ahead*, and the salon had a loyal unisex clientele, women customers finding the exuberant, preening male stylists highly entertaining. The boys flirted as they snipped, chattering away, 'you know, man, I quite like older women,' straddling their female clients, the radio tuned to Kiss FM. The women workers seemed overshadowed by these young studs, whose mates were always dropping by the salon to hang out. Roger Coutts popped in. Lee Murray came to Hair Hectik most Fridays to have his hair trimmed and spiked with gel, which he thought a very cool look, before he went clubbing. The barber found Murray to be a very vain man.

Not long after the stabbing Murray told Demetris that he wanted to disguise the new scar he had acquired over his right eye in the second Funky Buddha fight. Michael said he had just taken on a girl who might be able to help. Her name was Michelle Hogg. Family called her Chelle for short. Michael called her Miche, or Sweetie. She was slightly older than Murray and Demetris, born in 1974, the daughter of Jeff and Elizabeth Hogg, who lived in a semi-detached house on Shooters Hill, overlooking the streets of Plumstead where Murray and his mates grew up. Michelle later discovered that they had friends in common. The Hoggs were, however, respectable people. Jeff Hogg was a former Metropolitan Police officer, a constable with the River Police. Now retired from the force, he worked on the railways. Mum was musical. She played guitar in local pubs, and had the look of an ageing hippie. Michelle was multi-talented. She played the clarinet, painted, drew and made things. She was also a highly-strung girl who appeared much younger than her years, partly because she was so small and timid. It is also true to say that Michelle was a plain little woman, with prominent birth marks on her forehead and left cheek, blemishes she hid by wearing her hair long. Neighbours on Shooters Hill, who had known Chelle all her life, liked her very much. 'She is innocent in her outlook to life,' the lady next door told me, describing Michelle as a 'childlike character, sweet and naïve,' adding, 'Please paint Michelle in a kind light.'

After leaving home, Michelle rented a flat just around the corner from her parents, whom she still called Mummy and Daddy, in Vicarage Park, next to Plumstead Common. She had a boyfriend for a while, but lived alone in the flat, and made a good impression on her landlady. 'She was a very nice girl,' says Sylvia Purnell, 'a good-hearted, very likeable person.' Michelle worked for years on the make-up counters at Selfridges in Oxford Street, latterly employed by Estée Lauder: the same work Lea Rusha's girlfriend Katie did down in Tunbridge Wells. In the mid-1990s, Michelle took a course in theatrical make-up at the London College of Fashion, obtaining a BTEC Higher National Diploma in Theatre Studies, which included a course in prosthetics. She left Estée Lauder, worked briefly as a freelance make-up artist, then as a business manager with Diane Von Furstenberg, a brand of make-up products 'for glamorous women on the go', working out of Harvey Nichols in Knightsbridge. It was a sales job and nervous Michelle couldn't cope. One day after a bad meeting she quit. A friend introduced her to Michael Demetris, and, in July 2005, she went to work for him as a trainee hairdresser in his small, suburban salon, despite the fact the wages were half what she earned in the West End. 'I just wanted to cut hair,' she later said of this career change, claiming hair cutting was now her 'passion'.

The first time Michelle saw Lee Murray in the salon she was struck by how big he was. Looking up at the fighter, little Michelle felt that Lee filled the doorway at Hair Hectik. In November,

Michael asked Michelle to bring in her concealers and other specialist make-up products from home so she could do a special job on Lee, who showed Michelle the horrendous new scar over his right eye. 'I felt quite upset when I saw [it],' she says. 'I thought, *You could have died.*' She was wary of touching the scar, especially with alcohol-based products, but Murray insisted that she made him up so that the scar disappeared. He clearly had a good reason to want to disguise himself, and this was more likely to do with the robbery than pure vanity. The gang were much closer now to attempting the Tonbridge job, crucially because they had an inside man in the cash centre, and the use of disguises would be part of their master plan.

Chapter Five

THE INSIDE MAN

1

The gang's inside man was Ermir Hysenaj, pronounced Er-meer Hoo-sen-ay. He was an old friend of Jetmir Bucpapa's from Northern Albania. The boys were roughly the same age. Ermir claims to have been born in 1979, making him a year older, but much of what Ermir said before and after his arrest was a lie, with the result that his background story is hazy. He was the son of a mechanic, and grew up near Jet in the Tropojë region of Albania, attending the same school in Bajram Curri. Despite having the same background, the boys were very different both in appearance and personality. Jet was tall, athletic, lazy and stupid, with a hard, proud appearance. Ermir was a chubby, industrious and clever young man with a soft, moon-shaped face and spectacles.

Ermir claimed to have a sister and a brother named Ermal, which may or may not be true. It is not even certain that Ermir Hysenaj is his real name. It is one of several names he used for convenience in the UK, which he entered illegally in 1999, having smuggled himself by boat from Albania to Italy, then across the English Channel in the usual way. He presented himself to the

British authorities initially as a Kosovan refugee named Bekim Alia.

While this young man of many names waited for his asylum case to be processed, he settled in Hastings, on the Sussex coast, studying IT at college and earned a living packing books and doing freelance translation work. In September, 2000, he met an English girl named Sue Lee, a nervous older woman from Pembury in Kent. The couple married in 2003, the groom under the name Bekim Alia. They then moved to Crowborough, East Sussex, once home to Sir Arthur Conan Doyle, creator of Sherlock Holmes. Sue and Ermir lived in a flat in Eridge Road, before moving round the corner to Prospect Villas in New Road which, despite the name, was like stepping back a hundred years in time, for the cottages had hardly changed in that long, and their new next-door neighbour, Hilda Stiller, was almost as ancient, being in her nineties. Hilda became friendly with the young couple, whom she learned to call Sue and Nick, Nick being the latest in a series of aliases the young Albanian used. The story he told Hilda was that he was a Kosovan refugee.

Ermir, as we shall call him, for simplicity, was a good neighbour. Indeed he seems to have been in many ways a very nice young man. He endeared himself to Hilda by asking if she wanted anything when he went to the shops. The old lady kept a key for the couple, and fed biscuits to their dog, Aggy, an aged bull mastiff whom they had rescued from a bad home. Ermir and Sue weren't a flashy couple. Far from it: they didn't have a car or even money for much furniture. Hilda gave them a chair. 'Neither of us are materialistic, or into money at all,' says Sue. 'We are sort of hippy types.'

The authorities eventually discovered that Ermir wasn't Kosovan. As a result, in August 2004 his application for asylum was refused. He returned briefly to Albania, where he applied for a settlement visa for the UK, which was granted subject to review. So it was that Ermir came back to live with Sue and Aggy in Prospect Villas, Crowborough, and resumed his translating work, apparently the model of an honest, hardworking young immigrant.

But Ermir lived a double life. Just as he lied repeatedly about his identity and background, Ermir went to great pains to hide the truth about his friendship with Jetmir Bucpapa. Even Sue appears not to have known the truth, saying that, to her knowledge, Ermir only knew Jet for a short time in the UK, and the men never socialized. When Ermir first spoke to police investigating the Tonbridge robbery he maintained that he'd *never* known Jet. Then he said they'd been introduced in Café Costa in Tunbridge Wells in 2005 by a fellow Albanian. This would be his story in court, where he added that he eventually got involved in Jet's drug-dealing operation. But, as noted, the truth seems to be that Ermir and Jet knew each other from childhood. With that in mind, it is possible that Jet asked Ermir – his clever, hard-working and apparently respectable old pal – to try and get a job at Medway House, the gang thus carefully placing their own man inside. It was quite possible to do this.

Ermir's version of events is that he signed on with a recruitment consultancy named Beacon Contract Services, who didn't at first offer him a job at the cash depot. Neither did he ask the agency to place him with Securitas. 'I was just looking for any work.' The agency backs up his story. But Ermir was clever enough to know that this agency supplied staff to Securitas on a regular basis, and staff turnover at Medway House was high. Such a job might therefore be offered to him eventually if he was patient. This is exactly what happened. Initially all Beacon could find for Ermir to do was cleaning tables in Fenwick's in the Royal Victoria Place shopping centre, where Lea Rusha's girlfriend

Katie Philp worked. Jetmir did security work at the mall for a while. Then, at the end of 2005, bingo! Beacon sent Hysenaj for a job interview at Medway House.

In theory, all agency workers sent to the depot were security-vetted beforehand, but Securitas left the vetting to the agency, and in practice it was very difficult for employment agencies (more than one fed Medway House with staff) to check out the background of an east European immigrant who kept changing his name, whereby even his date of birth was uncertain. Some agency staff were sent to work at Medway House without being properly vetted. Apart from anything else, there wasn't time to check Ermir out thoroughly. He had his interview on 6 December 2005. Six days later he started work as a Cash Administrator.

2

From his first day in Medway House, Ermir Hysenaj was able to feed vital inside information to the gang about the Tonbridge depot. It seems that he passed this information to Jetmir Bucpapa, speaking in their own language on their mobile phones. Jet in turn told Lea Rusha who informed the others. As the inside information came in, the boys were able to draw up diagrams of the depot, and formulate a plan as to how to get past the security.

If we follow in Ermir's footsteps on a typical working day we gain a good idea of the levels of security in place at Medway House, and how the depot operated. Having travelled to Tonbridge by bus and train, Ermir first walked to the pedestrian gate on Vale Road and pressed the buzzer. Many cash depots have a turnstile pedestrian gate, so that only one person at a time can be admitted for obvious security reasons. Prior to the heist, Medway House had a simple iron gate which any number of people could walk through once it had been buzzed open. This was one of many security failings that were rectified after the event.

When Ermir pressed the buzzer, staff in the security pod looked out through the thickened windows to see who was at the gate, and checked Ermir against a staff list. When the gate was opened, Ermir crossed the yard and climbed seven concrete steps to the front door – a slab of grey metal reinforced with stainless steel. He was now standing with his face next to one of the glass portals, so staff inside could take a closer look at him and, if necessary, ask via the intercom for ID. A mirror was mounted behind, in case the caller was concealing anything. The doorstep was also watched by cameras. If they didn't open up quickly, there was a doorbell to push. Eventually the door opened and in Ermir went.

All this is relatively primitive security for a cash depot. Other buildings use biometric entry systems, whereby staff identify themselves by pressing their fingerprints to an electronic pad, or have their irises scanned. Such devices are usually used in conjunction with weight sensors underfoot which check the caller against a record of what this person should weigh. Doors won't open if a visitor is too light or too heavy. The idea is that, even if a gang cut off a worker's finger, and pressed the severed digit against the sensor, the door wouldn't operate. Certainly they couldn't just stroll in behind an authorized member of staff. But none of this sophisticated technology was employed at Medway House, which was basically an old cash centre run on the cheap.*

---

*Securitas denies it was run on the cheap. Security Director Paul Fullicks said in explanation of the relatively basic security at the depot: 'The level of security in place at that location was thought to be commensurate with the threat.'

When the front door slammed shut, Ermir found himself in the lobby of the building, its concrete walls painted grey. The lobby was brightly lit and under 24-hour CCTV surveillance. Ermir had been told when he got the job that there were more than sixty cameras scanning the depot, six of them hidden. He was being watched constantly. Pictures were recorded in colour on a hard disc, and additionally broadcast live to outside agencies.

There was a glass portal in the lobby, so Control Room staff inside the pod could see who had entered the building, and hold them if need be. Workers who arrived early for their shift could turn left and go upstairs to the staff room on a mezzanine level. Here for their comfort and convenience there were easy chairs, a TV, a microwave oven and fridge. Plant machinery was also housed upstairs. In order to enter the main part of the building, where the money is, staff had to come back downstairs and pass through a security door into the 'air lock', which is the depot's principal defence against robbers. Once through the first air lock door, the visitor was in a man trap, a short, sealed passage, at the end of which was a second door, which the pod controller opened electronically. In theory, the two air-lock doors couldn't be opened at once, preventing robbers from charging into the building.

While he was receiving his induction training at Medway House, Ermir asked his co-worker Matthew Harmer about these doors. 'He asked why both doors couldn't be opened at once,' recalls Harmer. 'I told him because the alarms would go off.' Ermir also asked whether there was 'steel in the walls', indicating perhaps that the gang were considering a ram-raid. Harmer thought these questions odd, but probably innocent. In truth Ermir didn't have to ask many questions to find out what the gang wanted to know. He was *given* most of the information. He was, for example, shown where the alarms were: little silver boxes mounted prominently on the walls. Initially, alarms were mounted lower down, so staff could press them surreptitiously in the event of a robbery, but there were too many false alarms with staff touching buttons accidentally, so the company moved them up onto the walls. This proved to be a mistake. Diagrams of the building were also displayed prominently on the walls, so the staff knew how to get out in an emergency; indeed staff showed Ermir where all the exits were and how to open them. It was a simple matter to memorize everything and tell Jetmir, who told the others, who drew up their own floor plans, marking doors and exits.

Once he was through the second air-lock door, Ermir arrived in the Secure Area, which was essentially an open-plan factory. First, he signed the registration book on the desk by the manager's office. Staff then went into the locker rooms opposite, one for men, one for women, where workers stowed their personal belongings, and put on special reinforced shoes, to save their toes from being crushed accidentally under the heavy cash cages. Ermir was told to leave his mobile phone in his locker. Mobile phones were banned in Medway House because of their cameras. (In fact, it was very difficult to obtain a signal behind the thick walls of the depot, but Ermir found a sweet spot in the men's locker room, and sometimes called Jet from here.) There were also strict rules about personal money. Anybody found with more than £20 inside the depot would be sacked. So Ermir had to leave his cash in his locker. Staff were subject to a body search before they went any further to make sure they complied with the regulations.

Securitas expected cash-centre staff to steal and they did. 'We would call it grazing,' admits Securitas executive Paul Fullicks. 'I would say there is a degree within the company [but] I wouldn't say it was commonplace.' Former executives say the practice

is indeed commonplace, with larger cash centres losing up to
£250,000 a year to staff stealing small amounts when the opportunity arises. Despite all the security, employees always found
ingenious ways to nick a few quid: rolling a note up and hiding
it inside a Biro, for example, or stuffing money into their underwear. A male worker was dismissed from Medway House after
money fell out of his pants. Staff were told not to wear baggy tops
for fear they would stuff cash up their jumper.

Also, cash-centre staff typically daydream about how they
would pull off a really big robbery. This is talked about all the
time within the industry. 'It's common speculation in every
centre how easy it would be to rob the centre,' says former
Securitas executive Erle Gardner. 'It [would] be canteen conversation . . . because the only time you realize how low-level security
is is when you are actually inside.' Management knew this. As
a result, they were deeply suspicious of all their staff, even those
with a perfect record. There is a saying in the industry that
model workers are the people you haven't caught yet. The company was also paranoid about what staff said about the depot
outside of work. Staff were warned *not* to talk about their work.
They were all vulnerable to criminals who might try to trick or
bribe them for information, or even kidnap them, and were given
an 0800 number to call if this happened (which Ermir thought
a bit of a joke).

Having cleared security, and put away his personal items,
Ermir walked into the part of the building called Desk Top
Processing (DTP). During the day, staff sitting at desks counted
relatively small amounts of money, for shops and such like, using
tills essentially. Money was put into plastic bags the size of carrier
bags, printed with the Securitas logo, the amount and customer details. The end of the bag was sealed to stop money falling
out. Staff used shopping trolleys, borrowed from Sainsbury's, to

wheel these plastic money bags to the loading bay for collection by van staff (who don't generally enter the secure part of the depot).

Just beyond the DTP, in the back left-hand corner of the depot, was the vault, in which the big money was stored. Ermir saw that the vault was a freestanding, double-height room, with a gap between its walls and the walls of the depot, which meant a ram-raid could never work. The vault door was also double: a solid-steel door and a second steel gate. Only senior staff could open both doors. To do so, they needed two keys.

Turning right, away from the vault, Ermir came to Customer Deposit Processing (CDP) where bulk consignments of money were dealt with. The nerve centre of this part of the depot was the CDP Room, which is where Ermir was sent to work on the 2–10 afternoon shift in December 2005. It was not a freestanding structure, like the vault, but the CDP Room had its own heavy steel door and a supervisor who checked everybody in and out, asking staff leaving the room to shake out their shoes and socks to prove that they hadn't stolen any money while they were working.

Throughout the day, large cash deliveries arrived at Medway House by van or lorry, the biggest vehicles being admitted to Loading Bay 1, on the north side of the building. The vehicles backed up to an internal loading bay, four feet high, inset into which was a scissor lift which raised to meet the tailgate of the vehicle. Bulk deliveries from the Bank of England came in green steel cages, which were unloaded by pallet lifter and manoeuvred through an air lock. Smaller van deliveries passed through a Transfer Unit, an internal hatch, which was more secure, because the loading bay doors didn't have to open.

Cash cages were trundled into the CDP Room where they

were 'split', that is opened up, and rubber bands and wrappers removed. A worker sitting at a desk sorted incoming notes by denomination into red plastic trays, removing Scottish bank notes and money from the Channel Islands; these had to be sent back to the Bank of England for repatriation. Ermir was one of those whose job it was to feed these red plastic money trays into the sorting machines. There were two such machines in the depot, the BPS 1000 and the smaller BPS 200. The big machine took up half of one wall and could count a thousand notes a minute, sorting soiled, torn and counterfeit notes into a reject tray, separating the rest into A–Fit and B–Fit notes, the former being of high enough quality to supply cash machines. The BPS 1000 ejected the money in standard bundles: fivers in bands of £500; tenners and twenties in £1,000 bands, and £50 notes in £2,500 bands. The money came out wrapped, with a label giving the amount, time and date. A worker combined these bands manually to make larger money bricks which they loaded into red cages called Super Sids, or blue Piano Cages (so named because they are the size and shape of an upright piano). These cages were wheeled to the vault for storage, bond stock clearly labelled 'PROPERTY OF THE BANK OF ENGLAND'.

Ermir liked his co-workers. He flirted with the girls, and got on well with the men, who tended to fall into two groups: older English blokes approaching retirement; or young immigrants like himself, who were generally brighter. The people were alright, but the job was lousy. Few of them enjoyed working at Medway House. The atmosphere of suspicion became oppressive, as did the fact they were working in a building without windows, with no natural light or fresh air. To go outside for a break, you had to repeat the whole security rigmarole, and few could be bothered to do so just to smoke a cigarette or buy a sandwich. Anyway, as Ermir discovered, the company didn't pay agency staff for a lunch break. They paid badly in fact, as little as £5.50 an hour, the going rate for manual work.

Although the company paid peanuts, they expected a lot from their staff and were quick to dismiss workers who fell short of their standards. Agency employees could be summarily dismissed at any time in the first thirteen weeks and often were. Workers were sacked for all sorts of reasons including lateness, drunkenness and theft. There was a very high staff turnover, especially in the run-up to the busy Christmas season when the depot was running at full capacity. Many staff left with a grudge against the company. Visitors to the depot were not impressed by the place, or its staff. Workers were using fire extinguishers to prop open security doors, in breach of regulations; there were broken locks that hadn't been fixed. The place was generally a mess. 'Inside, I have to say it was shoddy. It was grubby,' says cash-in-transit expert Jim Easton who worked with Securitas at the time. 'It was a little bit disorganized.'

3

The depot manager, Colin Dixon, was a big, middle-aged man of six foot three, overweight, with short, grey hair, spectacles and dimples. He was born in 1954 to Patricia and Thomas Dixon, raised on a council estate in Littlebourne, near Canterbury. Colin went to work for Barclays Bank as a teenager, marrying an eighteen-year-old bank clerk named Lynn Goodfellow, whose father was headmaster of Herne Primary School, just outside Herne Bay.

Some say Herne Bay is dull and full of old people, joking that 'you have to have a hernia to live in Herne', but Lynn loved the town and when she and Colin married they bought a house here, a four-bedroom detached property at 16 Hadleigh Gardens, a cul de sac on a hill overlooking the North Sea. They had a view across the sea to the Isle of Sheppey, and a shingle beach five minutes' walk away. Here the Dixons raised three children: Daniel and Dominic, with a long gap before their third and final child.

Colin went to work at Medway House in 1987, when it was still run by Barclays, and found himself employed, in the same job, by Securitas when the bank outsourced its cash operation in 2001. He earned a basic salary of approximately £30,000, plus benefits, the modest pay reflecting the fact that even the management of cash centres is considered a low-status job within the banking industry, a job given to solid, dependable, perhaps dull people. Years passed. Colin's life was one of uninterrupted routine. He did his job at the cash centre, overseeing people counting money. Lynn worked part-time for the Inland Revenue, counting money. The children grew up. Their eldest children moved away. The youngest child was with them, still at primary school.* The Dixons continued to live in Hadleigh Gardens, members of a stable, lower-middle-class community. Neighbours knew Colin worked in banking, but only one family in their street knew precisely what he did. 'He's very ordinary . . . a normal bloke, doing a normal job,' says neighbour Colin Boddington, who wasn't in on the secret. 'Pretty boring.'

Boring, except for the fact that Colin lived in the knowledge that he was at constant risk from what is called tiger kidnapping. This is when criminals stalk senior bank staff, then abduct and coerce them into helping them gain access to money, sometimes by holding their families hostage. In such cases there is often a

---

*The Dixons' youngest child cannot be identified, due to a court order, under the Children and Young Persons Act.

question mark over whether the victims were in cahoots with the gang, or innocent victims. The Northern Bank in Belfast had seemingly been robbed in this way the previous December. The gang escaped with £26.4 million, making theirs the richest cash robbery in British history at that time. With inside help from Ermir Hysenaj, the Tonbridge mob decided to carry out a tiger kidnapping on Colin Dixon. In doing so, they would break all records.

4

As 2005 drew to a close, and the heist gang dreamed of becoming rich beyond imagination, Stuart Royle's financial affairs worsened. Having failed to buy Redpits, Stuart and Kim Shackelton were living in the property in defiance of solicitors' letters asking them to leave. The owner Geoff Crabtree took them to court in October, with the result that they were ordered to vacate by 19 November, and told to pay Crabtree damages and costs of more than £9,000. Royle told the court that he still expected to be able to buy the house. 'Of course, he was really waiting for a payment for a certain event,' says one of his creditors. 'Even at the court case he said, "I should be able to complete in three weeks' time," or whatever, because he was obviously expecting some money.'

Just before Christmas, bailiffs closed down the latest incarnation of A Cut Above, apparently because Stuart hadn't paid the rent. 'They were there on Monday,' recalls a local shopkeeper. 'Tuesday they were gone.' As a result, Stuart's disabled car washer and tenant, Martin Bloe, lost his home in the flat over the shop. 'He couldn't get in and was forced to go back to live with his mother, brother and sister,' says carer Sue Broughton, who was sad to see her worst fears borne out. 'Martin was very upset . . . He was suffering seizures as well.'

In a desperate attempt to hang onto Redpits, Royle attempted a mortgage fraud. Kim contacted Promise Finance in Wolverhampton, telling the managing director, Alexander White, that she was living in a house called Redpits, which she wanted to buy. The cut-price hairdresser, whose salon had been closed, estimated her annual earnings generously between £120,000 and £150,000. She introduced Mr White to David Lawrence, her 'financial adviser'. This was Stuart Royle. He said Redpits had been valued at £750,000, but his client only wanted a £443,000 mortgage, which was agreed in principle.

While chatting with Alexander White, Lawrence mentioned that he'd recently lost £600,000 on 'an investment scam' and was going to court about it. This may have been a reference to Royle's unhappy investment in the Swiss real-estate scheme. Terry Lynch claims that during a meeting at Royle's house around this time he was threatened by the boss-eyed builder Sean Lupton over the money Sean and Stuart said he owed them. Royle was now saying that he wanted £3 million back from his original investment. Unable to pay him such a huge sum, and scared of what might happen to him when he didn't, Terry Lynch and his wife moved to a secret address. This was the chaotic state of Stuart Royle's life as the Tonbridge gang prepared in earnest for the robbery, which was now only weeks away.

Chapter Six

MOTORS, MASKS AND MAKE-UP

1

The inside man, Ermir Hysenaj, may have given the gang the name of the cash-depot manager, Colin Dixon, and passed on the fact that Colin was married with a young child. This was common knowledge within the depot, but vital intelligence to the gang who had decided to kidnap the Dixons, coercing Colin into helping them by making it clear that they would hurt or even kill his wife and child if he failed to comply, or double-cross them. First they had to find out where the family lived, of course, and, surprising as it may seem, they struggled for a long time to get the Dixons' home address.

Colin did not tell his work colleagues his home address, and Dixon is a commonplace name, which made the task of finding where he lived difficult. Also, Colin's home-telephone number was ex-directory. The gang had a physical description of the manager, of course, and it seems they attempted to follow him on his drive home from the depot. Murray may have been trying to do this on and off since the previous summer when he was first seen lurking around Medway House. But Colin had been trained to

take precautions. He and Lynn owned two cars, and they alter-
nated them, swapping between a silver Nissan Almera and a
dark-coloured Ford Ka. Also, Colin didn't use the same parking
bay at Medway House every day, and varied his journey to and
from work. He calculated he used at least 46 different ways home.
So it wasn't at all easy to trail him. But they kept working on it.

In the meantime the gangsters gave some thought to *how* they
would kidnap Colin and his family. Once they had the home
address, they could do so by force, bursting into the house, guns
drawn, but this was high-risk. It would be better to trick the
Dixons. The solution the boys arrived at was that two members
of the gang – it seems Murray and Rusha saw themselves in this
role from the start – would dress up as policemen and affect a
bogus arrest on Colin on his way home. Having transferred the
manager into the care of other members of the gang, who would
take him to a safe location, the fake coppers would then call at the
family home, tell Lynn Dixon that her husband had been in an
accident, and ask her and the child to come with them to the
hospital. When they had the whole family in their hideout, the
gang would make it clear to Colin that he had no choice other
than do what he was told.

There was a flaw in this plan. Cash-industry employees are
trained to be suspicious of anybody who stops them on the road,
or comes to their home unexpectedly. They are warned not to
automatically trust a person in police uniform, because criminals
can obtain police uniforms. If Colin was stopped by police in his
car, there was a standard routine he should have abided by. He
was trained not to get out of his car, but show the officer a
printed slip of paper that identified him as a cash-centre worker,
at which point he would offer to follow the police to their station where he would answer their questions. The gang were
either ignorant of this training, or confident Colin would not

follow procedure, because he was complacent or, as would later be suggested in court, he was in cahoots with the gang from the start. It is also possible the gang simply hoped for the best. As we shall see, there was an element of last-minute improvisation to the heist.

Even if Murray and Rusha carried out both kidnappings, they would need the help of others to transfer their victims to their lair, to guard them and take part in the robbery itself. Paul Allen could be relied upon to run errands and generally help out. Another old friend of Murray was also enrolled. Roger Coutts now became a core member of the gang. Usefully, he had access to an old ship container in his friend Nigel's car yard in Welling where they could stash some of the money after the raid.

Stuart Royle was just as active in the conspiracy as Coutts. Fat and middle-aged, he wasn't ideally suited to the physical work of robbing, but he had experience of following people. Recently, when his ex-wife Diane had met him in a pub with her new partner to discuss family matters, Stuart had the couple followed home, after which she says he threatened to have their house burnt down. Royle also played a part in trying to find Colin Dixon's home address.

Stuart's girlfriend Kim Shackelton opened an account with an online search company called Tracesmart, whereby users can search electoral rolls, birth, marriage and death records, and other databases of personal information to match names to street addresses. During the afternoon of 3 January 2006, somebody logged onto a computer later found at Cynthia Royle's bungalow, and used Tracesmart to search for a Colin Dixon in Kent. The computer produced eight possible matches, one of whom was the right man, giving Colin's full name, Lynn's name, their dates of birth and home address in Herne Bay. Whoever was searching the database apparently didn't realize they had found what they were looking for, assuming that the Colin Dixon they wanted was another man of that name living in Orpington, not far from Lee Murray.

Three days later, on Friday, 6 January 2006, there seems to have been a gang meeting at Redpits, where Stuart and Kim continued to reside in defiance of the court order to leave. Royle, Rusha, Coutts, Allen and Murray all appear to have attended. At least they all used their mobile phones in the vicinity at this time.* The boys were probably joined by the boss-eyed builder Sean Lupton, who may have ultimately helped the gang obtain Dixon's address. It is remarkable that Lupton lived so close to the Dixons. Furthermore, Lupton went paintballing with a local man named Tony Harun whose sister-in-law, Susan Grosvenor, had worked at the play school the Dixon child attended and occasionally babysat for the Dixons. These are striking coincidences, but that may be all they are, because at this stage the gang seemed to believe their Colin Dixon lived in Orpington. They were sending somebody to knock on his door to check.

Before this happened, Murray and Allen visited the Spy Shop in Chesterfield, Derbyshire, run by a former Royal Navy technician named Phil Stevens who sold surveillance equipment to customers including private detectives and jealous husbands who wanted to snoop on their wives. Murray bought a digital recording device together with a battery pack, attachment leads and,

---

*During the police investigation, mobile-phone records were examined in order to 'cell-site' the conspirators' movements in the days leading up to the robbery. This process allows experts to say that so-and-so was *at or in the vicinity of* a certain place on such and such a date. For the purposes of the story, cell-site evidence allows us to make certain assumptions about what the gangsters were doing on certain dates, such as 6 January 2006, when use of phones seems to put them in the vicinity of Royle's house.

most importantly, mini-spy camera and audio recording gismo, the camera body being the size of a 50-pence piece, the lens 3 mm in diameter. The package cost £399 plus VAT. Phil Stevens gave Murray advice on how to mount the camera on clothing, so it wouldn't be seen. The usual method was to glue the camera to a piece of card which would be stuck behind a button-hole, the tiny lens peeking surreptitiously through the hole. Stevens warned Murray to be careful not to get glue on the lens as he attached it. That evening, Murray drove back to Kent where he met up with Allen and Bucpapa at Rusha's house. They planned to give the spy camera to Ermir Hysenaj to film the inside of the depot.

The lads were also giving further thought to how they would get into Medway House. The basic plan was that Colin would be persuaded to help. But they couldn't all burst into the depot with him. It would be best if Colin went back to Medway House with one gangster, whom he persuaded the security guard to let in. That gang member would then overpower the guard in the con-trol pod, from where Colin could open the gates letting the rest of them in. In order to get the first bandit through the door, they would need a trick. Their simple solution was that the first gang-ster would, again, pose as a policeman. Although Murray and Rusha had apparently agreed to impersonate police officers to kidnap the Dixons, neither man wanted to go to the front door with Colin Dixon in police uniform. The problem was that they would have to show their face, and both feared they would be recognized by staff, or from the CCTV.

Murray and Rusha debated this matter in a telephone con-versation on 11 January 2006, a call which Murray inadvertently recorded on his mobile phone. Remarkably, the police later recovered the phone and downloaded the recording. At the start of the conversation the boys gabbled about how they couldn't sleep because they were so excited. 'I lay in bed all fuckin' night,' said Rusha, pretending to cry like a baby.*

'I'm [up] to four or five o'clock in the morning thinking,' concurred the man police identified as Murray, sounding appropriately dopey, though he always did sound a bit thick.

'I am and all . . . just thinking.'

'. . . a million, million routes.'

They discussed what the police would later claim was the plan to give the mini-spy camera to Ermir Hysenaj. Neither Hysenaj nor the depot were mentioned by name, but the context made it clear what they were talking about, and Rusha named Jetmir at one stage ('I phoned Jet anyway and I told him to get phone [sic] . . . well he can't do anything until tonight'). Jet was the conduit between Hysenaj and the others. Murray and Rusha debated how Hysenaj should wear the spy camera, whether it ought to go on his upper body or belt. Murray said that the 'geezer' he'd spoken to (presumably Mr Stevens) told him how to glue the camera to a belt, through the jeans, angled upwards. Murray thought this would be better than putting the camera on his shirt.

RUSHA: Probably better than up the top, yeah.

MURRAY: If they get it right . . . do you know what I mean . . . It'd be looking, like, up . . . so it'd get a lot more . . .

RUSHA: Yeah.

MURRAY: A lot more of the room. Do you know what I mean?

---

*Expert evidence heard in court indicated which speaker was likely to be Rusha and which Murray. Dialogue has been edited for clarity.

By 'the room', they surely meant the CDP Room, in which Hysenaj worked feeding money into the sorting machines. They wanted to fit the camera soon because Hysenaj was able to walk around the depot this week, 'pushing the cages', as Rusha said, rather than sitting or standing in one spot all the time, as he might be next week. 'So this is when we want it in there, now . . . Tomorrow, innit? . . . 'cos next week he probably might be sitting back down again.'

The fact the men were so inarticulate made their conversation hard to follow. Rusha and Murray also used a good deal of criminal slang. Rusha asked Murray for example: 'When are you gonna bring down . . . your bits and pieces, and we can go and get these . . . tools?' Tools means guns. When Murray said: 'I'm gonna have to take a trip over to fucking Holland, yer know, with it . . .' he may have been referring to taking a firearm to the Netherlands to have it modified, or to buy ammunition.

Rusha wanted to know who was going to be first to go up to the front door of the depot with Dixon. Whoever went to the door would have to show their face, and if the guard set off the alarm, as he said, 'you're fucking done'. Lea said he couldn't undertake this dangerous job because, 'the cunt . . . knows me'. A member of Lea's family was in fact a friend of a friend of a depot worker – an apparently innocent connection, as the police later checked it out thoroughly. This may have been enough to make him afraid he might be recognized. Also Rusha was a well-known, indeed a notorious character in Tonbridge. Murray was similarly reluctant to go to the door, his excuse being that he might be identified later because he was so famous:

MURRAY: Who do, who do you think is the best person to go to the door?
RUSHA: You.

MURRAY: I can't go.

RUSHA: Anyone, I don't give a fuck who goes to the door . . .

MURRAY: I can't show my face . . .

RUSHA: . . . The only thing is this geezer knows me name.

MURRAY: So we having newspapers and fucking telly . . .
When I have me come-back fights, they'll be all over the
newspapers and all the international papers.

RUSHA: Well, I could get . . .whatever . . . we'll get fucking
Paul or Kane . . . someone . . . anyone . . . I don't care . . .
I don't care if we pay a fuckin' knobby to come and knock
the fucking door.

It would be the Crown case that Rusha was talking in this last
paragraph about Paul Allen and a mate of theirs named Keyinde
'Kane' Patterson, while 'knobby' is criminal slang for a policeman. Rusha seems to be implying he knew a corrupt policeman
who might help them. He went on to talk about someone who
had 'two big sheds' in which were 'all the new things . . . the
proper . . . naughty bits'. This may have been a reference to
obtaining weapons from an underworld armourer.

'What . . . the geezer with them loud things?' asked Murray,
possibly meaning a loud gun. Criminals sometimes use guns that
make a lot of noise because the sound frightens their victims.

'Yeah,' said Rusha, becoming excited, 'it'd be like walking into
fucking . . . commandos . . . pressing buttons and all the walls will
be opening up . . . things everywhere . . . it's all on the walls and
shit.' The alarm buttons were on the walls.

Having talked the matter through, the boys seemingly decided
to send Ermir into the depot with the spy camera on Thursday,
12 January 2006. It is likely Bucpapa delivered the spy camera to
Hysenaj beforehand, and probably helped glue it on his belt. In
doing so the boys managed to make the exact mistake Phil

Stevens warned Murray about and got glue on the lens. Somebody had to take the camera back to Chesterfield immediately. Murray was busy, so he sent Paul Allen and Keyinde 'Kane' Patterson.

A Londoner of West Indian extraction, twenty-seven, six foot tall with a scar on his left cheek, Kane Patterson had recently faced a murder charge related to twin shootings. In October 2004, two men were shot dead at the Spotlight nightclub in Croydon, south of London, one of the victims being the doorman. Later that same night men pulled up alongside a car in Bristol and sprayed it with machine-gun fire, apparently intending to kill the men in the vehicle, but succeeding only in injuring the girls they were with. Despite the distance between Croydon and Bristol, police decided these shootings were the work of the same gang. Patterson was charged as a member of a conspiracy, but the charges were dropped due to insufficient evidence, and he was free at the time of the Tonbridge robbery.

Paul and Kane got to the Spy Shop so early it wasn't open. Allen called the shop number impatiently and got through to a message service, who informed Phil Stevens that a customer was 'outside the shop now, re: the camera with glue on the lens. Please advise when you will be arriving.' When Stevens turned up for work he found two scruffy men on his doorstep, one of mixed race (Allen) and one black (Patterson). They showed Stevens the camera with the jeans and belt. 'I told them the camera was no longer repairable, so I had to replace [it].' The cost was £99 plus VAT. 'At that point they asked me to fit it to the jeans and belt.' Stevens told them it would take a little time, so the lads went to McDonald's. At 10.44 a.m. Stevens rang Paul to say the camera was ready. He had glued it to a piece of cardboard, the cardboard to the jeans, reinforced by stitches applied by his wife, Mandy. The lens poked through an eyehole in the belt, and was

almost impossible to see. Having collected the camera, Allen and
Patterson hopped into their black Mercedes coupé, and shot off
to London. It may be that they wanted to get the camera to
Hysenaj in time for his afternoon shift.

At 11.20 a.m. two Nottinghamshire Police officers in an
unmarked car on the M1 clocked a Mercedes CLK 500 zipping
past them at 115 mph. They stopped the car and asked the driver
for his details. Paul Allen gave his name correctly, and his mum's
address in Woolwich. Keyinde Patterson also identified himself.
Apart from breaking the speed limit so extravagantly, Allen was
driving on an expired provisional licence, he didn't have MOT,
or insurance papers, and the car wasn't even his. He said he had
borrowed it from Kane's brother. The police informed Allen that
he certainly wouldn't be travelling any further in the car, which
they were impounding. Allen seemed OK about this, but
Patterson became 'extremely argumentative and aggressive,' recalls
PC Brian Avann. In fact, he locked himself in the car, refusing to
get out when the tow truck arrived. It was some time before the
officers managed to coax him out of the vehicle. In the circumstances it was good of the police to give Allen and Patterson a lift
to Loughborough Station, so they could complete their journey
by train.

During the drive to the station, Patterson's three mobile
phones rang constantly. 'I'm in a police car,' he told his callers, 'I'll
ring you back.'

2

The following Monday, Ermir Hysenaj received a visit at home
from Jetmir Bucpapa, Lea Rusha and possibly Lee Murray. They
had come to help Ermir get ready for work. He dressed casually

in a dark-blue, short-sleeve shirt and put on jeans fitted with the belt with the secret camera. Normally, Ermir wore his shirt outside his trousers. Today he tucked his shirt in, so as not to obscure the lens of the spy camera. The camera itself was almost impossible to see. The bulky recording device, battery pack and wiring was probably concealed in a bum bag in the small of his back, under his shirt, or in his underwear, which would have been off limits to depot staff doing a body search.

Ermir usually travelled to work by public transport but today it seems Murray gave him a lift, possibly dropping him in Strawberry Vale. Ermir was nineteen minutes early for his 2.00 p.m. shift. Admitted to the lobby at 1.41 p.m., he went upstairs to the staff room, came down again, walked through the air lock, queued to sign the register, put his things in the locker room, emerging at 1.53, with his shirt tucked into his jeans. His heart must have been pounding as he waited to be searched, but the staff didn't discover the spy camera in his jeans.

Ermir got a drink from the dispensing machine and strolled over to the CDP where he loitered outside the loading bay doors, sipping his drink and turning around and around in 360°, in order to record as much as possible of that part of the building with the spy camera. He glanced down repeatedly as he pirouetted in this way, as though checking the camera lens. At 2.03 he entered the CDP Room itself, where he worked, alongside other employees, on the BPS 1000 sorting machine. During the first half of his shift he repeatedly left his station to visit the locker room/toilets, as if he was unwell, walking back and forth through the building at least three times prior to the meal break at 7.00 p.m.

Most staff stayed in the depot for their break, using the staff room upstairs to eat food they had brought in. But Ermir hurried outside. He left the CDP Room at three minutes to seven, collected his coat and mobile from the locker room, and exited the building at 6.59 p.m., walking briskly along Vale Road towards Sainsbury's.

Three minutes later – by which time he would have been out of sight and hearing of any colleagues – Ermir used his mobile to call Jet, who was with Murray in Ryan's Pub in Southborough. Bucpapa and Murray left the pub and drove to Tonbridge, probably to take the recording device from Ermir. Jet and Lee then went to Jet's flat where they called Coutts, who seems to have been with Stuart Royle at Redpits. That evening, there was another gang meeting at Redpits, probably to watch the spy film Ermir had made. Ermir himself wasn't present, but Jetmir rang him repeatedly at home, probably with questions about what they were watching. At the end of the night Murray drove home to Sidcup.

Lightning Lee was soon back in Tonbridge, and continued to loiter about the area over the next two days, sometimes with Allen. On Wednesday evening Murray, Coutts and Bucpapa visited Jet at his flat, after which Murray and Bucpapa seemingly went to take another look at Medway House, where Jet was cell-sited twice before midnight and again just after, with Lee hanging around the area as late as 1.31 a.m. The following day, Bucpapa called at a house in Newstead Avenue, Orpington, saying that he was selling household goods. Jet sent a text to Lee Murray describing the man who answered the door as tall and slim with brown hair. This description did not fit Colin Dixon, manager of Medway House. They had the wrong man.

It was probably because of this latest dead end in the search for Dixon's address that Murray returned to the Spy Shop and bought a £500 electronic 'tracking device', a gadget which can be stuck magnetically to the underside of a car. Using satellite navigation, the device records the movements of the vehicle, relaying the information via an Internet signal to a personal computer. Murray, Bucpapa, Hysenaj and Coutts were all cell-sited at or in the vicinity of Medway House on Saturday, 21 January 2006. Maybe they were trying to work out a way to get into the compound to plant the device on Colin's car. This would not have been easy. On Monday, Murray, using the name Mark, left a message at the Spy Shop saying he now wanted a tracking 'stick', a smaller gadget which does much the same job. The same day he contacted JJN Electronics about buying a bug detector, which could be used to sweep a room for listening devices, and found time to pop into Smart Parts in Bexley to buy a black paintball mask. The invoice was made out to Lee Murray, who gave his mother's address in Abbey Wood. Lee additionally sent a text to Roger Coutts referring him to the website of a Liverpool hatters, Try & Lilly, who make police headgear.

The gang may have pulled off a quick robbery at this stage to pay for all the equipment they were buying. At 3.00 p.m. on Monday, 23 January, staff from a One Stop shop in Rusthall, near Southborough, were walking to the post office with £25,000 in takings when two hooded men grabbed the cash and made off in a Ford Granada. The police traced the car to Wateringbury Car Sales. When Stuart Royle was questioned about the robbery, he said that two men had picked the Ford up from his yard, then called in to say it had broken down, at which point his driver, Lea Rusha, was dispatched to collect it. Rusha was also spoken to about the robbery. The police suspected that he was involved, but there was insufficient evidence to charge either him or Royle.

Meanwhile, Roger Coutts made a quick trip to Cyprus look-ing for property to buy, quite possibly thinking ahead to what would happen after the robbery. The boys would be safe from the

British police if they got across the border into Turkish Northern Cyprus, a haven for British criminals on the run because there is no extradition treaty with the UK. There was another country even better suited to Murray, son of a Moroccan chef. His dad's homeland didn't have an extradition treaty with the UK either.

3

During the cash-centre robbery, the gangsters could wear paint-ball masks and balaclavas. But the robbers who posed as policemen during the kidnapping stage would have to show their faces, which put them at risk of being identified later by wit-nesses. It became apparent that, to remove the danger of being picked out of an identity parade, the men who impersonated police officers would have to transform their whole appearance. They would use wigs, make-up, even prosthetics.

On Wednesday, 25 January 2006, Rusha went shopping in central London with his make-up artist girlfriend Katie Philp, vis-iting specialist theatrical shops. First they went to Screenface in Notting Hill where they bought make-up and other products including brushes, sponges, crêpe hair and four latex noses, paying the £211.70 bill in cash. Then they called at Charles H. Fox in Covent Garden, one of the oldest shops of its kind in the world, with a client list that has included Charlton Heston – his wig for *Ben Hur* came from here. Lea and Katie found themselves in a shop stocked to the rafters with wigs, beards and moustaches, each of which has a splendidly descriptive name (try the Brigadier, Magnum or Poirot). There was also a range of prod-ucts for those with the skill to make prosthetic masks, which would be ideal for Big Lee, Little Lea and Kane. However, apply-ing wigs and prosthetic disguises is specialist work. For help, Lee

Murray turned again to his barber Michael Demetris. Lee apparently gave Michael a cock-and-bull story about having got an acting part in a Mixed Martial Arts computer game, for which he and friends needed to be made up as characters.

Meanwhile, the gang was obtaining vehicles needed in the robbery: some they stole, some they hired, others they borrowed or bought. Murray found one car on the *Auto Trader* website. It was an N-registration, burgundy-coloured Vauxhall Vectra, on sale with Cavalier City of Windlesham, Surrey. Murray rang and said he would be coming to see the vehicle the next day. With that arranged, he went online to shop for another tracking device, buying one from Spybuild.com in the USA, asking for the item to be shipped to his mum's house. If this was an attempt to be devious, he shouldn't have used his own e-mail address for the transaction: lightninglee@tiscali.co.uk was distinctive.

The following day, two young men showed up at Cavalier City to look at the Vauxhall Vectra. One of the men was Paul Allen. The second man may have been a friend of Murray's named Scott Needham who introduced himself to the staff at Cavalier City as Mark Scott. He said he was a scaffolder looking to buy a car with some mates who were chipping in a thousand pounds each. He took a cursory look at the red Vectra, which cost £3,999, made a phone call, then agreed to buy it without a test drive, which was unusual. When staff asked for his address for the paperwork, Mr Scott said he lived with his mum, and had to look on a piece of paper for her address. Company secretary Peter Vogel remarked that most people knew their mother's address. The buyer said his mum had moved recently. The address he eventually gave was 115 Tonbridge Road, Wateringbury: Stuart Royle's garage. 'He then handed me cash in bundles of a thousand,' recalls Peter Vogel. 'I offered him one pound change.'

'Keep it,' he said grandly.

As the buyer got into the car he leaned on the central arm rest, which broke. The salesman assumed he would complain, but this unusual customer tossed the broken arm rest in the back and drove off. The mob later fitted blue flashing lights and a siren to the radiator grille of the Vectra, and stored the car in readiness for the heist. It would be one of two fake police vehicles they used.

The gang also needed panel vans, into which they would transfer the kidnap victims after seizing them. The double benefit of solid-sided vans was that other road users would not see the Dixons and the Dixons wouldn't see where they were going. The boys decided to use Ford Transits and an old LDV Post Office van. There is a constant supply of decommissioned Post Office vans to the trade. One such vehicle was often parked outside Hair Hectik. It belonged to the hire company next door but one and had the registration number W664 KDA. The gang decided to acquire an identical vehicle and make up false plates for it using this same registration, so that if a witness took down the number during the raid the police would be led to the wrong people.

They found a suitable van advertised on the *Auto Trader* website, a 2001 Y-reg vehicle on sale for £2,300. Lee Murray called TW Motors of Essex on 30 January, using the name Peter, saying he was coming to take a look at the vehicle. Once again, he sent Paul Allen and Scott Needham in his place. A young man calling himself Mark Scott took a cursory look at the vehicle, then paid for it in cash. He again gave his address as 115 Tonbridge Road, Wateringbury. It seems that the London axis of the gang were, even at this stage, looking to double-cross their country partners, and were leaving clues that would take the police away from them to the likes of Stuart Royle after the raid. That is the theory of detectives who investigated the heist.

4

Finally, the gang found Colin Dixon's home address in Herne Bay. How they got the address at long last is unclear. The information could have come from Ermir Hysenaj. Murray may have used his tracking devices successfully. They may have had help from Sean Lupton. However they did it, Lea Rusha drove down to the coast on 31 January 2006, to take a close look at the address and obtain film of Colin Dixon's wife. They needed to see what Lynn looked like if they were going to kidnap her. Rusha made the journey in Bucpapa's VW Golf, and took Jet's mistress with him.

Raluca Antonela Radu was born in Romania in August 1980, the second youngest of eight children. The family lived in Oradea, near the Hungarian border, where her father worked as a vet during the dictatorship of Nicolae Ceausescu. These were difficult times for Romania, but the Radu household was apparently a happy and well-disciplined one. 'If my father ever suspected we stole something – even an egg or a flower, not that we did – we would feel the back of his hand right away,' says Raluca's sister Gianina. 'We knew the difference between [right and wrong]. We were well brought up.' Gianina married an Englishman named Paul McLaughlin, and set up home in Hastings, a town Hysenaj and Rusha had connections to. The McLaughlins ran a glass-import company. Raluca came to visit her sister and brother-in-law, and worked in their warehouse. She met a local man named Tony Millen, married him and set up home in nearby St Leonards. Raluca got a job in a nursing home.

Neither the job nor the marriage lasted. After separating from her husband, Raluca moved into a flat at 28 Dudley Road, Royal Tunbridge Wells, just off the main shopping district, near the Assembly Hall. It was a street of substantial Victorian town

houses, many of which had been subdivided into short-tenancy
flats, commonly let to students or new immigrants from eastern
Europe, after whom Dudley Road had been given the sobriquet
'European Street'. An enterprising girl, Raluca tried her hand at
pole-dancing and was on the books of an escort agency for a
while. Somewhere along the line she met Jetmir Bucpapa and,
despite the fact Jet was married, they began an affair. Jet also persuaded Raluca to help him in his preparations for the heist,
though, like Katie Philp and Kim Shackelton, Raluca Millen
would say that she had no idea that her boyfriend was mixed up
in a plot to commit kidnap and armed robbery.

Rusha later explained his reconnaissance trip to Herne Bay with
Raluca by telling a court he had been sent there by Stuart Royle
and Sean Lupton to check out an address for Terry Lynch, who
had done a flit from his home. Rusha was told that Lynch's wife
might come to the door. Because Lea didn't know what Mrs Lynch
looked like, he was given a bag with a secret camera in it to film
her. Because he felt carrying such a bag was 'poofy', Lea asked Jet
if Raluca would come with him and carry the bag. According to
this story, therefore, Raluca thought she was helping the boys collect a debt on the day she went spying in Herne Bay.

Lea and Raluca drove down to the coast on the afternoon of 31
January, parking up at the far end of Hadleigh Gardens. It was a grey,
damp day. They sat in the car for a while, listening to Invicta Radio.
At five o'clock, Raluca got out of the car and walked down to
number 16, chewing gum and breathing nervously. She paused occasionally to check her shoulder bag, inserted into the fabric of which
was a miniature camera, purchased from the Spy Shop. Raluca passed
a succession of neat, detached family homes, behind the curtains of
which were several retired people, including two former policemen
who kept a close eye on visitors. Being a no-through road, Hadleigh
Gardens was quiet, and visitors were conspicuous.

The close was built on a slope, the approach to the Dixon house on the down slope, so much so that Raluca had to descend a steep drive and a flight of steps to reach the front door. She rapped three times on the white PVC door, making sure her bag was positioned so she would film whoever answered. Under her arm she held a blue folder with an MOT symbol on it. Raluca intended to say she was looking for a man named Paul Smith of 16 Tyne Park. (Tyne*dale* Park was the next street.) This was a cover story that would give her time to film the woman she expected to come to the door.

When there was no answer, Raluca knocked again, stepped over to the window and rapped loudly on the glass. Lynn Dixon was inside, preparing dinner. She heard the knocking, but chose not to answer because it was late, her husband had a sensitive job and she wasn't expecting anyone. After several seconds, Raluca gave up. 'Ah, fucking bitch!' she exclaimed as she walked back to the VW Golf.

'She didn't answer,' Raluca told Lea.

'Didn't answer?'

'Three times I knocked. The windows as well. It was becoming suspicious. Sorry!'

They sat in the car. Raluca texted Jet; Rusha texted Royle.

5

That evening Murray and Rusha visited Michael Demetris at his salon, Hair Hectik. Murray, Allen, Coutts and Bucpapa were there. Lea's girlfriend Katie Philp, who'd bought bagfuls of specialist make-up products at Screenface and Charles H. Fox, was also there. Demetris, who would later be charged as a conspirator, but found not guilty in court, says Murray told him he needed to be made up for a video or computer game he would be acting

in. Philp was supposed to do the make-up. Michael, who wanted
to do more media work, took Lee aside and suggested Michelle
Hogg would be better for the job and Lee agreed. Demetris
phoned Michelle Hogg at home. 'Miche, can you make noses and
chins?' he asked her, as she recalls.

'I did them at college.'

Michael asked if she could also make moustaches and beards.
She said that she made a beard for a man playing Neptune.
Michael seemed satisfied with this reference, and told her he had
a special job coming up.

6

The gang needed two fake police vehicles. Having bought the
Vauxhall Vectra, they stole the second car. Just before midday on
1 February 2006 Edmund Lindsey drove to a friend's house in
Kingswood Avenue, Sanderstead, near Croydon, parking his grey
Volvo S60 outside while he delivered a parcel. When Mr Lindsey
re-emerged five minutes later, the car was gone. It was probably
stored with the Vectra at Stuart Royle's garage, where it was
seemingly fitted with false licence plates.

The red Post Office van was now at Stuart Royle's mother's
house. Stuart had been spending a lot of time at 33 Shaftesbury
Drive recently. His son Jimmy was living there, and Kim Shackelton
and others kept popping in and out. All in all, there was much more
activity than normal. 'Everybody was a bit worried, because [we]
saw all these cars coming and going and, you know, we couldn't
understand what was going on,' says neighbour Ann Berry, who
kept an eye on her elderly neighbour. 'Because she doesn't normally
have company.' The Berrys and other neighbours watched Cynthia's
ne'er-do-well son pacing about outside, talking on his mobile. A

young girl drove quickly into the drive, followed by other vehicles. Upon parking, the drivers hopped quickly out of their cars and dashed inside. Neighbours suspected Stuart was up to no good. But they didn't know the half of it.

Aside from the work of planning kidnap and robbery, Royle continued to pose as Kim Shackelton's financial adviser, 'David Lawrence', in order to try and get a mortgage for Redpits. Royle went up to Wolverhampton around this time with documents to show Alexander White of Promise Finance, the company he hoped would give Kim a mortgage. But the paperwork wasn't in order. Undeterred, Lawrence introduced other 'clients' to Mr White, including Katie Philp's mum, who apparently wanted to remortgage her home in Tonbridge; and Stuart's daughter, Chrissy, who now wanted to buy 33 Shaftesbury Drive. Chaotic and fraudulent, Stuart Royle's affairs were also darkly comic. Old Mrs Royle confided to Ray Berry that Stuart had recently asked to borrow £300 from her to buy a *bullet-proof vest*, 'because someone had taken a contract out on him'.

Now Stuart had this dirty great big van in Mum's drive. It looked like it had formerly had lettering on the side, of which traces remained (before it left Royal Mail's fleet, the Post Office insignia had been removed, but apparently not completely). As Ann Berry watched from her front window, men emerged from Cynthia's bungalow, stood on the little wall between the driveways, and began picking away the remains of the lettering. Shortly afterwards, the van was driven off. In the process, the driver damaged the driveway wall. Stuart assured Ray Berry that he would put it right. He said Mum was going to have a new wall built at the front, and when they did that, they'd rebuild the drive wall, too.

The next day the Berrys drove through Wateringbury and saw the red van parked by Stuart's sales office. It was stored here

for at least six days prior to the heist. Jimmy Royle was seen
cleaning the vehicle.

7

Back in London, Michael Demetris put his head around Michelle
Hogg's work station at Hair Hectik and told her that Lee Murray
was coming in for a chat.

Murray appeared a few minutes later and Michael ushered
them both into the staff room. Michelle was eating beef-flavour
Hoola-Hoops. She offered the bag to Lee, but he had other
things on his mind. 'He asked could I make moustaches and
chins. I said yes . . . He asked me if I could make moustaches and
beards. Yes, I could. I done it at college. I asked what the make-
up was for and he just said it was a job.' It seemed there would be
several people involved. She asked what he and his friends would
be wearing on the 'job'. He said suits.

Demetris popped his head round the door. 'Is everything
going OK?' Michelle said it was and shortly afterwards Murray
drove away in his new, banana-yellow Ferrari.

Soon afterwards Demetris called Michelle and asked her to
meet him at Murray's house, telling her to bring her portfolio and
a latex bird beak she had made at college as an example of her
prosthetic work, what she called her 'peacock's nose'. Michelle
had no sense of direction, and even though she checked the
London A–Z she managed to get lost on the short drive between
her flat and Murray's address. Later she was not sure where this
was. If she visited 32 Onslow Drive, Sidcup, Siobhan Lamrani-
Murray wasn't home. It seems Michelle may have gone somewhere
else, because when she arrived she was introduced to a woman
called Nicky, described as Lee's 'girlfriend'. The woman had a

little boy with her. This must have been Lee's mistress, Nicola Barnes, mother of young Lenie, who lived in nearby Erith.

Demetris was sitting on the sofa with Lee. 'Take your shoes off,' the barber told Michelle, as if to indicate the respect he felt due to Murray whom Michael treated as a celebrity. Michelle noticed a lap-top computer. On the screen was a swirling blue character with a bald head. The character was wearing what she recognized as a 'bald cap', a bit of latex that can be put over the head to make a person appear bald, or as the basis of a wig. Michelle showed the boys her portfolio and the famous peacock's nose. 'Michael was putting it on and mucking about with it.' Twenty minutes later she was ushered out. (Murray had a gang meeting later in Tonbridge.) Before they got into their respective cars, Demetris told his stylist he was giving her a week's leave to work from home making disguises for Lee Murray. She would get her salary and, as Hogg recalls he said, 'who knows, Miche, you might get some more'. Michelle liked the idea. Her boss rang her later at home saying he would be working with her on the Murray project. In fact, there would be four people to disguise, and arrangements were being made to take Miche up to London to get the necessary materials from Charles H. Fox. Questioned later by police, Hogg said she thought Murray was preparing for a party or a 'video or theatrical event'.

Michelle began her working holiday on Monday, 6 February 2006, as did Katie Philp, whom Rusha had persuaded to run errands for them. Murray had yet another woman helping. A friend of his named Sally Davison was shopping online for police clothing and insignia. Proving that you can get almost anything on eBay, Sally bought a police pullover, fluorescent Gore-Tex jacket and Kent Police badges through the website. Murray shopped for other items of police clothing mail order.

Murray phoned Michelle to say a friend of his was coming to

pick her up from home. She should meet him outside the One Stop shop at the top of Vicarage Park. A little after 11.00 a.m. that Monday Michelle walked up to the One Stop shop to meet a man who introduced himself as Kane. This must have been Keyinde Patterson. He bought her a Ribena drink from the shop, then drove her up to town in his Ford Focus. They chatted on the way. Michelle said her dad had been a policeman. Kane said he was an identical twin. Michelle was fascinated. She'd been a twin, too, but her twin hadn't survived.

Kane gave Michelle £400 cash and waited in the car while she bought materials from Charles H. Fox for making prosthetic 'pieces' — that is, latex noses and chins. These included alginate and dental plaster for the moulds, mud rock for modelling details, shellac and liquid latex. She also bought crêpe hair braids, eyeliner pencils and other items. After a coffee break, Kane drove Michelle to another shop in Warren Street. Then he drove her home. Michelle phoned Demetris, who said he'd be round later with 'a few friends'.

Demetris arrived at 14 Vicarage Park around 8.00 p.m., accompanied by Lee Murray and Kane, plus four people Michelle hadn't previously met: Rusha, Royle, Coutts and Bucpapa. Lighning Lee was wearing a green T-shirt with the words FUCKIN CRIMINAL printed on the front. There were hardly enough chairs for everybody to sit down. Michelle's main task this evening was to make casts of the faces of the men who wanted to be disguised, that is, Murray, Royle, Rusha and Patterson. Working with one man at a time, she smeared Vaseline over their face, eyebrows and hairline. She gave them straws to put up their nose, so they could breathe during the next stage, which involved smothering their face with alginate, which came in powder form, to which she added water. Michelle's first batch came out too runny. Murray went away and came back with a print-out from the Internet

showing her how it should be done. The next batch was stiffer.
Michelle had to work fast, because the alginate set in 2½ minutes.
With Demetris as her assistant, Miche poured the blue slime
over Murray's face. She says: 'Michael found it quite hilarious
seeing Lee Murray with alginate on his face and a straw in his
mouth so he took a picture of his face.' When the alginate set,
Hogg removed a hard, negative image of Murray's physiognomy,
which she could use to fashion a latex nose and chin that would
alter his appearance considerably. Lee had got alginate on his
FUCKIN CRIMINAL T-shirt. Michelle said she'd wash it for him, so
he peeled it off and gave it to her. She went through the same
casting process for Royle, Kane and Rusha. It took a long time
and life became more difficult when the boys asked additionally
for bald caps for Kane and Rusha. Michelle worked until it was
nearly dawn.

The next day she poured plaster into the casts she had
made the night before in order to create positive impressions
of Patterson, Murray, Rusha and Royle. Modelling clay and
mud rock could then be added to the noses and chins of these
plaster casts to alter the features. It was a simple matter to add
warts, score wrinkles, or make a larger chin. A square chin with
a dimple was created for Murray. The skill was not to overdo
things or the pieces would appear grotesque. When Michelle was
satisfied with the modelling, she could apply the liquid latex,
painting it on in layers each one of which had to dry before she
added the next. Finally, she carefully peeled away a rubbery
membrane which would be glued to the subject's face with spirit
gum. The liquid latex stank, and Michelle was aware that the
materials were carcinogenic, so she opened her windows as she
worked into the night.

On Wednesday, 8 February 2006, Coutts met up with Murray,
Allen, Rusha and Bucpapa in Tonbridge. Around 6.00 p.m.

Rusha was cell-sited in the vicinity of Medway House. He may have been taking pictures. A man was seen taking photographs of the building on 8 and 9 February. That evening the boys reconvened at Hogg's flat, where the bald caps were almost ready. Michelle had put thirteen coats of latex on each one, and left them to dry on the table. But when the guys were horsing about Roger Coutts knocked two wet bald caps together, ruining them. Demetris joked: 'Oh, Miche, you will just have to start again.' But Murray was furious with his friend. 'She's been grafting on this all day,' he told Coutts, who left the flat in a sulk. Lee had to text Roger to beg him to come back and pick him up. 'Come on man stop sulking we've got shit to do,' he texted at 9.42 p.m., and six minutes later: 'Come on Gurb, come back and get us. We are stuck.'

Maybe it was as a punishment that Coutts was sent back to stake out Hadleigh Gardens. He was on duty by 6.00 a.m. Thursday and appears to have spent most of the day in the area. At 3.20 p.m. he moved to Junction 7 of the M2 where it connects with the A229 Thanet Way, the dual carriageway Colin Dixon used every day, and the route the kidnappers would travel to snatch his wife. The gang would use Brenley Corner, as it is known, as a rendezvous.

Because of the accident with the bald caps, the manufacture of the disguises was now behind schedule. Murray spoke to Lea Rusha about getting Miche some help. 'Your bird, she can do this, she can help as well,' he told Lea, who brought Katie Philp to Hogg's flat at lunchtime on Friday. The girls worked at their slow, smelly task, with latex and plaster until Rusha picked Katie up in the evening. Michelle needed some more materials so Murray, Rusha and Philp went back to Charles H. Fox, buying several litres of liquid latex which they delivered to Vicarage Park. Up in her garret, Michelle was starting to feel like a slave. Katie wasn't happy either. She complained that Murray hadn't given her the right money for the stuff she'd bought.

8

Saturday night, Lee Murray and Paul Allen went clubbing at the SE1 in Southwark, south London, where they were joined by Kane Patterson and a mate of Lee's named Bradley Fitzgerald. The club was hosting a French-theme *Moulin Rouge!* evening and the boys had such a good time they decided to have a group photo taken by a professional photographer, who'd set up his equipment in the club.

Driving home from the SE1 around 6.00 o'clock Sunday morning, having picked up a girl, and probably the worse for drink, Murray crashed his Ferrari in the New Kent Road, then fled the scene, apparently having remembered to remove the car number plates before he did so (the car was later found without plates), but leaving two of his mobile phones and three of the photos he'd had taken at the club in the Ferrari.

Police called to the scene found Lightning Lee at a mini cab office at the nearby Elephant and Castle roundabout. As officers tried to question Murray about the accident, which he denied knowing anything about, he became agitated and aggressive, to the extent that the police tried to put handcuffs on him. Murray wouldn't let them. An off-duty constable who was passing lent a hand, and still the police couldn't subdue Murray. They called for reinforcements. A police van showed up and one of the constables sprayed Lee with CS/pepper spray which should have taken all the fight out of him. Remarkably, the spray had no effect on Murray, who was yelling at the constables at the top of his voice:

'I'll fucking smack you . . . You don't know who I am. I'm one of the world's best fighters!'

It took four police officers to cuff Murray and haul him off to Walworth Station where he was given a blood test and charged with assault, before being bailed. The case never came to court because the whole matter was overtaken by events. The Ferrari was impounded.

When he sobered up, Murray realized he had left two phones in the Ferrari, what the police refer to as 'mission phones' or 'dirty phones', that is pay-as-you-go mobiles bought anonymously, or in false names, by criminals who use them to plan a crime, then throw them away to destroy the evidence. The criminal principle is to keep one's domestic phone calls separate from criminal phone calls, because phone networks keep records of all calls made. The last thing criminals want is for their dirty phone to fall into the hands of the police, especially if the phones can be traced. Murray had left both his dirty phones in his car, now in a police pound. A disaster! Those phones would allow police to uncover his contacts with the other gang members. He had their numbers programmed into the phones next to their nicknames. The only ray of light was that the police were not yet investigating him. The robbery hadn't happened. With this in mind, Murray simply went to the Bluewater Shopping Centre near Dartford and bought a new mission phone.

One of Lee's first calls on his new phone was to Michelle Hogg, still slaving away in her flat. Katie was there helping, and Michelle needed all the help she could get because when Demetris came round he told her Lee needed *more* noses and chins. The gang may not have decided yet how many of them needed to be disguised. Did they need two teams of kidnappers, or could Murray and Rusha kidnap Colin Dixon *and* Lynn and her child? As with many aspects of the heist, details such as this seem to have been decided at the last minute. It is also possible that the boys wanted Michelle to make a selection of noses and chins for them to choose from.

The following day, Valentine's Day, the gang plus Michael Demetris met at Michelle's flat for a group make-up session. Murray, Rusha, Bucpapa, Coutts, Allen and Royle all showed up, staying until 10.00 o'clock, when the conspirators adjourned to Lee's house in Sidcup, possibly to discuss matters they didn't want Michelle to hear. Despite the amount of time the gang were spending at her flat, she insists she still didn't know what they were up to: she hadn't been told and hadn't guessed. Neither had Michael Demetris who was spending all this time helping Lee Murray simply in the hope, he says, that when the video game was produced Hair Hectik would be credited for doing the hair and make-up, thus boosting the profile of the little suburban salon.

The following night, Demetris and Murray returned to her flat, to inspect the noses and chins. Hogg says Michael Demetris cut Lee's hair and tinted it grey to make him look older. Demetris also apparently experimented with a wig, but only succeeded in making a mess. Barber and stylist were getting on each other's nerves. He said Miche could go back to work at the salon the next day.

In the morning her car wouldn't start. She hadn't used it for ten days and the battery was flat, so she was late getting to the salon. When she checked her phone she saw that Murray had been trying to call her. He wanted to come round again that evening. Michelle had arranged to hear her mum play guitar in a pub, but Lee insisted. He showed up about ten with Paul Allen. She fitted Lee with a false nose and a moustache. He left the flat in disguise, possibly as a test to see if people recognized him.

9

The boys had decided to use the red van in the kidnap of Mrs Dixon. Lynn and her child would first be abducted by two gang members, dressed as policemen and tricked into their car. This car would meet the red van, into which Lynn and the kid would be transferred. The gang decided to disguise the red van as if it was a fleet Post Office vehicle again, painted in Parcelforce livery. Royle knew just the guy to do this: his old mate Keith Borer, a 52-year-old ginger-haired lookalike for footballer Alan Ball.

Keith was a sign-writer. That is to say he made his living printing and fixing signs and transfers to shops and vehicles. A few years previously he made good money putting go-faster stripes on cars. Keith had enough men working for him at one time to run nine vans. He made car-number plates, too, until he received a visit from the police who pointed out that he wasn't authorized to do so. Then go-faster stripes went out of fashion and Keith lost the shops and the vans. He was living in a caravan now, at Yalding, next to the River Medway. Keith drove a Porsche, but business wasn't good. In fact, he was skint. He dreaded the bank statements. Sign-writing didn't pay much at the best of times, £200 was good for a job, and clients often bounced cheques on him.

When Stuart Royle called and asked, 'Can you make a van look like a Parcelforce van?' Keith replied that he probably could. He knew Stuart had no legitimate reason to disguise a van as a Parcelforce vehicle. He wasn't a postman. Nor was Stuart a policeman. Yet Keith agreed to make up small vinyl labels with 'POLICE' on them, suitable for mounting on a high-visibility jacket, and larger 'POLICE' signs, together with chevrons and coloured stripes, to disguise an ordinary car as a police car. Keith downloaded the Parcelforce logo and lettering from the Internet, and made arrangements to buy white reflective vinyl to make the 'POLICE' signs.

Rather like the children's TV character Mr Benn, Stuart Royle wore many hats at this stage in his career. Mr Royle was by turn gangster, car dealer, Post Office worker, policeman and financial adviser. Posing as David Lawrence, Royle was struggling to ensure that he and Kim Shackelton hung onto Redpits Cottage until such time as they actually got enough money to buy it. Promise Finance had referred Lawrence and Shackelton to an Ipswich firm, CBA Law, to do the conveyancing. But CBA Law discovered Royle and Shackelton had been given a court order to vacate Redpits, and only had until 22 February 2006, to remove their belongings before the bailiffs went in. Lucy Smith told David Lawrence this on 15 February. The bogus financial adviser somehow convinced CBA Law that Miss Shackelton could raise a £50,000 bridging loan for the property by 24 February.

Having bought a few days' time, Royle turned his mind back to the problem of the red van. He decided that Keith Borer could sign-write the vehicle in John Fowler's yard at Elderden Farm. Royle was in business with Fowler, of course, and he was in and out of the yard all the time. John was in France for a short skiing holiday with his son Jack. Royle rang him there on Friday afternoon. John said he would be home on Sunday, 19 February. Time was now pressing. It seems that the gang had decided to kidnap the Dixons Monday evening, robbing the depot in the early hours of Tuesday, which meant they were already into the last weekend before the heist.

The disguises were ready. Michelle was back at work at Hair Hectik, brushing her teeth in one of the sinks because she hadn't had time at home; everything was so frantic with the men coming round, and Miche working until dawn on the disguises. But Michael 'had a go' at her for brushing her teeth in his sink and, as a result, an overtired and highly-strung Michelle started to cry. She later claimed that they also had a straight discussion about the disguises. She told Michael she'd had enough and said: 'If anything dodgy is going on I don't want to be part of it.' She claims Michael replied: 'I've had a word with the boys and no one's coming round tonight.' He denies this.

Murray's men were taking it in turns to keep Colin Dixon's home under surveillance. Friday evening, Murray, Allen and Bucpapa appeared to have paid a call on Raluca Millen in Tunbridge Wells, after which Allen drove down to Herne Bay, where he was cell-sited into the early hours of Saturday 18 February (after which he went back to Hogg's flat). Bucpapa was in Herne Bay at 1.30 Sunday morning. That afternoon Jet and Stuart Royle visited Murray at home in Onslow Drive, Sidcup, where neighbours were becoming used to flashy cars pulling up, and 'tough-looking blokes' going into number 32 for what they later decided must have been gang meetings.

Around four o'clock Sunday afternoon Bucpapa, Royle and Philp showed up at Lee's house, before driving to Hair Hectik. Michael Demetris called Michelle at home at 4.20 – she was doing her ironing – and told her to bring the bald caps, latex noses and chins she had made, plus all her make-up equipment, to the salon.

The sign on the door was turned to 'CLOSED' when Michelle arrived, two hours late, but there was something like a party going on inside Hair Hectik. Stuart Royle emerged and helped her inside with her stuff, which she thought nice. The car dealer had grown a bushy white beard recently and his white hair had now been dyed a dark brown. Michelle thought it suited him. She saw Lea Rusha inside, at a basin. Michael was dying the roofer's brown hair ginger-red. Murray, Bucpapa and Patterson were also present. So was Katie Philp. The girls went to McDonald's to get some food, bringing it back to eat in the salon as Michelle started work on applying the wigs and latex disguises.

As various members of the gang and their associates came and went, Michelle and her helpers concentrated on the three men being disguised prosthetically: Murray, Rusha and Kane. It had been decided not to disguise Royle prosthetically after all. Michelle attached a false chin to Kane. Demetris wove extensions into his hair, and tried to stick a thick beard onto his face. In doing so he managed to get cotton wool stuck all over Kane's jaw. Kane complained indignantly that he was being turned into 'a black Father Christmas'. Michelle put a latex nose and chin on Murray and applied a false moustache to the cage fighter, while she says Michael trimmed his hair into a widow's peak and stippled fake hair onto his chin to give the appearance of stubble. Michelle thought the widow's peak made Lee look like Dracula. Demitris denies changing Murray's hair in this way, saying he was working on Lee's alopecia, a problem he'd developed recently.

The work took all night. They finished just before 8.00 o'clock on Monday morning, shortly before neighbouring businesses opened up. As Michelle prepared to leave the salon for home, she says Demetris told her that he wanted her to drive down to Maidstone later in the day to meet Lee and the others, in order to touch up their disguises, which weren't designed to be worn for a long period. Like stale sandwiches, the latex would curl up at the edges. Demetris denies he told Hogg to go to Kent and says it was Rusha who asked her to go. Either way, shattered though she was, Michelle agreed, and was given hand-written directions by Lea Rusha. Everybody hoped that she wouldn't get lost.

Chapter Seven

KIDNAP

1

Colin and Lynn Dixon celebrated their twenty-seventh wedding anniversary on Friday 10 February, 2006. The Dixons were in the romantic habit of taking this week as an annual holiday, partly because, in recent years, the anniversary coincided happily with their youngest child's half-term holiday. It seems that the mobsters took turns watching 16 Hadleigh Gardens during this vacation week for the Dixons, waiting for Colin to go back to work. They needed him at work for their plan to be effective, of course. It was Coutts' turn to be in Herne Bay in the early hours of Monday 20 February, and it may only have been when he saw Colin drive off for work that morning that the gang knew for sure Colin's holiday was over. Roger called Lee Murray at Hair Hectik, and the decision was made to nab Dixon that evening.

This was perfect timing for the gang, if they wanted to steal the largest amount of money possible from Medway House. Cash use fluctuates throughout the year, with an extra £2 billion drawn from cash machines across England and Wales daily during Christmas and New Year. After this spending bonanza, as the public tightens its belt, the stock of money held in regional cash centres builds up again, reaching a peak in the month of February. It is doubtful that the gang chose to rob Medway House in February for this reason alone. Getting Colin's home address, and having him at work, were more significant factors; and only senior Securitas staff knew exactly how much money was in the depot at any one time. Even so, the gang couldn't have chosen a better month to rob the cash centre.

There was a mundane factor limiting how much they could steal, however, no matter what month they chose. The lads needed to drive a lorry into the depot building in order to load up with cash out of sight of passing police cars, and the biggest vehicle that would fit into the larger of the two loading bays at Medway House was a 7½ tonne lorry with a loading capacity of 1,000 cubic feet (or 28 cubic metres). The use of two lorries was too complicated, and there was no way they could risk coming back for a second load, so one lorry load was all they were going to get. The main target for the gang would be the cash cages in the vault. The boys would struggle to fit more than twenty cages into a 7½ tonner, which gave them a rough idea of the maximum amount they could steal. They could get a lot, but they couldn't clean out the place.

It was apparently Stuart Royle's idiotic idea to *rent* the lorry. Villains don't usually hire their vehicles. Obviously, it leaves a paper trail. It would be better to buy a truck under a false name, or steal one. There was, however, an amateurish, bumbling side to certain members of this gang, especially Royle, who had been making enquiries about obtaining a suitable hire vehicle since 11 February, when he telephoned KTS Rentals in Faversham, Kent, using the name Ian, saying he was calling from C&A Cargo (one of Royle's many company names). 'He wanted a 7½ tonne box [lorry] with a tail lift,' says Sean Hughes of KTS. A rental vehicle of this type was reserved at C&A for Sunday 19 February, which meant Ian would have had to collect it on the Saturday. It may be that the gang originally hoped to rob the depot on Sunday night, but couldn't because Dixon wasn't back at work yet. In any event it wasn't until Monday that the lads obtained a lorry, which was then taken to Elderden Farm, John Fowler's place near Staplehurst.

Royle now owed Fowler approximately £80,000. The hope that cars sales, put through the books of Monarch Retail, would pay off Royle's debt had proved a vain one; Royle hardly sold any cars at Wateringbury. On top of this, along with many of Royle's mates, John had seemingly lost a large amount of money in the Swiss real-estate scam. Recently, Fowler had also been taken to Hastings County Court for non-payment of a small debt, indicating perhaps that money was tight for the Fowlers. Nevertheless, John appeared to be his usual cheerful self as he bought and sold cars that week. In the evening, the Fowlers relaxed in front of their large, flat-screen TV, and crackling log fire, over which were displayed a pair of antique rifles. The Fowlers were secure in their home, surrounded by their private acres and, beyond their fences, the gentle, green landscape of Kent described so well by H.E. Bates in *The Darling Buds of May*. John was a veritable Pop Larkin.

The car dealer maintains that he was never a part of the conspiracy to kidnap the Dixons and rob Medway House; he didn't know a thing about it. He was an Honest John, son of a Flash Harry, and he'd served time for fraud, but John wasn't *that* kind of crook. One tends to believe Linda Fowler when she says of her husband: 'He is not this way. He is not a bully boy.' John's story is that Slippery Royle, whom Linda had long warned him against, conned him into doing certain things to help the gang, including hiring the lorry used in the heist. John would later tell the police that there was no way he would have hired the lorry had he known what it was going to be used for, and indeed he would have been stupid to do so. Even so, the police believe that the gang used Elderden Farm on the night of the kidnap and robbery.

A lane ran alongside the Fowler property, on the other side of which were industrial buildings belonging to Hop Engineering, a company which made farm machinery. When staff came to work on the morning of Monday, 20 February, which was a freezing cold day, they saw a 7½ tonne white lorry parked next to Fowler's yard. This lorry was the exact type used in the raid, but curiously it was not *the* lorry. The boys may have had a last-minute concern about this vehicle, wherever it came from, because just after breakfast that morning Fowler telephoned KTS Trucks asking to hire *another* lorry. Fowler says that Royle told him he wanted the vehicle to collect some things from his defunct hairdressing salon in Maidstone, but he couldn't hire one himself, because he didn't have a credit card. So John hired it for him as a favour, with Royle promising to pay him back. They had done this before.

Royle was at Elderden Farm when Fowler called KTS. The sign-writer Keith Borer was also there, having come over to fix Parcelforce markings to the Post Office van, now parked in Fowler's yard. Keith was surprised at the size of Elderden Farm, 'a bloody great place', and sensed a heavy atmosphere as the yard gate was shut behind him. Despite the inclement weather, and his misgivings about the situation, Keith cleaned the side of the red van with Mr Muscle, then stuck on the bogus Parcelforce logo and lettering he had made for Stuart. The job took less than half an hour and Keith expected to be paid for his work in cash. Royle, typically, said he'd pay him later. That was four jobs in a row Keith hadn't been paid for. He left the farm feeling hard done by, cold and a little scared.

John drove to KTS around lunchtime, with his employee Mick

Tasker. John later said he was surprised to see what a large vehicle KTS had for him, far bigger than Stuart needed to clear out
his little shop; he could have done that with a van. This was a 7½
tonne Renault Midlum lorry, white in colour, with a drop-down
tail lift.

John rang Stuart. 'It's massive!' he said. Royle chuckled.

John told KTS he needed the lorry for 24 hours. If he really
intended to bring the lorry back before lunch on Tuesday, the
gang must have intended to kidnap the Dixons on Monday night,
robbing the depot in the early hours of 21 February. Fowler
charged the £130 rental, plus the £300 deposit, to his credit card.
He had to show his driver's licence plus two other forms of identification, so there was no doubt who had hired it. Fowler says he
handed the lorry over to Royle at a service area on the M20. The
evidence is that the lorry was then taken back to Elderden Farm
and that, somewhere along the way, it was fitted with false
number plates.

2

While John and Stuart were obtaining the lorry, Michelle Hogg
was running herself ragged to get down to Kent to meet the boys.
She had been up all night at Hair Hectik, disguising Lee Murray
and his mates, just had time to drive home to her flat, turn off the
lights and heating, and drink half a cup of coffee, before getting
back in her little car and heading down to Maidstone. She looked
at the directions Lea Rusha had written for her:

ON A2, TAKE DARTFORD CROSS, TURN OFF, GO
M25 GATWICK, TAKE M20 MAIDSTONE, JUNCTION
4 M20 HEAD TONBRIDGE.

Hogg was soon lost. She called Katie Philp, who put Lea on the line. He gave Michelle directions to the Chef and Brewer pub next to Royle's garage in Wateringbury, saying they would meet her there. Michelle arrived shortly before 10.00 a.m. When Lea and Kate showed up half an hour later they found Michelle asleep in her car. They took her into the pub for some more coffee. Lea scribbled return directions for Michelle on an order pad so she could get home later. Lea and Kate then got into Michelle's car and helped her follow a white van, almost certainly driven by Stuart Royle, to his mother's house in Maidstone. Bizarrely, the gang had chosen to use the pensioner's bungalow as base camp for the kidnap. Stuart let everybody in through the kitchen door, and led them through to the conservatory where Jetmir Bucpapa was waiting.

Michelle and Kate set to work, applying a latex nose to Rusha. 'He didn't like it, so it was removed,' says Michelle. Still they went to great trouble to change the roofer's appearance. Kate put special make-up on her boyfriend's face to give the appearance of broken capillary veins, as are often seen around the nose of an older person. Michelle stuck a ginger goatee to his face, to match his dyed-red hair.

It seems that Murray was with Kane Patterson and Paul Allen at Paul's girlfriend's house. Stacie-Lee Dudley, who ran a pub in Welling, lived in a former council house on the Lords Wood Estate on the outskirts of Chatham. The property was protected by high railings and a sophisticated video-intercom, as if she and Paul were worried about who might come calling.

After lunch, Murray, Allen and Kane drove from Chatham to Mrs Royle's bungalow to meet the others. Kane Patterson was grumbling about his disguise and Michelle could only agree that Michael Demetris had done a poor job. The wig he had put on Patterson looked awful, and Kane wasn't happy about the false nose that had been stuck onto his face. He said he wanted it to be flatter. Michelle improvised a solution in the most extraordinary way. Firstly she got two black rubber baby bottle teats, snipped off the ends, and pushed the flexible tubes up Kane's nostrils. This had the effect of flaring the nostrils, making his nose wider. Kane then asked for the skin around his eyes to be pulled back to lend him an Oriental appearance. Michelle tried sticking cotton tabs to his head, under the wig, but these didn't pull the skin tight enough. She needed elastic. 'I thought, *What else can I use*? I thought, my bra.' Michelle removed her brassiere, cut off the black straps, and stuck snippets of the elasticated material to Kane's skin, pulling his eyes into a slant.

When these weird, homemade disguises were complete, Murray led the boys into a separate room for a private gang meeting, emerging fifteen minutes later. Murray and Rusha should have left the house at this stage if they intended to kidnap Colin Dixon on his way home, but Murray remained at the bungalow until after 7.00 p.m., judging by cell-siting, by which time he had missed his opportunity. At 7.12, Ermir Hysenaj risked calling Jet from Medway House, possibly to find out what was going on, or to report some last-minute problem. It may be that the hold-up was to do with a change of plan about where the gang would take the Dixons after the kidnap. It's possible that they originally wanted to use Redpits. The bailiffs were expected any day now, however, and this may have put them off. It seems they decided instead to use Elderden Farm, and this may not have been convenient on Monday night.

About 8.30 p.m., Michelle drove home, and Stuart, Kim and Jet appear to have gone to Elderden Farm. Around 9.30 p.m., John Fowler's teenage daughter, Amy, was given a lift home by her friend, Nadine Jenkins. As the girls turned off Chart Hill Road, going towards the farmhouse, Nadine saw a white van and

white lorry turning towards the house. The drivers used a new
fork in the lane, which had been laid down for the convenience
of Hop Engineering. It joined the old lane between the engineering shed and the Fowlers' property. When Nadine tried to
pull out of the Fowlers' drive a few minutes later she found the
white van blocking her way. A man in a baseball cap came out
and moved it. This may have been Jet, who was in the area at the
time, speaking to Ermir on his mobile, after which he drove to
Tunbridge Wells to see Raluca Millen.

Here, then, was a pause in the frantic activity leading up to
the heist, but only a brief respite, because the gang decided to
make their move the following evening. The fact that the job had
been put back 24 hours gave them a bonus they may not have
appreciated at the time. Coming after the weekend, and before
the public start to draw money out again for the following weekend, Tuesday tends to be the day of the week that cash centres
have the maximum stock of bank notes. By clever planning, or
dumb luck, the gang were going to knock off Medway House on
a Tuesday in February, when the vault was filled to capacity.

3

It rained overnight and was cold when Colin Dixon got up for
work at 6.30 on the morning of Tuesday, 21 February 2006. His
was an early start because he had an hour-long commute to
Tonbridge. Colin put on black trousers, a blue shirt and loudly
striped tie, with a blue anorak. He slipped on his special work
shoes and picked up his black holdall in which he kept his Filofax
and a key fob that opened the pedestrian and vehicle gates at the
depot. He also picked up his wallet, notebook, mobile phone and
glasses case, in which he kept his spectacles, car keys and a swipe

card. Normally, Colin clipped a personal attack alarm to his belt, but he had recently sat on the device and broken it.

As he stepped out of the house into his drive, and smelt the ozone-rich sea air gusting about, Colin had a choice of two cars: the Ford Ka and the Nissan Almera with a pink gonk on its dashboard. Colin liked to alternate vehicles, but he had recently arranged to sell the Ka, and didn't want to put extra miles on the clock before the sale went through, so he was using the Nissan almost all the time now. As he started the engine, the morning news on the radio was of another bomb blast in Baghdad, further delays in the construction of the new Wembley Stadium and a 15 per cent jump in profits at his old firm Barclays Bank. Colin turned left on Beltinge Road, left again on Canterbury Road, and was soon heading west on the M2 with the sun rising in his rear-view mirror.

4

Lee Murray had been up since 4.30, gabbling on the phone with Paul Allen. This was the biggest day of their lives. During the next 24 hours the friends expected to both become multi-millionaires. But there was a lot to do before Lee pounced on Colin Dixon, on his way back home from work.

Thinking ahead to how they were going to split and hide the cash the gang had ordered a consignment of luggage, including a large number of cheap, Chinese-made holdalls and suitcases, branded Eagle and Monarch. The luggage was seemingly delivered to Fowler's yard overnight without his knowledge. When Hop Engineering worker Lee Ray came to work around 8.00 he saw luggage labels strewn in the lane, which he collected and handed to his boss, David Deacon. Ray also saw a white lorry parked next to Fowler's yard.

John Fowler was surprised to see the lorry when he woke up, doubly so when his daughter told him it had been there all night. He claims he rang Royle at 9.30 and asked him to move the lorry, which was blocking the lane. Royle was at his daughter Chrissy's house in Allen Street, Maidstone, just around the corner from his old salon. He came straight over to Elderden Farm to move the lorry, and asked John at the same time to call KTS to extend the lorry rental for another day, which Fowler did. John then started to go about his normal business, including making a deal to buy a black VW Beetle.

Waking up at home in Lambersart Close, Southborough, Lea Rusha put in a call to his girlfriend Kate at Fenwick's, where she had returned to work after her two-week break. Staff at the store were worried about Kate. 'She was not focused and had something on her mind,' says her boss Diane Rowbotham.

When Michelle woke up at her flat in London she saw that Michael Demetris had been trying to ring her. She claims that when she called him back, he said he wanted her to go straight down to Maidstone to touch up the disguises for the lads. He couldn't come himself because he had a meeting. Demetris denies he told Hogg to go back to Kent, and says he was spending the day visiting family in North London. Michelle set off in her car. Despite having done the exact same journey the previous day, she soon got lost.

Lee Murray was also driving down to Kent, to Chatham, where he met Paul Allen at his girlfriend's house. Roger Coutts joined them there, the three Woolwich boys forming a solid team. Their Albanian friend Jetmir Bucpapa was in Tonbridge keeping an eye on Medway House, where his mate Ermir Hysenaj would be working as normal later in the day.

It was cold and wet at lunchtime, rain alternating with sleet, when John Fowler drove the rented lorry to the Tamarisk Petrol Station on Linton Road to fill up with fuel, followed by Stuart

Royle in a green Peugeot car, which he parked outside the garage. Fowler paid for the petrol at 1.21 p.m. As Royle waited, he got out of his car and fiddled with his rear windscreen wiper in a way that attracted attention. 'He was looking across the fore-court as if he was looking for someone,' notes Jane Linfoot, who was in a car on the forecourt with her husband and her mother. 'I wondered if he was going to rob the petrol station.' Mrs Linfoot's mother, Evelyn Clifford, was so suspicious of the man with the green car that she wrote his registration number on her copy of the *Daily Telegraph*.

Stuart then drove to his mother's house, where the mob began to congregate in mid-afternoon. Neighbours had never seen so many people trooping in and out of the bungalow. When Ann and Ray Berry saw Cynthia at her door, they asked the old dear if everything was alright.

'Yes. There's nothing illegal going on,' was her peculiar reply.

'I'm not questioning you,' said Ann. 'I'm just making sure you're alright.'

'They're having a car dealers' meeting,' Cynthia explained.

When Ann asked Cynthia why Stuart's friends couldn't meet at his garage, the old lady said that the house was more conven-ient, grumbling only that Stuart's friends were treading muck into her bungalow: a typically neat old lady's house, the sideboards laden with knickknacks and family photographs, Scamp yapping at every visitor.

Just after lunch, Royle, Rusha and Bucpapa had to go and rescue Michelle Hogg who, despite having called Lea for direc-tions, had got hopelessly lost, and was sitting in her car in a dead end somewhere near Wateringbury. When they found her, Royle got into Michelle's car and directed her to his mum's house, while Lea and Jet followed in the Peugeot.

At the bungalow, Michelle reapplied Rusha's red beard. Kane

arrived still wearing the disguise from the day before, bra straps and all. Michelle stuck down the corners of his disguise. He was still complaining about the beard Michael had made for him, so Michelle gave it a trim. It looked a little better after that. Murray arrived about 5.00 o'clock, dressed smartly in a grey suit. He had a new false moustache, bushier than before, with a fuller beard. Michelle touched up the disguise. Paul and Roger also arrived. Neither was disguised prosthetically, but they both looked unusual nevertheless in that Michelle recalls they were wearing tight-fitting, black body suits, what Michelle described as 'Ninja-style suits'. Cynthia Royle's bungalow was now crowded with weird-looking people, wearing strange clothes and disguises. Stuart offered his odd guests coffee, cake and biscuits. Somebody sent out for pizza. Just as had happened the day before, the men then went into a room for a private meeting. Hogg overheard Murray speaking to Bucpapa, saying: 'Tell your mate . . .' Then she heard Bucpapa on the phone speaking in his native language, no doubt to Hysenaj, who would have been about to start his shift. The Albanian had been attending a training course in Hastings which meant he was working half-shifts at the depot. This evening he would only be at Medway House between six and ten.

5

Half an hour or so before Ermir came to work at Medway House, Colin Dixon handed over to the night-shift manager and went home. Colin tried to get away from work as promptly as possible at 5.30 p.m., because he had an hour's drive back to Herne Bay, and Lynn liked the family to sit down to dinner together between 6.30 and 7.00.

Born in London in 1977, Lee Murray is seen here, a couple of years before the robbery, as a young father with two of his three children.

Having been raised on council estates in south-east London, Lee Murray and his wife Siobhan moved to this suburban semi-detached house in Onslow Drive, Sidcup, in 2003.

On Christmas Day 2003 Lee Murray was involved in a violent road rage incident with lorry driver David Meyer (second from left) as Meyer was driving back to his house from Christmas lunch at the home of his mother Dorothy (far right), with son David (far left) and daughter Julia (third from left).

Lee Murray enjoyed a brief spell as a cage-fighting star, winning a major event in Las Vegas in January 2004. He is seen here (right) with his Dutch coach Remco Pardoel.

In September 2005, Murray got into two street fights outside the Funky Buddha club in London. He was knifed repeatedly in the second fight, and almost died of his injuries. He is seen here showing off the scars left by the stabbing.

Lee Murray's lifelong friend
Paul Allen.

Roofer Lea Rusha became a leading
figure in the heist gang.

Mechanic Roger Coutts grew up with Lee Murray in south-east London and
became part of the heist gang. Here he is fishing in happier days.

Car dealer John Fowler.

Stuart 'Slippery' Royle a few years before the heist.

Fowler's handsome home, Elderden Farm, near Staplehurst in Kent. The police believe the heist gang used outbuildings as 'the flop'.

Royle's rented home, Redpits Cottage, Langley, Kent, which he hoped to buy with the proceeds of the robbery.

Albanian clerk, Ermir Hysenaj, was the gang's inside man at the cash depot.

The other Albanian in the gang was Jetmir 'Jet' Bucpapa.

Ermir Hysenaj is seen here on CCTV inside Medway House, the Securitas cash depot in Kent, on 16 January, 2006, as he filmed the building with a secret camera in his belt.

The exterior of Medway House, the Tonbridge cash depot in which more than £200 million was stored. Note the fortified turnstile pedestrian gate which was only installed after the robbery.

Cash depot manager Colin Dixon is seen here with his wife Lynn on their wedding day in 1979. This is the only image of the couple in general circulation.

The hair salon in Forest Hill, south London, where Michelle Hogg says she disguised the robbers.

Inset: The Old Bailey heard that Hogg used elastic from her bra to disguise a robber.

Hogg lived in a top floor flat at this building near Shooters Hill, south-east London, and worked from home making the latex disguises for the gang. Note the wheelie bins by the door in which she disposed of the materials.

Inset: A display of make-up products found in Hogg's wheelie bin. She used these items to disguise the gang.

A few days before the heist, Lee Murray went clubbing with his mates at the SE1 in Southwark, south-east London. Left to right we see Paul Allen in a hat, Keyinde 'Kane' Patterson, a friend of Lee Murray's named Bradley Fitzgerald and Murray himself in the grey suit. At around 6.00 a.m. Sunday 12 February, 2006, a few hours after this picture was taken, Murray crashed his Ferrari driving home along the New Kent Road. He abandoned the car, leaving behind this and two other photographs, plus two mobile phones which later provided the police with invaluable evidence against the gang.

On the evening of Tuesday 21 February, 2006, Lynn Dixon and her youngest child were kidnapped from this house, their home at 16 Hadleigh Gardens, Herne Bay. The Dixons would never live here again.

Colin Dixon was halfway on his journey home from Tonbridge to Herne Bay on 21 February, 2006, when he was stopped by what he believed to be police on the A249. He pulled over on the right between the pub and the bus stop.

After the kidnapping, the Dixons helped the police create e-fits of the two 'policemen' who kidnapped them. Their memories were at times contradictory, but the man seen above was probably Lea Rusha.

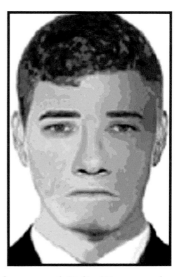

These are e-fits of the tall policeman who stopped Colin Dixon on the A249, seen firstly in his disguise, and how he would appear without the hat and beard. He bears a striking resemblance to Lee Murray.

PED GATE - Feb 22 '06 01:21:58

One of the remarkable aspects of the Tonbridge robbery is that the heist was captured on CCTV. The above image shows Colin Dixon letting 'Policeman' into the compound of Medway House via the pedestrian gate. Note the date and time on the police caption.

FRONT DOOR - Feb 22 '06 01:22:15

Seventeen seconds later, standing on the step of Medway House, Colin rings the door bell for attention. Policeman is behind him, head down.

LOBBY   - Feb 22 '06 01:22:31

Colin Dixon is now inside the lobby of the cash depot,
Policeman behind him, still with his head down, possibly with a
gun in one hand. Colin is pulling open the door to the air lock.

BLDG FRONT - Feb 22 '06 01:26:46

The white Renault lorry arrives at the depot gates, driven by
Driver (Stuart Royle) with Lynn Dixon and her child in the
back, guarded by an armed and nervous Hi Viz (Bucpapa).

FRONT DOOR - Feb 22 '06 01:29:07

Dressed from head to foot in black, more robbers arrive at the front door of the depot. Police believe this group included 'Lightning' Lee Murray.

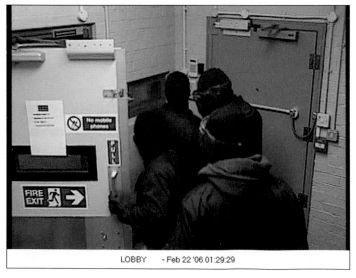

LOBBY - Feb 22 '06 01:29:29

Four robbers enter the lobby of Medway House, with Shorty (Rusha) opening the air lock door for his mates.

flashing lights in the radiator grille. I took it to be a police car [and] I thought they wanted me to stop, so I pulled over.'

6

Although the Three Squirrels looked like a normal pub, it operated as a private drinking club, featuring 'exotic dancers', and didn't open on Tuesdays. Just beyond the darkened public house was a bus stop where cars could pull over, so long as the Sittingbourne bus wasn't in the way. Rusha had taken a look at the area in January. It was perfect for them because it was so quiet. The landscape beyond was fields and woodland, spookily dark on a winter's evening.

With flashing blue lights behind him, Colin pulled over just short of the bus stop. The police tucked in behind him. Colin saw that there were two men in the car. The man in the passenger seat got out and came to his window, not to the passenger side as Colin expected, but crossing between the two vehicles to the driver's door, which was a dangerous place to stand with cars flashing past at high speed. Colin could feel the Nissan being buffeted in the slipstream of the fast-moving traffic on his right. Despite being such a very busy road, there was a paradoxical feeling of being in the middle of nowhere now he had stopped. The bus shelter stood empty. The Three Squirrels was shut. The building next door, Foley House Dog Kennels, appeared closed. There was nobody in sight save the policeman.

The officer was a tall man, wearing a dark jacket and a peaked cap with a chequered band. 'He told me to switch off the engine, and leave the keys in the ignition,' Colin later said. 'After that he told me to get out and go to the car behind.' Colin's training was clear. He should not get out of his car, but he did. This was the first of a series of actions Colin took on the night which would cause him to come under suspicion later on.

The tall police officer jostled Colin to the rear passenger door of the police car. Colin was told to get in and move to the far side, which he had difficulty doing because the driver's seat was pushed back leaving little room for a man as large as himself. The tall officer got in beside him. Colin noticed the man had freckles and a thin, ginger beard, which is confusing because police believe the kidnapper must have been Lee Murray, whom Hogg said had been given a grey tint. It was the much shorter Rusha who had been disguised with red hair dye. This is, of course, something Lee Murray could point to in order to back up his contention that he was not a kidnapper.

The tall officer snapped handcuffs on Colin, first his right wrist, then his left. When this was done the officer got out of the car to move Colin's car forward in the lay-by. Colin spoke with the driver who wore a fluorescent jacket with 'POLICE' on the back. Colin asked why he had been stopped. Without turning his head, the driver replied that a car with his registration had been seen several times the previous week speeding on the M2 and M20 at over 100 mph. Colin was astounded. He knew he couldn't have been caught speeding on those roads the previous week, because he'd been on holiday and hadn't used the motorway. And surely motorists accused of speeding weren't routinely handcuffed. Another thing that struck Colin as odd was that there was no police-type equipment in the car. At the least he would have expected a police radio. There was only a normal car radio, and it was tuned to Radio 1. Next to the radio the car clock showed the time was now 6.28 p.m.

The tall officer returned to the car, getting into the back with Colin, who asked to see identification. The men said their ID was at the station. At which point the driver accelerated into traffic. He sped down the dual carriageway to the junction of the M2, where he turned around and went back the way they'd come, over Detling Hill. Colin complained that his handcuffs were too tight. He was told they couldn't be loosened. The key was at the station.

Colin's car had been left in the lay-by, where it would be in the way of the next bus coming down the hill. So another gang member came along and moved the Nissan. Whoever did this had good local knowledge because they drove the car to the Cock at Detling, a quiet country pub which is difficult to find from the wrong side of the A249 unless you know the area. Stuart Royle could have found it, and he was cell-sited in the vicinity between 6.32 and 7.00 p.m.

Colin Dixon thought it prudent to make a note of what was happening. But when he reached for his notebook, the tall officer snatched it away. The Vectra proceeded to the M20, where they turned north, giving Dixon the impression they were heading for Maidstone Police Station, but they didn't take the correct exit. As if to cover themselves, the two fake policemen indulged in a little play-acting.

'Where are you taking him?' the tall policeman asked the driver.

'Tonbridge,' came the reply, apparently meaning Tonbridge Police Station.

'Why?'

'Because that's what we've been told to do.'

They left the M20 at Junction 4, turning onto the A228, and then continued south on the West Malling bypass into the hamlet of Mereworth, near Wateringbury. Suddenly the driver turned sharp left, in front of oncoming cars who flashed their lights in protest, at which point the driver said over his shoulder: 'You will have guessed we are not policemen. Don't do anything silly and you won't get hurt.' The driver turned right on Seven Mile Lane, travelling towards West Peckham. They pulled over suddenly. The driver took out a ringing mobile phone. 'Where the fuck are you?' he asked his caller, evidently having missed a rendezvous point. 'We just went past there.' Then he made a U-turn. The handcuffs were biting Colin's wrists. He wriggled to relieve the pain, which alarmed his kidnappers.

'We're not fucking about,' growled the tall officer, pulling out a pistol. 'This is a fuckin' 9 mm.'

The driver seemed to overshoot his rendezvous again, because he did a second U-turn, shortly after which they stopped behind a white van on the left-hand side of the lane. Colin noticed a rusty hasp on the rear van doors. He guessed the time was about 7.00 p.m., dinner time. Colin was told to get out of the car. As he walked into the headlights of the car, going towards the back of the van, he sensed two people flanking him. The double doors of the van were open and a man was inside with a balaclava on, a gun in his waistband. Colin thought there were two more men with the van, meaning he was in the hands of five bandits, two of whom would have been Bucpapa and Coutts, both cell-sited in the area around this time.

'I asked what side to get in,' recalls Colin, who was remarkably co-operative with his abductors from the start. At no stage did he resist, try to trick them, or escape. Despite being so meek he says that the men threatened and menaced him. When he raised his head to ask simply what side of the van to get into, for example, they told him gruffly not to look around 'or I would get a hole in me'. Colin swivelled himself in on his bottom. His legs were tied together, right over left. His spectacles were removed. A gangster whom Colin came to think of as 'Grunter' – because he didn't speak but coughed, sniffed and made grunting noises –

taped his eyes. Grunter also searched Colin's pockets, confiscating his mobile phone.

The doors were closed and the van drove off, with 'Grunter' guarding Colin in the back. Colin's perception was that they were travelling along country roads, splashing through puddles on what was a wet night. Occasionally there was light through the tape. 'Grunter' was flashing a torch. At length the van seemed to turn into a bumpy, potholed lane, then stopped. It seemed like they had been on a long journey to get here, but it may only have taken 20 minutes. Colin heard what he thought was the *clank* of a metal gate opening. The van seemed to turn 45° to the left, then 45° to the right, going up a slope, before getting stuck in mud. He heard the engine revving. Finally the van came to a halt.

The back doors were opened, but Colin was left sitting in the freezing cold as the gang went away to talk privately about what they were going to do next. It got colder. Colin heard rain on the back of the van, leading him to think the front was under shelter.

Police believe the gang had taken Colin into John Fowler's yard at Elderden Farm. If so, what of John Fowler? John had had a normal day. He'd been over to Seasalter to meet a couple who were interested in buying a bungalow he owned. John had also been trading cars. That evening a car dealer called at the house, while another man came over to talk to Linda about some computer work they were having done. Jack was off school sick and as the night drew in Dad was cuddling his boy in front of the fire watching TV. If the gang had brought Colin Dixon into his yard, John says he simply didn't know about it, while Linda insists that her husband would never have brought anything of this nature to their home. 'Why would you arrange for everything to happen at your house?' she asks.

While Fowler's yard is adjacent to the house, it is separate from the property, with its own entrance. A 440-yard lane runs from Chart Hill Road to the Fowlers' front gate, but, as noted, a new dog-leg extension had been built for the convenience of Hop Engineering. This extension was bumpy because it had not yet been surfaced. If the gang did bring Dixon to the farm it would make sense to use this track, which kept them away from the front of the house, while bringing them ultimately into the lane between Hop Engineering and Fowler's yard. The yard fence had its own gate with a metal fastener. Once inside this quadrangle yard, the gang would have been completely out of sight of the Fowlers in the house. If the van with the rusty hasp was parked in the yard under the lean-to it would have been partially out of the rain.

It so happened that the directors of Hop Engineering were holding their board meeting that night. The meeting started at 7.00 p.m. and ended at 9.30. Three times they were disturbed by the sound of doors slamming, vehicles moving and engines revving nearby. Concerned that there might be burglars prowling about, director David Deacon got up to take a look and saw headlights shining on trees between their buildings and Fowler's property. He also saw a white Transit van driving down the new track.

7

Having handed Colin Dixon over to their *compadres*, Murray and Rusha seemingly drove to Herne Bay to kidnap Lynn Dixon and her child. There was ample time to get down to the coast, and when they arrived they probably met other gang members who had been keeping the house under observation. It would be a disaster if Lynn went out before they had a chance to grab her.

Royle was in the area around this time. It may be that Murray and Rusha swapped vehicles with the car dealer, for although Colin had been kidnapped by two policemen in a Vectra, the second kidnapping was done by policemen in a Volvo S60, the car that had been stolen in Croydon. Again, the car was unmarked. Despite the change of vehicle, detectives believe that Murray and Rusha carried out both kidnappings.

Colin wasn't due home until 6.30, and the lads needed Lynn to fret a while before knocking at the door. If Lightning Lee and Little Lea waited in Hadleigh Gardens itself, they went unnoticed, and this was a street where neighbours took a close interest in who came and went. There had been a children's party that afternoon at one of the houses so there had been more cars around than normal, but the kids had long since been collected. Around 7.15 Shirley Wenman, who lived opposite the Dixons, walked down the road to her Red Cross meeting. She didn't see anything unusual. Nor did her husband John, a retired police sergeant.

Colin had been halfway home when he was kidnapped – 24 miles from Medway House, 25 miles to Herne Bay – which meant he would have been due home by now. His habit was to ring Lynn when he reached Thanet Way, twenty minutes away, so she knew to put the finishing touches to their meal. He didn't do so, which was the first thing that concerned her. Lynn called Colin's mobile. He didn't answer. Suppertime came and went and still Colin wasn't home. Around 7.30 Lynn took their child upstairs for a bath, then put the child to bed. Lynn called Colin's mobile two more times, and got his voicemail. She checked Ceefax to see if there had been an accident. She considered calling the police, but decided against it. Colin had said he was getting petrol. 'I didn't know if I was just panicking.' To take her mind off things, Lynn settled down to wrap some gifts for their child, soon to celebrate a birthday, and watched a programme on Channel Five called *Selling Yourself*.

The show was two-thirds over when at, 8.40 p.m., the door-bell went and the caller simultaneously banged on the door. Lynn rushed to the door to find two policemen on her step. She described one as very tall and lanky, with pale skin, a handlebar moustache and unkempt hair, which hung down from under-neath his policeman's cap. This sounds like Murray. She said the other man was short and stocky, possibly with a beard. This must have been Rusha, though it seems Lynn got the men mixed up to some degree.

'Are you Mrs Lynn Dixon?' asked Shorty.

When she said she was, the men told her they needed to come inside to discuss something. Lynn didn't think to touch the special panic button, just beside the front door. She let them in. The men then confirmed her fears. Colin had been in an accident, and was in hospital. She was naturally upset. They wanted to take her to hospital. She said she had a child upstairs in bed. The tall officer followed Lynn up to the bedroom. 'What do I say?' Lynn asked the officer, unsure how to explain to her youngest that Daddy had been in an accident. The policeman urged her to wake the child immediately and get the kid dressed. He waited while the youngster pulled on tracksuit bottoms, a coat and a woollen hat. Lynn went downstairs to get her handbag and mobile. She suggested that she might ask her neighbour to come in. The tall policeman said no. 'We don't want to distress anybody else.'

One of the officers had Lynn's mobile. He put it in her bag. Lynn got her coat, some children's books and a Robinson's fruit drink for the child. They all left the house at approximately 8.50 p.m. Lynn set the house alarm as she departed. The officers' car was parked in front of the house next door. The child got in the back first. Both men climbed into the front. As Lynn got in the back she noticed that the car radio was tuned to Magic FM. Suddenly suspicious, she asked the men for identification.

'Oh, it's in the boot,' one of the men replied.

Lynn screamed. The officer in the passenger seat reached behind and put a gloved hand over her mouth. Lynn felt the car door close on her foot. 'Why are you hurting my mummy?' yelled the child. Lynn was allowed to free her leg. The men warned her that they were armed. They wouldn't harm her or the child so long as they kept their heads down and remained quiet. Realizing that getting upset wasn't helping, Lynn calmed down and told her child she was alright. This all happened in seconds as the car sped out of the close.

As they drove at speed out of town, Lynn asked after Colin, assuming that the men had her husband, too. She was told that her husband was alright. She then told her child that so long as they did what the men said they wouldn't be harmed, and the youngster seemed to accept this, though the child was confused as to what had happened to Daddy.

The men in the front were speaking almost constantly on mobile phones, their conversation cut only as they shot through the Chestfield Tunnel. Around 9.05 p.m. they reached Brenley Lane, just off Brenley Corner, where the Thanet Way joins the M2. Lynn saw a man in overalls and a balaclava waiting in the back of a red Parcelforce van. There seems to have been several men with the van, some of them possibly in Royal Mail clothing. It is likely that Royle was one of them. The kidnappers wanted Lynn and the kid to get out of the car one at a time. Lynn refused, saying they wouldn't be separated. 'We're not going to do anything silly,' she reassured her kidnappers, and so she was allowed to hold the child's hand as they were put into the back of the van together. A police jacket was thrown over them, the door closed, and they set off, being thrown about by the motion of the vehicle. As Lynn tried to sit upright she explained as best she could to her child that they were not going to hospital, after all; the men just wanted money.

At about 9.45 p.m. at the end of a long and uncomfortable drive they came to a bumpy lane, then stopped. Lynn was very concerned for her child, who now wanted to go to the toilet. The side door of the van slid open – allowing Lynn a glimpse of a dark building with a light on in a frosted window – and the child was taken a few steps to urinate in the open before being brought back. Time passed. Every few minutes the door would open so the kidnappers could check on them. Lynn asked how long they would be kept there. It was freezing cold, and her legs were numb. Mother and child rubbed themselves for warmth and cuddled up close. Then they heard shouting.

8

Although Lynn didn't know it, Colin was only a few yards away in his van. Before Lynn arrived, his shoes had been removed leaving him in stocking feet. Still blindfolded and handcuffed, he was extremely uncomfortable and cold. Colin heard various sounds including a train in the distance and a motor running. A man was in the driver's seat of the van, and each time his mobile rang he got out to answer it, evidently so that Colin couldn't hear what was said. 'Grunter' got in and out, too, while another man came to the van periodically to interrogate him.

This man asked about Colin's phone, which had rung with a call from a person identified in Colin's address book as AAAA, a code the gangsters thought suspicious. Colin explained that this was his wife. He had their home number programmed in his address book as AAAA so it would come up first in the menu. The questioner asked what Lynn would do if he didn't arrive home on time. 'I told him that she would ring me.' The kidnapper wanted to know what she would do next. Colin predicted that she would ring his work.

'Then what?'

She would ring the police. This was a real risk to the gang until the point that Mrs Dixon was kidnapped, assuming that the Dixons were innocent victims.

The gangster then quizzed Colin about Medway House, asking how many people would be working there tonight, though one might imagine the gang would have known this from Ermir Hysenaj. Maybe it was a test question. Colin answered honestly that there would be approximately fourteen people on duty. He was asked about the position of alarms, and told the kidnappers where the buttons were.

Colin heard a car and two vans arrive. 'We have your wife and kid,' he was told. 'If you do as you're told no one will be hurt.'

Colin asked how he could be sure they had his wife and child. The kidnappers went and got Lynn and the kid, opening the sliding door of the red van and walking them around to the white van, which was parked nose-to-nose with theirs. 'There were a number of people with balaclavas and with guns,' Mrs Dixon remembered, 'and there was Colin.' Her husband was sitting on the edge of his van, eyes taped, handcuffed. Although blind, Colin knew it was his wife the moment she spoke. 'She kept asking if I was OK.' Colin had been warned not to speak, but he couldn't help but ask Lynn in return if they were alright.

After this brief reunion Colin was interrogated further, particularly about the CCTV system at Medway House. The man asking the questions was under the impression that information from the cameras was stored on a CD-type disc, which he wanted to remove after the robbery. Colin said there was no such disc, rather pictures were recorded onto a hard drive which could not be taken out easily. Now that he knew for sure the gang had his wife and child, Colin was telling the gang everything they wanted to know, though in fact he had been remarkably chatty from the start. The gang rewarded his cooperation by bringing Lynn and the child back to the Transit to sit with Dad. Colin was in acute discomfort because the handcuffs were cutting off his circulation. Lynn reached across to him, but her touch made Colin wince with pain. Lynn told the robbers that their child needed to pee again, and again the youngster was taken into the yard. Lynn saw what looked like a garage, but she was more concerned about being separated from her child. 'I could feel that she was upset [by this],' Colin later said.

Colin was told to get out of the van. He wriggled to the edge, where the rope around his ankles was untied and the handcuffs removed. Colin managed to stumble ten paces or so before his feet began to shake, having been bound so long. 'Help him' ordered someone, and two men supported Dixon into a building. Colin couldn't see where he was, but he smelt car paint. The tape was then removed from his eyes, he was given his glasses back, and ordered to look down.

Spread out before him on a green tarpaulin were two plans of Medway House, one drawn with a ruler and one freehand. Next to these were a pistol, a shotgun and a machine gun. 'I thought the guns were put there for my benefit, to intimidate me.' Five men stood around Colin as he studied the plans. The lettering showed the artist to be a poor speller. The vault was labelled 'valt'. Also, the terms used were not those Colin would employ. The CDP Room was referred to as the 'Counting Room', the Control Room as the 'Security Room'. The plans were not architecturally correct in all respects. Some walls were not shown. Doors hinged the wrong way. But a partition wall built in the

DTP within the last two weeks was on the plans, showing that the gang had up-to-date inside information.

Colin's legs were failing him, so he kneeled. As he did so, he was asked questions about the plans, including the location of alarms. Turning momentarily to his right, Colin saw a gun at his head. It looked like the tip of the barrel was lined with copper. This made such an impression on the manager that he started to think of the man holding the gun as 'Copper Tip'. This may have been Lee Murray. The kidnapper asked Colin where the gang could leave him and the rest of his staff after the robbery; Colin suggested they might lock them in the staff room. Surprisingly, the mobsters had not thought this through. Indeed, it became apparent that there were several aspects of the robbery which weren't planned. They didn't even seem sure how they were going to get into the building.

The men had Colin's bag. Inside, along with his Filofax, house keys and a Peter Kay DVD, they had found a black key fob and a swipe card. They assumed that Colin could let himself into the depot using these. He had to explain that the key fob only opened the pedestrian gate in the fence, while the swipe card worked internally. He couldn't let himself into the building. He had to ring the bell like everybody else. His interrogator asked who would be on duty in the control room. Colin thought it would be Aaron Moore who, he said, had a problem with his shoulder. One of the ruffians snarled that if Moore caused any problems they'd 'blast him'. 'Copper Tip' wanted to know what would happen if they all turned up at the depot in a police car with flashing lights. 'I said that I didn't think this would be the right thing to do.' Colin was asked what would happen if he turned up in a less ostentatious way with a single officer. He thought Aaron would let them in. He was asked whether CCTV engineers who had been installing new cameras would be working this evening. They had originally been scheduled to be on site, but Colin had authorized a change in their work hours that meant they wouldn't be back until the weekend. The questioner also knew that air-conditioning engineers had been in the depot recently and wanted to know if they would be there tonight. Colin wasn't sure. The engineers had a deadline to work to, so it was possible.

Colin said the duty manager would be Alun Thomas. 'We know about him because he spells his name funny,' said the gangster. 'He spells is A-l-u-n.' Again this showed a remarkable depth of knowledge. In fact, the bandits seemed to know the names of all the supervisors, mentioning Kamrul Islam and Ken Moody-Smith, though they mispronounced both names. Colin said that supervisors and shift managers had alarms clipped to their clothing. If activated, these sent a message to a call centre which alerted the police.

The manager was quizzed again about fixed alarms, including a specific alarm by the door in the CDP Room. Colin said he couldn't remember on which side of the door this alarm was situated. 'You're the fucking main man,' he was told angrily, 'you must fucking know.' Colin suggested that if staff were moved to the centre of the CDP Room, they wouldn't be able to touch the wall alarms, wherever they were, which got a more favourable response: 'That would work.'

The interrogation was over. Colin's glasses were taken away and tape was put back over his eyes. He was led outside to the Volvo S60, and told to sit in the front passenger seat. In addition to the driver, three gangsters got in the back. If the police are right, one of these must have been Murray. If Colin hadn't been blindfolded, he would have seen a man no longer dressed as a police officer but clad from head to foot in black: mask, boiler suit, gloves and boots. Murray looked like a member of the SAS, or indeed a member of the heist gang in *Ocean's Eleven*, a film the gang seem to have taken inspiration from. As the George Clooney figure, Murray was going to be timing his mob. Police believe he wore a stopwatch on a lanyard. All the men going to rob Medway House were dressed like Murray, save for Kane who went as a policeman. He was the only robber who would show his face, heavily disguised by Hogg and Demetris. It seems he was driving the Volvo to the depot.

Lynn and her child were ordered out of the white van. Lynn saw that it had started to sleet. They were warned to keep their eyes down. Nevertheless, Lynn caught further glimpses of the buildings and the vehicles the gang were using. A member of the gang yanked her hood down over her face. Mother and child were then taken through a gate with a metal handle. In the lane Lynn saw what she later described as a 'large white van'. It was the 7½ tonne Renault truck hired by John Fowler, who had apparently retired to bed having noticed nothing unusual in his yard this evening. There were at least four kidnappers around the Dixons now, and another man in the lorry rearranging pallets. Lynn and her child were made to get onto the tailgate lift which raised them up so they could get into the lorry, where they were ordered to sit down.

Seven men were going to rob Medway House. The police believe that behind the disguises, six of these men were Lee Murray, Kane Patterson, Lea Rusha, Roger Coutts, Jetmir Bucpapa and Stuart Royle. Detectives initially believed that the seventh masked robber was Paul Allen, and indeed this was the Crown's case during his subsequent Old Bailey trial, but the Crown ultimately conceded that, while Allen was a conspirator to kidnap and armed robbery, he wasn't one of the men who went armed into the depot on the night. No other candidate for robber number seven has been suggested. Four were in the Volvo.

Royle drove the lorry. Bucpapa was in the back, wearing a high-visibility jacket (the police later code-named him Hi Viz as a result). He was standing guard over Lynn and their child, with a gun and a torch. A seventh man drove the Vectra, which was to be used as a getaway vehicle. At approximately one o'clock on the morning of Wednesday, 22 February, these three vehicles drove towards Tonbridge in convoy. There was nothing for Lynn and her child to hang onto and they were thrown about in the back of the lorry. Hi Viz turned his torch on them sporadically, and Lynn saw that the man was fiddling with his gun in an alarming way. She would have been even more frightened had she known that, between them, the gang were armed with a 9 mm pistol, a pump-action shotgun, a Skorpian machine pistol and an AK47-style automatic rifle.

Chapter Eight

ROBBERY

1

The gang seem to have split up en route to Tonbridge. Stuart Royle may have driven the lorry ahead, with the arrangement that they all meet at Wateringbury, before travelling together for the last part of the journey. Royle was cell-sited in the vicinity of his garage just after one o'clock on Wednesday morning, at which time he received a call from Sean Lupton, with whom he was in contact throughout the night.

The gang may have split up to be less conspicuous on the road, but this seems to have led to them losing each other. The men in the car Colin was travelling in were obviously trying to liaise with somebody else. He couldn't see where they were going, but they performed two U-turns, and he heard a robber say into his mobile: 'Where are you?' Colin overheard another call in which a gangster said: 'You're nearly there.' A robber told the driver to flash his lights.

The Volvo stopped, the tape was removed from Colin's eyes and he was given his spectacles back. 'Look down, pretend you're asleep.' They set off again, and stopped again. Colin figured they were close to the depot now. His handcuffs were removed. Someone got out of the car.

Unlike the other industrial units on Vale Road, Medway House was in operation through the night, with several cars in the floodlit car park. The robbers knew they had to move fast. Colin had warned them, helpfully, that the staff were entitled to a break at 1.30, at which time some of them would come outside for a smoke. The robbers wanted to get in before that, and they arrived at the gates with minutes to spare at 1.21. Luckily, the air-conditioning engineers had just left.

The Volvo approached the depot first, stopping short of the gate. The driver handed Colin his key fob. Colin got out of the car, followed by the robber in police-style clothing, including a cap and fluorescent jacket with 'POLICE' printed on the reverse. For obvious reasons, the real police later code-named this robber 'Policeman'. An Old Bailey jury would hear that he was probably Keyinde 'Kane' Patterson. Colin took Policeman into the compound through the pedestrian gate, using his key fob, then led him up the steps to the front door. Under his cap, Policeman's face was uncovered, though he may have been wearing a prosthetic mask. At 1.22 a.m., Colin rang the doorbell, putting his face to the thick glass portal to make eye contact with Aaron Moore, but the man he saw inside was Gary Barclay.

2

'Tonight, it's Control Room Surprise,' Alun Thomas told his night-shift staff earlier that evening. Once a month the man in the Control Room was swapped at short notice with a CDP worker as a security precaution, and Alun decided that tonight was as good a time as any to carry out this routine procedure, making the regular man Aaron Moore change jobs with Gary Barclay, a relatively new agency worker who wasn't familiar with all the controls, or correct security procedure.

Gary had just caught a glimpse on CCTV of a car outside the gates of the depot when the doorbell went. Glancing out of the glass portal he saw Colin Dixon looking in at him. There was no reason for his boss to be returning to work so late. Correct procedure would have been to ask for an explanation, even ID, but Gary simply buzzed Colin in.

It was only when Gary looked through the internal portal into the lobby that he saw Colin was with a second man in police uniform. This time Gary really should have demanded an explanation. Unexpected visitors were a major security risk. But he assumed Mr Dixon had brought a police officer to the depot for good reason, probably because 'someone had to be escorted off site'. There had been problems in the past with stealing and so forth. He opened the first air-lock door without asking either man a single question. When this steel door slammed shut, Colin and Policeman were obliged to turn left and walk away from the Control Room towards the second air-lock door. They were in the man trap. If Policeman had got no further, the robbery could not have taken place. But Gary opened the second door without question, allowing both men into the Secure Area, at which point security was fatally breached. Colin used his swipe card to open the door to the corridor that led to the Control Room and within moments they were with Gary in the pod.

Colin spoke briskly to Gary. As he later recalled: 'I told him to do what the bloke said, because he had my wife and child.' Policeman had removed his cap, pulled a balaclava over his face and replaced the cap, so his features, even if he had been wearing a mask, were obscured, though Colin could see naturally dark skin around his eyes.

'Get on the floor,' Policeman told Gary, speaking in a muffled voice, possibly because of a prosthetic mask. He was brandishing a pistol. 'Nothing will happen if you do what you're told.' Gary got down on the floor immediately, taking his cue from a poster on the canteen wall which advised staff: DON'T BE A HERO. 'I decided [to] do exactly what I was told, then I would be OK. I also decided at that time not to look at anyone . . .'

Policeman ordered Gary to put his hands behind his back, then clipped handcuffs on so tightly they pinched his skin. Colin stepped across to a CCTV camera which was pointed directly at them. Although he couldn't do anything about the sixty or so other cameras in the depot, Colin chose to move this one, because, as he later explained, he felt that it might unnerve Policeman. In fact, he may have been trying to do something clever. Tilting the camera should have sent an alarm to Kent Police Headquarters. But nobody came running to their rescue.

Colin told Policeman that Gary could be seen through the door panel by anybody walking past to the toilet. 'You better move his feet.' Policeman did so. Then, without being told to do so by Policeman, but, as he would later explain, remembering an order he thinks he had been given by the gang on the way to the depot, Colin pressed the green button that opened the vehicle gate, allowing the Volvo into the car park. The time was 1.24 a.m. Two minutes later the white lorry appeared at the barrier, with the Vauxhall Vectra behind. The gate was wide open, but the vehicles paused. There were pressure pads in the tarmac before and after the gate. The gang seemed wary of these, so much so that the driver of the lorry (code-named 'Driver' by Kent Police, probably Stuart Royle) actually reversed, obliging the Vectra to back into Vale Road. One or more people then got out of the lorry. The gang evidently decided it was safe to proceed because the lorry then moved into the compound and backed up to the second loading bay.

Colin pressed the red button that closed the vehicle gate. As he did so, four robbers ran across the car park and mounted the steps to the front door. They all wore black boiler suits, black boots, black gloves and black balaclavas or masks. Only the robbers themselves know for sure who was behind each mask, but the men varied sufficiently in height, build and equipment to be given code names by Kent Police, who later worked out who they thought each robber was.

Two of the men were unusually tall. One wore a Darth Vader-like paintball mask over a balaclava helmet, carried an AK47-style assault rifle, and had a stopwatch round his neck, earning him the code name 'Stopwatch'. The police believe this was Lee Murray. The second tall man wore his boots tucked into white socks, apparently had a ballistic vest on under his boiler suit, wore what looked like a gas mask, carried a torch and had his hood pulled up over his head, earning him the code name 'Hoodie'. Police later surmised this was Paul Allen, though it was eventually accepted in court that he wasn't an active robber and didn't handle any firearms. The third, much shorter man wore a blue ballistic vest over his boiler suit, which was of a slightly different type to the others. Police called him 'Shorty', and believe he was Lea Rusha. At the start of the robbery he brandished a Skorpian machine pistol, though the boys passed their weapons between them as the need arose. The fourth and final man on the doorstep wore a balaclava, probably had a ballistic vest on under his boiler suit, and was otherwise so unremarkable that the police called him 'Mr Average'. They believe this was Roger Coutts.

Colin pushed the button to open the front door at 1.29. Stopwatch (Murray), Shorty (Rusha), Mr Average (Coutts) and Hoodie entered the lobby, Hoodie taking up the rear. Two seconds later the air-lock door was opened and they entered the man trap, doubled-backed along the parallel corridor, then stormed the Control Room where they sat Gary Barclay up, put yellow tape over his eyes and a rubbish sack over his head. 'Don't worry, you won't get hurt,' a robber told Gary in what sounded to him a Kentish accent, though that may be misleading. During the robbery the hostages – who were frightened and bewildered, and unable to see clearly who was speaking to them – heard accents they would describe variously as African, South African, Kentish, London and Scottish. Often they contradicted each other.

While the robbers were asking Gary Barclay about access to the 'electricity room' upstairs a woman walked past the door. 'Who is that [and] where have they gone?' Colin was asked. He said he couldn't see. So Stopwatch went to find out.

Gary Barclay was asked if the camera in the corner of the Control Room was the only one in the room. He said it was, catching a glimpse under his blindfold of a rifle on the floor beside him. He feared he might start hyper-ventilating. Most of the gang then left the Control Room, Colin walking in front of them past his office into the open-plan Desk Top Processing (DTP) area, where two staff members were chatting. Alun Thomas, the grey-haired duty manager, was talking with supervisor Melanie Sampson, one of the most experienced members of staff, about Colin, funnily enough, when they looked up and saw Colin standing there, 'pale and clammy, almost puffy,' as Mel later recalled.

'I'm sorry, Alun,' said Colin.

Thomas saw three men behind the boss, dressed in black. 'Initially, I thought they were policemen, because of the type of clothing they were wearing. [Then] the guy immediately behind Colin raised a gun and told me to get down.' Alun hit the deck so fast he broke his glasses. Mel also got down quickly, sensing these men were not to be defied, and put her hands behind her back. A robber patted her down, found and confiscated her attack alarm. Mel smelt manure on the robbers' boots, as if they had come from the country. They took a bunch of keys from Alun. Then they bound their hands behind their backs with black plastic cable ties, made into handcuffs by looping one through the other, like the gang in *Ocean's Eleven*. 'You're being awkward, fella,' a robber admonished Alun as he tried to get the ties around his wrists.

3

The woman the robbers had seen walking past the Control Room was Anca Deiac, a 20-year-old Romanian. She had been in CDP Room splitting a cash delivery from Barclays. Her break started at 1.30, and the first thing she did was go to the loo. Anca was in a cubicle in the ladies when she heard the door open and someone coming into the room. When she opened the cubicle door Anca was confronted by an armed man in black.

'Get down! Get down!' he shouted, pushing her to the floor. He was so rough with her that she cut her lip as she scrambled to get on the ground.

The robber asked if she had a mobile telephone, or scissors, bizarrely, though perhaps she misheard because he was speaking very fast. She had so much trouble understanding him she thought he might be Scottish. 'Where's Mel?' the man demanded, meaning Melanie Sampson, apparently unaware his colleagues had already found and subdued her. Mel was one of the staff members they knew to have a personal attack alarm. If Mel actuated her alarm the police would be down on them in seconds.

'She's outside.'

The robber told Anca to get up and marched her outside, holding her hands behind her back. Anca then saw Mel and Alun being trussed up. Alun saw Anca, and noticed she was crying. Colin Dixon was overcome by guilt. 'At that specific moment, I remember thinking "Oh God, what have I done?" If I hadn't stopped [my car], if I hadn't co-operated we wouldn't have been standing here.'

The gang now had four members of staff in their power: Barclay, Thomas, Sampson and Deiac. There were ten more workers in the CDP area, and one of these people was now walking towards them. Like Anca, Mark Garrott had just started his break, and was coming over to talk to Alun about booking some leave. He had only taken a couple of steps towards the DTP when he met Colin and the robbers striding the other way. 'Get down!' the bandits yelled. Mark saw a gun. 'Stay calm. Whatever you do, think of your family.' He didn't need telling twice. 'I thought, *Holy cow!* [I'd] better do what they say.'

The noise of the BPS 1000, and the thickness of the walls, meant that the remaining workers didn't yet know robbers were in the building. No alarm had gone off and they were all still working normally in the CDP Room. Colin knew there was a very good chance that one of these workers would touch a panic button on the wall if the robbers startled them, so he made sure he entered the room a step ahead of the nervous and excitable armed men.

Aaron Moore, who would usually be Control Room Supervisor, was working in the CDP Room with two older men, Lyn Clifton and Michael Laughton-Zimmerman. A heavyset young man named Tony Mason was also in the CDP, together with Sarah Hudson, Patrick Robinson, a young South African named Ndumiso Mnisi, agency worker Shahraiz Nabeel and a Nigerian named Olowajesiku Oluwakemi, whom everybody knew as Kenny. These nine people were working as a team to unpack and split money, sorting the cash into red trays, and feeding these trays into the processing machines. White-haired Lyn Clifton was one of those workers collecting the processed money from the dispensing pockets of the BPS machines, wrapping the money in plastic and loading it into cash cages which, when full, were secured with two padlocks, each requiring a different key. There was a lot of noise and the team was concentrating, because they were working against the clock, Lyn slightly behind schedule. So they didn't notice the robbers at the door until they heard Colin yelling.

'Get away from the walls!' Colin shouted at his staff. 'Do what they say, they've got my wife and child!'

An armed robber who entered the room with Colin was also shouting and swearing, saying all sorts in his excitement, but demanding mostly that they: 'Lie face down. Hands behind your back. Eyes closed.'

They did what they were told, except Kenny, who was listening to his iPod.

'Get out! Get out!' the robber screamed in Kenny's face, startling him so badly he dropped the money he had in his hands.

No one put up a fight. None of the workers attempted to touch an alarm. Nevertheless, they were treated roughly. Lyn Clifton, 60, who suffered from arthritis, screamed with pain as he was pushed to the ground. Sarah Hudson thought she might never see her husband and children again. Once the workers were all face down on the floor, the robbers searched their pockets. A pair of handcuffs was clipped onto Clifton's wrists. Mr Average fastened cable ties on the others. 'Let's get these fucking things on,' one of the robbers chided him, and in his hurry Coutts pulled the ties too tight, cutting off circulation and breaking the face of Michael Laughton-Zimmerman's wristwatch. The hostages were soon in severe discomfort. Then they saw Anca being led into join them, with blood on her face.

4

Colin was ordered back to the Control Room, where he lowered the rising ramp in front of Loading Bay 1. Then he raised the roller door, allowing Driver (Royle) to back the lorry inside. Colin was then taken back to the CDP where Mr Average was finishing tying up the staff. Stopwatch stood over them with the AK47 while a roll-call was taken. 'When I call your name I want you to answer,' said a gangster, reading from a staff list. 'Alun?'

'Yes.'

'Ansa?' This and several other names were mispronounced.

While roll-call was completed, one of the robbers, possibly Hoodie, took Colin to the loading-bay doors. There was an inner door and an outer door to Bay 1, secured by what is known as a four-way bolt, the space between the two doors being another air lock. Colin held the outer door open with his foot as he reached across and opened the inner door.

The lorry was already in the loading bay. Inside the back of the vehicle, Lynn Dixon was in a bad state. She had been shaken about on the drive to the extent that she felt she might throw up. She had also suffered the humiliation of having to urinate in the lorry. Then during the past few minutes she had heard shouting. Lynn was extremely apprehensive about what might happen next. When Hi Viz stood up, gun in hand, and ordered them to move, Lynn feared that he was about to kill her and her child. Instinctively, she shielded the body of the little one.

As Lynn prepared to die, with her arms around her youngest,

the door of the lorry rolled up with a clatter. Two robbers in black were standing on the loading bay. The tail lift of the truck was raised to meet them. The men shouted at Lynn to get out of the way. Mother and child shuffled to the side, and cowered with their faces to the inside of the lorry. A robber got in and grabbed some black plastic cable ties. Hi Viz fetched metal pallets the gang had brought with them to load the money. The bullets Lynn expected didn't come.

Seven bandits were now inside Medway House, each with a job to do. Hi Viz remained with the lorry for the most part guarding Lynn and her child. As we have seen it was Mr Average's responsibility to tie up the staff, after which he became a thief. Others were herding the fourteen worker hostages from the CDP to the DTP area, picking them up roughly and frog-marching them through the cash centre.

'We need to get them all together,' said a robber.

When they had been moved into the DTP, the staff were made to kneel facing the wall, hands behind their backs. Some lay down on the floor. All were in pain. Many were scared for their lives. Policeman stood guard with a gun. The robbers yelled constantly – orders like 'Keep your heads down!' – and some seemed especially jumpy. There was no knowing what they might do. When Mel Sampson dared wriggle her fingers to try and ease her discomfort she was told sharply to stop moving by the robbers who were watching for tricks. This was the last thing on the minds of the hostages. They were more concerned with their discomfort.

Some of the robbers showed a smidgeon of humanity. When Lyn Clifton yelped again with pain, because of his arthritic arm, one of the gangsters told a colleague, 'Sit him in that chair,' then asked the night worker: 'How are you doing, Old Timer?'

'Struggling,' replied Clifton.

A robber asked if anybody would like water, and brought cups from the drinks machine to those who requested a drink, holding the cups to their lips.

Now that the workers were all tied up, the gang asked Colin Dixon about the vault. 'How much money have you got in there?' one of the robbers wanted to know.

'Two hundred,' replied Colin laconically, meaning £200 million. 'How much are you about to take?'

'About half.'

There were two doors to the vault, a solid-steel door and a steel gate. These doors were locked with two keys, plus two dial locks, the combinations changed regularly, new combinations passed orally between the shift managers. Colin asked Alun Thomas if he had the keys to the vault. He didn't. They had to be retrieved from the two buff-coloured wall safes mounted outside Colin's office, opposite the toilets. Each safe held one key. Normally, two members of staff had to work together to get the keys, each knowing one combination. Dual Control, as it is called, is a fundamental principle of cash-centre security, meaning no one member of staff can unilaterally gain access to the most secure area of the building. Highly unusually, Colin had recently overridden Dual Control and given himself access to both keys and combinations, so he could open the vault on his own. This was even more irregular than Colin's decision to get out of his car when stopped by police earlier in the evening. 'That's something that would never, ever be allowed,' comments former Securitas executive Erle Gardner.

Colin went to the small wall safes, tapped in the codes, and opened the doors. He took out the keys, walked past his staff to the vault, the stand-alone structure with extra-thick walls in the far, left-hand corner of the depot, fitted the keys into locks, top and button, spun the combination dials and swung open the doors. The time was approaching 1.42 a.m. as the robbers marched Colin inside the vault, hands on his head.

The robbers discovered the inner sanctum of the cash depot to be a large, square room with a concrete floor, brightly lit, and filled with blue, green and red cash cages. The smaller cages were stacked on top of each other three high. They were packed solid with money bricks in colour-coordinated wrappers: green for fivers, blue for tenners, red for twenties and yellow for fifties. This was what £200 million looked like.

The cages were far too heavy to move manually. The gang needed a machine. The depot had a Lansing power lifter with prongs which slid under the cages, but it was tricky to operate. First they needed a key. Colin found it for them. As he did so the robbers moved the hostages again, realizing they were in the way. Clifton, sitting on an office chair on castors, was simply wheeled aside. Others were treated more roughly. 'Just move them out of the way,' ordered one of the more strident robbers. 'I don't care how.'

When he had the key to the power lifter one of the robbers turned the machine on and tried to manoeuvre it into the vault, but kept getting it jammed in the narrow doorway. The robbers asked Colin who knew how to use the fucking thing. The gang were becoming increasingly nervous, shouting, swearing and behaving very aggressively. Sarah Hudson recalls: 'One of the males was ranting and raving about the fork lift, and who was the driver.' It was established that Tony Mason was the man they needed. Mason has the distinction of being the only member of staff who made any attempt to thwart the robbers during the heist. Although he knew perfectly well how to glide the power lifter into the vault, Tony deliberately kept bashing the machine into the door frame. He was trying to get it wedged. One of the nastier robbers stood over him menacingly, growling that the fat fucker was fucking them about.

'Colin, you'll have to do it,' said one of the bandits.

The manager tried, but failed. More helpfully, he pointed out that there were fully loaded cash cages outside the vault, including two green Bank of England cages each containing £3.5 million. The robbers didn't need the power lifter for these, they could use the smaller pallet lifter. But they had problems with this machine, too. It needed to be primed, by pumping it up. Colin started to prime it for them, but the robbers seemed to suspect a trick and told him to stop. 'You've done something that you fucking shouldn't have done,' Hoodie told Dixon menacingly, pointing a gun at his head. He was told to kneel down and say nothing while a robber took over. They finally got the pallet lifter to work and used it to move two cash cages to the lorry.

Frustrated by the fact that Tony Mason still hadn't got the power lifter inside the vault, members of the gang pushed past him, clambered up onto the cages, cut the padlocks, and started scooping out armfuls of money, which they carried to the loading bay, throwing it into the back of the truck. Lynn and her child had to dodge out of the way.

Policeman was standing over Tony Mason when, at 1.53, he slid the power lifter into the vault. Mason then used the machine to pick up two cages, one on top of the other, deliberately choosing cages of lower value, and moved them out of the vault through the depot to the loading bay. In contrast to the frantic activity around him, Tony took his time. When he reached the lorry he paused while Hi Viz re-arranged the cages already onboard to make room. Tony saw Lynn and her child inside the vehicle. None of the other hostages had seen Colin's family up to this point. Tony was struck by the look of fear on the child's face.

Tony Mason had a final trick to play. The tailgate of the

Renault was 6–8 inches lower than the platform. It was possible to drop down onto the vehicle, but Tony knew he would never be able to get the power lifter back onto the loading bay. So the gang found the machine stuck in the entrance to the lorry. Angry and frustrated, they heaved the power lifter over the side so it crashed to the floor, then marched Tony back to join his co-workers. He found them in a pitiful state, pleading for their cable ties to be loosened. Their hands were numb and, because most were kneeling, so were their legs. Michael Laughton-Zimmerman feared he was about to have an angina attack.

The gang carried on ransacking the depot regardless, grabbing money anywhere they could. Using the pallet lifter with more success than the power lifter, Policeman transferred several pallets of cash into the truck. Stopwatch, Hoodie and Driver were in the vault, busting open cages and throwing money into shopping trolleys which they wheeled to the lorry – a 'supermarket sweep' of more than the usual value. However, this was not an efficient way to load the lorry, which was becoming full even though they had taken less than half the contents of the vault.

Shorty (Rusha) moved Lynn and her child out of the vehicle, and made them stand with their faces to the wall of the loading bay. Lynn tried to amuse her child by playing a word game. When she touched the wall as part of the game, Shorty snapped: 'Don't do that. It's a pressure point.'

'How would I know that?'

At times Shorty seemed almost caring, asking Lynn how she was doing, to which she retorted pluckily: 'What am I expected to say to that?' When she told him she had been tricked into leaving home by men who told her that her husband was in hospital, the robber seemed surprised – an example perhaps of how much confusion the hostages had about who was who, because Shorty was almost certainly the small policeman who came to the house to tell Lynn her husband had been in an accident. Or maybe Shorty didn't want to own up to being the one who had played this low trick on Mrs Dixon.

5

On his knees in the DTP area, Colin had no idea where his family were. He hadn't seen them since they were in the vans. Time passed. Colin felt his back ache. He asked a robber if he could move and was told to be quiet. Although the hostages didn't know it yet, the robbery was coming to its conclusion, and the gang were thinking about what to do with the hostages. 'Colin, let's go and look at the electricity room,' the manager was told, suddenly yanked to his feet.

'I will have to get the keys,' he said, knowing that the key to the electricity room was in the Control Room.

'No, you won't, I've got them.'

They went upstairs to the electricity room, but the gangster was concerned that if they put the hostages here they might be able to trigger an alarm. The men then looked at the staff room, but they couldn't find a key to lock the door. The robber took Colin downstairs where they met another member of the gang. 'Where are you going?' one masked man asked the other.

'To find the key to the staff room.'

'You don't need it,' replied his partner in crime. 'We can lock them in these,' meaning the cash cages, an idea which apparently occurred to the gang at the very last minute, showing again how sketchy their plan was.

6

The robbers cut the hostages' cable ties so they could climb into the blue Piano Cages, which were about five feet high, locking the mesh doors with padlocks and, in one case, a pair of handcuffs. They were all in physical discomfort. 'This hurts me! This hurts me!' Ndumiso Mnisi squealed as the gangsters cut his ties. They told him to shut up. 'My legs had gone numb and when I was lifted up to go in the cage I just fell on the floor,' recalls Anca Deiac. The robbers picked her up and stuffed her into a cage with Mel. Women were kept apart from men, some of whom went into cages in pairs. Lyn Clifton was put in a cage with Aaron Moore. Others were put into cages on their own. It was one of the most frightening parts of the heist for the hostages who feared they might all be killed now that the gang had what they came for, if only to ensure there were no witnesses.

The robbers put the pallets they had brought with them back into the lorry with the money and the pallet lifter which they stole for later use. Then they closed up the lorry. One of the robbers brought Lynn and her child into the main building. 'Stop when I say stop,' the robber told them. The child obeyed as it had throughout. Hoodie wheeled over a Piano Cage, into which they were both put, the kid first. Then they physically lifted Lynn in. Driver reminded mother and child, 'Keep your head down, keep your eyes closed,' before rolling the locked cage across to join the others. So it was that Colin turned to see his wife and child being wheeled towards him: their youngest crouched next to Mum, knees up, head down, terrified.

The gang had been inside Medway House just over an hour. Remarkably, no alarm alerted the local police. As mentioned, the

primary reason for the location of Medway House on Vale Road
was that it was in the triangulation of three 24-hour police stations, the nearest 300 yards away. Police cars were patrolling the
area. They may well have driven past the depot while the raid was
in progress. Yet all the electronic equipment protecting Medway
House failed to inform Kent Police that a robbery was being
conducted under its nose, and even though live CCTV images of
the depot were being transmitted to outside security monitoring
companies nobody noticed anything amiss. Lee Murray and his
cohorts, not the brainiest bunch, had succeeded in outwitting
Kent Police and one of the world's biggest security companies,
not to mention the Bank of England, whose bond money they
had now stolen.

As the raid came to an end, Stopwatch marched around the
place like a Commando, confident and cocky. Others showed
signs of fatigue. Some pulled at their clothing as they got hot and
sweaty, revealing glimpses of their skin. One robber appeared
ready to throw up. But taken as a whole they were a disciplined
crew. Though they didn't load the lorry as efficiently as they
might, they worked until the lorry was more or less full. They
then took the time to lock up their captives, and they exited the
building in good order. The robbers even remembered to gather
up the cups they had drunk from, which would, of course, have
their DNA on.

Colin was the last hostage to be put into a cage. The gang
asked him if his key fob would open the loading-bay door and he
told them it would. Shortly after that, Driver (Royle) and Hi Viz
(Bucpapa) got into the cab of the lorry, where, for an unknown
reason, Hi Viz gave Driver his fluorescent jacket. At 2.33 a.m.,
Driver drove the lorry out of the loading bay, turning sharp right
towards the gate. In doing so, he clipped the striped blocker in
front of the second bay. The lorry stopped. Hi Viz (no longer

wearing his jacket) got out to inspect the damage. The guard rail of the truck was scraped and one of the reflectors had been knocked off. He climbed back into the cab and they drove out of the depot compound, turning left on Vale Road.

Within two minutes, Stuart Royle received a call from Sean Lupton, who seems to have been waiting for them at Elderden Farm. Two minutes after that, at 2.38 a.m., as the lorry was barrelling along Hadlow Road, Jet decided to call Ermir Hysenaj. The boys must have been bursting with excitement to share the news of their success. Ermir didn't answer his mobile. It was, after all, the middle of the night. But an electronic record of this attempted call remained, as with all the calls the gang had made over the past few weeks, creating a trail for the police to follow.

The remaining five robbers lingered in the depot to make sure their hostages were secure. They had parting words of advice for their victims. 'Don't be silly,' they told the people they had terrorized, and caged like animals, 'and don't forget we know where you live.'

One robber added sarcastically: 'Thank you for the co-operation.'

Another – the aggressive lead robber – said, 'Come on, let's rock 'n' roll!'

With that, they left the building through the lobby, the way they entered 75 minutes earlier. The time was now 2.44 a.m. The robbers got into their cars and sped off into the night, each one a multi-millionaire.

Chapter Nine

THE FLOP

1

The hostages heard the robbers drive away from the depot, but were so cowed by their experience that they weren't immediately confident they were safe, and made no attempt to escape from the cages. Colin Dixon asked Lynn if she and their child were alright, and if anybody was injured. There were grumbles of pain and discomfort from his staff. Anca's face was cut, and Lyn Clifton had an aching shoulder where he had been manhandled. Everybody was shocked and frightened. Other than that, they were unharmed. Colin told his child that the men hadn't been using real guns, but replica plastic weapons, because they were making a film.

The hostages became bolder. One worker kicked his cage. 'When they didn't come back to shoot us we knew they had fled,' says Alun Thomas. Mel Sampson announced that she had a padlock key in her pocket, but she couldn't reach it. There was a weak point in the cage in which Lynn and her child were locked, and Colin encouraged them to widen the hole in the mesh, urging his child to wriggle through the gap. The youngster made

a few attempts before succeeding, then retrieved the key from
Mel's pocket. By 3.00 a.m. everybody was out of the cages.
Surprisingly, however, they didn't hurry to sound the alarms or
call the police. Colin told his staff that they should 'wait a while'.
He later explained himself by saying he didn't know whether
some of the robbers were still outside the building, and might
come back, though this was illogical. Even if they were outside,
they couldn't come back in unless he let them in.

Still Colin waited. Everybody got drinks from the machine. The
smokers lit up, even though they weren't supposed to smoke inside
the depot. Colin took off his jacket and tie, and commended his
child's bravery, putting his hand affectionately on the child's head.
He suggested everybody write down what they could remember.
Staff had noticed all sorts of quirky details about the robbers,
especially their footwear which they had all been obliged to
stare down at. Several noticed that the men had mud on their
boots. Mel smelt manure. Lyn had seen the brand name Magnum
on one boot. Michael was impressed by how organized the robbers
seemed to be, working together as a team. Others were surprised
by the gang's familiarity with their difficult drinks machine, which
proclaimed itself out of order, but would nevertheless dispense cold
water when asked. The staff knew this, but how did the robbers
know it?

Colin mentioned to Alun Thomas that he had a feeling the
gang knew where they both lived. They obviously knew where
Colin lived, but from what they said he believed they had Alun's
home address, too. This scared Alun so badly that he rang his
wife, Alison, and told her to leave the house immediately, which
she did. All this was before anybody had raised the alarm. It was
3.14 a.m., half an hour after the last of the robbers left, that
Colin went into his office with Alun and activated an alarm.
When there was no immediate reaction, Alun impatiently rang

999 as well. As he says: 'In a situation like this, minutes seem like hours,' which makes Colin's decision to delay seem especially strange.

Colin then made a phone call to Steve Morris, a former special-branch officer who worked as Security Inspector for Medway House, waking Steve's wife at home in Ashford. Mrs Morris tapped her husband on the shoulder. The couple were used to false alarms in the night. 'Steve, we've been turned over,' Colin told Morris, jolting him fully awake. The minute he put the phone down, Steve called Kent Police, and then started ringing his bosses at home, including his superior at Securitas, John McGlade, and their boss, Tony Benson.

Meanwhile, two uniformed constables arrived at the depot gates in a squad car, joined minutes later by another pair of constables. When the staff were sure that these were genuine police, they let them in. PC Kevin Brigden took charge of the situation in the first few moments, directing colleagues to check the CCTV tape so they could put out a general alert for the getaway vehicles.

2

The robbers had been clear of the depot for well over half an hour now, ample time to get to what criminals call 'the flop', the place where villains rest after a job and divvy up the spoils. The police believe that at least some members of the gang went back to John Fowler's yard at Elderden Farm, though Fowler says he knew nothing about it if they did, and indeed he and his wife suggest it is inconceivable the gang used their property in this way at a time when the whole family was asleep in bed in the main house, adjacent to the yard, though separate from it.

Even if the gang did come back to Elderden Farm, as the police believe, it seems likely that they stopped on the way, possibly at Redpits to drop off some of the loot. It seems that Jetmir Bucpapa and Sean Lupton were at Redpits during the night, talking with Royle, who was cell-sited in the vicinity of Elderden Farm from about 3.30 a.m. It is unlikely he was alone if indeed the farm was used as the flop. The principal gang members would have wanted to be present when the cash was shared out.

The hire lorry was too big to get through the gate of Fowler's yard, so if the lads did bring the cash back to Elderden Farm they had to park in the lane. There would have been no one about at Hop Engineering to see them. The Fowlers' neighbours, including the Salmons who lived directly behind the farm, were sound asleep. In the freezing cold, pitch-dark, country night the boys must have gathered around the back of the lorry, marvelling at the mountain of money they'd carried away. There must have been a moment of jubilation, slapping each other on the back, jumping up onto the tail gate, tearing open plastic bags of money, rubbing their faces in the cash, inhaling its delicious inky smell.

Celebrations had to be brief, though. The practical problems of sharing out and hiding the loot were pressing, and the task was as immense as the haul, which weighed almost five tons, though they couldn't have known this. Nor could they have known exactly how much they had taken by value. Although the cash bricks and cages were all labelled, as to their content and value, to add up the figures required more time, patience and indeed intelligence than this mob possessed.

They had stolen the pallet lifter from the depot, probably to help them unload the cages which were far too heavy to move manually. The first job must have been to get all the cages out of the lorry. Then they had to break the cages open and remove the money bricks. They also had to get the loose money out of the lorry, some in bags, which they filled during the robbery, more in three supermarket trolleys which they had also carried away. Having made a pile of money, the process of dividing up the spoils may have been 'one for you, one for me', each man watching carefully as their heaps grew in size and value.

Some of the money was in brand-new, consecutive notes, fresh from the Bank of England. The individual gangsters didn't want too many of these, though the boys would pay off at least one person who had done work for them with such money. There were quite a few people to take care of. Apart from the sign-writer Keith Borer, there was the inside man, Ermir Hysenaj, not to mention the three girlfriends who had, as they would later insist, helped the boys without knowing what they were really up to. Surely the lads would want to reward Katie Philp, Kim Shackelton and Raluca Millen for their innocent services. Then there was the barber Michael Demetris and his ditzy make-up artist Michelle Hogg, both of whom had apparently been duped into helping the gang. There were others who would demand payment, mates in the underworld, car dealers, money launderers, armourers, contacts who had helped with this and that. Some could be palmed off with new fifties. In truth, even the used fifties were of limited value to the gang being notoriously hard to spend. The green bags of fivers were also not especially desirable. It was the blue bags of used tenners and the red bags of twenties that were the main prize, and most of the stolen money was in red bags. Fortunately for the robbers, none of the cages or bags were booby-trapped with exploding coloured dye, or fitted with tracker devices.

In a couple of hours it would be dawn, shortly after which the working day began, with staff arriving next door at Hop

Engineering and Netbox5 from 8.00 a.m. Neighbours would also be up and about. It was essential that the lads were on the road with their shares before that. As the gang divided up the money they packed the cash into cheap black and tan holdalls and tartan-pattern suitcases, luggage bought especially in bulk. To store all the cash would require 75 such suitcases. They didn't have time to unwrap the money. For the most part, they stuffed it into these bags still in its plastic sleeves, along with labels identifying the money as the property of Securitas or the Bank of England. The labels often stated that the money had been processed at the Tonbridge depot, giving the date and time it went through the BPS machine. Finally, the boys hauled their individual shares away to their own secret hiding places.

Once again, what of John Fowler while all this was going on? According to evidence later heard in court, at 5.30 a.m. somebody telephoned the main house at Elderden Farm from the garage workshop in the yard. There was a 17-second conversation. But Fowler insists the first call he had that morning was from a car-dealer mate named Glyn Mercer (who also went by the name Locking). Glyn called from his home about a car he was driving up to Hull for John. Glyn said the car wouldn't start. Fowler says Mercer rang back a little later, at 6.30, to say he had the car going and was on his way. When Fowler came downstairs for breakfast he says he found the white hire lorry parked outside again, and rang Stuart Royle to remonstrate with him for blocking the lane. Fowler says the upshot of this conversation was that he agreed to move the lorry for Royle.

The lorry was full of incriminating evidence, including empty cash cages, red plastic money trays, a Sainsbury's shopping trolley and scraps of paper printed with Securitas and Bank of England details. All had to be disposed of. It seems that Royle asked his girlfriend Kim Shackelton to help John with this clearing-up job.

Royle called Kim at home in Maidstone at 5.07 a.m. When she called him back from her mobile half an hour later she was on the A20 driving to meet them.

3

The first genuine police officer on the scene at Medway House called CID at Tonbridge Police Station who in turn contacted DS Andy Nicoll of the Serious and Organised Crime Unit, getting Andy out of bed at 3.30 a.m. with the banal statement that there was 'a bit of a job on'. An imposing but genial officer, tall and broad, with cropped silver hair and a goatee, Nicoll sat up and listened as he was given the basic information: a Tonbridge cash-centre manager, his wife and child had been kidnapped and cash had been stolen from the depot. 'How much?' asked the detective sergeant.

'It might be up to a million pounds.'

'Ouch!' exclaimed Nicoll, who started calling senior colleagues. 'A million quid's a lot of money,' he pointed out the obvious fact. 'Do you want me to deal with it?' The answer was yes, for now. So DS Nicoll drove to the depot, arriving at the same time as another DS, Dick Cater.

The two detective sergeants were now told that a lot more than a million had been stolen, and DS Nicoll made further calls as a result, warning his bosses that they needed more staff on the scene. As he waited for reinforcements, Andy Nicoll took care of the Securitas workers, some of whom were still trembling. 'It was an atmosphere of disbelief. Nothing like this had happened to anybody.'

DS Cater took Colin Dixon aside. From the start, the cash-centre manager would be treated differently to the other hostages.

When Securitas' Security Inspector Steve Morris arrived at the depot a few minutes later he found Colin, whom he knew, to be surprisingly calm. 'He was acting as if it was a normal day.' Shortly after this the Dixons were all taken to the Victim Suite at Tonbridge Police Station, where they gave forensic samples to DS Anthony Bartlett. Part of the process involved putting Sellotape on their clothing to remove hair fibres that may have been picked up during their ordeal. Forensic officers even dug the fluff out of Colin Dixon's turn-ups. The next job would be to get Colin into a car, with DC John Wood, and retrace his journey of the night before so they could start appealing for witnesses to what the police were realizing had been a tiger kidnapping.

Back at the depot, Securitas executive John McGlade, a hugely fat man, was making a rough estimate of how much money was missing, based on CCTV footage of the robbery. As McGlade did this, his colleague Steve Morris toured the building. A few weeks prior to the robbery there had been a security review, with Steve making recommendations to management for ways to improve security. None of these changes had been made. There were glaring problems and irregularities including broken locks and blind areas which weren't covered by cameras. The bars in the vehicle gate were so wide apart a man could squeeze through them, as Steve now demonstrated. Although there were live CCTV pictures of the depot available to two outside agencies, on a monitoring system called TeleEye, and the system was functioning properly during the heist, live pictures of the depot were not online during the robbery because no alarm had been raised that would prompt operators to call up the images. 'We wouldn't routinely, 24 hours-a-day have somebody watching every monitor,' explains Paul Fullicks, one of several Securitas executives who now hurried to the depot.

Scenes of Crime Officers (SOCOs) had arrived. They put on

their trademark white Tyrex suits, and blue disposable gloves, before commencing a fingertip search of the cash depot and its car park. They soon found items of interest: snippets of black cable ties, which they put in bags to be DNA-tested; a pair of handcuffs attached to a cash cage; and a broken reflector lens. DS Nicoll put on a white suit and went into the vault with the Securitas people. Estimates of how much was missing had gone up considerably from the initial million quid. They now thought it might be £20 million.

Just before dawn, PC Brigden took the night-shift workers upstairs to the staff room to be body-searched. Clearly the gang had inside information, and everybody was under suspicion. Working with senior people from Securitas, police searched workers' cars and lockers. The staff were held at the depot for hours. Apart from answering questions, they had to give DNA samples, and surrender their clothing to the police. Somebody was sent into town to buy tracksuits so the staff had something to wear. When the police were finally finished with them, much later in the day, staff were simply told to make their own way home. It was only when the workers protested that Securitas organized taxis. When they did finally get home, the night workers were too wound up and upset to sleep. Sarah Hudson wrote two words in her diary – 'Armed Robbery' – then sat and stared at the page in shock.

4

A bonfire was ablaze at Elderden Farm. It had been alight since at least 7.30 when one of the Fowlers' neighbours, Maurice Donnelly, looked out of his window. The Fowlers insist this was a routine bonfire, set by staff working for John, but the police believe the gang may have been burning evidence, possibly including the personal belongings of Lynn Dixon and her child, including her glasses case and a Chanel scent bottle. It appears that mobile phones may have been thrown on the fire. The remains of phones were found in the ashes.

Mobiles belonging to Royle and Coutts, used constantly in the run-up to the kidnap and robbery, went dead on Wednesday, 22 February. Mobiles used by other gang members, including Murray, Rusha, Allen, Bucpapa and Hysenaj, all ceased operation over a broader period of 21–23 February. As the mobiles were disposed of, the chatter between the gang fell off dramatically. On the eve of the heist, the gang made 218 calls and texts between the dirty phones identified by police. Three days later they made only 67 calls.

Whether or not the gang burnt any of these phones at Elderden Farm, the mob had a huge amount of stuff to get rid of: everything they wore during the kidnap and heist could be used in evidence against them, including their boiler suits, masks, gloves and boots. Then there were the latex disguises and wigs, and all that had been used in their manufacture; the guns and ammunition; the cars, vans and lorry; and the various electronic gadgets they had bought; together with the receipts that came with every purchase. Above and beyond all this, there was the money, dozens of suitcases full of cash, and the masses of branded plastic and paper it was wrapped in, together with the cash cages, shopping trolleys and pallet lifter.

The gang stole a total of seventeen cash cages and three Sainsbury's trolleys from the depot; that much is clear from the CCTV footage. It seems likely that three of these cages and two of the shopping trolleys were dropped off by the gang on their way to Elderden Farm, if indeed they ever came to the farm. It is possible these items were dropped off at Royle's place, Redpits. That left fourteen cages and one trolley in the back of the lorry, which was parked next to John Fowler's yard early that morning.

Lee Ray saw it when he came to work at Hop Engineering around eight o'clock. The cages were highly distinctive: they were large, brightly coloured and unusual in shape. They had to be disposed of without delay.

John Fowler later told police that when he rang Stuart Royle on Wednesday morning to ask him why the lorry was back at the farm, Royle asked him to drive the lorry to meet him at a service area on the M20. John agreed. When he got to the service area, John claims to have had another conversation with Royle in which Slippery asked him to dump some stuff off the back of the lorry before it was returned to the hire company at Faversham. It was due back around lunchtime. They agreed that this fly-tipping might conveniently be done at a place near Detling called Friningham Farm. John's mate Glyn Mercer (aka Glyn Locking), the man who was apparently driving to Hull for John that morning, rented a yard at Friningham Farm to store used cars. Stuart said Kim Shackelton would go with John to help him.

In going to Friningham Farm to dump the cages, John and Kim were very close to where Colin Dixon had been kidnapped the night before. Indeed, they probably passed the Cock in Detling where Colin's Nissan was still sitting in the car park, having been left there overnight by the gang. Opposite the pub is the Pilgrim's Way, the ancient route across the North Downs travelled for centuries by Christians heading to Canterbury Cathedral. Driving along the Pilgrim's Way the motorist soon reaches Coldblow Lane, a quiet lane overhung with trees, which climbs Detling Hill. At 8.45 that morning, local resident Ann Day was driving down the lane on her school run when she met a white lorry coming the opposite way. She pulled over into one of the little muddy recesses in the lane to let the lorry by, noticing a man and a woman in the cab.

John continued to the summit of Detling Hill where there is an old RAF transmitter tower, a relic of the Battle of Britain. He turned left opposite this tower into a private track called Back Farm Road, bouncing down the hill, through puddles and potholes, into the yard of Friningham Farm, run by 61-year-old Paul Burden. Farmer Burden's house is to the right. John turned left to reach the bit of land Burden rented to Glyn Mercer (whom he knew as Glyn Locking) to park a motley collection of fifty used vehicles.

It so happened that Ann Day lived on Friningham Farm. She rented a flat overlooking Glyn's car yard. When she got home from the school run, Mrs Day noticed the white lorry she had seen in the lane was now in the yard. The tail gate was down and the man and woman were unloading. Watching from her window, Mrs Day witnessed the woman pushing a shopping trolley back and forth from the lorry to the yard. She saw what looked like red plastic boxes in the trolley.

Ann Day telephoned her landlord. Having been up since before dawn tending to his newborn lambs, Farmer Burden was in his kitchen at 9.30 eating a late breakfast when Mrs Day called. 'She rang me up and told me there was a lorry chucking off some stuff and she thought I ought to know.' Burden rang Glyn, who told him that a lorry he had bought was indeed on the farm 'chucking off some rubbish' which they'd clear up in a couple of days. That was good enough for Burden who went back to his breakfast. When he emerged from his farmhouse a little later he saw the white lorry driving off his property, but thought little of it and went back to his work.

Chapter Ten

OPERATION DELIVER

1

Around the time that John Fowler and Kim Shackelton were dumping the cash cages at Friningham Farm, Detective Chief Inspector Tim Smith arrived at Medway House to take charge of the police investigation. At 9.00 a.m. DCI Smith called his boss, Detective Superintendent Paul Gladstone, a quietly spoken Geordie with overall responsibility for Smith's Serious Crime Unit, and the parallel Major Crime Unit, both within Kent Police. 'This is far bigger than we thought,' Smith told his Super, adding that representatives from the Bank of England were on their way down from London. The DCI had received a call from their car, under police escort on the motorway.

Surprising as it may seem, D. Supt. Gladstone hadn't previously been aware that there was a cash depot in Tonbridge holding £200 million plus. The fact there was such a remarkable building on his patch would have been on a 'contingency list' somewhere, along with other sensitive county sites, but Medway House wasn't a place he'd had reason to deal with before. In fact, he wondered why the Bank of England were sending people down to talk to them. He asked Tim Smith to arrange a meeting at Tonbridge Police Station so they could find out what the panic was.

2

In the City of London, the Governor of the Bank of England, Professor Mervyn King, was arriving for work. He strode into the building through the impressive entrance on Threadneedle Street, across the marble Front Hall, and out through French windows into the Garden Court. Although the Bank presents blank fortress walls to the world, it is built around a secret garden, planted with mulberry trees in recognition of the fact the first paper money was made from mulberry bark. The trees are small and somewhat weak, propped up by wooden staves. Their roots can't grow deep because the Garden Court is merely a shallow tray of soil sitting on top of three subterranean vaults of cash and bullion containing the wealth of Old England.

Stepping back into the building on the north side of the courtyard, Professor King entered his ground-floor office. The desk has been used by every governor since 1795. Almost every type of crisis has assailed the Old Lady of Threadneedle Street over the centuries. There have been anarchistic plots, world wars, the Great Depression and recession. Still the news that greeted the Governor this morning was extraordinary. It was the job of the Chief Cashier, Andrew Bailey, whose signature appears on every bank note, to inform the Governor of a 'very big event' overnight. Criminals had kidnapped the manager of the Securitas cash depot at Tonbridge, and coerced the man into helping them steal a considerable sum. A senior Securitas executive on the scene had viewed the CCTV and, based on the cages counted as stolen, he concluded that 'no less than £51.5 million' was missing from the depot, at least half from bond, which meant in effect that the crooks had stolen from the Bank of England itself, just as if they had raided the vaults downstairs.

The Chief Cashier hastened to add that the robbers 'didn't clean the place out' (it was overwhelmingly tempting to talk in criminal parlance). They had left behind far more than they had taken. Also the £25 million stolen from bond was 'off balance sheet', the meaning of which was clear to Professor King, but requires a little explanation.

Companies such as Securitas do not have the wherewithal to buy billions of pounds from the Bank of England. Yet they store billions for the bank. To resolve this paradox the Old Lady has invented financial limbo. So long as its bond money is secure in cash centres, such as Medway House, locked up and marked Property of the Bank of England, it is deemed 'off balance sheet' – neither the property of the security carrier, nor classed as money 'in issue'.

Even though Securitas doesn't own this money, the company undertakes to look after it, which means insuring themselves against theft. It was insurance that concerned the Bank of England first thing Wednesday morning. The Governor didn't know for certain whether Securitas' insurers – including Lloyd's of London syndicates – would cover such a massive loss. Securitas was of course fully insured, but that didn't necessarily mean the insurers would be able or willing to pay up, especially if there had been any irregularities at the depot. It was always possible that they might find an excuse to baulk at taking such a hit. Down in Tonbridge, at the police station, representatives from the bank were explaining this to D. Supt. Gladstone. They told him they weren't so worried about the missing cash, but the potential repercussions. If the insurers didn't cover the loss, Securitas Cash

Management might go bust, and have to close all its eleven cash centres. As there were only 28 such centres in England and Wales, such an event could trigger a national emergency.

As of 10.30 on the morning of 22 February 2006, the Bank of England was facing the alarming possibility that the Tonbridge robbery might cause England to run out of money. So serious was the situation that the Governor's private secretary placed a call to the Chancellor of the Exchequer, Gordon Brown.

3

Securitas' Steve Morris had downloaded the CCTV from the computers at Medway House and given the data to the police. A young detective, Stewart Catt, would be given the task of reviewing every second of film from all sixty cameras in the depot. He was looking first at the robbers, of course, but he would also go back four months to watch the behaviour of all the staff prior to the raid in order to try and identify an inside man. If DC Catt had not already worn spectacles, the experience of viewing 152,000 hours of film may well have given him four eyes.

Other officers were knocking on doors in Vale Road asking residents if they had seen anything. 'We was amazed to know the amount of money that was there,' says Jean Wilkins, who lived in the nearby railway cottages, but typically she hadn't seen a thing. 'Obviously we was in bed at the time.'

The Dixon family was still at Tonbridge Police Station. Lynn Dixon telephoned her mother, Pamela, to say that she and Colin and their youngest had been kidnapped and held hostage while Colin's work had been robbed, but they were with the police now. 'We're safe, we're all safe,' she wept.

While the police had a duty to care for the Dixons, they

inevitably looked quizzically at Colin, who was interviewed for the first time that day while the events of the night were fresh in his mind, his story then picked over during 26 subsequent interviews. Colin told detectives that he had been kidnapped on his way home by two men in a dark-coloured saloon car with flashing blue lights, the men posing as police officers. They handcuffed him and took him at gunpoint to a building where it was made clear that he and his family were in danger unless he answered their questions and, moreover, got the gang into the depot. The way Colin told the story, he had no choice other than to cooperate. But was he a criminal posing as a victim? The police knew there must have been at least one inside man. There almost always is in such cases. They made it clear to Colin from the start that 'one line of enquiry' they would be pursuing was that *he* was the inside man.

The police checked Colin's personal and financial situation. Tony Benson told them everything he could about Colin's work history with Securitas. Dixon had been with the company a long time. A married man with children, he was the type of person they found most trustworthy. He had just celebrated 27 years of marriage. Colin would have to be a psychopath to turn around, the following week, and put his wife and child through such an ordeal. But there were reasons to wonder about Colin.

In the first place he should never have got out of his car. As Paul Fullicks says coolly: 'He acted in a manner which wouldn't normally be expected.' When Colin arrived at Medway House in the early hours, Gary Barclay should not have buzzed him in without questioning him about why he was there. 'None of your bosses turn up at that sort of time in the morning!' exclaims Steve Morris. 'Colin was a man of habit. He worked nine to five.' Colin could have flashed a red card he had in his wallet or held an ID card upside down to tip off Barclay that something was wrong.

He didn't. It was also true that Barclay hadn't behaved as he should, which prompted the question: was he in on the robbery? The police discounted this scenario when they discovered Barclay was only on the job that night as the result of Control Room Surprise.

It was Colin who brought Policeman into the depot, fatally compromising security. Once he was inside, Colin had opportunities to press silent alarm buttons without being seen. Unlike the other hostages, he was not tied up during the raid, and he wasn't watched all the time. But he chose not to operate the alarms that would have brought the police to their rescue.

When it emerged that Colin had given himself access to both wall safes, there was considerable surprise within Securitas. This went against the fundamental principle of Dual Control and was, as Paul Fullicks says plainly, 'obviously a breach of procedure'. Colin hadn't told his superiors he was making this radical change to security at the depot, something which would never be officially sanctioned. Furthermore, Steve Morris discovered that Colin had programmed short-cut codes into the safes so he didn't have to remember long numbers. It was all too easy for Colin to open the vault on the night.

Colin's colleagues had mixed feelings about the man. Some praised him highly. 'Colin is the nicest person possible, and he had the highest integrity,' says fellow worker Jackie Howse. Lyn Clifton points out the obvious glaring fact, however: 'They wouldn't have got in the building without him,' going on to express a general feeling of having been let down by the company, not just Colin. 'It shouldn't have happened. We thought we were safe. We all thought we were safe. There was no way anybody could get in that place, so we thought. We had precautions that should have been taken, and weren't that night.'

Talking to the police, Colin conceded that when they watched the CCTV it would look like he was helping the robbers, 'and I was, but I was helping for one reason: the safety of everybody there and myself . . . If I co-operated with them they would leave us alone [and] we would be safe and Lynn and [my child] would be returned to me.' But Colin had been *exceptionally* co-operative. He opened doors and moved cameras without being asked. It was Colin who suggested that Policeman move Gary Barclay's legs so staff wouldn't see him. It was Colin who ordered his staff not to touch the wall alarms. Without Colin, the gang wouldn't have pulled off the job.

4

While the cash-centre manager explained himself to the police, the gang and their associates were starting a new day. Michelle Hogg had come into work at Hair Hectik as normal. Michael said there was lots to do. But when she got to the salon, Michelle found she didn't have any clients booked and felt suddenly so fed up with Michael 'treating me like a slave' that she turned around and went home. 'I'm tired,' she told him. 'I'm exhausted.'

Lea Rusha and Jetmir Bucpapa turned up at the salon a little later. Lea wanted the red dye washed out of his hair. After this was done, the lads drove into London. Around lunchtime Jet spoke on the phone with his friend Rebecca Weale. 'I remember him saying he was tired, and he sounded tired,' she says.

After his hard night, kidnapping and robbing, Stuart Royle had crashed out at his daughter's house in Allen Street, Maidstone. The exhausted robber didn't stir until after two o'clock that afternoon. His movements are known because Royle was foolish enough to continue using his phones after the robbery, phones which were later seized and analysed by the police. Murray and others dumped or destroyed their dirty phones after the job, showing how professional they could be. Royle was still making calls. He needed to get the Vauxhall and Volvo cars scrapped. His first call was to a pal named Roger Sugden, who asked: 'When do you want it done?'

'As soon as.'

Sugden was busy, so he referred Royle to a mate in banger racing. He couldn't help either, and passed Royle to a man named Clyde. Nobody could scrap the cars at such short notice.

5

Back in London, the Bank of England received welcome news. The insurance syndicates behind Securitas Cash Management *would* cover the money missing from bond. By the time the Governor went for his lunch the bank had been repaid its £25 million in full. This was of course only an estimate of what the gang had stolen from bond, but it was understood that adjustments would be made when a full audit had been done. A lot more than £25 million had been taken from the depot, at least as much again, but Securitas' insurers were able to handle that claim, too, which was good news for all but the Lloyd's names involved. Still, Professor King asked his deputy, Sir John Gieve, to undertake an immediate nationwide review of cash-centre security.

As the Bank of England was being repaid its money, a very different transaction was being conducted in Maidstone. Between catching up on his sleep, and trying to find a scrap dealer, Stuart Royle called the sign-writer Keith Borer. 'We've got your dosh. We've put a drink in with it,' Royle told him, suggesting they meet outside Maidstone Prison, just around the corner from Chrissy Royle's house.

Keith drove to the rendezvous in his Porsche. Soon after he parked, Stuart opened the door and slipped into the passenger seat. 'There you go,' he said, giving Keith an envelope. 'Have you heard?'

'Heard what?'

'You haven't heard?'

'No.'

'You will do!'

When Royle left, Keith put the envelope in the glove compartment and drove home. He stopped on the way to roll a cigarette. He put a hand in the envelope. It felt fat. When people said 'a drink' that usually meant a tenner. He reached in and drew out handfuls of new £50 notes. 'I couldn't fucking believe it!'

6

It had been a quiet day at the Ferrari Press Agency, the south London news agency that sent a reporter to Lee Murray's house after the Funky Buddha fight. Part of the daily work of Adam Gillham and Matthew Bell, the two young men who ran the agency, was monitoring Kent Police for anything of national significance. 'It was a very, very quiet day up to that point,' says Adam, who was scrolling through his e-mails when he saw a bulletin from the press office at Kent Police: a snippet about an armed robbery at a 'security depot' in Tonbridge. Robbers had got away with a 'substantial amount' of cash; and police were appealing for witnesses who may have seen a white Renault truck. Adam wrote a short news story, catch-line RAID, which began: 'Detectives are hunting armed raiders who tied up members of staff at a security depot and escaped with a large amount of cash . . .'

He sent this all round the daily papers at 1.00 p.m., knowing the story was unlikely to be used. 'Armed robberies very rarely make it unless someone's been shot.' In this case, nobody had even been injured. A little later Adam's partner, Matt, took a call from the *Sun* news desk, asking for more information about the Kent robbery. 'There's no need to get excited. You won't be interested,' replied Matt, but the *Sun* news desk was excited, telling Matt they had heard from their political reporters, who had the tip from the Treasury, that the robbers had got away with between forty and sixty million. 'Oh fucking hell! What a great story!' exclaimed Matthew, and so the chase began.

As reporters, photographers and camera crews scurried down to Tonbridge, and editors began redesigning their front pages to accommodate the breaking story, John Fowler was going about his normal business, which included visiting John Davis at the Seat dealership near Maidstone to talk about buying some cars. The TV was on in the office when Fowler arrived. 'John was looking at the screen,' says Davis. It was a news flash about the robbery. John turned the volume up. 'That wasn't anything to do with you?' Davis asked jokingly. John muttered something about just being interested because it was local, and said he'd come back tomorrow for the cars.

Michelle Hogg had caught up on her sleep when her mother called to tell her there was something on the TV about a robbery in Tonbridge. Mrs Hogg knew Michelle had been doing a make-up job down there. Michelle claims this is the moment she began to realize what she had been mixed up in. 'I just thought, *Oh my God!*'

Keith Borer tells a similar story. He says that when he saw the TV news he knew the money Royle had given him must have come from the robbery. But he didn't call the police. He called his girlfriend, Brenda. They'd had a tiff on Valentine's Day and Brenda had left him. Keith implored her to come back, which she did. Helpfully, she counted the money for him. There was over £6,000 in the envelope, mostly in brand-new £50 notes. 'At one minute I was ecstatic. The next minute I was on the floor,' says Keith, who hid the cash in his caravan, then went down the pub.

As Keith was knocking back the drinks, the press were meeting D. Supt. Paul Gladstone at Maidstone Police Headquarters, a big brick building on the outskirts of town. 'Nobody was hurt, but the manager and his family are extremely shocked,' the superintendent explained the basics to the media, without giving away the name of the depot manager. 'They were threatened with extreme violence by the gang and underwent a terrifying ordeal. This gang were highly sophisticated and organized. This was clearly a robbery planned in detail over time – someone must have information that will help us in the hunt for the robbers. A very substantial sum of money running into millions of pounds has been stolen and we are determined to bring the robbers to justice.' Anyone with information was urged to telephone. The police weren't giving a figure for how much had been stolen, but ITN announced £40 million during its 6.30 evening news.

Ermir Hysenaj had enjoyed a day off work. His agency had texted him earlier to say staff weren't to go into Medway House today, and indeed they enquired as to whether Ermir might want counselling to cope with the shock of what had happened to his colleagues in the robbery which was now all over the news. Far from needing counselling, Ermir was going out to celebrate. He and Sue had tickets for the Levellers, Sue's favourite band, at the Assembly Hall.

While Ermir enjoyed the show, Michael Demetris was paying a visit to Michelle Hogg, whose account of the meeting differs crucially from his. Michelle claims she didn't want to see him

when he called, but at 9.30 that evening the barber showed
up at her flat with 'a grin like a Cheshire Cat'. Michelle saw
the diamond glint in Michael's teeth as they sat on her little two-
seater sofa where Lee and the boys had so often sat squeezed
together. By her account, Michael said: 'So, Miche, how does it
feel to be part of history? Nuts, isn't it? I knew you could do it."
He said he'd just been with the boys. They were 'lying low', and
they wanted to give Michelle some money for what she had done
for them. She claims to have declined the offer.

Then he said: 'If the police come here . . .'

'What do you mean?' Michelle asked in alarm.

'They probably won't, but if they do . . . you're just a make-
up artist and know nothing about it.' If the police asked about
Lee Murray, she was to say she only knew him as a famous cage
fighter. And she should delete Lee's name from her mobile. *OK,
sweetie?* Michael Demetris denies this conversation took place,
saying that when he visited the flat that evening he told Hogg that
Lee Murray had been in the salon that afternoon to have his hair
cut – as in fact he had – and Lee had paid Michael £400 for the
all-night hair and make-up session for the computer game project they'd been working on, which was now apparently over and
done with. Michael said he'd give Michelle £100 of this money.
He recalls Hogg was behaving strangely, as if she knew what had
really happened, while Michael himself was still totally oblivious
to the fact that Lee had pulled off a robbery in Kent in a Hair
Hectik disguise.

Michael told Michelle she could keep the unused make-up
materials they had bought, but after he left her flat she decided
to get rid of everything. She fetched a pair of scissors and cut the
bald caps into tiny pieces, in the same frantic manner she cut up
letters and photos at the end of a recent unhappy relationship. She
put the scraps into bin bags, together with everything she and

Kate had bought from Screenface and Charles H. Fox, including brushes, hair braids, a false moustache, plaster moulds, soiled cotton wool pads and sponges, tubs of hair dye, tins of grease-paint, Vaseline, modelling wax, dental plaster and eye-liner pencils. She also threw away notes she'd made. When the bags were full, Michelle lugged them down to the green wheelie bin outside the front door. Then she went back upstairs to smoke a joint to calm herself down.

As Michelle got her head together, Colin and Lynn Dixon were coming towards the end of a very long and stressful day, during which they had both been interviewed at length. Lynn, who hadn't been blindfolded during her ordeal, was able to give Kent Police detailed information about the journey she had been taken on, the vehicles the gang used, and the place where she'd been held. She described a yard with a garage-like building on one side and a dark-brick building on the other side. There had been a light on in a frosted window. Colin hadn't seen as much, but he was able to describe details such as the green tarpaulin on which the guns and maps were set out.

As night drew in Colin and Lynn began to realize not only that they couldn't go home this evening, they might *never* be able to go back to Hadleigh Gardens. They were witnesses, and would be called to give evidence in court if the men were apprehended and charged. In the circumstances the Dixons were clearly at danger from the gang. If they went home, they might receive intimidating visits. They might be murdered. So the Dixons were taken from the police station to a safe house, which they would share with three officers. One of these, PC Lorraine Brown, would be with the family 24 hours a day. The idea was to safe-guard, comfort and debrief the family while keeping a close eye on Colin. PC Brown decided at the outset that Colin was behaving strangely for someone who had just been through such an

ordeal. She wrote in her notebook: 'He doesn't appear to be concerned that he and his family have been kidnapped.'

In contrast to her husband, Lynn Dixon was very emotional.
She cried a lot and refused to watch the television news because
she thought it would be too upsetting. She would also refuse to
look at the newspapers, the first editions of which were being put
to bed with the same sensational story on page one. The *Daily
Mail* splash headline read 'KIDNAP GANG'S £40 m ROB-
BERY'. The *Sun* ran with 'BIGGEST HEIST IN HISTORY'.

7

As the national newspapers were distributed across the country in
the early hours of Thursday, 23 February, the temperature plum-
meted. It was freezing at 8.00 a.m. when 18-year-old Ricky
Clark ventured outside the family pub in Kent. The Clarks ran
the Hook & Hatchet, on the edge of a wood at Hucking, a
couple of miles from where Colin Dixon had been kidnapped.
Ricky had volunteered to take his mum to Gatwick Airport this
morning. When the teenager returned home, the pub was covered in snow and the only vehicle in the car park was a Post
Office van. There was no sign of a postman, however. Ricky
noticed two sets of tyre tracks in the snow behind the van, but no
snow under the vehicle. He worked out that somebody had left
the van there overnight, or very early that morning, before it
started snowing, driving off in a second vehicle after the snow
began to settle. When he went inside, Dad was reading about the
robbery in the paper. Ricky persuaded his father that the van in
their car park could be connected to the robbery and they called
the police to tell them as much.

Forensic officers found the van full of evidence that left them in no doubt this was the vehicle Lynn Dixon and her child had been in. There was a paper towel with the child's left footprint on. There was also cardboard and plastic wrapping that went with a certain brand of cheap, imported luggage, and a grey glove which they swabbed for DNA. Inside the glove compartment was a sales invoice which showed that the van had been bought on 31 January by Mark Scott of 115 Tonbridge Road, Wateringbury. Was this a clue deliberately left by Lee Murray and his London mates in order to send Kent Police haring off after Stuart Royle, rather than themselves? If so, it worked.

8

The investigation now had a name. DS Nicoll, who became the Case Officer, had the honour of choosing 'Operation Deliver' from a prepared list of code names. 'Sounds like an Adam Ant song,' his colleagues told him, as in 'Stand and Deliver', but that seemed appropriate. Along with the name, the operation had an office. D. Supt. Paul Gladstone set himself up in a room on the first floor of McCann House, a new annex to Kent Police head-quarters. He had an early meeting here with his chief constable, Michael Fuller.

Fuller had been at home with the flu when news of the robbery broke. He heard about it on the TV. When he saw the robbery described as record-breaking on the news he decided he better drag himself into work and make sure Gladstone had everything he needed. 'It meant drafting in detectives from around the force, so we ended up with this huge investigation team,' says the chief constable. 'This is before we made the telephone appeal. We wanted the officers in place before the telephone lines were actually publicized.' One hundred officers were marshalled, with shifts rearranged so another 200 support staff could be on hand when needed, including forensic officers who were directed to fast-track evidence for Operation Deliver. 'The scale of the crime [required] commensurate resources,' Fuller continues. 'Large numbers of support staff, not only detectives, is a luxury we don't normally have. It meant that we were able to get some very fast results.'

Adrenalin was running. 'The first two weeks were very exciting,' says the chief constable, who watched pundits talking about the robbery on TV, saying how professional the criminals were, and what a hard job Kent Police would have catching them, and decided to prove the experts wrong. 'I'd watched people saying, "They'll never solve this, they'll never catch anybody for this" and also criminals, or reformed criminals saying, you know, "Whoever did this crime has done a good job, and I hope they get away with it" and I think that riled me, really, and made me want to [prove them wrong]. It presented a challenge, which I always relish, and there's no doubt all the officers working on the case relish the challenge . . . they positively enjoyed it.'

There was a political dimension to this, too. In November 2005, the Home Secretary had announced that he wanted to merge smaller constabularies such as Kent to make larger, more efficient regional police forces. It was argued that small forces were not good at handling major incidents, and Kent might be merged with Sussex and Surrey. Fuller submitted a detailed report to the Home Office arguing the case for his force to retain its autonomy, and he was waiting for a reply when the robbery happened. Although he says Kent Police met all the Home Office criteria for a stand-alone force, Operation Deliver would be seen as a test of their capabilities. Fuller was therefore determined that Kent Police would solve the Tonbridge robbery *on their own*.*

So when Mike Fuller's officers received an early offer of help from Scotland Yard's Flying Squad, otherwise known as the 'Sweeney'†, the acknowledged experts in combating armed robbers, the response from Maidstone was lukewarm. 'They were interested in offering help. But as it was we didn't need their help,' says the chief constable.

It was the Flying Squad, however, who came up with Lee Murray's name. They told Kent Police that the word in the capital was that Murray was mixed up in something big. 'There was liaison in relation to that,' admits Mike Fuller, but Murray was just one of many names his officers had at this stage, and he wasn't a priority. In fact, it was some time before Kent Police started to take a close interest in the cage fighter. There was simply so much else to do, and the investigation was moving incredibly fast, 'far faster, clearly, than the people involved thought that we would,' says Fuller. 'I think that [the gang] under-estimated the speed with which we'd be on top of them.'

9

The rental company KTS started calling John Fowler at 8.30 Thursday morning, asking when he was going to bring their lorry back. It was two days overdue. Fowler assured them he was on his way, but he had some errands to do first.

After unloading the lorry at Friningham Farm, John had

---

*Plans to amalgamate regional forces were later abandoned.
†Rhyming slang: Sweeney Todd = Flying Squad.

parked it in a service area on the M20 where it remained overnight. The vehicle was in fact given a parking ticket. Before returning the lorry to the depot, John paid the fine and repaired some minor damage. Stuart Royle had clipped a riser ramp leaving the depot on Wednesday morning, damaging the offside guard rail and its reflector lens. John obtained a replacement rail for £37.60, the receipt for which was later found shredded at his home.

Fowler then drove the lorry to Shampooz Hand Car Wash in Chatham, which shared a forecourt with the Auto Barn car lot, run by a mate of Royle's named Daniel Brunning. The men had mutual friends in the traveller community. Royle called Brunning repeatedly the day after the robbery, and sent him a text that read: 'Can you get me a new phone, mate? Meet the other fella before you meet me.' Fowler later claimed that Royle booked the lorry into Shampooz for a clean, and he simply drove it there. One wonders why Fowler was so obliging towards Royle, who owed him thousands of pounds. Surely Royle should have been doing errands for Fowler? Yet John was acting as Slippery's delivery boy. Also, there is no onus on customers who rent vehicles to have them cleaned before they are returned. On top of which, Thursday was a lousy day to use a car wash. It was snowing when John arrived at Shampooz. The car-wash workers – an Albanian named Burem Isufi and two Lithuanians called Stonkus and Popovas – were standing around idle. John was their only customer.

'He said he wanted a full valet,' says Burem Isufi. 'He was quoted £100 and he seemed happy to pay this.* He wanted the lorry cabin cleaned, the rear of the lorry steam-cleaned and the

---

*In his police interviews Fowler denied paying for the car wash.

outside washed.' It took the men 40 minutes to give the vehicle a thorough going over. When the job was done, Fowler headed off to KTS. Staff were pleased to see him rolling into the yard at 12.40. Unusually, the returned vehicle was pristine clean. Indeed, it was still wet from its wash.

While this was going on, detectives made two breakthrough arrests acting on 'received information'. In plain English, somebody tipped them off. Information had flooded into Kent Police headquarters in the aftermath of the robbery and detectives had already spoken to many people including salon workers at Hair Hectik, who told them that Michelle Hogg had been making masks and wigs for 'an inside job'. The story was that Michelle was expecting £50,000 for her work on this job. Police suspected her boss was involved, too.

Around 1.00 p.m. on 23 February, within 36 hours of the gang leaving Medway House, detectives went simultaneously to Hogg's flat in Plumstead, and to Michael Demetris' parents' house in Bromley. The barber Demetris was arrested first on suspicion of being part of the conspiracy, and taken to Tonbridge for questioning. He became the Number 1 suspect in the case, not the first in rank of importance, but the first to be nicked. The list would grow to include 29 suspects. Officers began a search of Demetris' home and salon. As they did so, Lea Rusha tried to call Michael on his mobile, unaware that the barber had already been arrested.

A couple of miles away, DC David Ecuyer was trying to get an answer from the top-floor flat at 14 Vicarage Park. He had pressed the bell repeatedly and suspected Hogg was in, but she didn't answer. At 2.30, the detective was given permission to force the front door. He found Hogg on the landing. She said she couldn't hear the door from her flat. DC Ecuyer arrested the hairdresser for conspiracy to commit armed robbery. He said the police knew she had made masks used in the heist. She didn't have to say anything, but if she did it could be used in evidence. Hogg burst into tears.

10

That afternoon Kent Police held a press conference at head-quarters presented by Assistant Chief Constable Adrian Leppard who had been chosen as the public face of the investigation, allowing Paul Gladstone to get on with the detective work. It was important to have a dedicated officer who could address the public directly via television-news reports. 'Psychologically, forces want to have continuity so when somebody's making appeals for public help, the public recognize him,' explains Sky's crime correspondent Martin Brunt who had set up his satellite truck outside headquarters. 'They tend to be rather avuncular [officers] who will encourage people to phone in, if they've got information. If you've got different cops every day making appeals there's no continuity, people aren't so keen to phone in . . . that's the psychology.' Kent Police also knew they had a problem in asking the public to help solve a bank robbery. 'There's this public view that this is a victimless crime,' Brunt explains. 'That's what the police battle against in trying to get information.'

When the cameramen were ready, ACC Leppard announced a reward of up to £2 million for information leading to the recovery of the money and the successful prosecution of the gang. Behind the scenes the police had worked with Securitas and its insurers to come up with this reward, which didn't mean anybody supplying any snippet of information would get £2 million. It was a reward of *up to* £2 million, payable only on certain conditions, the figure designed to catch the public's attention. It was reported as the largest reward ever offered in the UK, dubiously. Larger rewards are sometimes paid for information about robberies, but they aren't always publicized. 'It's not like a lottery where you present a cheque in front of a photo-call,' observes Securitas' PR consultant Carl Courtney. 'The type of people who can typically provide this information quite often, obviously, don't want to be named.'

Having grabbed the media's attention with the £2 million reward, Adrian Leppard asked for information about a red van he announced had been found at Hucking, and the depot manager's Nissan Almera, which was still missing. Police also needed to find the white lorry. They released CCTV images of the Renault at the gates of Medway House to help the public. Then Paul Fullicks of Securitas answered questions. 'Managing people in security environments is always very difficult,' he told reporters, making it clear that the company suspected an inside job. 'We continually review our security to try and eliminate those weaknesses, [but], without doubt, in this instance people have been the weak link.' Leppard finished on a confident note, however. 'We will catch these people,' he said, knowing of course that detectives already had two suspects in custody.

Michael Demetris and Michelle Hogg were being questioned at Tonbridge Police Station. Hogg, who had no previous convictions, didn't say much. Instead, her solicitor handed detectives a written statement from his client:

> *I have committed no crime as far as I know. I may have done some work innocently without any knowledge of how my work would be used. I would like to assist the police further so I could establish my innocence but I am terrified as to what may happen to me and my family if I say too much. I do not think the police could protect me or my family from harm. I am really distressed and shocked to be arrested for a robbery and I had no idea that I had any connection to such a serious or indeed any crime. I am very sorry that I cannot help the police but I am too scared to do so.*

That evening police began a forensic search of Hogg's flat. They also went through her rubbish, in the nick of time before the dustmen emptied the bins. In amongst the detritus of Michelle's life, SOCOs found all the make-up materials she had thrown out, together with a Charles H. Fox itemized receipt for £400. Officers were interested to recover a man's used razor and a cigarette butt (used razors and cigarette ends yield excellent DNA results). One of the most intriguing finds in the bin was a pot of flesh-tone greasepaint on the back of which had been written 'LEE M.' Could this be the Lee Murray the Flying Squad had mentioned? Also in the bin were handwritten notes giving directions to what police discovered was the home address of a man named Jetmir Bucpapa in Tonbridge, and a map showing the way to a garage in Wateringbury which had the same address as Mark Scott, the registered owner of the red van. It was a simple matter to discover that the owner of the Wateringbury garage was one Stuart Royle. Police also found a map in Michelle's bin giving directions to a house registered to Royle's mother.

There was more evidence inside Hogg's flat, including orange hair fibres which matched those taken from the clothes of Colin Dixon and his child. Pieces of shredded paper in a kitchen drawer were reconstructed to reveal notes, in Hogg's childish hand, about how she apparently intended to disguise her clients. One note was headed 'Stuart', underlined by an arrow pointing to 'Shiek' (sic), underneath which she had written:

Indian Turban
wider nose
Teeth
Cheek bones

Hogg had thought of making Royle up as a Sikh, which she mis-
spelt 'Shiek'.

There was another note about someone called 'Lil Lee',
underneath which were the words:

Older
cheek bones
wrinkles

Did 'Lil Lee' mean 'Little Lee', indicating that detectives should
be looking for a Big Lee, too? Police found more notes in Hogg's
flat, about 'Facial Life Casting', and a copy of her curriculum
vitae, which informed them that she had worked as a make-up
artist in London department stores since the 1980s and was 'a
team player' used to working to 'tight deadlines [in a] fast-paced
environment'. She also possessed 'good telephone skills'. These
were indeed all qualities Michelle Hogg had brought to her work
with the heist gang.

11

Thursday night there was a pub quiz at the Cock in Detling.
During the evening a customer pointed out to the landlord,
Colin Howarth, that the silver Nissan Almera in the car park
matched the description of a car Kent Police were appealing for
information about on the TV. Howarth called the police, who
arrived at the Cock at closing time to recover Colin Dixon's
motor.

Almost simultaneously, the grey Volvo and the burgundy
Vauxhall used in the kidnapping and robbery were being driven
along Burberry Lane, which crosses open country near Redpits

Cottage, and parked in a field. Both cars were then set alight. They were still burning when the fire brigade showed up around midnight, the firemen in turn calling the police. It was fortunate that the emergency workers got to the scene fast because they were able to salvage useful evidence before the cars were burnt out. In the boot of the Vectra was Colin Dixon's briefcase. The remains of a siren unit and blue lights were recovered from the grille of the vehicle, showing that it had been used as a bogus police car. In the foot well of the Volvo was ammunition for a 9 mm weapon, as well as a magazine clip to a Skorpian machine pistol.

While these were lucky finds for the police, taken together with what had been recovered at the cash depot, the red van, and most especially Michelle Hogg's flat, it showed the heist gang was not as slick as police had originally thought. Rather detectives seemed to be dealing with a mixed bunch of robbers, some of whom operated like professionals, with others who were, frankly, amateurish, and in the wake of this spectacular robbery the criminals seemed to be panicking.

Chapter Eleven

BANG! BANG! BANG!

1

Michelle Hogg was questioned again, about what had been found at her flat, on Friday, 24 February. She didn't have anything to say and the police decided to release her on bail without charge. The same went for Michael Demetris. That was not the end of the story, though. Later in the day detectives met Michelle, her parents and her solicitor, secretly at the Black Prince Hotel in Bexley in order to discuss the possibility that Michelle might become a Crown prosecution witness. Hogg declined the offer. She was clearly scared, however, caught between her fear of the gang and a possible criminal charge. Considering what had been found at her flat, it seemed likely that the police would charge her unless she did a deal.

Friday was the birthday of the Dixons' youngest child. The family celebrated the event as best they could in the police safe house. Later, Lynn went with officers to retrace what she could remember of her kidnap route, giving detectives vital information. There was no prospect of going home to Hadleigh Gardens. The press now had the Dixons' address. Reporters and photographers were staking out the house in Herne Bay in the expectation the family would return eventually. As they waited the reporters talked to the Dixons' neighbours, few of whom had much to say about the family, or the events of Tuesday evening. Neighbour Steve Hutton says typically: 'It was really an ordinary night. There I was decorating. My wife was watching telly and someone was being kidnapped. It was just quite bizarre.' Across the road, retired police sergeant John Wenman was visited by a TV reporter with cameraman. 'I didn't see anything or hear anything,' John told them.

'Can we film you saying that?'

He closed his door, opened it again, and told them he hadn't seen or heard anything. They went away satisfied.

The Dixons' middle child, Dominic, aged 21, then showed up at the family home and spoke exclusively to a reporter from the *Sun*, which acquired a number of family photos of Colin, Lynn and their child. 'They should be made to suffer just as they made my family suffer. They should have guns held to their heads and see how they like it,' Dominic told the paper excitedly. He said the first he knew of the robbery was when he saw the television news and recognised Medway House as the place where Dad worked. 'I knew roughly what he did for a living, but I had no idea of the scale of the money stored in the depot. I thought it was closer to one or two million quid.' When he tried to telephone his parents, Dominic discovered that their mobile phones were switched off. He still hadn't been able to make direct contact. He said his mother was 'calm and organized, so I think she'll be struggling to cope' and Dad was 'so straight and sensible, and brilliant with money. If you dropped a tenner, he'd run down the street after you.'

2

Just after 9.00 o'clock that morning, Stuart Royle walked into Brandon Tool Hire in Upper Stone Street, Maidstone, and told the manager that he needed to cut up some metal. Brian Denyer suggested a petrol-driven STIHL disc cutter, assuming that the customer wanted to hire a machine. Royle asked if there were any for sale. It so happened that a pair of new cutters were in stock. 'How much would it be for the two of them?' the customer enquired, evidently having a lot of metal to cut up.

The manager quoted a price of £395 each plus VAT. With the discs it added up to just under a thousand pounds. 'He pulled a large bundle of notes out of his pocket and started to count them.' Having laid out £500, Royle went to get the rest of the money from his car. When he'd handed over the full amount in cash, the manager asked the customer for his name for the guarantee. Royle said he was Paul Nicholls, and gave a Maidstone phone number (Stuart's number with two numbers juxtaposed). Denyer told him that the cutters needed to be assembled. His mechanic would do this, if the customer would like to come back in an hour, which he agreed to do, driving off in a BMW. Mr Denyer made a note of the registration number in case the money he had been given turned out to be fake. Indeed he was so suspicious of such a large cash payment that he took the money straight to the bank.

When he returned to his shop, Brian Denyer found his mechanic in the car park helping Paul Nicholls load the disc cutters into a white Transit van, which was parked alongside the customer's BMW. There was a second man with them, John Fowler, who at 11.34 that morning visited a nearby Texaco station to fill jerry cans with petrol, which would have been needed to fuel the cutters. Later somebody drove the Transit van to Glyn Mercer's yard at Friningham Farm, leaving it there with the disc cutters and the petrol cans in the back. The intention must have been to cut up the cash cages that were still in the yard, but this didn't happen.

John had other things to do. He rang his car-dealer mate David Johnson and arranged to pay him cash for a black VW he'd bought earlier in the week with a post-dated cheque. John drove up to Brands Hatch to meet Johnson, and gave him £4,500 in readies. There is no evidence that this was anything other than a legitimate transaction.

3

Disposing of the stolen money was almost as big a problem as stealing it. The gangsters seem to have adopted a policy of dividing up and hiding their stash, in large and small amounts, sometimes putting millions in one place, other times hiding a single bag of cash, with a few thousand in it.

Murray gave a holdall of money to his wife. It contained £38,000, mostly in £50 notes. Siobhan Lamrani-Murray later said she thought Lee had earned this money cage-fighting (even though he hadn't fought in over a year, and never won this much). Mrs Lamrani-Murray didn't pay the money into the bank, as most people would. Nor did she keep it at home. She chose to leave it with a girl she had grown up with named Ria Anderson, telling Ria that she was thinking of moving and needed to store some things temporarily. Ria gave Siobhan a key to her house, 46 Pitfield Crescent, Thamesmead, a tatty property on a rundown housing-association estate. Siobhan put the bag in the spare room. Ria's mum, 48-year-old Myra Anderson, worked with her boyfriend in the Queen's Arms pub in Plumstead, where Lee, Siobhan, Roger Coutts and Paul Allen all grew up. Myra knew them, and their mums. Myra had a criminal record, for forgery, but she insists that she knew nothing about the Tonbridge robbery, and had no idea Siobhan Lamrani-Murray had stashed £38,000 in her spare bedroom.

It was a similar story when Lea Rusha and Jetmir Bucpapa gave a couple of money bags to an acquaintance of theirs named Chris Bowles, apparently on the pretext that Rusha was having domestic problems with Kate, and wanted to store some things temporarily. Christopher Bowles is a short, powerfully built man of 48, a former British judo champion who competed in the 1980 Moscow Olympics. Thirteen years later he was arrested in connection with conspiracy to supply ecstasy, a Class-A drug. The CPS didn't proceed with the case. More recently, he had made a living teaching judo in Tonbridge to students such as Lea Rusha. Bowles lived with his family in nearby Hildenborough, driving a gold sports car and a white van. He put Lea's money bags in the van, having no idea what was in them.

Bowles had a judo class on the morning of Friday, 24 February. Afterwards he went to his van and, at this stage, decided to look inside the bags he was holding for Rusha. He saw a balaclava helmet and a gun. This sent him into shock. He got into the van and started driving, his head in a 'blur', driving down the M20 until he came to the Ashford International Hotel, a large, conference-style hotel two junctions south of where the gang turned off the M20 to kidnap Colin Dixon. It was 11.00 a.m. when Bowles pulled into the car park, about the same time Royle and Fowler were collecting the disc cutters in Maidstone. Bowles parked next to a sign warning him that 'vehicles and contents are left entirely at owner's risk', then went inside the hotel, where he paced around for a while, before walking out again, across the car park, past his van, towards Sainsbury's. He didn't come back.

Shortly after Bowles left the scene, two uniformed police constables, Martin Mason and Craig Chalmers-Stevens, pulled up next to the van in their patrol car, having been directed to the hotel by 'information received'. It would later be hinted by defence barristers in court that Bowles himself tipped off the police. The time was now 12.24, just under an hour since Bowles had walked away from the hotel. PC Mason tried the van doors and found them unlocked. Two plain-clothes detectives arrived to join the constables, followed by an inspector. When everybody was assembled, PC Mason slid back the door. The vehicle was piled high with judo suits, gym mats and punch bags. There was also a black zip-up bag, inside of which the constable found a bullet-proof vest and a black balaclava, tucked inside of which was a gun.

More police were summoned, including a specialist search officer named Sgt. Glen Craddock, who identified the gun as a Skorpian machine pistol, matching the weapon used during the robbery, compatible with ammunition found in the Volvo. The gun was loaded with live rounds, establishing that the robbers used real weapons in the heist. The blue ballistic vest and black balaclava also appeared to match items used by the robbers. A single orange hair was recovered from the balaclava. It matched hair found at Michelle Hogg's flat, hair on Colin Dixon's jacket and hair on his child's woollen hat.

These were all very significant discoveries, but they paled beside what police found when they opened two tartan-pattern suitcases in the back of the van. When Sgt. Craddock opened the first case, splitting the plastic sides with a scalpel in case the bag was booby-trapped, he discovered the suitcase was packed with bank notes, a mixture of £5, £10, £20 and £50 notes, most still

wrapped in Securitas plastic, together with a dispatch note showing that the money had been processed at Medway House only
fifteen minutes before the robbery. It added up to £825,500. The
second suitcase contained £545,000, a total of over £1.3 million.
Once the money was photographed, forensic officers wrapped it
in grey plastic, and transferred the bundle to their van. The cash
parcel was so heavy SOCOs staggered under the weight. They
continued to look through the van for any other evidence. If the
police didn't in fact already know who owned the vehicle, it was
easy enough to find out. Chris Bowles' business cards were in the
glove compartment.

While the van was being searched, Kent Police were giving the
press an e-fit of the bogus policeman who kidnapped Colin
Dixon. The first e-fit showed an unsmiling young, white man
with a wiry, ginger beard which didn't match his dark eyebrows
and hair. There was a second e-fit of the same man without the
beard and the peaked cap, to indicate to the public what he might
look like normally. The suspect was estimated to stand six foot
one inch tall. 'This is the face of one of the armed robbers,' ACC
Adrian Leppard told reporters. 'We have callous, professional
gangsters to catch and we will bring them to book.' The picture
reporters took away for publication and broadcast was a good
likeness of Lee Murray.

4

Friday evening, Paul Burden was eating a solitary supper in his
house on Friningham Farm while his wife took a turn with the
lambs. Paul kept an eye on the TV news as he ate, taking keener
interest when the robbery came up on the news because of the
local connections. He saw that police were appealing for

information about a white Renault lorry, and talking about a £2 million reward. Burden remembered something his tenant Ann Day had told him a day or so ago about people unloading stuff from a white lorry in his yard, and rang Mrs Day. 'What day was that that they was chucking out those cages?' he asked. She couldn't remember. 'Well, come on, put your thinking cap on, there's a £2 million reward.' She still didn't seem to remember much.

Grumbling to himself, Burden called the police and gave a female officer the gist of what he knew. 'Would you do us a favour?' asked the officer. 'Would you go and have a good look to see whether it's still there?' When he finished eating, Burden went up to the yard he rented to Glyn Mercer, ringing the officer back from the scene.

'There's these crates here,' he told her, shining his torch on the cash cages.

'What colour are they?'

'Well, there's blue ones, and red ones, and green ones.'

'Don't touch anything. Sounds if that's what we're looking for.' She took down directions to the farm, which was not an easy place for townsfolk to find in the dark, as Burden knew.

'I'll put some floodlights on so as they can find it,' the farmer told her, for he had floodlights that could be seen from the A249, 'if you've got your wits about you.' Then he sat down on a hay bale, and waited. 'I thought, as soon as I go down home they'll come.' Some time later the police rang back saying they were in a lay-by on the A249, 'the opposite side of A249, not even the right side of the bloody road, still looking for me'. Finally the exasperated farmer saw cars coming down the lane and he showed the police what he had found. In amidst the second-hand cars were seven blue Piano Cages, six green Bank of England cages, one red Super Sid and a shopping trolley. All were empty and, intriguingly, three cages and two trolleys the police knew had been stolen from Medway House were missing.

Farmer Burden didn't get rid of the police until eleven o'clock that night and they came back early on Saturday morning to begin a forensic examination of the yard. He told them to get on with what they had to do, but to keep the press away because he was busy with lambing. He also asked for some officers to stay at the farm overnight in case 'them buggers' came back and tried to give him 'a thundering good hiding'. The police promised, and when Glyn Mercer came driving into the yard a little later they arrested him.*

Apart from the cash cages and shopping trolley, the scene-of-crime officers found plenty of other evidence in the yard including Securitas tags, padlocks, cellophane packing, on which fingerprints were found, two Eagle luggage labels, and scraps of paper identifiable as having come from the Securitas depot. There was even a sheet of paper printed with the words 'NCS BOND FACILITY PROPERTY OF THE BANK OF ENGLAND', which was apparently all that remained of the Bank of England's bond.

5

The police investigation had grown so quickly, generating so many leads, that D. Supt. Paul Gladstone was overwhelmed by work in McGann House. One day he looked up from his desk to see a line of eleven detectives waiting for his decision on one thing or another. It was too much for him and DCI Tim Smith to deal with, so he recruited a second deputy.

---

*The car dealer was released without charge.

Mick Judge was the head of the Major Crime Unit at Kent Police, the CID team that worked alongside Tim Smith's unit. Whereas Tim combated organized crime, Mick spent most of his time investigating murder. 'My bread and butter is murders,' as he says, with a smile. Despite such a grim workload, Mick was a jolly fellow, chubby and grey at 44, with an affable, boyish demeanour. Gladstone thought the smiling DCI would be particularly useful to them because of his experience using the computerized Home Office Large Major Enquiry System (or HOLMES, after the great detective), which murder squad officers commonly use to collate information and generate leads. Because of the huge volume of information coming in about the robbery, Gladstone was going to use HOLMES to process the data in Operation Deliver. Mick started work with the team first thing Saturday morning. Ultimately, he would take over and lead the investigation. His first day was very busy. The weekend as a whole was even more eventful.

As far as the press was concerned, the highlight of Saturday was getting a statement from the elusive Colin Dixon, whom they had not yet seen or heard from. Disappointingly, they still weren't going to. Colin's statement was read out by Securitas executive Paul Fullicks:

The night of Tuesday February 21 was simply the worst night of my life. But more than that, it was the worst night in the lives of my wife Lynn and our [child]. The terror of what happened and the horror of what might have happened is with us in every waking moment. This horrific experience angers me beyond belief. We are a normal, law-abiding family and no one should suffer as we have done. For the criminals to use me is bad enough, but to kidnap my wife and child and put guns to their heads and threaten them with death is something so frightening no words can convey them today.

Colin spoke of the 'greed' that motivated the gang, while for him and his family the evening of 21/22 February had been a matter of 'survival'. He thanked the police, and he urged the public to call with information to 'help capture these terrible people and ensure they are punished. No one should have to experience such an ordeal at their hands again.' One of the people who rang the police hotline in response to Colin's statement was Jane Linfoot, who recalled having seen a man in a green car behaving oddly at the Tamarisk Service Station on 21 February, so much so that her mother had written down his registration number. This would later be part of the trial evidence.

The press were starting to hear rumours about Olympian Chris Bowles, who was questioned by police on Saturday, having attended the station by appointment. That is to say the police didn't go busting into his house with guns drawn and drag him down to the station. He was invited along for a chat. Bowles told detectives he had simply done his friend, Lea Rusha, a favour by storing some bags for him in his van. When he saw what was in the bags, 'I panicked. I didn't know what to do.' Despite the fact that Bowles was the last man in possession of a van containing £1.3 million in stolen money, and a loaded machine gun, the police were completely confident he was not a robber, or a kidnapper, and he was released without charge the same day. Detectives were much more interested in finding Lea Rusha, and his friend, Jetmir Bucpapa.

A routine check on the police database revealed that Rusha had a record for violence. The Tonbridge gang were heavily armed. Indeed, their weaponry went far beyond the usual sawn-off shotguns favoured by blaggers (because they are easy to obtain and hide). These boys were properly tooled up. They had machine guns. So when the police went to raid the homes of Rusha and Bucpapa, they did so ready for a shoot-out.

Although the raids were timed to coincide as much as possible, police approached Bucpapa's address in Tonbridge first. Around 3.00 o'clock Saturday afternoon, police cordoned off Hadlow Road, causing major traffic congestion as shoppers tried to drive in and out of the town centre. When the area was clear and secure, Sgt. Derek Lockwood led a team of six armed officers towards the Bucpapas' ground-floor apartment. They wore dark overalls, ballistic vests and carried semi-automatic weapons.

Inside, Rebecca Bucpapa was heating up some chilli con carne for a late lunch. She had been at work during the morning, and planned to go for a swim after she had eaten. As she stirred the pot, Rebecca became aware of a Land Rover outside the house and saw police with guns pointed at her windows. 'I lifted the curtain [and] opened the window and asked them what was going on and what did they think they were doing. They asked who I was and did I live here. Was Jet at home?' She said he wasn't. They seemed unconvinced. 'I could hear them making plans to break down the front door.' So she let them in the back.

'They literally dragged me out of the house. I didn't have any shoes or socks on. I was frightened. I did what they said. They were shouting, "Don't panic! Everything's fine!" There were dogs barking. One of the dog handlers stood with me. He was yelling. Someone else came over and asked him to calm down a bit.' Rebecca was made to wait in a van while the officers moved through the flat, checking every room in case Jetmir was hiding. They tossed a pair of shoes out for Rebecca. 'I asked them if they were Immigration. I was asking them, "Are you taking him away?"' They told Rebecca they were investigating the Tonbridge robbery, then took her to the station to make a statement.

Once Sgt. Lockwood's team had 'cleared' the flat, a second, 'containment team' secured the property. A third search team put on white overalls and blue gloves, then went through the flat with

a video-camera, filming the scene and seizing evidence. It was a
pleasant little flat. There were flowers in a vase, a teddy on the
bedroom floor. Next to Ted was a Nike bag inside which police
found an anti-bugging device. Outside, they recovered Jet's VW
Golf. The Sat-Nav was programmed with postcodes and
addresses relating to Herne Bay.

6

A second firearms unit was simultaneously raiding Lea Rusha's
house at 12 Lambersart Close, Southborough. 'I heard some
banging, and I thought, *What's that about?* I looked out and there
was a load of police cars,' recalls neighbour Robert Neve, who
saw officers with rifles trained on Rusha's semi, which was scary
because the two houses adjoined each other and Robert's wife
and children were home. 'I thought, *Blimey!* I went and told
everyone, and [we] looked out the back.' The Neve family saw
police marksmen at the bottom of next door's garden, guns
pointed at the house, while officers broke open the patio doors.

As with the Hadlow Road search, the first team moved
through the house methodically announcing themselves as armed
police. When they had cleared the property, the men in black
handed over to a uniformed containment team, while SOCOs
put on their white suits and blue gloves for the search, which
took three days, and revealed a treasure trove of evidence.

In a bag in the living area they found plastic cable ties, and a
book about wigs; an MOT certificate for a vehicle registered to
a company owned by Stuart Royle (that name again); and paperwork linking Rusha to Jetmir Bucpapa. Upstairs in the kids'
bedroom, next to the bunk beds, they found a media centre
bought from the Spy Shop in Chesterfield, from which police

downloaded a recording of a woman knocking on the Dixons' front door.

The master bedroom was at the back of the house. It was very untidy, with clothes, shopping bags and paper scattered over the floor, together with an artificial rose, evidently a love token to or from Katie Philp. Her make-up was arranged on the chest of drawers, next to which was a leather armchair, behind which PC Andrew Farthing found two pieces of folded A4 paper. When the officer unfolded the pages he beheld two hand-drawn plans of Medway House, with areas marked 'safe', 'counting room' and 'office'. On one of the plans somebody had additionally scrawled:

Yellow = 50
red = 20
blu = 10
green = 5

Although the writer evidently couldn't spell, this is the correct colour-coding of money bricks in the depot, not the sort of information a roofer might be expected to keep at home. There was little doubt these were Lea Rusha's documents. They were found in his bedroom, written in his hand, marked with his fingerprints. Behind the chair police also found a card on which was written the Ordnance Survey grid reference for Medway House.

There was a tool shed in the garden. In amongst the usual junk left in any shed, police found two rucksacks, one of which contained postman clothing, including a fluorescent Royal Mail tabard with 'JET' printed on it, a Royal Mail shirt and a mail bag. Inside the second rucksack were two black balaclavas of the type worn in the robbery, cable ties and tape, and a multi-band scanner pre-tuned to police waveband. In a pocket of a Puma rucksack was a Magnum air pistol, a type of airgun prohibited in the UK because it looks like a real gun and can in fact be lethal. In a chest of drawers were ten shotgun cartridges. On the floor was a blue boiler suit, of the same colour and design as those worn by the robbers, only with a tear at the left shoulder. (Five robbers wore identical overalls during the heist, one was dressed as a policeman and the sixth man, Shorty, wore a slightly different pair. Rusha may have rejected this damaged pair at the last minute.) Also in the shed was a black refuse sack in which were sign transfers printed with the word 'POLICE'.

7

Halfway between Whitstable and Herne Bay on the Kent coast lies the village of Tankerton, the principal buildings of which are ranged along Marine Parade overlooking a broad swathe of grass – known as Tankerton Slopes – below which is the sea. Tankerton Slopes is raised up above the beach and there are fine views to Herne Bay. One can see the water tower on the hill that marks where the Dixons lived. There is also a flagpole, some rusty cannons and a wooden shelter. At weekends, Tankerton Slopes is popular with walkers.

Just after 1.00 p.m. on Sunday, 26 February, 2006, a blue BMW hurtled down Marine Parade in the direction of Herne Bay pursued by two cars. One of these cars got ahead of the BMW, forcing it to halt by the shelter. As members of the public watched, armed men leapt out of the cars trapping the BMW, produced guns and fired at it:

BANG! BANG! BANG!

The noise was startling. 'We were sitting down to lunch,' recalls resident Douglas Gilbert, whose house overlooks the Slopes. 'We heard three bangs, peculiar bangs.' Like several witnesses, Mr

Gilbert only realized the armed men in the road were police officers when they pulled police caps from their pockets. A few doors
down, 16-year-old Gala Jackson-Coombs was watching *Scooby Doo
2* when the unusual noises drew her to the window. 'Of course, it's
Tankerton, so you don't expect something huge to be happening.
And when we went to the window, there were all these policemen
outside [and] they had these huge, huge guns strapped to them.'
Gala assumed this was an exercise, 'because we didn't expect them
to have these huge guns tied to them with a piece of string'. In fact,
these were Heckler and Koch submachine guns on lanyards. The
officers had used the weapons to shoot out the tyres of the BMW.

One of the armed officers, PC Spencer Duffy, now opened the
driver's door and yanked out a fat man with white hair. 'Can you
confirm you are Mr Stuart Royle?' he asked politely.

'Yes,' puffed the car dealer, who had shaved off his beard and
had his hair cut short since the heist.

'I'm arresting you on suspicion to commit robbery.'

Police had traced and trailed the BMW having failed to find
Royle at any of the places associated with a man who seemed to
have no fixed abode. They had followed the BMW from
Maidstone, choosing to stop Royle here on an open stretch of
road by the sea for the sake of public safety. It turned out that
Royle was travelling with a friend named Tommy Love.
Detectives believe Stuart was on his way to meet Sean Lupton,
and wondered, in retrospect, whether Royle might have led them
to more of the stolen money if they had been more patient. But
it was easy to be wise after the event.

One of the places police had been looking for Stuart was his
mother's house in Maidstone. In fact, they broke the door down
when she was out. When Cynthia came home that afternoon
from having Sunday lunch with her son, Andrew, she thought at
first that she'd been burgled. Then a policeman came to the door

and explained it was Stuart they were after. During their search of the bungalow, police recovered a Compaq computer used to do the Tracesmart search for Colin Dixon's home address. Over at Redpits, officers found a list of people who were owed money by car dealer Terry Lynch. Royle was on this 'debt list'. Next to his name was the word 'mug'. Also on the list was John Fowler, who was apparently owed £47,500, and Lee Murray, who was owed £14,000. All these names were fed into the HOLMES computer, which would have matched Murray to the man the Flying Squad were talking about, and indeed to the abbreviated name Lee M. written on a pot of greasepaint at Hogg's flat. There was so much going on, however, that Kent Police still didn't go looking for Murray.

Over the next few days police also searched Chrissy's Royle's rented house in Maidstone, where Stuart and Kim had been staying. Parked outside was a white Ford Courier van which detectives took a close interest in. When they went to Royle's car yard at Wateringbury they found handcuffs, a registration certificate for a red LDV van and a scribbled memorandum about needing a new number plate for a Volvo S60.

8

The BMW Royle was arrested in was one of three vehicles bought by John Fowler the previous week. Police now knew of the connections between Royle and Fowler. John's name was on the company records of Monarch Retail as well as numerous documents recovered from Royle's addresses. It was time to speak to Mr Fowler.

By his own account, John hosted a dinner party at Elderden Farm Saturday night. He spent the first part of Sunday at home fiddling with cars, including a car for his daughter, Amy, who was about to start a new job. He watched Jack play in a school hockey match, bought petrol, did some paperwork, then made up the fire so there was a good blaze going when his father-in-law, Derek, came round for Sunday lunch. They sat down to eat at four o'clock.

Afterwards, John borrowed his wife's Porsche Cayenne and drove to Maidstone Hospital, apparently hoping to find a man who had a logbook for him, but also seemingly going to speak to his car-dealer mate Glyn Mercer, who was visiting the hospital after being released by the police. John rang Kim Shackelton. It may be that she told him Stuart had been arrested. She must have heard by now; the police were all over every house they had ever lived in. As Fowler left Maidstone Hospital at 6.20, two plain-clothes policemen seized him by the arms and told him he was under arrest on suspicion of conspiracy to commit robbery.

By Sunday evening, the police had both Royle and Fowler in custody. Royle was first interviewed at Canterbury Police Station at 10.22 p.m., by detectives Jane Murray and Kane Clifford. They asked about the red van, which they had retrieved from the pub at Hucking. They were sure it had been used in the robbery, and it was registered to Royle's garage. Stuart admitted he'd had the van on his lot, saying it was supplied by two brothers, Terry and Ian, on a 'sale or return basis'. He had used the vehicle briefly to move some personal belongings, before returning it to the brothers on 18 February. The van's original registration number was Y697 BOA. During the heist it carried a W-registration. Royle explained this by saying there were trader plates in a mail sack in the back of the vehicle. He'd touched the plates, so his fingerprints would be on them. A commercial sales invoice showed that a Mark Scott – not Ian or Terry – had bought the van. Royle said he had no idea who Mark Scott was. He said he'd seen his van on TV in connection with the heist, which made him 'a bit panicky'. He assured the officers his panic wasn't to do with guns in the van. Nobody had mentioned guns.

The interviews continued into the early hours of Monday, at which time Royle said there was a roll of adhesive material in the van, giving a description that fitted the vinyl found at Rusha's house. Stuart hinted that he knew what the adhesive roll was used for. In fact, he was so concerned when he saw the van on television in connection with the robbery he'd phoned his solicitor. The police asked why he hadn't phoned *them*. Royle said he was worried about the safety of his family – an excuse he used repeatedly.

John Fowler's first interview started shortly after Royle's, and was conducted at Maidstone by detectives Pamela Chapman and Ray Bovis. In contrast to Stuart, John was calm, relaxed and talkative. He answered all the officers' questions and made a point of addressing them by their first names, making jokes and self-deprecating comments, charming them as a salesman would.

After telling the officers he knew nothing about the robbery, apart from what he'd read in the papers and seen on TV, John explained his business relationship with Stuart Royle: 'Give and take. He takes and I give.' He described Royle as a 'dirty and smelly' man who ran his office like he did his life. 'It's in shit order.' Stuart spoke in half-truths and had a high opinion of himself. Asked if they spent time together socially, John said Linda wouldn't have Stuart in the house! It was because he owed them so much money, John estimated about £80,000. John explained that he set up Monarch Retail so Royle could pay him back. While Royle still owned Wateringbury Car Sales, he was supposed to put the profit on cars he sold through the Monarch bank account to eke out the debt. The problem was that Slippery had only shifted three cars since January, and the cheque for one of those had bounced.

9

It seems that the arrest of Royle and Fowler was the signal Lee Murray had been waiting for, possibly having deliberately left clues to draw the police away from him, towards the bickering car dealers, and the rest of the idiots Lee found himself associated with. As he would later make plain to me in correspondence, Lee didn't have a high opinion of most of the gang. He called them 'the wallies'.

Lee Murray and Paul Allen had become official suspects in the heist investigation on Saturday 25 February, but the cage fighter had not yet been spoken to by police. They had too much else to do. 'The information we got was changing every hour,' says DCI Mick Judge. 'It was a massive task. That was the hard bit: keeping a view to hold the picture together.' It was, however, only a matter of time until detectives came calling at 32 Onslow Drive. Murray had to skedaddle, and he decided to do so with his best mate Paul Allen.[*]

Since news of the heist had broken there had been talk in criminal circles, and speculation in the media, as to how the gang would get away with the money. It was commonly thought they would take their millions abroad as soon as possible. Rumour had it that the gang had invested in an elaborate escape route which involved taking a boat to South Africa, while another theory was

---

[*]Murray would claim that he left the UK for entirely innocent reasons, of course.

that they had flown to South America. There was also speculation about the gangsters fleeing to Thailand (where Fowler owned a holiday home). In truth it would be virtually impossible for any members of the gang to fly out of the country with any stolen money, let alone 75 suitcases full. Imagine going through security with that sort of luggage! It was also too risky to use Eurostar. The simplest and safest way was by cross-Channel ferry to France. Customs officers at the docks rarely stop and search vehicles leaving the UK, being more concerned about people smuggling contraband into the country. Even then checks are desultory. It was a small risk to put a few suitcases in a car, not millions, just spending money, and drive out.

Late Sunday night Lee and Paul drove to Dover, with a friend, in Lee's black Mercedes, and caught a late ferry to Calais, probably thinking there would be even less chance of being stopped if they travelled at an unsocial hour. They were right. Before the sun rose on Monday morning, Lightning Lee and the Enforcer were driving north to Amsterdam, free as birds.

Chapter Twelve

FINDING THE MONEY

1

After arresting John Fowler, the police came to search his house. Linda Fowler was arrested and taken to Maidstone Police Station for questioning, suspected of being the woman seen with John dumping the cages at Friningham Farm.* With Mum and Dad in custody, provision had to be made for the care of the Fowler children, two of whom were working towards their GCSE exams. The Fowlers' neighbours awoke on Monday 27 February to find themselves within a cordoned-off crime scene, a quarter-mile in diameter. There was a police checkpoint on Chart Hill Road, with officers challenging anybody who wanted to pass, and police with dogs were patrolling the fields and footpaths. When John's mechanic, Norman Underdown, cycled to work that morning he was told that his boss had been nicked. Norman expressed surprise, and told the police he hadn't noticed anything unusual at Elderden Farm the previous week. He had seen

---

*After being held for three days Mrs Fowler was released without charge.

Slippery fiddling with a red van in the yard, 'but I didn't take a lot of notice'.

The search of Elderden Farm commenced in earnest on the Tuesday, 28 February. It was a big property, and the operation continued until 7 March, involving many officers. At first glance, Fowler's yard seemed to fit the description Colin and Lynn Dixon had given of the place where they had been held. Walking through the garages and sheds in a tight group, hands in pockets, so as not to disturb any evidence, detectives noticed a green tarpaulin, smelt car paint and heard the hum of an electric motor (a cesspit pump), all things Colin had mentioned in his interviews. There was also a lean-to under which a van, if parked, would be partly out of the rain. It all seemed to fit.

Down at the station, Fowler himself continued to be talkative and apparently helpful. He told detectives Bovis and Chapman – or Ray and Pam, as he called them – that he'd seen the red van on Royle's forecourt and helped start it for Jimmy Royle and Martin Bloe ('he's a bit simple') who were cleaning it. Asked why he had gone to Maidstone Hospital on Sunday, he said he wanted to see a man named Chris Hayman, who was visiting his sick mother, and had a logbook John needed. More generally, John gave the officers an account of his character and lifestyle at Elderden Farm.

John said he was a man of routine, a family man and *Daily Mail* reader, who liked his creature comforts. He was proud of his business acumen and his home, which he estimated to be worth £1.5 million. He talked about his marriage, portraying himself as a loving, if henpecked husband. After a hard day's work, supper and a glass of wine, he admitted he was often 'sold out' in front of the fire by 9.30 p.m. Linda was not impressed with this, and would sometimes go up to bed and leave him. (At one stage John asked the police to erase a bit of the tape where he felt he'd gone too

far in disparaging his dear wife.) He said Linda hated Stuart
Royle. If he rang and she picked up the phone, she'd say, 'It's that
Stuart again! I told you not to deal with him.' John didn't like
Stuart much either. He considered Slippery a thoroughly untrust-
worthy fellow, who might well be involved in a crime of this sort
and may have duped John into doing certain things to help. John
was adamant he hadn't helped *knowingly*. As he said: 'I'm not
involved in the robbery. I don't know anything about it. I thought
I was just helping somebody else.'

It all started when Stuart asked him to hire a van so he could
clear some things out of his barber shop. Royle didn't have a
credit card, so John agreed to do him a favour, as he, Joe Soap,
had so many times before. He was amazed when he saw the vehicle Royle wanted him to hire. 'I thought, Jesus Christ! This isn't
a van, it's a whacking great thing . . . I phoned Stuart, and I said
to Stuart, "What do you want this bloody great thing for?"'
When John later saw an identical lorry on the TV news he called
Royle and asked: 'Is this a coincidence, or am I being put in the
frame here?'

'Relax,' Royle told him. 'Everything's cool.'

Fowler said he then received an anonymous phone call. 'Mr
Fowler?' a man asked roughly.

'Who's calling?'

'It don't matter who's calling. I know where you live. I know
your wife and family. I know where they are. I know where your
boy goes to school. I know what time he goes to school. Keep
your nose clean and no one gets hurt.' John connected this call to
Royle and the lorry. 'I thought I was doing somebody a favour
and it's caused me grief.'

In summary he told the police nothing untoward had happened on his property, 'to my knowledge', and argued that it
would be 'a nonsense' for him to hire the lorry using his real

name, driver's licence and credit card, if he had known what it was to be used for. This was a strong point. 'I think bank robbers are mugs,' he went on. 'I just wouldn't have the balls to do it.' Also he was already a rich man. 'I live in a nice house. I do nice things. I don't need to rob a bank.'

2

When Lea Rusha and Jetmir Bucpapa heard that their homes had been raided by the police, they decided to lie low in the London area, booking into the Premier Lodge in Barking, to the east of the city. On Monday morning the lads met a solicitor named David Turner in Greenwich, after which they drove, in a black VW Beetle, to meet Jet's sister who was living in Creek Road, Deptford. As they approached the flat, around 1.40 p.m. Monday lunchtime, the lads were ambushed by armed police, who shot out their tyres.

'I heard the screech [of car tyres] then four bangs,' an eyewitness told the *Sun*. 'I saw a police officer pointing a handgun at the car.' Rusha leapt from the driver's side, only to be grabbed by PC Mark Jewiss, who 'assisted him to the ground where I handcuffed him . . . I said, "I'm arresting you on suspicion of robbery," cautioned him and he made no reply.' The same went for Bucpapa, who was plucked from the passenger seat. The police found £500 in Rusha's pockets. When they did a check on the VW, it was linked to John Fowler.

Rusha and Bucpapa were taken to Gravesend Police Station for questioning. The search of Rusha's home had by this stage yielded a mass of evidence against him, including the media centre used in the spying mission to the Dixons' home. This gadget also implicated Bucpapa, because his DNA was on it.

When the police downloaded the film they saw that it started with a couple (Lea and Raluca Millen) sitting in a car with a crack in the windscreen, identical to a crack in Bucpapa's VW. Additionally Bucpapa and Rusha were linked to the Ashford van, in Rusha's case by DNA on the balaclava. When police asked the boys about all this, Jet said he was completely innocent; Rusha said nothing at all. The police got no further with either of them.

Stuart Royle now told the police he had also decided to exercise his right to silence. But as in most aspects of his life, Stuart was inconsistent. He continued to issue occasional statements and answer questions as the mood took him. There was an erratic quality to his interviews which is not in line with the way professional criminals behave. Often, they say nothing at all in interviews. Royle couldn't seem to make up his mind what to do or say. Detectives asked him, for example, about a note found in his sales office in which he had written down the details of a matt grey Volvo S60 beside which he had started to write 'need new plate', as in need a *false* number plate. Royle said he didn't know anything about this, but suggested the aforementioned Terry or Ian could have written the note. A little later he conceded the note was 'obviously' about a number plate for a Volvo. He denied any knowledge of the Vauxhall Vectra, however, bought by a man using his address. 'I've never seen it and I do not know Mark Scott.'

As interviewing officers persisted in trying to get a truthful, or at least sensible, answer from Royle, the total amount of money he had been party to stealing was revealed. It had taken Securitas and the Bank of England almost a week to do an audit, during which time estimates published in the press had risen steadily. The final tally was £52,996,760,* a bigger haul than any comparable

---

*A slightly higher figure, £53,116,760, was given out by Kent Police at the time.

British robbery. The recent Northern Bank raid had netted £26.5 million, a previous cash record for the UK, and about the same value as the gold bullion stolen famously from Brink's-Mat in 1983, when adjusted for inflation. The Great Train Robbery of 1963 would also be worth a similar amount in modern terms. There had been bigger robberies in wartime, especially abroad: notably the looting of the Reichbank in 1945, and the theft of £572 million from Iraq's Central Bank in 2003. Other crimes of very high value included a money broker's messenger in the City of London being relieved of bonds worth £292 million by a mugger in 1999; while the value of raids on safety-deposit centres – such as a Nice branch of the Société Générale in 1976 – were notoriously difficult to value because box owners were so secretive. In terms of a verifiable peacetime cash robbery, however, the £53 million Tonbridge job set a new British and indeed world record, and was recognized as such in the new edition of *The Guinness Book of Records*.

Having made criminal history, the heist gang were a shambles. Eleven people had been arrested to date, and, though some had been released on bail, detectives had three of the suspected seven robbers in custody, which is to say Royle, Rusha and Bucpapa. They also had Fowler. 'When you look at the arrests you get Hogg and Demetris* Thursday; Royle Sunday. By the next week we've got Rusha and Bucpapa. Within a week of the robbery we've got our main players all in custody,' comments DCI Mick Judge with pride. Police had recovered most of the vehicles used in the heist, including the Renault lorry, which they seized from the hire company. They had also found the best part of one and a half million pounds of stolen money. Looked at another way,

---

*Hogg and Demetris were subsequently cleared of all charges.

almost £52 million was still missing, as were key members of the gang, including its ringleader.

The Flying Squad thought the country coppers had moved too fast, making easy arrests when they might have done better to watch and wait, and thereby catch the big man. 'The Flying Squad's view was that Kent had gone for what they call "easy wins",' explains Sky's Martin Brunt, who has excellent contacts within Scotland Yard. 'The Flying Squad advice was, "No, don't do this so fast. Sit back and watch where they go . . . See who they associate with, and in the long term it'll bring you better dividends." That was the Flying Squad view and the two sides, the two forces, fell out big time over this difference of approach.' Kent Police deny there was a rift. But there is a tinge of irritation in Mick Judge's voice when he says: 'It's all very well this watch and wait stuff. It's all about recovering money.'

3

More money was found on Tuesday at Elderden Farm where scores of officers were conducting a fingerprint search of the house, its outbuildings, and grounds. Officers in waterproofs had waded through the River Beult, which crossed the Fowlers' land, looking for clues; divers descended the wishing well; police used a cherry picker crane to take a look down the chimney. The army came and laid a metal track over the muddy field so police could take a look at an old bonfire. They put a tent over it and sifted through the remains painstakingly, removing two burnt mobile phones and items which may have belonged to Lynn Dixon and her child. One of the workers from Hop Engineering came forward with luggage labels he had found in the lane; the labels went with the type of luggage found with the money in the van at the

Ashford International Hotel and the packaging in the red Post Office van.

The first real excitement for the police at the farm came when they opened the boot of a green Peugeot in Fowler's yard and found £30,000 in red plastic Securitas bags. The registration number of the car fitted that provided by the family who had seen a man behaving strangely at the Tamarisk Shell Station on 21 February. There were also two empty Red Bull cans in the car. DNA swabs from the cans matched Lea Rusha's DNA profile. One match was so good the chance of error was one in a billion.

In the interview room, John Fowler told police that the green Peugeot belonged to Stuart Royle. He went on to tell them there was more money at the farm. 'I'm very, very concerned about my position,' Fowler said, 'not only about the police, but the intimidating phone call [I told you about].' It was because he was scared that he had not been totally candid with detectives so far, but he had now decided to tell them everything, 'because I've got nothing to hide'. He admitted dumping empty cages and shopping trolleys at Friningham Farm, before returning the lorry to the hire company, insisting that he didn't know what the cages were. Stuart asked him to do this. Kim helped. He said Kim drove to meet him at the farm, rather than them going there together.

After dumping the cages, John said he left the lorry at the M20 services, and went home where, later in the day, he sold two vehicles, a Land Rover Discovery and a black VW Beetle, to two unnamed men who agreed to pay a total cash price of £9,500. The mystery men collected the cars on Thursday, then returned the Land Rover complaining that there was a problem with its immobilizer. Fowler said he tried to repair this on Sunday morning and, as he did so, he made an astonishing discovery: in the back of the car there was a black bag filled with cash. 'I just went cold. I thought, *Fuck me! Jesus Christ!*' he told the police. 'I was panicking . . . If I leave it there and somebody finds it I'm in big shit.' He decided to hide the bag in his orchard. If the men came back, he would give them the money. He estimated there was as much as £15,000 in the bag, and assumed the men who bought the cars were connected with the robbery. He said his fingerprints might be on this money because he had handled it while hiding it in the orchard.

A call was put through to the search team at Elderden Farm and PC Claire Boichat was sent to look in Fowler's orchard. At the foot of a dead tree, she found a black bag hidden under some logs. Inside the bag was a very large sum of money, much more than Fowler estimated. It was £105,600. The money was not in Securitas wrappings, and couldn't be traced to Medway House, but the police assumed it had been stolen from the cash centre. Although it wasn't in coloured plastic, the money had been bundled up with cardboard and cellophane to make money bricks. The police wondered whether the gang had parcelled up more of the money this way and, if so, why. The bricks weren't suitable for burial. Water would get in and the card would rot. Nor were the bricks sufficiently well-sealed to be smuggled out of the country in fuel tanks, as drugs are sometimes transported. The favourite theory was that the money had been made up into bricks to be fitted in the cavity between two courses of blockwork in a new building, as if it were insulation. The police had seen this done before. Whatever way you looked at it, hiding £105,000 under a tree in your garden was a very peculiar thing to do.

Yet Linda Fowler refused to entertain the possibility that John had been involved with kidnap or robbery. 'As far as I'm concerned, my husband is totally one hundred per cent, one hundred and *fifty* per cent, innocent of it all,' she told me, adding that John would never have anything to do with any crime against children, and it was absurd to think he would bring criminals to their home. She blamed Stuart Royle for everything.

Meanwhile, Royle was giving police an account of his movements over the period of the kidnap and robbery:

Since being evicted from my property on the 3/2/2006* my life has been chaos, my oldest son and Kim have gone to live with my daughter. I've been spending a lot of my time since then trying to buy my property back . . . It will be difficult to account for my whereabouts last week, my life has been chaotic. I would have been working on my car lot or travelling around Kent looking at vehicles. I was also sorting out loans or mortgage requirements for example . . . I was probably sleeping at my daughter's some nights or the odd nights at my mother's, I also spent the night sleeping at my office at my car lot. You're asking me to account for a period of time that's in a bit of a blur. The previous three weeks were the same chaos. I really cannot be specific. My family have been split up and I was trying to buy back my house and run a business all at the same time.

He went on to say that it should be obvious that he wasn't an armed robber and, despite their ups and downs, he didn't think John was a robber either. However, Stuart wanted to know whether Colin Dixon had been arrested, which made officers' ears prick up. 'Do you know any reason why he should be?' they asked the car dealer.

'No, I'm just curious why he's not under arrest.'

4

Lynn Dixon had been shown five albums of photographs of Elderden Farm and a police film of the property to see if she recognized it. She said she couldn't be sure, because the photographs

---

*The date Shackelton and Royle were due to be evicted from Redpits.

and the film had been taken in daylight, and she was abducted at night. She asked to be taken there after dark.

In order to re-create her journey of 21 February as exactly as possible, detectives put Lynn into the back of a police van. Branching off Chart Hill Road, at about a quarter to eight in the evening, they drove to Elderden Farm on the new track, causing Mrs Dixon to remark that 'the way in was bumpy like that night'. When they pulled into the yard, parked and opened the door, Lynn said: 'This is the right place . . .'

'Is this the venue?' DC Darren Reynolds asked her, to be sure.

'I am convinced, yes.'

5

The search of Elderden Farm made front-page headlines the next day, 1 March 2006, the national press seizing on John Fowler as the likely Mr Big behind the world's biggest cash heist. Fowler was described in his regular newspaper, the *Daily Mail*, as a 'multi-millionaire car dealer', living on a £2 million country estate which, as journalists noted assiduously, included tennis courts and a swimming pool. When the *Sun* obtained a collect* photograph of Fowler, drink in hand, winking at the camera, they ran it on page one under the splash headline: 'HELLO, JOHN, GOT A NEW MOTOR?' Inside were more collect pictures of the car dealer with a stripper at an office party years earlier. In one picture he was drinking vodka from a woman's shoe. 'This is the "Arthur Daley" crook whose home was swooped on yesterday in the hunt for the £53 million Securitas blaggers,' the newspaper told its readers. 'An army of police

---

*A 'collect' picture being one journalists collect from the public, typically an informal snapshot.

was last night scouring car dealer John Fowler's farm in Kent.'

In the interview room, John Fowler's charm was beginning to wear thin. He reminded the police that he was sixty years old, grumbled that his police cell was uncomfortable, the food diabolical and he had a splitting headache. By the time the interviews had concluded the previous evening he didn't know whether he was coming or going (or as he put it, 'I didn't know if I was punched, bored or counter-sunk'). He told them: 'My brain is now becoming scrambled. If I have misled you I'm sorry.'

He wanted to make some changes to his story. John had told the police originally that he'd gone to Maidstone Hospital on Sunday to see a man named Chris Hayman about a logbook. This was not quite true. He had seen Hayman at the hospital, but he went to the hospital primarily to visit Glyn Mercer, knowing Glyn had been arrested at Friningham Farm over the cages. 'I wanted to apologize to Glyn, to tell him I didn't drop him in it intentionally.' (So now Fowler was admitting to discussing the robbery with others, something he had previously denied.) He also said he knew the cages he removed from the lorry were from the robbery, but he didn't make that connection until later. When he dropped the lorry off at KTS he hoped his 'involvement' would be over, '[but] it just went on and on'.

Asked about the red van, John said he'd seen the van being worked on at Elderden Farm. Again he blamed Slippery, who had called him to ask if a sign-writer could do the work in the yard because 'the Pakis' at the Shell station (the Wateringbury petrol station was managed by an Asian) didn't like him doing work on their forecourt.

Then John said: 'I've just heard a bombshell this morning that [the Dixons] were possibly held in my buildings. I find that absolutely incredible and I'm very scared about it.' He insisted he was in bed with his wife during that night and she would con-

firm that. DC Bovis told Fowler that he didn't think the car
dealer was a robber or a kidnapper, necessarily, but he did think
Fowler helped plan the job and obtained the lorry for it. 'Ray, I
didn't,' John told him. 'You think I'm telling porkies [but I'm
not] . . . If I was planning to do a bloody bank robbery, I would-
n't have done it in my back yard, that's for sure!'

Fowler then introduced a new aspect to the story. He said that
Stuart Royle had telephoned him the previous Friday saying he
had left two hessian sacks in the yard building they called the
Stables, asking John to bring the sacks to him, which he did,
meeting Royle in the car park of the electrical store Comet at
Borstal. Fowler refrained from looking in the sacks. 'I didn't want
to know what was in [them],' he told the interviewing officers,
though he had 'a bloody good idea'.

POLICE: Did you believe there was money in these sacks?
FOWLER: I think there could have been . . . I didn't think it
    was [Stuart's] dirty laundry, that's for sure, but how it got
    into my stables I don't know.

The last he saw of these sacks was when he put them in the boot of
Royle's car. The police had not recovered the sacks. In fact they never
found them. Two sacks could have contained millions of pounds.

Fowler again made the point that it wouldn't make sense for
him to be involved in a robbery that was linked directly to him
and his home. 'That would be a very foolish thing to do.'

'It would, and it has been,' Ray Bovis replied.

After a break, Fowler admitted he hadn't been entirely honest
during the course of his police interviews. 'I have lied,' he said. 'I
admit that . . . but generally, most of this, I have told you the truth.'

In his interviews, Royle was now saying he couldn't tell the police
any more because he was fearful for the safety of his family. Detectives

pressed on, nevertheless, telling Royle that Fowler said he asked for the lorry to be hired. Royle made no comment. He was told that John said Kim went with him to dump the cages. Stuart said Kim regularly helped them out. Royle was asked about handcuffs found at his garage, and whether he was the man who bought the disc cutters from Brandon Tool Hire. Royle had no comment.

As Royle was being questioned, the sorry saga of Redpits Cottage was coming towards its conclusion. On Tuesday, 28 February, Kim Shackelton had called her conveyancing solicitor at CBA Law to ask whether a £50,000 bridging loan for the cottage had arrived in their client account. Kim said the money was being sent by a friend of hers called Onal Tevfik. 'I told her we hadn't heard anything from this gentleman,' recalls CBA solicitor Lucy Smith, who took the opportunity to warn Shackelton that she was about to be evicted from Redpits by bailiffs, and advised her to remove her personal belongings forthwith. 'She was pretty upset,' recalls Smith. 'She started crying [and] put the phone down.'

Shortly after this conversation, Smith received a call from a man whose name she thought was Upton, but the Old Bailey later heard was Sean Lupton. He identified himself as another friend of Kim. He said she was too upset to speak, but could Miss Smith double-check to see if the bridging loan had now arrived. When Lucy Smith spoke to her cashier she found that £20,000 had been wired to them on 24 February, another £30,000 arriving that day. She called Lupton back to tell him the good news, and tried to call Shackelton, but her phone was turned off.

6

Ermir Hysenaj had not been back to work since the robbery. In fact all work had been suspended at Medway House, which was sealed off by police as a crime scene. Detectives and Securitas executives were busy going through the files of all their agency staff, which included looking at the personnel folders agencies kept for each employee sent to the depot. In many cases these folders proved thin reading. There seemed to have been virtually no vetting done in some cases. 'I was opening up folders and they were blank, there was nothing in them,' says Security Inspector Steve Morris. 'You'd get a name, for example Dave Smith, no address, no date of birth, or photograph.'

Ermir's agency had found him a new job at Uckfield Post Office. He started there on Monday, 27 February. He and Sue were asleep in their flat in Crowborough on Thursday morning when armed men came to the door. Despite the fact the police were standing directly outside Ermir and Sue's ground-floor bedroom window, it took some time before the couple opened up. What seemed like a division of officers then charged in. As Aggy barked hysterically, and Sue protested, Ermir was arrested and taken away for questioning. When Hilda next door discovered what had happened she expressed astonishment. As she said: 'We all liked him.'

Police interviewed Ermir at Tonbridge Police Station in the presence of his solicitor. They had been led to his door because he was a known associate of Jetmir Bucpapa, whom they already had in custody, the only associate of Bucpapa who worked in the cash depot. When detectives suggested to the Albanian clerk that he had been part of the conspiracy to rob Medway House, he exclaimed: 'It's laughable!' He denied asking questions at work about the operation of the security doors, or whether the walls of the building were reinforced, and denied drawing plans of the depot. Although he had many English and Albanian friends in Kent, he didn't know anybody named Jetmir Bucpapa. He also denied knowing Fowler, Royle and Rusha. He said he knew

Colin Dixon was the boss of the cash depot, but he didn't know where Mr Dixon lived. When he was told it was Herne Bay, Ermir said he'd never heard of the place. The police told Ermir that they had found a cash card in his wallet in the name Ermal Kulic. Ermir said this was his brother, using a false surname. He had borrowed Ermal's card, with his permission, when he ran short of money. Ermir was talkative and relaxed throughout this interview and, at the end, he was allowed to return home, thinking perhaps he had got away with it, though he must have been concerned to learn that Jetmir was charged this same day with conspiracy to rob.

7

At Canterbury Police Station, detectives were coming to the end of the time they could hold Royle without charge. The car dealer was not at all happy. Like Fowler, he complained that he hadn't had a proper night's sleep since he was arrested; his neighbour in the cells made far too much noise; his ulcer was playing up; he didn't have his glasses, and he hadn't had any decent hot food. (Royle had turned his nose up at the microwave meal the police offered him, asking instead for a Chinese takeaway. The request was denied.)

Thoroughly disgruntled, Royle sat down again with officers at 8.00 p.m. on 2 March 2006, and this time he had a lot to say, some of it very strange indeed. Regarding the subject of kidnap, he told the police that Kim's son, whom Royle regarded as his own, had gone missing in August 2004 when a 'policeman' removed him from school.* In light of this, Royle wondered

---

*Royle didn't report this incident at the time. When it was subsequently investigated it was found that the boy had merely wandered off for a while.

whether the Dixons had been kidnapped by real police officers, as opposed to men merely dressed up as officers, though he conceded that most police weren't 'bogus'. He made an intriguing comment about the suspects the police had rounded up. 'I would doubt that you have the right people in custody,' he said. He didn't actually know who they all were, but could guess, 'because I'm relatively intelligent.' He then said John had asked Kim to go with him in the lorry to Friningham Farm. Royle implied that this was to do with the robbery, thus implicating his friend, though he added that Kim was unaware of the connection.

Trying to understand how Royle fitted into the gang, the police asked him: 'You are not Mr Big, are you?' Stuart replied that he was not, adding: 'I honestly don't think you've got a prayer of finding the right people.'

POLICE: Stuart, do you know who the right people are?
ROYLE: I could certainly recognize them. I just don't know.
POLICE: And how have you become involved in this then?
ROYLE: Um, I think accidentally.

Royle seemed to be on the point of making a confession. He asked if he and his solicitor, Gordon Crowe, could talk with the police off the record, but was told this wasn't possible. Then he said: 'I think you'll find that everybody who you might view as a suspect in this has children,' adding that he didn't think any of the people arrested had been 'willing participants'.

'So why haven't they been willing, in your words?'

Royle talked vaguely about a feeling that his family, and the family of others, were at risk. He too seemed to think he was a potential target. 'I never assumed for a minute you would be uncovering these clues whilst I was in custody. I thought you'd be uncovering these clues whilst I was dead,' he said melodramatically, before again implying that Kent Police officers had some involvement in the heist. With that, Royle was charged.

8

John Fowler was the first to step into the dock at Maidstone Magistrates Court the next day to face charges of conspiracy to rob and kidnap and handling stolen goods. A bespectacled, grey-haired man, Fowler looked a good deal older than the cheeky car dealer pictured in the *Sun*. He was joined in the dock by Stuart Royle, also charged with conspiracy to rob. They ignored each other. Royle was uncharacteristically subdued, perhaps because he found Kim Shackelton in the dock, too. His girlfriend trembled as she heard she was charged with handling stolen goods (that is disposing of fourteen cash cages with Fowler at Friningham Farm). Like Fowler, she had been picked out of a video identification parade by Ann Day. Shackelton's lawyer asked for bail, which was denied, and the unhappy trio were led away to their cells.

The arrest of Shackelton brought the saga of Redpits to an end. Stuart and Kim had fought like fury to keep hold of the cottage, despite repeated orders to get out, apparently convinced that they would get the money to buy the house from somewhere. With both in custody, estate agent David Page gained entry to the Langley property to have a look round before putting Redpits on the market again for Geoff Crabtree. Page was surprised to find the cottage full of Stuart and Kim's personal belongings, including a pet hamster. As to the £50,000 wired to CBA Law as a bridging loan, when Lucy Smith became suspicious about the transaction she reported it to her superiors and asked the sender of the money for identification. The money was then frozen by the courts pending a police enquiry into money laundering.

9

The Graves Industrial Estate is an old coal yard behind Welling Corner, not far from the suburban homes of Lee Murray and Roger Coutts. Mrs Min Graves, an elderly member of the family who has owned the yard for years, still managed the place, collecting rent from her tenants, who were mostly car mechanics or engineers turning lathes, fixing carburettors and doing MOT checks.

Around 2.45 on the afternoon of Thursday, 2 March, two plain-clothes Metropolitan Police officers slipped down the lane of the industrial estate to unit 7a, where Nigel Reeve ran ENR Cars. As detectives Nicholas Sergeant and Sean Augustine turned the corner, 43-year-old Derek 'Del Boy' Evans was spraying a car in the yard. The officers identified themselves to Evans and told him they were executing a warrant to search for stolen car parts and paperwork. (This was a ruse to cover the fact that an informant had told Kent Police there was stolen Securitas money in the yard. The Met were conducting this call on behalf of Kent Police because Welling is within Greater London.) DC Augustine searched Evans, and retrieved keys to a rusty old ship container in a walled area just across from the garage. Nigel had rented this space from Mrs Graves as extra storage for the cars he was buying and selling with Roger Coutts. Roger's power boat, the *Shakey Jakey*, was in the compound next to the ship container. Evans seemed very nervous as the police went to the container. DC Sergeant recalled: 'I was holding onto his arm in order to make sure he didn't escape.'

Detective Augustine opened the ship container to reveal twelve holdalls packed with Securitas cash, totalling £9,655,040. A bin bag in the main garage building contained another £50,000. The police asked Del Boy who these bags belonged to. He said he didn't know. As he was in possession of the keys, they took him down to the station for questioning about this vast haul, almost £10 million.* Uniformed officers stood guard over the money while plain-clothes detectives visited neighbouring workshops, such as Telmic Engineering next door, asking if anybody had any information about Del Boy, or his boss Nigel Reeve. They discovered that Nige – as he was known – had just driven over to Spain with a van-load of furniture. He and his girlfriend had a villa on the Costa Blanca which they were fixing up.

Nigel was having a beer in a bar in Javea, Spain, the following day when he saw his yard flash up on Sky News. The TV reporter was saying that £9.6 million had been found in his Welling garage. They showed pictures of the garage, with the sign over the door that gave his mobile-phone number. Nigel's mobile started ringing almost immediately. 'Where's the rest of the money then?' It was the first of a stream of calls from members of the public who thought this a funny prank. The joke calls from England cost Nigel £500 before he had the mobile number cancelled.

Nigel told everybody who asked seriously that he had nothing to do with the robbery and he had no idea the money was in the ship container. He telephoned Kent Police to tell them the same and when he got back home he went voluntarily to Tonbridge Police Station to give a statement, emerging after

---

*Evans was later released without charge.

several hours without being charged. He even brought his van back to the UK for police to do tests on. Nigel got the impression that the police suspected him of being involved in the heist. He was a close associate of Coutts, who had become a suspect; he also knew Roger's friend, Lee Murray; the cage fighter brought his cars to Nigel to be repaired. And Nigel had money problems. He was £1,400 behind in rent to Minnie Graves at the time of the heist, which might be a motive to make some illicit money. Then there was the fact he had driven a van to Spain directly after the job. 'I know what the police is thinking, and I know what everyone else is thinking: that I've taken a big load of money out to Spain. I know they think I've done that,' he says. 'But I honestly haven't.'

10

There was another find on Thursday at Friningham Farm. The cash cages and other items had long since been taken away for forensic examination when a detective telephoned farmer Paul Burden to request another meeting in his yard. 'How long's that white van been parked here?' the officer asked the farmer, pointing to a white Transit van. Burden replied that the van had been there all the time. In fact, the police had been parked next to it while they searched the yard. He went back to work grumbling about coppers who couldn't catch a cold.

The van was linked to Elderden Farm. Norman Underdown had worked on it there on 24 February and the tax disc was from a Land Rover Discovery on the property. At first, detectives thought this may have been the van in which Lynn and her child were abducted. When she looked at the van, Mrs Dixon said it was not the right one. The find was significant nonetheless. A new STIHL disc cutter was in the back, along with green plastic petrol cans. The other cutter was never found. Police believe it was with the three missing cash cages.

11

Jetmir Bucpapa came before magistrates on Friday, 3 March, charged with conspiracy to commit robbery. He smiled up at his wife, Rebecca, sitting in the public gallery during the brief hearing. The case was committed to the higher, crown court, with Bucpapa remanded into custody in the meantime.

After lunch, Rusha stepped into the same dock. Prosecution counsel outlined the weight of evidence against him. The court heard about police finding theatrical make-up, a book on how to put on a false beard and moustache, drawings of Medway House, a gun, ammunition, handcuffs and police-style livery at his home. Additionally, Rusha had been 'completely matched' to DNA on a balaclava retrieved from the Ashford International Hotel. Reporters chuckled as they made their notes. Judging by what they had heard, Rusha seemed the most inept robber in Britain. Lea maintained a tough-guy demeanour, whistling as he was led away, but he clearly had little to be happy about, and indeed further evidence of his criminal stupidity was about to come to light.

Just off the main London Road, which runs through Rusha's hometown of Southborough, is Sheffield Road, which leads into Castle Street, at the end of which is a cul-de-sac of lock-up garages owned by an elderly lady named Peggy Stapley. Mrs Stapley lived adjacent to the garages in a bungalow built by her late husband. Originally there were stables at the end of the road for the large houses nearby. Trevor Stapley converted the stables into lock-ups, the largest of which he rented to a mechanic named Kevin Worsell who was like a son to the couple. Since Trevor died, Peggy Stapley had remained in the bungalow, drawing a small rental income from the lock-ups, comforted by the fact that Kevin continued to fix cars in the yard.

It was two days after Peggy's 75th birthday, on Friday, 3 March, that she first noticed something funny. A white van made repeated trips down her private road to the lock-ups, apparently visiting the second garage from the end, which Mrs Stapley rented for ten pounds a week to a neighbour named James Hughes, a former prison officer. The following evening Peggy heard a car shoot down, '*Broooom!* And then in seconds reversed all the way back at great speed. 'I thought, "Who the heck's that?" So I went out to the gate to have a word, but by that time he'd gone.'

Sunday was frosty. When Peggy glanced out of her window in the afternoon she saw scores of police by the lock-ups, many armed, their vehicles parked all the way down the lane: forensics, dog units, the works. 'Can you tell me what's going on?' she asked the police, as they sealed off her road with police tape: 'CRIME SCENE – DO NOT ENTER'.

'I can't divulge anything at the moment, Madam.'

'I do own this [land] and I live here. Surely I have a right to know.'

'Well, I'm sorry, no.'

Wondering what was going on, Peggy telephoned her daughter who hurried over to comfort Mum. Soon the police came knocking at the door, asking sheepishly if they could use the loo. Peggy and her daughter found themselves making tea for everybody, which was appreciated by the police on a bitterly cold day, and the whole story came out. The car Peggy had heard reversing at high speed down her lane the previous night was the police having received a tip-off about one of the lock-ups. (It was amazing how many tip-offs the police were getting, and the information they received was excellent.) Having got the garage open, in amongst a lot of old furniture, the police found eighteen bags – a mixture of chequer-pattern laundry bags, Monarch holdalls and Eagles suitcases – stuffed with Securitas money, mostly still wrapped up. There was a huge amount, £370,500 in one Monarch holdall alone. The total came to £8,601,990. Also in the lock-up was a sawn-off shotgun, another shotgun compatible with ammunition recovered from Lea Rusha's tool shed and a shoebox containing a photograph of Lea and Katie Philp.

As with the Welling hoard, the Southborough money was in a lock-up owned by an unsuspecting little old lady, putting one in mind of the character Mrs Wilberforce in the classic Ealing comedy *The Ladykillers*, which concerns another bunch of hopeless robbers. 'Tis strange, isn't it?' says Mrs Stapley, who noticed the similarity and quite enjoyed the excitement, though she groused about the press. 'Ah! It was horrendous. I've never seen anything like it. All those great big cameras you see on telly. And there was *Daily Mirror*, *Daily Express*, *Guardian*, [Kent and Sussex] *Courier*, *Kent Messenger*, *Sun*; and they were standing up on the coal bunker trying to get photographs looking down the yard . . . Then the phone starts and we had some girl from Sky on the doorstep. She just wouldn't move. And I refused to speak to her.' Having said no to the young lady, Peggy went into her lounge to watch live coverage of what was happening on TV. She was mortified to hear a reporter tell viewers – as she remembers it – that an old lady living in a bungalow at the crime scene had not been arrested 'at this stage', as if to imply Granny might be brought forth in handcuffs soon.

Mrs Stapley was quickly ruled out of the enquiry, though she continued to receive visits from the police. 'It's very strange the way they go about these things, because it must have been ten days, a fortnight later, that they came back and went through the

bins. Well, the bins had been emptied a week or more before.'
Then CID officers turned up asking for a statement. Peggy said
she'd already given one. The officers apologized, saying they had
been drafted in from another force, at which point one was
interrupted by his mobile. 'He answered it and he said to the
sergeant, "Oh, Rob, we're in the wrong place. We should be at
Sidcup, not Southborough." So they went off. My God! What
did that cost?'

Although Peggy rented her lock-up to James Hughes, he had
sublet it to a local man named Jason Hodge (aka Jason Bennett),
who said he wanted to store some furniture. Jason was Lea
Rusha's cousin. Jason didn't pay James his rent. 'He was supposed
to give me £10 a week, and he was an absolute nightmare with
the rent . . . to this day he still owes me £20!' Somebody – James
denies it was him, though he admits helping the police with their
enquiries – then tipped off the police about the lock-up. When
the dust had settled, James Hughes asked Jason if he had any idea
how £8.6 million came to be in the lock-up. He says Jason told
him he knew nothing about it, but he had lost the garage key
prior to the robbery.

The lock-up wasn't a clever hiding place. Not only was it
sublet from a former prison officer, Peggy's neighbour, William
Fuller, was a retired policeman who had CCTV cameras in his
yard. As a result, he was able to give Kent Police video footage
of men visiting the lock-ups at 2.47 p.m. on Thursday, 23
February, 36 hours after the robbery. It was snowing as a white
van and a silver Fiat coupé drove up to the garages. At least two
men got out and spent seventeen minutes loitering around the
yard (the actual lock-up was out of view of the camera) before
driving away. It was enough time to load the garage with money
bags. And surely it was no coincidence that Lea Rusha drove a
silver Fiat coupé.

12

Three days after the robbery, Roger Coutts and his pregnant girlfriend Fiona Neary went on a skiing holiday to Switzerland.
They returned a week later on Saturday, 4 March, and were on
their way home to Welling when their taxi was stopped by the
police, and Roger arrested.

Officers searched his business, Northfleet Transit, a short drive
south of Welling, where they found a copy of the *Kent Messenger*
from 24 February, with a ring around an article by a former
police officer headed: 'Thieves will now have to be careful who
they trust.' Detectives also searched Coutts' homes. Although
Roger and Fiona were living in a rented house in Welling, they
owned a maisonette in neighbouring Bexleyheath. They had
been trying to sell this property, in Harding Road, at the time of
the heist. 'They weren't exactly the friendliest of people,' says
Harding Road neighbour Jacqueline Wall, 'and they had all these
mates . . .' Neighbours had observed that Fiona and Roger lived
well for a young couple with a baby, and another on the way. She
worked in a shop. He ran a small garage. Yet they drove expensive cars, latterly a black BMW; they went on foreign holidays;
and had apparently spent a lot of money remodelling their flat.
'How on Earth can you afford to [live] like that?' asks Jacqueline
Wall. Which touched on the other problem neighbours had with
the couple: their mates.

Rough types were constantly coming to the flat, usually driving flashy cars. They hung around in front talking loudly to
Roger, or loitered by the garages. Pat Mitchell, whose flat overlooked the lock-ups, had watched Roger and a friend loading
black bin bags into the garage. 'It was all very suspicious what I
saw going on.' She informed the police. They didn't do anything

about it at the time, to her knowledge, but police were crawling all over the garage now. They were also in the house. Searching the cupboard under the stairs, police found a boiler suit of the type worn during the heist and a pair of Magnum-brand black boots covered in mud; while upstairs in a wardrobe was a black balaclava.

Down at the station Roger was told about these finds, and that a substantial amount of stolen money had been found at ENR Cars, to which he was linked. He declined to answer questions, but with the help of his solicitor, Jatinder Sokhal, he gave the police a brief statement, saying that he ran a business which repaired vans, and bought and sold vehicles on the side with Nigel Reeve at ENR Cars. 'I deny any involvement in the offence for which I have been arrested.' Police took a DNA sample, and released him on bail.

13

By mid-March eighteen suspects had been arrested, five of whom had been charged: that is Fowler, Royle, Shackelton, Bucpapa and Rusha. All were in custody, the men in Category-A cells at HMP Belmarsh, Britain's highest-security prison, located just outside Woolwich, south-east London, close to where Lee Murray and his mates grew up. Others who had been questioned and released included significant characters such as Hogg, Hysenaj and Coutts, who could be re-arrested at any time. D. Supt. Paul Gladstone's team had also recovered £19.7 million of stolen money and collected a vast amount of evidence.

Looked at from another perspective, most of the £53 million was still unaccounted for, and it was becoming clear that detectives didn't have all the key players. Most notably, they still didn't have the ringleader. When Chief Constable Michael Fuller addressed the media on Monday, 6 March, 2006, he gave journalists a hint of the direction Operation Deliver was now going. 'We will do everything humanly possible to retrieve all the stolen money and track down the criminals involved,' he said. 'Our aim is to ensure that no one profits from this crime. We will do whatever it takes and go wherever we need to in the world to achieve this aim.' The search for the money and the gang was moving abroad, where Lee Murray was on the run.

Chapter Thirteen

THE ROAD TO MOROCCO

1

Lightning Lee Murray left the UK at the end of the busy weekend when the white van full of money was found in Ashford, the cash cages were recovered from Friningham Farm, police raided the homes of Rusha and Bucpapa, and arrested Royle and Fowler. While all this activity was going on, Murray slipped across the English Channel with Paul Allen, then drove to Amsterdam where they booked into the Holiday Inn. Lee knew people in Amsterdam from when he came to the Netherlands to train with Remco Pardoel. His contacts included a fight promoter named Marc De Werd, and a Moroccan mate of De Werd's named Aït Assou, who had a house in the city. Lee and Paul moved into Assou's home while they thought about what to do next.

If Murray was indeed the ringleader of the Tonbridge gang, he surely had a claim to the lion's share of the £33 million the police had not yet recovered. Gang members who were now in custody obviously had difficulty hanging onto their share of the cash, and one must assume that Coutts, Bucpapa and Rusha had lost most of their money in the police raids on the lock-up garages in Welling and Southborough. Murray may well have only brought a few hundred thousand in cash with him to Holland, if indeed he brought any cash at all, but as we shall see he soon had access to much more. Murray would say he acquired this wealth from cage-fighting and legitimate business ventures. The police believe otherwise.

If indeed he brought stolen cash with him from England, Lee would have an immediate problem to deal with. While he could buy basic comforts with cash, Lee couldn't finance a life on the run with bags of twenty-pound notes. He needed to feed his cash into a bank account.

Introducing dirty money into the banking system, and thereby laundering it, is one of the biggest challenges facing a successful bank robber, and Murray couldn't solve the problem by depositing his cash in a new savings account, in Britain or abroad. British banks are obligated to file a Cash Transaction Report regarding cash deposits of *any* amount that seem suspicious. Even a modest cash deposit from a new customer can alert bank staff. During the first few days of the police investigation into the heist, a south London nurse tried to pay £6,000 into the Portman Building Society in Bromley. The money was banded with Securitas wrappers. She was arrested immediately, and questioned overnight before it was established that hers was an entirely innocent transaction. Imagine what would have happened to Lightning Lee if he turned up at a high-street bank with a million pounds, itself only a fraction of the outstanding money. It is for this reason that criminals traditionally stash their loot in garages, and with mates, as the Tonbridge gang did. But when it came to moving *millions*, more sophistication was required.

Having got some money abroad, things were easier. Still, banks on the continent would look askance at a stranger trying to make a large cash deposit. So-called 'secret Swiss bank accounts' are not that easy to open, and Swiss banks are as likely as any others to alert the authorities if they have suspicions that their customers are trying to launder the proceeds of crime. First things first, sterling had to be changed into the more widely accepted euro. There were people in the Netherlands who could help Lee, in return for a commission. Detectives later speculated that the cage fighter may have handed a relatively small amount of cash, which he had brought with him, to local criminals who couriered it to associates in major European cities, such as Paris, that are also popular tourist destinations, where the money can be exchanged for euros by runners simply doing a tour of the *bureau de change*. These euros could then be drip-fed into regional bank accounts controlled by Murray's associates, ultimately paid into an account in his name, or simply couriered back to him and Paul in cash.

Buying and selling property is an excellent way to launder money, and Murray's plan was to invest his cash in bricks and mortar in Morocco. As we have seen, Lee's dad was Moroccan. The former cage fighter had a half-sister, named Nora, in Casablanca. Lee and Siobhan visited Marrakesh for a wedding in 1995, and it seems Lee returned to Morocco on at least one subsequent occasion. That was the extent of his connections to the country prior to the robbery. But there was a compelling reason to make his home here now.

The fact that Lee's father was Moroccan meant Lee had a claim to Moroccan nationality and, crucially, the Moroccan Penal Code prohibits Moroccan citizens from being extradited to face trial abroad. Also there is no extradition treaty between the UK and Morocco, partly because the North African kingdom practises capital punishment and Britain is unwilling to send prisoners to their deaths. If Lee could get to Morocco, and claim nationality, he would be out of the reach of the British authorities, and free to invest his money.

Lee didn't have a Moroccan birth certificate, however, and the

chances were that he would have to go to court at some stage to
have his claim to nationality endorsed. He would need Dad on
hand as a witness. For years now Brahim Lamrani had resided in
the UK, latterly in a scruffy council flat on the Woolwich
Common Estate. Despite this, and the fact that he and Lee had
always had a difficult relationship, on 21 February 2006, that is to
say 'kidnap day', Brahim Lamrani returned to Morocco, where he
stayed for the next ten months.

2

Before Lee and Paul set out for North Africa, they got themselves
into a nasty scrape in Holland that almost ruined everything. On
Thursday, 2 March 2006 – the day police found £9.6 million in
Welling – the boys went shopping in PC Hoofstraat, one of the
premier shopping streets in Amsterdam. Around 4.30 p.m. they
visited a jewellery shop, quite possibly intending to buy something. They had plenty of money to spend. Indeed, their pockets
were stuffed with wads of euros as a court would later hear. But
the body language of these two rough and burly men was such
that the shopkeeper called the police, saying he feared he was about
to be robbed. The police came straight away, picked Murray and
Allen up, and took them to the police station.

Lee and Paul protested their innocence. There was no evidence to charge them with any crime. But the police wanted to
see identification before they released the Englishmen. Lee and
Paul didn't have their passports with them, so they called their
friends to bring the documents to the station.

The boys must have sweated bullets as they waited for their passports. If Kent Police were now actively looking for them, there was
a good chance that their details had been circulated by Interpol.

When the Dutch police checked their passport details, the game would be up. But when the passports came, the Dutch simply let the Englishmen go. Kent Police had not yet realized the full significance of Murray and Allen. There was no Interpol alert for their arrest.

The experience of being picked up by police was, however, a very close call. It was also reminiscent of the other brushes with the law the boys had had in recent months, starting with the day Murray was stopped by police outside Medway House. It seems that Lee decided to flee Amsterdam as a result. First he called his old mate Mustafa Basar and asked him to come out to Amsterdam and collect his Mercedes. Mus hadn't been doing much recently. He was lame from a motorcycle accident, single and broke at 27, living alone in a flat in West Sussex, round the corner from his mum Doreen. He agreed to do the errand for Lee.

The following day, Friday, 3 March 2006, Lee and Paul left the Netherlands in a gold Mercedes, possibly with a box of euros in the boot. They drove to Spain, a favourite bolthole of British criminals on the run. There were many places the boys could stay out of sight, possibly in a friend's holiday villa on the coast with satellite TV and access to the British newspapers. That way Lee could keep in touch with news from home. He would have been amused to read about the enterprising hotelier in Tonbridge offering Tonbridge Robbery weekend breaks, and about the court appearances of the 'wallies' he had left behind. He could hardly believe his ears when he heard the Southborough stash had been found in a lock-up for which the rent hadn't been paid.

3

Although Kent Police had not been looking for Murray when he was picked up by Dutch police on 2 March 2006, they realized soon afterwards that the cage fighter was somebody they had to speak to. Lee Murray kept coming up in the enquiry. The Flying Squad had first mentioned the name, which was written on the debt list recovered from Royle's house. It was also seemingly written in abbreviated form on a jar of make-up at Hogg's address. Murray was an associate of Roger Coutts, with links to ENR Cars. Most significantly, perhaps, there was a DNA link to the fighter. Lee's DNA was on file with the Metropolitan Police because he had given a mouth swab when he was arrested after crashing his Ferrari in London just before the robbery. The profile matched DNA swabs taken from latex scraps in Michelle Hogg's bin, and the glove police found in the Post Office van at Hucking. As if that wasn't enough, Murray was a dead ringer for the e-fit Colin Dixon helped police make of the tall policeman who kidnapped him. All things considered, Murray looked like being a robber and a kidnapper.

Paul Allen was never far from Lee, and Paul was now an official suspect, too. On 15 March, DCI Mick Judge sent officers to Chatham to speak to Allen's girlfriend, Stacie-Lee Dudley. They found £5,000 in cash in the glove compartment of her car. The money was seized and she was arrested, later released without charge. The next day police went to see Lee's mother, Barbara, his wife Siobhan and his cage-fighting associates. Nobody seemed to know where exactly Lee was, except that he might be on the continent with Paul.

The fact that Murray was now a suspect in Operation Deliver, with Kent Police making active enquiries about him, leaked to the press. Martin Brunt of Sky News recalls typing Murray's name into Google and being surprised by how much information there was about this suspect. 'It was a remarkable story, you know: you get the names of villains and you Google them, do some research, and you very rarely find out anything interesting.'

But Lee Murray had his own lurid website, with pictures of him in his Hannibal Lecter mask in Las Vegas. There was abundant biographical information about his troubled youth and propensity for getting into fights, culminating in the stabbing outside Funky Buddha, which had made the national papers in 2005. When Brunt reads all this he says, '[Murray] became a very much more interesting figure.'

The reporter put together a package for the evening news. 'Sky News has tonight learnt the identity of one of the men police want to talk to over the £53 million Securitas robbery,' the newsreader announced on 16 March 2006. The report began with footage of Lee fighting, taken from his website, Brunt informing viewers that the cage fighter was one of a number of people detectives were looking for; he mentioned the Funky Buddha stabbing, Murray's recovery, and his plans to return to the ring, concluding: 'But now Mr Murray's career is on hold. His family and manager say they don't know where he is.'

Simultaneously the *Sun* and the *Daily Mail* were printing similar stories about Murray. 'A notorious martial arts fighter is suspected of being one of the masterminds behind the £53 million Securitas heist,' wrote Stephen Wright in the *Mail*. 'Detectives think Lee 'Lightning' Murray may have been in charge of the logistics and planning of Britain's biggest cash robbery last month.' The *Sun* reported that Murray was believed to have fled to Spain.

4

Police arrested Siobhan Lamrani-Murray and took her to Gravesend for questioning. Siobhan had £1,650 in her handbag. They searched the Sidcup house thoroughly, recovering £14,000, which could not be linked to the robbery, and a large amount of new, American-made fitness equipment matching equipment found at Redpits. It was all part of the same stolen shipment. Apart from the keep-fit equipment, Kent Police now had the luck to recover Lee Murray's Ferrari, which had been in the police pound in Charlton since 12 February. Hitherto, police hadn't taken much interest in the yellow sports car. Now they went over the vehicle meticulously, and were surprised and delighted to find two mobile phones in the vehicle. Analysis of the calls made on these phones revealed not only who Lee had been in contact with prior to the crash, but where he and his fellow conspirators had been when they spoke to each other. Even better, Murray had inadvertently recorded himself talking to Lea Rusha, apparently about the robbery. DCI Judge allowed himself a smile.

Police then raided 46 Pitfield Crescent in Thamesmead, having watched Siobhan visiting the address. Ria and Myra Anderson were down at the Queen's Arms when a neighbour rang to say police were inside their house. They raced over. 'To be honest with you, my language was a bit salty,' says Myra Anderson. Police had already found Siobhan's £38,150 in the spare bedroom. The Andersons were nicked. 'When they arrested us, they said, "You've heard of the Securitas robbery?" We're like "Yeah." "This is what we're here for."'

Down at the station, Myra Anderson expressed astonishment that a bag full of cash had been stored in her house. 'I had no knowledge it was there.' It was of course a 'helluva lot of money' to have in the house; it sounded 'very stupid' to say she knew nothing about it, but that was her story. 'It was just a bag, with no knowledge of what was in the bag. It was nothing to do with us. We weren't nosey. We didn't look in it.' In her interviews, Siobhan Lamrani-Murray said that Lee earned the money cage-fighting.

The police told the three women that the cash was being seized.

If any of them wanted to make a case for having a legitimate claim to it, they would have to go to court and prove where it came from. Otherwise, it would be forfeited under the Proceeds of Crime Act. All three were then released without charge. The story appeared in the *Sun* under the headline 'HEIST: THREE WOMEN HELD'. None were identified, but the paper reported that one was a friend of Lee Murray, the man 'on the run'. The article also linked Murray to the Welling garage where almost £10 million had recently been found, reporting that Murray and 'a business pal' were now believed to be in Europe. Murray would have found out quickly that Siobhan had been nicked, the money bag found and his name splashed over the papers. It was time to make another move.

5

Murray and Allen entered Morocco on Saturday, 25 March 2006, travelling with a third man, probably their pal from Amsterdam, Marc De Werd, in the gold Mercedes. It seems the lads put the car on a ferry in Algeciras, then crossed the Strait of Gibraltar to Ceuta, a Spanish enclave on the North African coast. Entry into Morocco is three miles down the road from Ceuta at the border town of Tetouan.

Moroccan border police and customs tend to process visitors to their country slowly, insisting travellers fill out multiple forms, with additional paperwork for those bringing cars into Morocco. Security appears to be tight. At the same time this particular border crossing is notorious for being a place where drugs are smuggled, and people are trafficked. The Moroccan authorities have a reputation for accepting bribes. It may well be that Murray arranged to pay an official to overlook the fact that he was bring-ing a large amount of cash with him to Morocco, as much as

€400,000. However, Kent Police do not know for sure how Lee got his money into Morocco, only that he had access to a massive amount once he arrived.

Having crossed the border, Murray and his friends dumped the gold Mercedes and hired a taxi to take them to Rabat, the capital of Morocco, 250 kilometres away on the Atlantic coast. During this very long taxi ride Murray had ample time to look around at the country he had come to live in. Although close to Europe, Morocco strikes the European visitor as exotic. Lee was now in Muslim North Africa. In some ways it is a pleasant land. Lee felt the warmth of the sun. The streets are lined with palm trees and bougainvillaea. Traditional Moorish buildings are decorated with spires, arches and brightly-coloured tiles. There are many quaint sights. Alongside the cars and motorbikes on the roads men ride donkeys, often pulling carts laden with animal skins. Older men wear the *djellaba*, sometimes also the fez. Highways are lined with posters of the king, Mohammed VI, known to his subjects as 'M6'. His kingdom is evidently striving to modernize, but the roads are pot-holed and between the many new buildings there are stretches of dirt, strewn with rubbish. Cattle and goats graze wherever they can find grass to eat, even in the cities.

As the sun goes down, the wail of evening prayer reminded Murray that he was in an Islamic country, albeit a liberal one. Women take a subservient role in society, though few wear the full burka. Alcohol is permitted, but most people don't drink. Men are more likely to spend their evenings in a café smoking and drinking mint tea. This was all very strange to Lee Murray. Lee wasn't a Muslim (though he has apparently since converted). He didn't speak Arabic, or French, as many Moroccans do. He couldn't read the street signs, nor newspapers, or understand the television. Without a guide, he would struggle to get around town. It is hard to believe that Morocco is a country he would have chosen to come to, leaving his family and friends behind, had Morocco not offered a refuge from British justice.

The fact that Murray and Allen chose to come to Rabat is doubly surprising, considering where else they could have gone within Morocco. Casablanca is a larger, more vibrant city; likewise Tangier is an exciting town; Marrakesh is popular with tourists; while a younger crowd is drawn to the resort of Agadir. Faced with these options, Murray chose a city of commerce and administration, with a reputation for being a dull sort of place, with a faded, French colonial atmosphere. Murray came to Rabat because Aït Assou owned a villa here, in a residential suburb of the city called Souissi, where members of the Moroccan royal family, government officials and foreign diplomats reside.

The boys met Assou at a water tower in the suburb after their long drive from Tetouan, then followed him to his house, the Villa Samira. Like most of the properties in the neighbourhood, the villa was largely hidden behind a wall. There was a spiked metal gate at the front, with a resident caretaker named Moussaffia Abrik in the gatehouse. Other staff included a housemaid. The villa was a large, two-storey building, the windows fitted with bars or roller shutters, so security was excellent. It had satellite TV, a landscaped garden with barbecue area, swimming pool, pagoda and cabana. Paul and Lee were given adjacent bedrooms at the back of the house, overlooking the pool.

The villa also had the benefit of a metal strongbox, into which Murray poured approximately €400,000 – money he had either brought with him, or arranged to pick up when he arrived. He and Paul each had a key to this richly endowed piggy bank, and agreed to withdraw money as they needed it, leaving a note of what they had taken. It was essentially their petty cash.

Having brought them to Rabat, Marc De Werd went back to

Holland. A few days later Aït Assou also travelled back to Holland, though he returned regularly to Rabat to check on his house guests. So it was that Lee and Paul began to settle into their new life in Morocco.

6

Back in England, on a fine spring morning, the Dixons' youngest child went back to primary school, not to stay, but to say good-bye to friends and teachers. The Dixons were moving. Securitas had bought their old home at Hadleigh Gardens – Colin and Lynn were in no position to handle the sale themselves – and the family had relocated to a new, secret address. It was reported in the press that they were going to live in Australia under the Witness Protection Scheme. In truth, they didn't move far at all. But they made sure that their new address in the area was as much of a secret as possible, even a secret from their victim support offi-cer, Lorraine Brown, whom they arranged to meet henceforth at a neutral location.

In fact, there had been a deterioration in relations between Colin and the police looking after him. Colin had been inter-viewed many times since the heist and was generally patient and talkative with detectives. His demeanour changed when he was asked about taking photographs of Medway House staff with his personal camera, evidence of which had been found in his office at the depot and on his home computer. Using a personal camera inside the cash centre was against company rules, and the police were suspicious in case Colin had taken these pictures to help the gang. When first challenged about this, in March, Colin claimed he didn't remember taking any pictures of the depot and staff, even though the pictures were on his home PC. When detectives pressed him, Colin wouldn't give them a straight answer. 'He seemed to close up,' noted PC Brown, who told her superiors she didn't think Colin was telling the truth.

There were an inordinate number of rules to worry about working at Medway House and it was inevitable that staff broke some of them in order to do their job. It was hard for Colin to admit this, however. He needed to stay on good terms with Securitas, who had relocated him, and whom he still worked for. At the same time he had to get along with the police, who were lining him up to be their star witness in the forthcoming robbery trial. It was anyone's guess when this trial would start.

Police were still pursuing leads and questioning suspects, including Ermir Hysenaj who was rearrested on 4 April and asked about his normal journey to work at Medway House. He maintained that he always travelled by bus and train, then walked to the depot. Yet CCTV showed that he got a lift to Medway House on 16 January 2006, and he seemed to behave out of character in the depot that day. Police showed Hysenaj images of himself mooching about the loading bays with his shirt tucked into his belt, whereas he customarily wore his shirt outside his trousers. Putting their cards on the table, the police suggested to Hysenaj that he was wearing a spy camera on his belt. They wanted to see this belt and the jeans. Ermir said he no longer had them. He was shown a photo of Jetmir Bucpapa. Having denied knowing him in earlier interviews, Ermir now said he *did* recognize the young man, but knew him as Hajdar. He had known him for about a year.

Ermir was released again without charge, returning home to Prospect Villas, Crowborough. Sue was off work with depression, and the couple spent most of their time together at the flat, or walking Aggy. It was more than a month since the police had first raided their home, and Sue found herself watching Ermir (or

Nick as she called him) to see whether there was anything in his
behaviour that betrayed guilt. 'If you are that close to another
person you would pick up on even a slight change if they were
worried about something, or they were nervous about something, or they were concerned, and [his] behaviour was absolutely
exactly the same as it was previous to [the arrests], no change in
him whatsoever. He didn't do anything different, and he didn't
attempt to leave the country.' Sue decided to trust her husband.

It was therefore a rude awakening when police conducted
another dawn raid at Prospect Villas on 11 April. Aggy went
berserk as police hauled Ermir away for a second time, while officers subjected the flat to another search, looking specifically for
those jeans and that belt. 'This has left me and our pet dog trau-
matized. The dog is so stressed out I've had to take her to the
vets,' Sue complained to a local reporter. 'The police arrested him
before and when they did they turned our flat upside down and
left it in a complete state. They even ripped up our floorboards.
Now they've done it again. I can't cope with all this, it's getting
me down.'

In contrast to his anxious wife, down at the police station
Ermir was relaxed and talkative. He denied having asked to work
at Securitas. Rather he was registered with Beacon Contract
Services for any job that came up, and they offered him work on
the night shift at Medway House. Asked again whether he knew
anybody named Jetmir, he denied it, only to be told that somebody of that name was programmed into his phone. 'Oh! This is
a guy that I haven't seen for about eight years,' he replied. 'He
came from the same village I come from in Northern Albania.'
Shown a photo of Jetmir Bucpapa, Ermir said this man was
Hajdar. They'd been introduced by his brother Ermal in Café
Costa in Tunbridge Wells. Ermir saw Hajdar socially. He couldn't
say for sure whether Hajdar was his real name, though, explaining

that Albanians often use false names in the UK because of their immigration status. The police told Hysenaj they had information he'd spoken to Bucpapa seventy times on the telephone. 'Seventy? *Seventy?*' Ermir asked, incredulous. 'I haven't even spoken to my wife seventy times!'

Detectives then asked Ermir why £2,500 was paid into his bank account in 9 January, 2006, and what he knew about a further £8,800 being paid into Ermal Kulic's account in the weeks preceding the robbery – that is the account he had access to with the card they had found in his possession. It was a lot of money for a man like Kulic who, according to Ermir, worked in Pizza Hut. Almost as much again was paid into the account after the robbery, a total of £16,000. 'I have no explanation,' said the Albanian. 'It does seem a lot.' Detectives believed that this was Ermir's payment from the gang, in whole or part, for his inside information, and he had banked the money in dribs and drabs in Ermal's name to hide it.

The police told Ermir again that they had strong evidence he had been secretly filming in the depot on 16 January. He denied it. Asked where the clothes were that he had worn on that day, he said he'd put them in the recycle bin behind Waitrose in Crowborough.

POLICE: Why did you get rid of all those clothes?
HYSENAJ: Why? Because I like new.

That evening Hysenaj was charged with conspiracy to rob Medway House. As a result, Hysenaj, along with Bucpapa, became famous back home in Albania, where many people took a perverse pride in two of their young men being linked to the world's biggest robbery. A few days later, police arrested Jetmir's mistress. When DS Nicholas Fullerton searched Raluca Millen's flat in Tunbridge Wells he found a green shoulder bag with a hole in it, behind which the spy camera had been mounted for the reconnaissance at Herne Bay, film of which they had recovered from Rusha's address. After two days of questioning Raluca was charged with conspiracy to rob and kidnap, to the amazement of her family. 'I laughed! I said, "No, come on, what?"' recalls her sister Gianina. 'She is not that sort of person.'

When Raluca appeared before magistrates on Saturday, 22 April, her family heard the prosecutor explain why Kent Police believed Raluca had spied for the gang on the Dixons, and that she had been less than truthful in interviews. 'This defendant was arrested two days ago and interviewed about these matters. She effectively lied to police for two days,' Paul Chamberlain told the court, adding that the defendant had eventually admitted to making a surreptitious film of 16 Hadleigh Gardens, though she denied any connection to the robbery. 'Her story changed every time a further piece of evidence was presented to her. Her eventual story was, yes, she was there, she made a film but she was doing it without knowledge of others.' In support of his contention that Millen should be remanded in custody, the prosecutor added that Millen might have access to the missing money and she might attempt to leave the UK.

'I will never leave the country!' Raluca protested, before being led back to her cell.

7

A large number of suspects were now in custody. Gang members under lock and key had to rely on friends and family to protect their interests on the outside. Stuart Royle received regular visits from his son Jimmy, who remained loyal to Dad, as did Chrissy

Royle. Jimmy was chauffeured up to HMP Belmarsh by his dad's mates, including Tony Gaskin and Clamper Craig. Gaskin claims he was approached by somebody close to Stuart, asking if he would be prepared to move stolen money on Royle's behalf. 'We were asked to go and move £2.5 million.' Gaskin says he was told the money was in the sports hall next to Herne Bay Railway Station, that is the hall where Royle's mate Sean Lupton ran a boxing club. Gaskin says he turned down the request to move this money because the cut he and his associate were offered was too small. 'At the end of the day we were only offered a hundred grand out of that. To be honest with ya. Do you know what I mean? And it's not worth the cost.'

Prior to the robbery, Jimmy Royle had been staying with his grandma at her bungalow in Maidstone. As we have seen, Stuart persuaded Cynthia to sign papers allowing him to raise a loan to put down a deposit on Redpits, a plan that had ended in utter failure. The most unhappy consequence of this was that old Mrs Royle now lost her home. Payments on the loan her son had taken out had not been kept up, and as a result her house was repossessed.

Just before the bailiffs came to change the locks, Cynthia, now aged 78, went next door to say goodbye to Ray and Ann Berry. 'Everybody felt sorry for her, because of what happened, because she said all she wanted was to finish her days in her little bungalow,' says Ann. 'She was ever so upset.' Cynthia moved into a small flat on the other side of Maidstone. It was not nearly as nice as her bungalow. 'I feel like it's being in a prison here, but there's nothing I can do. I can't see I've any hope,' she told me, 'I can't see how I can ever buy [another home].'

Stuart's main concerns were the forthcoming trial and, just as importantly, what was happening with the money the police had not yet traced. There were stashes of cash all over south London and Kent, with a power struggle going on for control of the loot. The robbers and their associates were suspicious of one another. Evidently, the gang had been grassed-up repeatedly. Otherwise police wouldn't have been able to make so many arrests so quickly – picking up Hogg, by prime example, the day after the robbery. When the police raided ENR Cars, and the Southborough lock-up, they went straight to the money. It was the same story at the Ashford International Hotel. The information they were getting was superb.

The gang members were highly suspicious of anybody taken into custody for questioning, then released, such as Michelle Hogg, suspecting that they had been offered a deal by police. In Hogg's case, they were right, though she had so far turned down overtures made to her by Kent Police. Those suspects who were charged, and held on remand, were not necessarily trusted either. The fear was that they might also be tempted to turn QE (Queen's Evidence). Threats and beatings were dispensed inside prison as reminders not to grass, with people on the outside making threatening phone calls and paying house calls to family members. Jimmy Royle complained to police that he had received threatening text messages. A rumour went around that two masked men had gone to Elderden Farm after dark to threaten Linda Fowler, who henceforth adopted a policy of not answering her door. 'I don't answer the door, because I don't know who is at the door.'

Then Paul Allen's girlfriend's pub burnt down. In January, Stacie-Lee Dudley had become joint licencee of the Forester's Arms in Welling, a short distance from ENR Cars. In the early hours of 25 April 2006, local resident Charlie Hagon was woken by a tinkling sound. When he looked out of his window he saw the pub next door was ablaze; the flames were above the roof. The tinkling was glass coming out of the windows. The police suspected arson. Somebody, perhaps, wanted to send a message to Paul.

Just over a week later, on 5 May, Mick Morrell, a large, lugubrious detective constable, knocked on Keith Borer's caravan, at Yalding. Police knew from their enquiries at Elderden Farm that Stuart Royle had hired a signwriter and Borer's number was in Royle's mobile phone. The DC found a Xerox envelope in the galley kitchen, inside which was £1,350 in brand-new, sequential £50 notes. There was another £50 in a floppy disc case, and Keith had more cash on his person. In total, police recovered just over £1,400. The fifties were part of a batch of new notes released by the Bank of England in November 2005, and stored in Medway House in one of the cash cages ransacked by the robbers on 22 February. Police also recovered a Dell computer from the caravan. Analysis of the hard drive would show that somebody had done an Internet search for Parcelforce logos before the robbery.

'I will tell you everything,' Keith told DC Morrell nervously, even before the detective had read him his rights. 'I got money from these people, not millions. I [did] the vehicle for [Royle]. I've done work for him before,' he blurted out. Down at the station, Keith unburdened himself further. He said he was in a bad state. He had been living on his nerves and whisky for the past few weeks. 'I've just been so scared. I've been so worried the past few weeks, months. It's been like a bubble waiting to burst,' he told DC Morrell and DC Linda Robb. 'I got a call, "Could you do a Parcelforce van?" I said "Yes."' He downloaded the Parcelforce logo, made the sign, showed it to Royle, who asked him to fit it to the van. He met a man at Staplehurst who led him to the yard where he did the job. '[Stuart] said, "What do I owe you?" I think I said, "A couple of hundred quid." He said, "I'll sort it out tomorrow."' The next day Keith drove to Maidstone

Prison. A man in a balaclava opened the car door and – 'bosh!' – threw an envelope inside. Keith drove home, stopped on the way, looked inside, and saw there was £2,000 in the envelope, ten times what he expected. When he got home the TV news was all about the robbery and he realized it was linked. Indeed, he saw that the notes he had been given were sequential. But Keith was so skint he kept the money and spent it. 'I just thought, "take the money and run."' He'd bought petrol, food and bits of shopping. The police had what was left.

Borer said Royle had also asked him to make some reflective 'POLICE' stickers. He did so. It was easy to do, using white vinyl and the Helvetica font. 'He didn't say what he wanted them for,' Keith told Morrell and Robb. 'It could be for fancy dress parties . . . anything . . .' He didn't dream that Royle wanted 'POLICE' signs because he was planning kidnap and robbery. When pressed to explain why he accepted this unusual commission, Borer cited his finances. 'This year has been exceptionally bad, financially. It's been absolutely awful. There's not been enough coming in.'

POLICE: You think that's why Stuart approached you?
BORER: Probably, yes, Muggins.

As the interviews progressed, Borer changed his story slightly. He now said it was Royle who gave him the money at Maidstone Prison, not an anonymous man in a balaclava. That was all. Borer swore on his son's life. But he was still lying. A few minutes later, Keith told the officers there was actually £6,000 in the envelope, three times what he had told them earlier. He'd been so amazed by the amount that he went down to the pub and got 'absolutely pissed'. During subsequent days, as he watched the story develop on the news, he became more worried about what he had been mixed up in and started

drinking heavily. Like Royle and Fowler, Borer told the interviewing officers that he was very frightened. 'I'm worried
about my life . . . I'm absolutely petrified.' At the end of these
interviews, Keith was released on bail.

8

Lee Murray and Paul Allen were now enjoying the high life in
Morocco as house guests of Aït Assou, who came and went, travelling between Amsterdam and Rabat. On one of these trips
home Assou brought a friend to keep the Englishmen company,
an American named Nick Stark. He also arranged for the boys
to hire a Moroccan chauffeur and translator named Adnane
Ghannam, for 200 dirham (£12.50) a day. Ghannam liked Lee
and Paul at first. 'They give me the impression [of being] great
gentlemen,' as he says in his stilted English. Ghannam had previously worked for a hire-car company and he drove Paul and Lee
around in a rented Renault Clio initially. Then they bought a
blue Mercedes for 360,000 dirham (£22,500), which was a great
deal of money in Morocco. Ghannam saw that the Englishmen
had no idea of the value of money in his country.

They established a daily routine whereby Adnane would swing
by Villa Samira at nine o'clock each morning to take the lads to
a café for breakfast, then wherever else they needed to go that day.
'Wherever they go, they go together.' Paul and Lee often asked
him to drive them to Agdal, an up-market district of Rabat where
they patronized the LPG Café, McDonald's and the Pressto laundry. The boys rented a flat around the corner at 20 Rue Jbel for
6,000 dirham a month (£375), from a cousin of the King.
Anybody who lived well in Rabat brushed up against relations of
M6, but it is remarkable how closely Lee and Paul associated with

the Moroccan establishment. Not only was the Agdal flat owned by a relative of Mohammad VI, it was next door to the regional office of the United Nations. So each time Murray and Allen visited they walked past police on a street under CCTV surveillance. This didn't seem to concern them at all.

The Englishmen used the Agdal flat as a business address for two import–export companies they set up. The companies allowed them to open accounts with the Banque Populaire and Attijariwafa Bank in Rabat. As a result they were able to move large sums of money into Morocco. One payment of €900,000 came into Murray's account from Dubai. Paul Allen also opened a bank account. Aït Assou brought substantial amounts of money into the country when he visited the boys, though he declared this money properly at customs. One way and another Murray now had access to a great deal of money, and he lost no time in making his first investment.

Murray entered into negotiations with another cousin of the King, a man known as Moulay Yousef, to buy a mansion round the corner from Villa Samira for the equivalent of £500,000. Unlike Stuart Royle's farcical attempts to buy his dream home in Kent, Murray was good for the money. The vendor was first paid a deposit, then the balance without a hitch. The house was on a new road, partly undeveloped. There was a vacant strip beside the property used to graze animals and tip rubbish. Neighbours on the other side included some of the most prominent people in Rabat. The house itself was an ugly concrete villa decorated with pseudo-classical details. The metal front door was flanked by columns, which supported a massive triangular entablature, as one sees on a Greek temple. There were bars or shutters over every window. The place had a fortified appearance.

In addition to the purchase price, Murray spent three million dirham (£187,000) making the villa even more secure, and still gaudier inside. Workmen raised the height of the perimeter wall on top of which Murray had surveillance cameras fitted, with a video-intercom at the gate. But most of his money was spent on interior decoration. 'He wanted everything to be just right. All the marble was to be in black, maroon and beige, but he kept changing his mind all the time,' Moulay Yousef commented. 'One room was for his 7-year-old daughter, another for his 2-year-old son and another one was for his parents. He also wanted [a] large room for a guard and chauffeur.' The décor might be described as 'gangster chic', reminiscent of Tony Montana's house in the movie *Scarface*. There were stone floors, inlaid with an intricate star pattern in the living room, which was furnished with cream leather sofas, an elephant tusk lamp stand, a harp-shaped book shelf and gold chairs in the form of giant sea shells. The whirlpool bathroom was decorated in the style of an Olde English pub with a specially commissioned mural celebrating Murray's UFC victory over Jorge 'El Conquistador' Rivera.

The size and cost of the house was completely out of proportion with the lifestyle Murray had hitherto led in England. A council-house boy, who had only recently moved up to a semi in Sidcup, Murray was now establishing himself in the style of a Moroccan prince. So was Paul Allen, who asked their chauffeur to call him Prince. Prince Paul bought a mansion round the corner from Lee's new place for £312,000. This house had ten bedrooms and, like most large residences in Souissi, came with a resident caretaker: in this case a midget. Paul ordered extensive renovations before moving in. While the work was carried out, the friends continued to lodge together with Nick Stark in the Villa Samira.

Murray was looking for other properties to buy, taking a particular interest in the seaside community of Harhoura, a Moroccan

Malibu south of Rabat. Lee and Paul rented a villa here for a while, mostly as a place to take girls, whom they picked up at the nearby Platinum Bar. Adnane Ghannam says that some of these girls were prostitutes. The boys also frequented the Chameleon Bar, adjacent to the city's most expensive hotel, the Tour Hassan. 'It was magical,' says their chauffeur of the high-rolling evenings they enjoyed together on the town. Paul drank heavily when they went out. Lee contented himself with a beer and a cigar. At the end of their evening, the lads would routinely tip the doormen two days' wages.

When they wanted to join a gym, the Englishmen signed on at L'Institut Moving, the most expensive gym in the city, frequented by members of the royal family. Lee and Paul also took up golf, which only the very rich play in Morocco. When the boys grew weary of Rabat, they visited Casablanca, Marrakesh or Agadir, where they stayed in the most expensive hotels and gambled heavily in the casinos. One night, Murray walked away from the tables in Marrakesh with six million dirham (£375,000).

The boys loved to shop. They shopped in the Rabat medina for what they would call antiques, that is to say the vulgar furniture they were filling their mansions with. They also came to the market to buy cell phones, purchasing a remarkable number for cash. Apparently concerned the British police might track their calls, Paul and Lee used a phone once, then destroyed it.

When it came to recreational shopping, Lee and Paul didn't want to bargain in a market. The boys wanted expensive, brand-name designer items from shops they had heard of, preferably in a Western-style shopping mall. There was only one such place in Morocco, the Megamall, and fortunately for them it was just up the road from their villa, very near the gym. Rabat's Megamall was small by British standards, a fraction the size of Bluewater at Dartford, for example, but genuinely exclusive, being far too expensive for most Moroccans. The lads visited almost every day. They often ate breakfast, lunch and dinner in the cafés and American-style fast-food outlets, patronizing Domino's Pizza and Quality Burgers in the basement. They hung out in Amando's Café on the top floor, where the stools were upholstered in yellow leather, the same colour as Lee's Ferrari. The lads bought armfuls of casual clothes at Tommy Hilfiger, always in extra-large sizes and paid for with cash. Lee purchased fifteen new watches in the jewellery stores, the most expensive costing over £35,000. They also bought gifts for their lady friends at Gabbana.

Apart from the women they picked up in bars, Lee and Paul flew girls in from the UK. Each man had more than one lady in his life and, with their newfound wealth, the boys were treating the girls to something they really wanted: cosmetic surgery. Paul and Lee were paying for no less than five women to go to the Belvedere Clinic back in London to have 'procedures' costing approximately £3,000 each, including nose and boob jobs. The boss of the Belvedere Clinic was named Richard Tickle. There was much merriment within Kent Police when detectives discovered that Paul and Lee had sent the girls to a man who became known inevitably, in the style of the *Carry On* films, as Dr Dick Tickle.

One of their lady friends was an exotic dancer girlfriend of Paul's named Jade Bovingdon, who arrived in Rabat on 7 May to spend a couple of weeks with Paul, who took her to the beach house at Harhoura. Lee's mistress Nicola Barnes visited with their two-year-old son, Lenie. A few days after she left, Siobhan showed up, having taken the Eurostar to Paris, where she caught an Air France flight to Rabat. Murray told his household staff that Siobhan mustn't know Nicola had just been there. '[He] told me to shut my mouth and to say nothing to his wife,' says Ghannam, who drove both Lee's women to and from the airport.

The house party grew in May when Nick Stark flew in a girl-friend from England, an exotic creature who claimed to be a world champion kick boxer. They all went to Casablanca on a shopping expedition, during which Lee and Paul spent 100,000 dirham (£6,000) on clothes. They also ate out at the fanciest restaurants. Adnane Ghannam estimated that, when they were on a spree like this, the boys were spending the equivalent of £2,000 a day. Murray told his driver he made his fortune as a cage fighter, but Ghannam was not convinced. He tapped Lee's name into Google and discovered that his boss was wanted by the British police in connection with a robbery. The chauffeur started to notice that, when he drove Lee and Paul around town, they were being followed by unmarked police cars. Murray noticed, too. He wondered if Siobhan had been followed to Rabat, and asked Aït Assou if there was a way to get the police off his back.

9

Murray and Allen had managed to slip into Morocco before Kent Police had a chance to pick them up, which was 'unfortunate', as Chief Constable Michael Fuller concedes. Getting them back from Morocco would be a huge problem. First the police had to find the Englishmen. The process started in April 2006, when DCI Judge made contact with the Moroccan authorities in Rabat, asking for assistance. The Moroccans reported back in May that Murray and Allen had entered their country on 25 March, and were currently living in the capital. Helpfully, the Moroccans placed the Englishmen under surveillance. This was done by a special division of the Moroccan police known as the Direction de la Securité Territoriale (DST), who watched the Villa Samira day and night.

At the same time, Kent Police had Siobhan Lamrani-Murray under surveillance. When Siobhan and Stacie-Lee Dudley set out to visit their respective partners in Rabat, Kent Police officers in plain clothes followed the girls onto the Eurostar. Unfortunately, when they got up to visit the loo, Siobhan and Stacie-Lee recognized the Kent coppers, returning to their seats laughing about it. What they didn't know was that a woman sitting opposite them, texting on her mobile phone, was a Flying Squad officer in plain clothes, relaying their conversation to Scotland Yard: just one example of the way Kent Police and the Met stepped on each other's toes during the investigation.

Even Inspector Clouseau would have had little difficulty trailing Murray and Allen around Rabat. The fact Lee and Paul were English made them stand out in a city that receives few British visitors, while most of those who do visit are business people rather than flashy young men in T-shirts and jeans, their arms decorated with tattoos and Rolex watches. The boys made no attempt to be inconspicuous. On the contrary they attracted attention. When Murray went clubbing, he asked to have a DVD of his Vegas fight shown on TV so everybody in the club knew what a star he was. Lee and Paul also fraternized with local criminals, with whores and drug dealers, from whom Paul bought cocaine. But that wasn't the end of their stupidity.

10

One night in May, Lee, Paul and Nick took their partners out to dinner at Piccolo's in Rabat. Afterwards they returned to the Villa Samira where Nick's kick-boxer girlfriend stayed overnight, sleeping in the room with the strongbox. The following day Nick and his girlfriend got into an argument, which ended when she refused to stay another night under the same roof as him, and checked into the Golden Tulip Hotel. Then she flew home to England with Paul's dancer girlfriend, Jade.

With the girls gone, Lee, Paul and Nick settled back into a bachelor routine, eating and shopping at the Megamall, working out at Moving and hitting the clubs at night. After a week or so, Lee decided to do his accounts. When he opened his strongbox, approximately €200,000 was missing.

Lee and Paul accused each other. 'You're supposed to write down what's taken from the box!'

'Yeah, of course I did.'

When they had blown off steam, the friends tried to work out who had stolen their money. Suspicion fell on Nick Stark, and his kick-boxer girlfriend, who had spent a night in the room with the box, before the argument which resulted in her checking into a hotel. Lee and Paul thought the tiff might have been play-acted for their benefit. They confronted Stark, who denied it, casting aspersions instead on the people who worked for them in the house. 'Nick blamed me and other staff,' says the caretaker Moussaffia Abrik. 'Lee and Paul also wanted to question Adnane, because he is always with Nick.'

The chauffeur Adnane Ghannam arrived for work as normal at the villa at 9.00 a.m. Tuesday, 30 May, 2006. His first job was to drive Nick Stark to breakfast, after which Stark wanted to go to the gym. They returned to Villa Samira around 4.30. Adnane sat in the car outside in the street and smoked a cigarette. Aït Assou emerged from the house with a man who introduced himself to the driver as police lieutenant Simohamed. This was not a real police officer, but one of three Moroccans paid by Assou to come to the villa that day posing as police in order to interrogate the staff about the missing money. The use of bogus policemen is strikingly similar to the trick the heist gang pulled in Kent. Ghannam was immediately suspicious of this policeman, and asked for identification. The 'policeman' responded by bundling him inside the compound, cursing.

When the gate closed, Paul Allen stepped forward. 'Go inside, you son of a bitch,' he told Ghannam, pushing the chauffeur towards the cabana by the pool. The cabana became an interrogation chamber. 'Simohamed beat me. Paul beat me. Lee beat me very, very, very tough.' Lee Murray slapped Adnane around the face. 'I'm going to kill you, motherfucker, if you don't tell me where's my money,' he threatened, adding: 'We've been beating people for nothing.' This was a reference to the fact that other members of the household staff had already been given the third degree. They had not cracked, though, reinforcing Murray's belief that Ghannam had the answers they wanted. He didn't like Adnane anyway. The driver was clever and talked too much. 'Now you're going to tell me where's my money, you funny guy.'

Ghannam says the beating continued for thirty minutes, during which time he received blows to his body and head, breaking two teeth and causing him to bleed profusely. They stopped the beating around 5.15, leaving Adnane locked inside the cabana. Adnane listened apprehensively through the locked door as Lee and the others yelled about what they were *going* to do to him next, Murray working himself up into a rage. When Lee unlocked the cabana door, he was foaming at the mouth. 'They've been shouting, screaming, talking for about fifteen minutes and he was getting very nervous and the spit was coming out of his mouth,' says Ghannam. 'He was more than angry.'

The Moroccan crept nervously out of the cabana and across the lawn, making for the gate. As he did so, Lee Murray picked up an iron bar that was lying on the ground and again asked Ghannam where his money was, accusing the driver of helping Nick Stark steal it. 'I could not say what I didn't see [or] what

I didn't know!' wails Ghannam. 'I couldn't give them a [false] answer. They could check in one minute and they are going to find out I'm a liar.' So Lee hit him with the bar, belabouring his back and shoulders, causing the smaller, older man to raise his arms in self-defence. 'I was beaten like a dog.'

Ghannam scampered out through the gate, and crossed the highway to the other side of the road, where he stood in a daze. Although he was on a residential street, in an expensive neighbourhood, with passing cars, nobody came to his aid. Instead, Murray caught up with him. In his concussed state, Adnane became mesmerized by Lee's eyes, which seemed to open wider as if he stared into Ghannam's. He had the bar behind his back as if he didn't want people to see it.

'Pick him up!' Lee ordered his henchmen, who dragged the chauffeur back into the compound and sat him down in the gatehouse.

The men now became solicitous towards the chauffeur. They attempted to treat Ghannam's wounds, using a local remedy which involves rubbing red pepper seeds into cuts. Ghannam was given money, almost a month's wages. Lee then informed the chauffeur that they were all going for a drive, during which he was to point out where he had taken Nick Stark.

Ghannam was put in the back of the Clio, between Lee and one of the fake policemen. Assou and a second bogus cop were in front. As they drove into town, Ghannam formulated a plan. He lied to his captors that he was a diabetic. 'I told them that I must have a bottle of water. I felt very, very, very weak. I was not strong enough to talk.' They pulled into a Shell station on John F. Kennedy Avenue. 'The man on my right side got out of the car and went to buy the bottle of mineral water.' Lee remained in the car on his left. Ghannam looked out of the window over Lee's shoulder, tricking Lee – 'stupid as he is' – into turning to look the same way. Adnane seized his opportunity and got out of the car.

The second he was clear of the vehicle, the chauffeur screamed abuse at Lee and Assou and the two bogus cops in order to make a scene. Service-station staff turned to see the commotion. Lee couldn't risk dragging Ghannam back into the car in front of so many people. 'Calm down. It's nothing,' the cage fighter told his hysterical driver. He promised to give him more money and to take him to hospital. When Ghannam continued to shout and scream, Murray and his henchmen drove off, with a warning: *Don't go to the police.*

It was 6.30 p.m. Ghannam went home briefly, then took himself to hospital. Later he called Nick Stark, telling him that Murray had beaten him because Lee and Paul suspected he had helped Stark steal their money. Surprisingly, Stark was still at the Villa Samira, and continued to live there. It seems Murray wasn't ready to take the American on directly. He was a much more formidable character than Ghannam, and under the protection of Aït Assou. Lee had chosen instead to try and beat a confession out of their older, weaker driver. The attack on Ghannam had been cowardly, showing Lee once again to be a bully. It was also foolish, because the next day Ghannam went to the authorities.

Chapter Fourteen

BOSH!

1

Three days after Lee Murray assaulted his Moroccan driver, DCI Mick Judge decided he had enough *prima facie* evidence against Murray in connection with the heist to ask a magistrate for an international arrest warrant, which is tantamount to a charge in criminal law. Once the suspect is picked up the police have to proceed straight to court; there is no opportunity to question them. The warrant was granted in Maidstone on 2 June 2006. Ignorant of this significant development, and not knowing whether Adnane Ghannam had gone to the police or not, Lee and Paul stayed put in Aït Assou's villa in Rabat, inviting two friends over from England to keep them company.

One of these friends was Mus Basar, the man who had recently collected Lee's black Mercedes coupé in Amsterdam and taken it back to London. Since then Mus had been arrested by Kent Police, who found £14,000 in cash in his flat in Crawley, and released on police bail. Lee now asked Mus to drive his car to Morocco, which he agreed to do. 'Mus didn't tell me, because he knows I worry too much,' says his mum Doreen, who'd hoped that Mus had put these old associations behind him. Lee's second call was to another old mate, Gary Armitage. As with Mus, Gary's adult life hadn't amounted to much. Admittedly he'd had a poor start. Dad, a professional criminal and alcoholic, who was absent during much of Gary's formative years, drank himself to death in 1997. Like his father, Gary had got into a cycle of getting into trouble and spending time in jail. He was under investigation for using an imitation firearm when Lee invited him to Rabat for a holiday. As with Mus, Gary chose not to tell his nearest and dearest where he was going. 'He had a phone call and he was invited out to some friends in Spain,' says his sister Kelly, having been told less than the whole truth by her brother, which wasn't unusual. 'He doesn't tell me everything . . . there's always things you are never going to know about them.' Kelly expected Gary back soon, though, because his girlfriend, Lisa Guidotti, was pregnant with his first child. 'He said he'd be back in a week.'

Gary flew to Rabat on 18 June, to find Mus had already arrived in the Mercedes coupé, a highly conspicuous vehicle in Morocco, not least because of its UK plates. Apparently unconcerned about this, the lads set about having a good time: working out at Moving, shopping and eating at the Megamall, partying at the Platinum and Chameleon bars with the local drug dealers and floozies. During the day they watched the FIFA World Cup on TV. England was progressing through the rounds and optimistic fans thought the team might go all the way to the final. It was a good time to be lounging around the TV with a beer, a joint and a line of coke, and this was what they were doing at the Villa Samira towards the end of June. The only cloud on the horizon was news from the UK, on Friday, 23 June, that two more men had been arrested in connection with the heist. Both were charged over the weekend with money-laundering offences.

Despite this development the lads went out for dinner in the Megamall on Saturday evening as if they hadn't a care in the world. The following day was warm and sunny. Gary Armitage had originally been due to fly home, but he had decided to change his ticket because he wanted to stay and watch the football with the lads. England was playing Portugal at 4.00 o'clock in the World Cup quarter-final. The boys didn't have much to do until kick-off so they got up late, taking their time to shower and dress. Lee put on jeans and a black shirt; Paul selected a red Dolce & Gabbana T-shirt. Under the D&G logo was the legend 'Delicious & Gorgeous'. They went to the Megamall for breakfast, then came back to the villa, all four friends leaving again for the mall later in the day in the blue Mercedes. They were going to watch the match on a big screen in one of their favourite cafés. As they left the Villa Samira, the Englishmen noticed they were being followed by a Fiat Uno commonly used by undercover police in Morocco, but continued nevertheless.

2

As Murray and his friends strolled towards the south door of the mall, two Englishmen were leaving the building by another exit. DCI Mick Judge and his DC, David Ecuyer, a Swiss-born officer who spoke French, usefully, had brought Murray's specially obtained European arrest warrant to Rabat to show the Moroccan police, whose responsibility it would be to pick Murray up. The British coppers had become frequent visitors to Rabat over the past few months, building up a working relationship with their Moroccan counterparts. Initially Mick stayed at the Tour Hassan, wanting to be as comfortable as possible, also to give the

Moroccans the correct impression. He had to check out of the luxury hotel in a hurry when he discovered that Lee and Paul were frequently to be found boozing in the bar downstairs.

During their visits to Rabat, the British officers found the Moroccan police helpful, but there were significant cultural differences to get used to. When the Englishmen were first invited into police headquarters in Rabat they heard a sound long since gone from British police stations, the *rat-a-tap-tap* of typewriters as officers typed up their reports. They discovered that low-ranking Moroccan detectives had cars they couldn't drive if they had exceeded their petrol allowance. It was all a bit of a joke. But when DCI Judge went upstairs to see the top brass, he saw that senior Moroccan police had every facility, including computers on their desks.

It was hard to get used to the difference in procedure, too. The Moroccans couldn't understand the painstaking way DCI Judge went about his investigation, accumulating evidence he hoped would pass muster in a British court. The Moroccans took a much more direct approach to crime-fighting. If they wanted to arrest somebody, they did. At the same time there were strict rules in place regarding the working relationship between the Moroccan and visiting British police. Mick had to be careful to go through the correct diplomatic channels at all times, and he didn't want any hasty arrests. Rather, he wanted a softly-softly operation, giving him time to gather evidence, and hoping Murray would lead them to the missing millions. Judging by his spendthrift ways, Lee had access to very large sums. This game had gone on long enough, however.

DCI Judge met the local police in Rabat over the weekend of Saturday 24–Sunday 25 June. The Moroccans explained they had a plan to arrest Murray at home on Tuesday 27th. At 10.00 p.m. Saturday night they called Mick back to the station to tell him

things had changed. They had received intelligence that Gary
Armitage and Lee Murray were due to fly to Paris the follow-
ing morning. Murray had booked the tickets. Sunday morning
Mick Judge and DC Ecuyer went with the Moroccan police to
Rabat Airport to watch the 7.00 a.m. Air France flight to Paris.
The plan was to arrest Murray as he went through immigration,
but not the others. If Paul, Gary or Mus were there they would
be restrained, to make sure they didn't intervene, then let go.
Mick didn't have enough evidence as yet to ask for Paul's extradition. He was happy to wait until Paul's visa expired and the
Moroccans simply deported him. As it turned out, Murray didn't
show up at the airport. He had changed his mind again. The
Moroccan police said they would have a rethink and, in the
meantime, they suggested that Mick and his DC went somewhere nice for their Sunday lunch. Their driver took them to the
Megamall. The English detectives had just finished eating, and
stepped outside to bask in the sunshine, when Murray and his
pals showed up, trailed by a small army of Moroccan police.
Having heard the boys were coming to the mall to watch the
game, the Moroccans had decided to nick the British here and
now, possibly to impress the detectives from Kent Police, who
swear they had no warning of what was about to happen.

3

The security man on the south door, Said, knew Lee and Paul.
He says: 'The English came almost every day. They ate here and
shopped here and the shop owners were always pleased to see
them because they tipped generously.' Unusually, when the lads
got out of the car this afternoon, they didn't come straight into
the mall, but hung around outside the south door, Lee sitting on

a planter, Paul pacing up and down nervously as he used his mobile phone. Then he too sat down. 'I went to ask Lee not to sit outside; it's not allowed,' says Said. 'I asked Paul to stand up. I put my hand on his shoulder and he didn't seem to know I was there.'

Paul was distracted by what looked like a large number of police vehicles on the far side of the car park. 'Let's go in,' he told the others. Inside the door, the mall splits into two paths, which curve around an atrium. The Englishmen chose the left path. As they walked past Tommy Hilfiger (which was closed on Sunday, as were most of the shops), the Moroccans made their move. Armed officers swarmed across the car park and punctured the tyres of Lee's Mercedes, in case he tried to use it for a getaway. Others drove their cars over grass verges, like the Keystone Kops, apparently in order to seal off the area. Mick Judge and Dave Ecuyer became alive to what was happening when they saw police blocking the Routes de Zaërs outside the mall. They watched in amazement as a motorcyclist tried to go through the road block, and was kicked off his bike by a policeman. Having guessed what was going on, Mick called his Moroccan minder to come and get them. When he didn't receive an answer, he called the consulate to send a car urgently.

The mall was in uproar. '*Bosh!* They all [charge] in the Megamall,' recalls Gary Armitage. 'They all come running in and, like, we knew we weren't going to get away. They all had guns.' The Englishmen split into two groups, Paul and Lee running down the left side of the mall, Mus and Gary heading towards another exit, Mustafa unable to run fast because of his gammy leg. Police caught Lee first, outside Al Hassania Voyages. Paul was stopped further on by the pharmacy. The police claim Murray and Allen started to fight the officers, martial-arts style, injuring their men. The boys tell a contrary story. 'We was all getting our heads smashed in and had guns put in our face,' alleges Gary, who insists they surrendered immediately. 'They broke all my ribs and bashed us right up.'

Although it was a quiet shopping day, there were members of the public in the mall, and many ran screaming at the sight of guns, assuming a terrorist attack was under way. The Megamall is next to a royal palace, and Morocco is plagued by Muslim terrorist groups who think Mohammed VI too liberal. There are regular bombings and other outrages. Fearing this was what was happening, shop staff hid in toilets. Women customers fainted. Al Jazeera flashed news of a possible terrorist incident.

Mick Judge and Dave Ecuyer had been picked up by a consulate car which followed a high-speed convoy taking Murray, Allen, Armitage and Basar – hooded so they couldn't see where they were going and tied hand and foot – to the Villa Samira, where Moroccan detectives ordered the caretaker Abrik to open up. Paul, Gary and Mus were held in a parked police car outside on the street, while Murray was driven into the compound. From the start, Lee was given special attention. DCI Mick Judge was asked by the Moroccan police to look at what they had in the vehicles. 'I thought they'd found the money!' Instead, he was shown four prisoners, whose pillow-case-type hoods were momentarily flipped up. He identified Murray and Allen by sight. The Moroccan police searched the villa, and interrogated the staff roughly. 'The police seized me,' recalls Moussaffia Abrik. 'They handcuffed me and they beat me [and] they searched the house.' The police didn't find much money in the house, but they did discover amounts of hashish and cocaine, the latter being a serious offence in Morocco. Having seized these drugs, the police took the English prisoners downtown to the *Police Judiciaire*. Gary Armitage: 'Then [they] left us with blindfolds on for like two and a half days on the floor, hand-cuffed, foot-cuffed, no water, no toilet, nothing. It was just unbelievable.'

4

Lee Murray's British lawyer, Derek Parker, soon heard about his client being arrested in Morocco. Realizing that Kent Police would now try to extradite Murray to stand trial for the heist, and somehow guessing that Murray wouldn't want to come home, Parker telephoned the Foreign Office to ask for the name of an English-speaking extradition lawyer in Rabat. They referred him to Abdellah Benlamhidi El Aissaoui. Parker called his office and left an urgent message.

The next morning the newspapers carried the story. 'Man held at shopping centre said to be martial arts fighter and raid master-mind,' declared the *Daily Mail* over a menacing picture of Lee Murray. D. Supt. Paul Gladstone spoke to journalists in Maidstone. 'He was arrested for robbery, kidnap and other offences linked to the £53 million Securitas raid,' he told them, establishing a clear link between Murray and the heist. 'We are grateful for the help of the Moroccan authorities and the Foreign and Commonwealth Office in this matter.'

Although Murray's arrest had been carried out at the behest of the British, once Murray and his pals were in custody the Moroccans insisted that they investigate allegations about crimes committed in their country before consideration was given to the extradition request. Murray and Allen were charged with posses-sion of hard drugs, assaulting police officers during the arrest and false imprisonment of Adnane Ghannam. Basar and Armitage were charged with possession of drugs and assaulting the police.

On Wednesday, 28 June, all four lads were brought before a
judge in the courthouse at Salé, just across the Bou Regreg
River from Rabat, for a preliminary hearing. The British press
had arrived in force and a *News of the World* photographer
snapped a terrific picture of Lee and Paul being led into the
court in handcuffs: Murray looking furtively around as if searching for an opportunity to make a break for freedom; Allen
grinning broadly as if he didn't have a care in the world. Both
were unshaven, wearing the same clothes they had on when they
were arrested, Paul's T-shirt still declaring that he was 'Delicious
& Gorgeous', though he didn't smell so good after three days in
the cells.

The case was adjourned. Until their trial, Murray and his
friends would be held in the adjacent prison, known simply as
Salé Prison. While they were in town, British reporters did a little
background research on Lee Murray's life in the sun. It became
evident that Lee and Paul hadn't maintained a low profile in
Rabat, and that their cover story convinced few local people.
'They said they were businessmen,' a cab driver told the
Guardian's Duncan Campbell. 'But they didn't look like businessmen because they had tattoos.' Campbell reported something
else about Murray that aroused suspicion in Rabat, probably
without him realizing: 'Neighbours thought the men were gay
because it is unusual for men to live together [in Morocco].'

Salé Prison is a large penitentiary surrounded by a high concrete wall, on which squabbling seagulls perch. It is a mixed
prison, men and women are held here (not, of course, together),
as are convicted felons and those awaiting trial. Salé is considered
a modern, well-run prison by Moroccan standards. Inmates are
allowed to wear their own clothes and most are permitted to
socialize freely, the men enjoying marathon communal games of
soccer and basketball in the exercise yard. The four Britons were

segregated, however, kept in single cells in a high-security prison block with round-the-clock guards. To Murray it was a dungeon, a filthy hole overrun with rodents and cockroaches. 'We didn't see no one,' says his mate Gary Armitage. 'We was down the block for the whole time, single cells, with two guards outside everyone's cell. We would come out of the block once a month to see the solicitor, and every time we come out we had like five guards with each of us . . . We only come out on our own [to] exercise on our own, and you're allowed like one hour a day each to come out and try and get a little bit of food in you, and that's it: banged-up.'

The only way the lads could chat between themselves was to stand at their cell windows and talk through the bars to each other. Visitors were very welcome. Derek Parker came from Bexleyheath to see the lads, but as weeks stretched into months their most frequent visitor was Abdellah Benlamhidi El Aissaoui, the Moroccan lawyer Parker had engaged on Lee's behalf. He ended up representing all four Englishmen.

'Call me Ben,' said Abdellah when they met. At the age of 55, Ben was overweight to the point of corpulence, with grey hair, a neat little moustache and spectacles. He spoke excellent English, with an American accent, having been educated in the United States, and had a cheerful, affable manner. The boys liked him. Ben liked them, too, though he had to concentrate to understand what they said. Good though his English was, Ben wasn't conversant with the demotic language of south London, with 'geezers' and 'wallies', 'bosh' and 'bollocks'. His clients' conversation was made more challenging by their disregard for grammar, making, for instance, liberal use of the double negative, which had the effect of expressing the opposite to what they meant (Gary: 'I got fuck all to do with no robbery'); they substituted 'f' for 'th' and 'ink' for 'ing'; on top of which they had a propensity to swallow their words, and swore almost constantly. Ben found Gary particularly hard to understand. Lee less so. Despite his limited vocabulary, Ben didn't think Lee stupid. 'He seems to be very sharp. Every time I talk with him his mind is alert and present. You cannot [fob him off]. Everything you say to him needs to make sense.'

Realizing the boys were usually hungry when he visited, Ben started bringing them pizza and coke from Pizza Hut. Pizza could be obtained from any number of cafés in Rabat, but the boys only wanted Pizza Hut. Lee took charge of the food and shared it out, making sure that the guards got a slice. This was part of his status as a big man in the prison, 'the Boss' as Gary and Mus called him. Despite a number of pizza deliveries of this kind, the boys soon lost weight. Prison food was poor and Lee and Paul couldn't obtain the steroids and food supplements they had used for years to bulk out their physiques. At the same time, the boys could buy all sorts of comforts. They sent Ben out to get television sets for their cells. Lee had a DVD player, even the use of a mobile phone. A prisoner can get almost anything in a Moroccan prison, if they pay. 'It's really just unbelievable,' says Ben. 'It can be a five-star hotel.'

Gary and Mus didn't have as much money and didn't enjoy the same privileges. They also received fewer visitors. Whereas Siobhan and Stacie-Lee came out regularly to see Lee and Paul, Gary's girlfriend stayed away. As did his sister Kelly. 'I'm not willing to fly on a plane to Morocco on my own,' she told me, at home in Thamesmead. 'I get lost going to Bluewater in my car.' Doreen Basar came to visit her son, Mus, and was 'disgusted' by the conditions he was being held in. As to why her son was there, it was the old story. She said her angel had got 'mixed up in a bad crowd'.

5

The day Lee Murray was brought before a judge in Rabat, Roger Coutts was appearing before magistrates in Kent. Roger had first been arrested at the beginning of March. His home was searched, and he was released without charge while forensic tests were carried out. Analysis of mobile phones implicated him heavily in the conspiracy; he was a known associate of Lee Murray; and there was lots of DNA evidence against him. He was now rearrested and brought back to Tonbridge Police Station to explain himself. Coutts refused to answer detectives' questions, but issued a series of statements prepared with his solicitor.

Told that his DNA had been found in the red van, Coutts said he might have done repair work on the vehicle. He admitted knowing Lee Murray; Lee was a customer of ENR Cars. The police told him they knew each other better than that. They had grown up together, and had recently been on holiday with their partners to Barbados. Coutts had even tried to buy Murray's house. 'Lee Murray is a friend of mine. We grew up on the same estate in Woolwich,' Roger conceded. 'I have never denied my friendship [with him].' Told that police had found blue overalls and a balaclava at his house that matched the garments used in the robbery, Coutts explained that he used the former for work, the latter for paintballing, as anybody down at the Duchess of Edinburgh would confirm. Despite having Jet's phone number programmed into his mobile, Coutts denied knowing Bucpapa. He said he only knew Michael Demetris as his barber and had only been to Herne Bay in the *Shakey Jakey*. Told that his DNA was on cable ties found inside Medway House, Coutts said that this was 'impossible'. It wasn't, and he was charged with conspiracy to rob and kidnap.

'He was one of the robbers inside the depot,' Paul Chamberlain told Maidstone Magistrates on 28 June, warning the bench that Coutts had connections in Cyprus. His solicitor didn't make a bail application and Coutts was hauled off to join his pals in Belmarsh, his next court appearance scheduled for the Central Criminal Court in London, better known as the Old Bailey, where the Securitas robbery trials would be heard.

The same week Katie Philp was arrested. Since Lea had been picked up, Kate had left Fenwick's to work in London at Harrods 'to avoid any further publicity' as her boss told police. She was still living at home with mum in Tonbridge, though. Police searched the address, recovering a make-up box inside of which were Charles H. Fox products. They charged her with conspiracy to rob and kidnap.

Detectives then went back to Yalding to speak to Keith Borer. They showed him vinyl 'POLICE' signs recovered from Rusha's shed, together with rolls of backing paper, and oddments of coloured vinyl that appeared to have been used to make police livery. Borer had already admitted Stuart Royle asked him to make up 'POLICE' signs. He said these might be them, telling detectives that some of his customers did occasionally want police signs. 'They use them for jokes sometimes, stag nights, all sorts of things,' he explained unconvincingly. Going back to the money Stuart had paid him, Keith now said he thought it was £6,100, and having given this as his third and final answer, Keith was charged with handling stolen goods: that is the money in the envelope.

Michelle Hogg had been the second person arrested in connection with the robbery. Having been questioned, and had her flat searched, she was released without charge. During the following five months Hogg had a series of secret meetings with Kent Police to discuss the possibility of becoming a Crown prosecution witness. She declined their repeated offers, gambling perhaps that they didn't have enough evidence to charge her.

Michelle didn't return to work at Hair Hectik, but she had enough money to go on holiday to Spain with Mum in July 2006. Elizabeth and Michelle Hogg's plane had just touched down at Gatwick at the end of their vacation, on 12 July, when they were asked to leave the aircraft before the other passengers. As they did so, Michelle was met by police. They rearrested the hairdresser, who started shaking so badly with fear she had to be given a wheelchair, then drove her to Kent to be interviewed. 'I have now lost complete faith, for the first time in my life, in the police,' this child of a police constable told the officers, angry about the way she had been arrested at Gatwick. She said she felt humiliated. 'I feel there is nothing I can tell the police to make them treat me as a decent person,' she went on, peevishly, telling her solicitor she felt she had been 'emotionally raped by the police'.

The police told Michelle they had accumulated a great deal of evidence against her since their last encounter. They showed her a long list of items recovered from her flat and bin, and explained the DNA evidence and phone records that also connected her with the other suspects. Faced with all this evidence, Michelle said she was too frightened to be completely candid, but she made some admissions. 'My boss asked me to do him a favour,' she told the police, referring to Michael Demetris, whom she would blame for everything. She said Demetris introduced her to friends of his who wanted to be disguised for a party, or video production, or something that involved buying specialist make-up. Michael gave her time off work to do it and said it was nothing to worry about. 'Because he's my boss, I done what he said.' He told her she should think of it as a 'working holiday', though Michelle grumbled that she still hadn't been paid.

The police asked where she got the money for the items she bought. She said one of the men who visited her flat gave her £200. Detectives showed Michelle a NatWest bank envelope they had found torn up at her flat, and pieced back together. On the envelope were directions to Cynthia Royle's bungalow, using the nearby Saxon Chief pub as a landmark. Hogg admitted travelling to the house on Monday, 20 and Tuesday, 21 February 2006, in order to touch up the disguises she had made for her 'clients'. She said somebody else helped her, but wouldn't say who this was. 'I'm not prepared to say the names of any people who called or sent a text to my phone or *vice versa* because I fear for my safety. I will say that the people I was told to work on in relation to make-up and prosthetics did contact me quite a lot in early February, to check on how advanced the work was going . . . At no time did anyone mention any criminal activity and at no time did I suspect such.'

Did she not question what these disguises were for? Michelle said she asked Demetris repeatedly for an explanation, but he declined to give one, which she thought 'weird'. The police then asked what she and Katie Philp had been talking about for so long on their mobile phones on the night the Dixons were kidnapped, by men they believed were wearing the prosthetic masks made by Hogg. 'I feel totally helpless,' the hairdresser replied, losing her composure. She babbled: 'I've been involved in something I know nothing about and I wouldn't have been involved in it had I known.' The fortnight she worked with these men had been 'awful, because I just felt like I had been taken out of my life and put somewhere . . .' When she saw news of the robbery on television she realized what had been going on and threw the prosthetic materials out. 'I didn't want to keep anything. I was so shocked. I didn't want it to be part of my kit.'

At the end of these interviews, Hogg was charged with

conspiracy to rob and kidnap, appearing before magistrates on 14 July 2006. Family members including father Jeffrey, a wheezy, tired-looking ex-copper of 55, watched from the gallery as she was remanded in custody and hauled off to Holloway Prison, an experience which triggered a nervous breakdown.

While Hogg and her co-defendants prepared their defence in the UK, there were further developments in Morocco. In mid-July, Aït Assou, who had hosted Murray and Allen at the Villa Samira, returned to Morocco from Holland. As he came through customs, he was arrested and charged with offences including kidnapping Adnane Ghannam, and holding him prisoner while he was beaten. Around the same time, Ghannam claims to have received a visit from four men – a Moroccan and three Dutchmen – offering him the equivalent of £7,000 to change his story. He refused. Moroccan police then arrested a 42-year-old hospital worker named Houssein Al Fadiani, and charged him with kidnapping and assaulting Ghannam while posing as a policeman. Both Assou and Al Fadiani were held in Salé Prison as they awaited trial, segregated from Murray, Allen, Armitage and Basar.

6

That autumn police raided a series of properties in and around Herne Bay, bringing the hunt for the missing money very close to where the Dixons had made their home. At dawn on Thursday, 9 November 2006, detectives searched the sports hall next to Herne Bay Railway Station, where Tony Gaskin claims he was told Stuart Royle had £2.5 million stashed, money Gaskin further claims he was asked to move back in April. Police had spoken to Gaskin, 'an off the record *chat*, they like to call it'.

The wheel clamper told them what he had been asked to do, but said he didn't know whether the information was 'a load of old bollocks', as was so often the case with Royle. Anyway, it was 'too dodgy', so he didn't get involved. When the police came to look in the sports hall, there was no money to be found.

That same morning Kent Police raided the nearby home of the builder, Sean Lupton, recovering two substantial bundles of cash totalling £10,450. Sean's teenage daughter sobbed as police led Dad away for questioning. Sean himself didn't seem bothered. Interviewed at Canterbury, he explained the money away by saying he was often paid in cash. He needed cash in hand to buy building materials. Asked where he was on the night of the Tonbridge robbery, he said he was at home with his wife, as she would confirm. Therese Lupton did so. But phone records seemed to show that Lupton was in the vicinity of Elderden Farm in the early hours of 22 February, calling Stuart Royle's mobile just two minutes after Royle left the depot, for example. Later that night Lupton was cell-sited at or near Redpits, when he and Therese said they'd been in bed at home in Whitstable. Perhaps Sean had been sleep-walking.

Police had found paperwork in Lupton's house linking him to a white van, the crushed, burnt-out remains of which had been found in a field in Sussex. Despite its condition, police established that the van had a hasp on the back and believed it may have been the vehicle used to kidnap Colin Dixon. On Lupton's kitchen table police found a strange, hand-printed letter which began: 'SEAN LUPTON TALKS TO [sic] MUCH. STOLE MY MONEY. TONBRIDGE ROBBERY . . .' before going onto refer to 'GIRLS [and] DRUGS' and ending with what read like a threat: 'PEOPLE DON'T LIKE IT.' Therese told the police that the note had arrived anonymously in October.

The police went down to the beach and had a look in the

family's beach hut. Nothing. They went to see Sean's mate, Tony Harun, a 41-year-old curtain salesman, raiding his business and the Herne Bay council house where he lived with his common-law wife. Here too police found an amount of cash, which they seized. From under the couple's bed, detectives fished out a copy of the anonymous letter they had seen at Sean Lupton's house. Harun was arrested and interviewed. His DNA matched swabs taken from the rear number plate of the red LDV van used in the robbery, but he was released without charge, grumbling about it all being Lupton's fault. 'He's the reason I'm in this bloody mess.'

The police also released Lupton without charge. He returned home as if nothing had happened. Therese Lupton says she demanded to know what was going on, but she didn't get much change out of her husband. 'He just said they asked him about this and that, about his connections with Royle, but it was nothing to worry about.'

A month later, on Tuesday, 12 December 2006, Lupton drove his white Ford Transit van to Capel-le-Ferne, a village near Folkestone, to meet a client who wanted a price for some building work. Lupton gave a quote and, at approximately 6.00 p.m., telephoned Therese to say he wouldn't be home for dinner because he was going on to price another job in West Sussex. His wife later claimed Sean also said he was going to see an under-world figure, 'a very hard man [who] I'll call Mr X'. Sean didn't return home that evening, and he didn't call. The next day Therese phoned the police. A week later Sean's van was found in Aycliffe, near Dover. On the face of it, Kent Police treated this as a straightforward missing-person case, and appealed to the public for information about Sean, whose photograph they distributed to the press. But there was a deeper mystery here.

There were clear links between Lupton and the heist gang,

notably with Stuart Royle. It seems that Lupton was at the flop
after the robbery. Having had his collar felt in November, he
may have decided to do a flit with his share of the money. Police
outlined a scenario to Therese Lupton whereby a criminal who
has decided to disappear will make sure his family are provided
for, then drop out of sight for a while, during which time he
won't get in touch directly for fear police will find him, but
eventually he will make contact. Therese pointed out bitterly
that Sean *hadn't* left them provided for. She was struggling to
meet the mortgage. And he hadn't been in touch. Also, he
hadn't taken any of his belongings. He had surrendered his passport to the police when they arrested him, which made
travelling difficult, and he hadn't used any of his credit or debit
cards.

Christmas came and went without Sean sending word home.
He also missed family birthdays. Therese says she then received
a visit from the murder squad. Kent Police were still treating
Lupton as a missing person, but they told her they wanted to
check every angle. His wife began to think the worst. 'I don't
know where he is, whether he is dead or alive,' she says, but she
didn't want him back. 'If he's alive, he's out of order [because] it's
cruel to do that to your own children . . . When you hear your
children crying themselves to sleep at night, it's not very pleasant . . . If he's been murdered, well then he must have been
murdered for a reason, because he's been involved in something.'
There was the intimation of a threat in that note – 'SEAN
LUPTON TALKS TO MUCH . . .' But Kent Police didn't seem
interested in the note. In fact, they were fairly confident that Sean
Lupton had done a flit to Turkish Northern Cyprus. They didn't
know exactly where he was on the island, but believed he was
alive and well, and knew that even if they found him there they
wouldn't be able to extradite him.

7

There was a similar situation with Lee Murray in Morocco, though in this case Kent Police did at least have Lee in custody and they were willing to do everything it took to try and get the fighter home to face trial. Lee was always a much more significant figure for them than Sean Lupton.

Lee and his Moroccan lawyer Ben were now fighting a legal battle to prove that Lee had a claim to Moroccan nationality, because of his father, and therefore could not be extradited to face trial in the UK. This was not a simple matter. One problem was that Lee lacked a Moroccan birth certificate. Ben had to try and get one retrospectively, his task complicated by the fact that Lee's parents hadn't registered their marriage in Morocco.

In the meantime, Ben tried to improve Lee's public image in his adoptive country. Local press coverage of Murray's arrest had been lurid, reporters not feeling the need to rein themselves in, as the British press would, because of the mere fact Murray hadn't stood trial yet. The magazine *Maroc Hebdo* described Murray typically as 'a hardened criminal', the mastermind behind 'the heist of the century'. Ben now gave interviews to the Arabic press about his client, whom he referred to as Moulay Ibrahim Lamrani, making the best of Lee's Moroccan antecedents, telling journalists that Moulay Ibrahim was a great Moroccan sportsman and wealthy businessman who had nothing whatsoever to do with the Kent robbery. Why then didn't Lee return home to the UK to see his family and clear his name? Ben's answer was that his client believed that the British police had made up their mind that he was guilty, based on his association with other suspects, and he had no chance of a fair trial. Also the British were convinced Lee was guilty because of the money he had spent in

Morocco, which seemed out of proportion with what he had earned before coming to the country.

Following his arrest, Lee had approximately €3 million in his Rabat bank accounts (£2.12 million), apart from which he owned a £500,000-plus mansion in Rabat and a £250,000 house in the UK. There was ample further evidence of wealth, and profligacy. The clothes Lee left unclaimed in the Pressto dry cleaners when he was arrested were worth £7,000. Where had all this money come from? Ben said Lee told him he had more money than the British thought he should have because he hadn't paid income tax on his earnings as a cage fighter (apparently unconcerned that tax evasion is a serious offence). The argument was preposterous anyway, because, as we have seen, Murray never earned a living wage from MMA. The biggest fight of his life, in Las Vegas, earned him about £3,000.

Even more risible was Lee's new contention that he couldn't return to the UK because he would be a victim of British racial prejudice 'because of his Muslim or Arab race' in Ben's words. Although he was born and raised in England, to an English mother, and looked and sounded like a typical South Londoner, Lee Murray was now posing as an Arab – the Sheikh of Sidcup, perhaps. This despite the fact that Lee privately had contempt for Moroccans, or at least those who ran the judicial system in his adoptive country. As he wrote to me from his dungeon in Salé, 'this lot couldn't arrange a bunk up in a brothel, they have the brains of demented earth worms'.

Paul Allen was also trying to play the race card. 'He says he wants to become a Muslim, and he is choosing the name of Omar,' Ben told me one day, 'and he wants to remarry Stacie-Lee according to Islamic marriage.' Setting aside the fact that Paul and Stacie-Lee had never been married, it was remarkable how Paul copied everything Lee did, even when it didn't make sense to do so. Unlike his friend, Paul didn't have a Moroccan father, so he had no prospect of Moroccan nationality and there was no point in adopting Moroccan ways in this cynical fashion.

Months passed without any discernible progress. In January 2007, a delegation of Moroccan law enforcers visited London to discuss closer co-operation between the two countries, including a possible extradition agreement. Morocco wanted the UK to extradite a Moroccan who had been tried and found guilty in absentia for involvement in terrorist bombings in Casablanca. The British wanted Murray. The inference from the Moroccans was that they might do a swap. The British made it clear that this was impossible. Still, they wanted Murray, and they now made an official request for Paul Allen as well.

The boys were brought before a judge in Salé on 7 February 2007. After seven months in jail, Allen, Armitage and Basar looked gaunt and scruffy, as if they had been sleeping in their clothes. Murray – the Boss – appeared better fed and better dressed. He also held himself erect in court, with a sense of pride that set him apart from the other defendants. The Englishmen and their two co-accused Moroccans, Aït Assou and Houssein Al Fadiani, were surrounded by more than twenty armed police officers, with relatives sitting in the public benches at the back of the courtroom. 'You are originally, Moroccan, that's right?' the judge asked Murray in Arabic. 'Do you speak our language?'

When this question had been translated, Murray replied: 'I understand just a little bit, but I don't speak it.' Via the translator, the judge proceeded to interrogate Murray and his co-accused in a rather confusing way. There wasn't a linear process of calling witnesses for examination and cross-examination, building up a narrative, as one sees in a British court, the evidence of witnesses being weighed by a jury. Here the judge sat alone with a case file, asking questions and calling witnesses as he saw fit.

Murray denied charges of kidnapping Adnane Ghannam, holding him prisoner, and assaulting him; also assaulting police officers and possessing 18.5 grammes of cocaine. He conceded that he had hit Ghannam around the head once, not with an iron bar but a wooden bar, though he admitted he had drawn blood. Lee excused the attack saying he was angry with Ghannam partly because the driver wanted a pay rise. As to the arrest at the Megamall, Lee insisted it was the police who beat him and his friends, not the other way around.

'We found cocaine in the house, it's yours?' the judge asked suddenly.

'Nope, it's not mine.'

'Do you take drugs?'

'Never.'

'And what about your friends, they take drugs?'

'I've never seen anyone of them using drugs.'

Asked about the money that went missing from Villa Samira, Murray said he believed Nick Stark took it. The judge said Murray's remarks were not consistent with a statement he made in police custody. Murray said he was interrogated by police when he was blindfolded, and he wasn't confident his words had been translated accurately. Also he had been 'scared'.

Murray was told to sit down, and Paul Allen was called before the bench. He claimed he wasn't at the villa when Ghannam was beaten, but said the drugs at the house were his. The judge asked a police officer to give evidence about what had happened at the Megamall when Murray and Allen were arrested. The officer said Allen had assaulted him and his colleagues, which prompted Allen to interject angrily, accusing the officer of assaulting *them*. Gary Armitage complained that the police gave him a black eye. The judge said the police report showed Armitage 'fell down' and injured himself. Moving on, the judge asked Armitage whether he used drugs. Gary said he smoked hashish in Morocco, but hadn't used cocaine. Mustafa Basar said he didn't use drugs at all.

Turning to the other defendants, the judge questioned Aït Assou about the bogus policemen at his villa. Assou admitted paying the policemen 3,000 dirham (£187), saying he did so with Lee's knowledge, indicating that it was Murray's money he used, 'because I'm the one who takes care of Lee's money, and when I asked him about that he said it was OK'. But he insisted that they were real policemen, at least he thought so. Why Assou and Murray should find it necessary to pay the police wasn't explained. Finally, the hospital worker Al Fadiani denied that he had posed as one of these bogus officers, maintaining that it was simply his misfortune to bring medical reports for Assou to the villa the day all hell broke out.

The Moroccan Crown Prosecutor recapped the story of how Moroccan police went to arrest Murray at the Megamall in response to a UK warrant; rather than surrender peacefully the Britons fought back, injuring officers; and when they took them to their villa they found hashish and cocaine. He went into the details of how Murray and Allen had seemingly entered Morocco with €400,000, which they locked in a box at Villa Samira, only to find themselves robbed. Assou brought police to the villa to investigate the theft, but they were not *bona fide* officers. The prosecution claimed Al Fadiani was one of these fake policemen. Ghannam was then beaten and held in the house, which amounted to kidnap. The prosecutor claimed Assou and Al Fadiani were party to this, and concluded by saying it was especially outrageous that foreigners should treat Moroccan police as these Englishmen had.

Ben told the court that Kent Police believed Murray to be one of the organizers of the Tonbridge robbery. As a result they were applying pressure to the Moroccan authorities to hold Lee while a way was found to extradite him and Allen for trial on this much bigger matter. That was the context. Ben then went on to question the evidence against his clients. He pointed out that Armitage and Basar weren't even in Morocco when Ghannam claimed he was beaten, so it was absurd that they should be charged in connection with it (as they now were). Ben didn't understand why the prosecution case was that cocaine was found *inside* the house, when it was found in a car, and he argued that Lee had not kidnapped Ghannam, though he conceded Murray had beaten his driver. Finally, lawyers for Assou and Al Fadiani said their clients were innocent of all charges.

Judgment was given on the evening of 21 February 2007, exactly a year after Colin Dixon was kidnapped. The judge pronounced Murray not guilty of kidnapping and imprisoning Ghannam, but guilty of assaulting the driver, for which Murray, together with Assou, was ordered to pay Ghannam 5,000 dirham compensation (£312). Murray was also found guilty of assaulting the police, and ordered, together with the other four Britons, to pay 5,000 dirham damages to an officer who had sustained serious injury; Murray was additionally found guilty of possession and use of drugs. His sentence was eight months in prison, plus a 10,000 dirham fine (£624), and compensation to Ghannam and the police officer, on top of which Murray and the other Britons had to pay 303,100 dirham (£18,944) to Moroccan customs for the illegal possession of drugs.

Allen was acquitted of kidnapping and falsely imprisoning Ghannam, but found guilty of assaulting police and drug possession. He too was given an eight-month sentence, plus a 10,000 dirham fine, in addition to which he had to share in the compensation to the policeman and customs. Armitage and Basar were acquitted of kidnapping and false imprisonment, but were found guilty of assaulting police and possession of drugs. They were sentenced to four months apiece, ordered to pay 5,000 dirham each and share in the compensation payments.

The hospital worker Al Fadiani was cleared of all charges. But Aït Assou was found guilty of kidnapping Ghannam, and allowing his home to be used for illegal acts, for which he was sentenced to three years in prison, a stiff sentence that caused him to break down and weep.

In contrast the Britons appeared jubilant. All were now convicted felons, convicted of charges of assault and possession of drugs, something Murray always maintained he had nothing to do with. Their relatives also seemed pleased. 'I'm very satisfied with the judgment,' Lee's mother, Barbara Lamrani, told reporters. Ben on the other hand said it was a severe judgment, and they would appeal. In fact, all parties appealed, including the Crown prosecutor who thought the sentences too lenient.

Having more than served their time already, Gary and Mus were released from Salé Prison in the early hours of the following morning. As they waved goodbye to Lee and Paul, and thanked them for the holiday, the boys had high hopes of all being reunited soon. In fact, Murray and Allen were on a list of prisoners due to be released on Sunday. But Kent Police lodged an objection on the grounds that the extradition request was still active and the release was cancelled at the last minute. Lee and Paul asked Ben angrily how this could have happened. 'You are in Morocco,' he told them with a shrug. 'Everything is possible.' This was not what the lads wanted to hear. 'They got very frustrated with me.'

Ben warned Lee that if the British extradition request failed there was provision in law to try him in Morocco for the robbery. When they talked this over they decided it might be to their advantage. If the Moroccans let him walk free when the fines in the local case were paid, Murray would effectively become a prisoner in exile, like the train robber Ronnie Biggs had been in

Brazil for years, unable to come home for fear of arrest. Ben: 'I said, "Listen, it's better for you to be tried here [for the robbery], because we get rid of it, we'll fight it, and then you'll be given a [verdict], we don't know which one, either guilty or not guilty, then if we don't like it we can appeal it, and then whatever sentence, you know, you pay it, and then you are free, home free, you can do anything, you can travel anywhere. There is no one that can touch you."'

8

Back home, the matter of the £10,450 seized from Sean Lupton came before Maidstone Magistrates on 6 March 2007, which was the last opportunity Lupton had to prove he had a lawful claim to the money. But there was still no sign of the builder, who had now been missing almost three months. In court, Kent Police made it plain that the money was linked to the Tonbridge robbery, and they believed Lupton was involved in the heist. The Chairman of the Bench ordered the cash forfeited under the Proceeds of Crime Act.

The £38,150 seized from Siobhan Lamrani-Murray's friend's house came before the same court a few weeks later. 'The money was seized because it was believed to be from some kind of unlawful act,' Laura Harsant, a financial investigator with Kent Police told the court, adding: 'In interviews, Siobhan Lamrani-Murray said the money was hers and was given to her by her husband. She hasn't asked him any questions as to where the money comes from.' The magistrates were told that there had been no response from Mrs Lamrani-Murray, or her lawyers regarding the seizure of the money, which they also ordered to be forfeited under the Proceeds of Crime Act.

Siobhan was in Rabat, where I reached her by telephone. 'My 'usband's told me not to speak to no one about giving any information out about my life, my kids' life, my husband's life, or anything to do with anyfink,' she said, unhelpfully. She was more talkative in an interview Ben set up with the Moroccan newspaper *Al-Ayyam*, as part of his campaign to improve Lee's public image. They met the reporter and photographer in a hotel. Siobhan looked anxious and much older than 26 in the photo that was taken, a weary woman with a fag in hand. 'I don't believe my husband was involved in this robbery,' she told the reporter, her true manner of speaking lost in translation, as was her name. The paper called her by a Moroccan name, Chiva. She asked rhetorically why Kent Police had 'made [Lee] out to be the main character', arguing that her husband was 'not a member of the Mafia', but a devoted family man, claiming he was 'paying the price of his popularity'. (Siobhan and Lee share an exaggerated sense of Lee's celebrity.) 'Morocco must not extradite one of its citizens to another country.' When the reporter suggested that Lee had fled to Morocco as a fugitive from British justice, she objected hotly: 'This is not true. We all decided to come back for good to Morocco a long time [ago].'

Siobhan remained in Rabat a few more days. Paul's girlfriend, Stacie-Lee, had gone home, but Gary and Mus were still around, together with Gary's girlfriend, Lisa, who had brought their baby son Archie Ray to see his dad. Although the boys were out of prison, they hadn't been given their passports back and couldn't leave the country until the appeals were heard and the fines paid. Gary and Mus each faced a bill of £5,439. And when they went home, Kent Police would want to talk to them about their adventures in Morocco. They were especially interested in Mus, having found £14,000 in cash in his flat. When I tried to discuss this with Mus, he said he wasn't 'talking about this to no one'.

Gary was more amenable. He said he was resigned to being arrested on another matter when he got home, 'and go on remand until my trial', but unconcerned about any questions Kent Police might have for him regarding the heist. 'You can't be nicked for coming on holiday and seeing someone, can ya? They can fink what they like . . . In England, you've gotta prove things. It ain't Morocco, England, is it? In Morocco they can come out with any old bollocks and you get nicked for it. In England, you've got to prove it.' In the meantime, he and Mus were kicking their heels in the Relais Mercure on Rue de Tunis.

The next significant court date in Morocco was 2 May 2007, when Ben produced a retrospective Moroccan birth certificate for Lee Murray. To his frustration, the judge said this wasn't enough to make him a Moroccan, and adjourned judgment on the matter so Ben could find more proof. The judge did however reach a decision on the extradition request for Paul Allen. He ruled that Allen should go back to the UK. 'It was kind of expected,' said Ben, who told Allen they could appeal. 'We talked about it and he said, "No" . . . he's ready to face the charges against him.'

Despite the ruling, nothing happened immediately because the appeal hadn't been heard and the fines remained unpaid. The biggest fine, the one all four Britons had to share in, amounted to less than £19,000. One might have thought this was small beer to Murray, but he had cash-flow problems. His bank accounts in Rabat had been frozen. The Moroccan authorities had seized his mansion and his two Mercedes cars. Murray hadn't paid Ben's legal fees, and was negotiating with the *News of the World* to see if the paper would pay Siobhan's 'travelling expenses' to and from Rabat in return for an interview with Lee.

Months passed without any discernible progress. DCI Judge likened dealing with the Moroccan authorities to trying to herd cats, but realized there was nothing he could do but be patient. Allen would be sent home at some stage to stand trial, and even if the Moroccans didn't extradite Murray they were promising to try him for the Tonbridge robbery in Rabat on behalf of the British. Justice was being done, in a strange way.

Chapter Fifteen

THE OLD BAILEY

1

Murray and Allen were embarking on their second year in Salé Prison when the first robbery trial began at the Old Bailey in London in June 2007. There were eight defendants in what became known as Trial I: Rusha, Royle, Bucpapa, Coutts, Fowler, Hysenaj, Hogg and Borer. All except Borer were charged with the same three counts: that is conspiring with Murray, Allen, Philp, Millen 'and other persons' to kidnap the Dixons; likewise conspiracy to rob Securitas Cash Management; and conspiracy to possess a firearm. Borer stood accused of handling stolen goods: the £6,100 he said Royle gave him for sign-writing the red van.

To make life easier, it had been decided that the three girl-friends charged – Philp, Millen and Shackelton, the latter accused only of assisting an offender (that is helping Fowler dispose of the cash cages) – would be put into a second trial. It was hoped that Allen would be back from Morocco in time to join them, pos-sibly Murray, too. In the meantime, the women were free on bail. All eleven defendants had entered not guilty pleas to all charges.

Because of fears that criminal associates might try and bust defendants free from court, Trial I was conducted under armed police guard in Court 8 of the Old Bailey, a large, ugly room at the far end of the second-floor corridor in the modern, bomb-proof extension to the famous building. Court 8 had an unusually capacious dock, suitable for cases with many defendants, with a Perspex screen to stop them escaping. The defendants – bar Borer and Hogg, both of whom were on bail – were brought to court each morning in an armoured truck from HMP Belmarsh, police stopping the traffic on Newgate Street as the portcullis gate to the courthouse was opened. The truck descended to the underground cells, from where the defendants were brought up to Court 8 by lift. They were escorted into the dock by nine prison officers, who sat with them throughout the hearings. Borer and Hogg, the latter accompanied to court by her parents, and a family friend named John Selley, a former police sergeant, entered the courtroom by the main door, and were searched before they were let into the dock to sit with the other defendants.

Each of the eight defendants had a barrister and he in turn had a junior, all wigged and gowned, the desks in front of them laden with case files. Most defendants also had a solicitor's clerk taking a note of proceedings. The cost to the taxpayer for defending each of the eight defendants on legal aid was approximately £500,000. DCI Mick Judge led a large team of Kent Police officers to court each day. There were also several representatives from the Crown Prosecution Service, which had engaged the distinguished QC, Sir John Nutting, to present their case. Tall and skinny, with owlish glasses, wearing a black silk robe, the straggly ends of which look like feathers, Sir John lived in a nest of box files facing the judge's dais. He was flanked by his junior, a florid QC named David Jeremy; the duo assisted by a younger barrister who sat behind them. This three-man prosecution team cost the taxpayer £600,000, adding to a legal bill of about £4.6

million, which would be more than doubled by other court costs. Presiding over everybody was the Honourable Justice Sir David Penry-Davey, an exceptionally tall and patient judge of 64 years (the same age as Sir John) with a good sense of humour and a reputation for being a softy. Other people in Court 8 included two clerks, the usher, a shorthand typist and a pack of journalists, the latter squeezed into seats next to the dock.

A full court was further encumbered by computers, television screens, a PA system and hundreds of fat lever-arch files – files of exhibits, photographs, maps, and statements – loaded into cardboard shelving units, stacked three deep in places, and prone to collapse under the literal weight of evidence. There were no windows, and the inadequate ventilation system meant that some parts of the courtroom became very warm during proceedings, while others remained chilly. Screams of fury and despair from other parts of the building occasionally intruded via the air vents, reminding one that the Old Bailey is a vortex of human misery. Court was also often interrupted by loud banging or drilling from builders working next door. Early in the trial the builders drilled through a pipe that led to a flood, which caused large brown water stains to form on the ceiling, where the marks stayed, like malevolent clouds over our heads, until the end.

Jury selection took a day and a half. Dozens of prospective jurors were paraded before His Lordship, and most had an excuse as to why they couldn't commit to a trial which, he warned, might last until November. Jurors rarely talk in public about their experience, but after the case one of the jurors selected for the trial came forward to tell me his story. Juror Number Nine, as I shall call him to protect his identity, a man in his mid-30s, was living in Surrey when he received a letter asking him to report to the Central Criminal Court. The summons came at a good time for the man who had just sold his business, a sandwich bar, and was temping as a recruitment consultant while he decided what to do next. 'I was aware on the day of my jury service starting that this trial, Securitas, was starting as well,' he recalls. 'Having said that, it's totally random [where you are sent]. There are eighteen courts at the Old Bailey . . . When they said, "You're going to Court 8" we didn't know what was happening in Court 8.' He became Juror Number Nine in the case, simply the ninth person sworn in, taking his place on the green jury seats alongside three men and eight women, all drawn from within the M25. They were a cross-section of ordinary working people, 'about as middle England, middle of the road, as you could get'.

2

As soon as the jury was sworn in, Sir John Nutting rose from his nest, fluffed out his feathery robes, and began his opening speech in a voice richly theatrical and grand. The case before the court was a record-breaker, he said, involving what was said to be the 'largest amount of money ever stolen in this country'. It was also a human story, whereby the manager of the Securitas cash depot in Tonbridge had been kidnapped and held hostage along with his wife, child and fourteen members of staff: innocent people surprised in the dead of night by masked men with guns. 'And the motive for this crime?' Sir John asked rhetorically. 'Greed, pure and simple . . . the prospect of dishonest gain almost beyond the dreams of avarice.'*

---

*Quoting from *The Gamester*, by Edward Moore (1712–57): 'I am rich beyond the dreams of avarice.'

Some of the jurors cast a nervous glance at the dock. Although they were behind a screen, the defendants – save Hogg, a snivelling wreck – had an intimidating appearance. Rusha in particular had the look of a tough guy, a stocky little man in an open-neck shirt, with a disagreeable expression. It wasn't necessarily easy to meet their gaze at first, but Juror Number Nine made a point of doing so. 'At the start some of the girls said, "I'm not even looking at the dock! . . . I can't even look at the defendants!" [But] I was like, *I want to see what these guys look like, I want to see reaction.*' After a short time, Juror Nine noticed that Fowler, Rusha and Bucpapa seemed to want to make eye contact, too, and it wasn't long before jurors and defendants were all smiling at each other like neighbours meeting on the bus. 'I will smile at anyone,' says Juror Number Nine. 'I'd rather smile at someone than scowl.'

Mindful perhaps that the crime might appear glamorous, Sir John told the jury sternly: 'There is nothing very courageous about kidnapping women and small children.' He then introduced the defendants one by one. Rusha was 'at the heart of these conspiracies . . . surely one of the robbers and he may well have been one of the kidnappers'. Royle was also a central character, possibly a kidnapper and a robber. Bucpapa was the link to the 'inside man', Ermir Hysenaj. Coutts may have been both a kidnapper and robber. Fowler, who was linked to the conspiracy via his association with Royle, supplied the lorry in which 'the booty' was hauled away, and allowed his home to be used as 'the flop' (Sir John enjoyed criminal slang). Hogg's role was to disguise the men who kidnapped the Dixons, and possibly one of the robbers as well, something she had essentially admitted to, though she claimed not to know why. 'Borer is not charged with conspiracy'. He helped disguise a van used in the kidnapping, for which he was paid in stolen money, and as a result he stood charged with handling the proceeds. Glancing up at the public gallery, Juror Nine noted how few visitors the defendants had in court. Keith Borer's dad came this and most days, but often Mr Borer was the only relative in the gallery, and some of the defendants didn't appear to have any supporters. 'I think they found out who their friends are.'

Sir John explained that the jury didn't have to work out which defendant was behind which mask during the robbery. 'The charge of conspiracy simply involves an agreement by two or more persons to pursue a course of conduct which, if carried out in accordance with their intentions, amounts to the commission of a criminal offence . . . It is not necessary for each defendant to conspire with all of his co-defendants, or all of the co-conspirators. It is enough if he agreed with one of the others to further these kidnappings and/or this robbery.'

It was also important the jury understood that not all the participants in the crime were in court. 'There are two men currently in prison in Morocco,' said Sir John, introducing the 'co-conspirators' Lee Murray and Paul Allen, whose photos were put on screens around the court. 'Both [were] at the very heart of this conspiracy. Murray and Allen fled to Morocco soon after the robbery . . . the Crown hope to secure their return to this country for trial early next year.'

Other co-conspirators not in court were Rusha's partner, Katie Philp, who Nutting said helped Hogg with making the prosthetic masks; Bucpapa's mistress, Raluca Millen, who spied on Mrs Dixon; and Royle's girlfriend Kim Shackelton, who helped dispose of evidence*. Sir John said there was a third group of people, 'suspects' the police wanted to interview in connection with the case, but couldn't put their hands on, or concerning whom the CPS had decided there was insufficient evidence to prosecute. In

*All three women were later cleared.

this category Sir John put Michael Demetris, Sean Lupton and Keyinde Patterson, who, he said, might be in the West Indies.

Having got thus far, the judge called a halt to the day's proceedings, warning the jury before they went home that such a high-profile case was bound to attract publicity, and they had to pay attention to the evidence rather than what they read in the newspapers or saw on television. As Michelle Hogg left the building, Sky News tried to film her and she became hysterical, running into the street. Her mother tried desperately to calm her down. A white van then pulled up, apparently by pre-arrangement, and Mrs Hogg and family friend John Selley bundled the accused into the back. It was the first of many bizarre incidents involving Michelle Hogg, who henceforth wore large, black, movie-star glasses on her journey to and from the Old Bailey.

Coverage of the case in the morning papers was overshadowed by the fact that Tony Blair was stepping down after ten years as Prime Minister. As Blair handed over power to Gordon Brown on Wednesday, 27 June 2007, Sir John Nutting told Court 8 that mobile-phone, or 'cell-site' evidence would be an important part of the Crown's case. Every time a mobile makes a call, the signal is picked up and relayed via a cell site (or radio mast), and mobile-phone companies retain coded records of these calls, allowing the police to find the actual cell sites used. An expert can thereby predict where the user of the phone was when the call was made, sometimes within a very small area, which meant the jury would be given an indication of the gang's movements.

'Two of the most consistently active conspirators in planning this robbery [were] Lee Murray and Paul Allen,' said Sir John, adding that there was evidence Murray had been planning the robbery as early as July 2005, when police found him in Strawberry Vale, next to the depot. Murray had subsequently purchased electronic spy equipment, and directed suspects to places they could buy police clothing and other items that seem to have been used in the heist; a friend of Murray's bought Kent Police badges on eBay; while police had recovered £38,150 from a house Murray had access to in Thamesmead. Furthermore, Murray's DNA was on prosthetic material found at Hogg's flat. 'Make no mistake, the Crown suggests that Murray was at the hub of this conspiracy.'

Remarkably the police had obtained a recording of Murray and Rusha discussing the robbery on a mobile phone. Sir John read from the transcript, the boys' rough language comical in the mouth of a baronet who had been educated at Eton. The fact Ermir Hysenaj didn't start work at the cash depot until December 2005 seemed to indicate, as Sir John put it, that the robbery may have been 'but a gleam in Mr Murray's eye' when he was caught lurking around Medway House the previous summer. The QC added that Murray's friend Paul Allen was also 'a central player'. Allen purchased spy equipment; he bought the Vauxhall Vectra car; he was in regular phone contact with the others; he took his turn spying on the Dixons; and he left his fingerprints on key items of evidence.

While the Tonbridge gang got away with just short of £53 million, Sir John revealed that they left behind almost £154 million. The only reason they didn't take more was 'because the robbers could not fit any more cages into the back of that 7½ tonne truck'. He said the robbers divided up 'the swag' at Elderden Farm. Arrests were made quickly, Hogg being picked up the day after the robbery. The jury were shown photographs of the mass of make-up and prosthetic materials found in her bin, together with hand-written notes apparently showing how she intended to disguise the men. The DNA of Murray and Rusha, possibly also that of Kane Patterson, were on latex scraps in the bin. A cigarette butt in the bin had Paul Allen's DNA on it.

As the other gang members were picked up, searches of their addresses added to the haul of evidence, especially in the case of

Rusha, whose home was a treasure trove of incriminating items, as was the van found in Ashford with £1.37 million inside and a 'robber's kit' of balaclava, bullet-proof vest and gun. Rusha's DNA was on the balaclava. Taking all this into account, Sir John suggested to the jury that 'it would be a truly astonishing coincidence if Rusha had not participated in the robbery, if not also in the kidnapping of Mrs Dixon,' who spoke of a short policeman coming to her door. Police had found £8.6 million in bags in a lock-up rented to a cousin of Rusha. Coutts' DNA was on one of these money bags. There was also DNA evidence against Jetmir Bucpapa, who was arrested with Rusha. Neither man had answered police questions. More evidence was found at Bucpapa's home, however.

Upon arrest, John Fowler tried to shift the focus of the investigation from himself onto Royle, with whom he had been in regular contact by mobile leading up to the heist. Quoting from a police interview, Sir John told the court how Fowler had insisted to detectives in the interview room that he had 'been 100% up front with them', then commenting to the jury with a flourish, 'But *of course* he hadn't.'

Juror Nine was impressed by Sir John, and his opening speech. The man was entertaining and likeable. 'He is flamboyant when he wants to be, he can make a joke when he wants to, he can be serious . . . He's the full part.' Opening speeches are not evidence, however, and now the jury had to concentrate on the witnesses, the first one of significance being Colin Dixon himself. Before Colin made his entrance, he was upstaged by Stuart Royle.

3

During the first week of the trial, Slippery Royle appeared uninterested in proceedings, sometimes sitting with his feet up in the dock. Behind the scenes the former car dealer had sacked his counsel, Ian Jobling, then reinstated him. But their relationship was breaking down, and Royle was generally troublesome.

On Monday, 2 July, Ian Jobling rose to inform His Lordship that Royle hadn't got into the prison van to come to court this morning because his back hurt and the short journey from Woolwich was apparently too onerous without a 'warming pad' he required. Royle also wanted a special chair in the dock. Preposterous though this sounded, Justice Penry-Davey delayed the start of Colin Dixon's evidence in order to telephone the prison. 'It seems to me your client is raising difficulties of one sort or another,' the judge told Jobling when the court reconvened, 'and there is no indication in my judgment that [Royle] is unfit to be here.' The case would proceed.

The police had kept Colin Dixon under wraps ever since the heist. Only one photograph of the cash-centre manager was in general circulation, a picture taken at his wedding to Lynn way back in 1979. The man who strode into court in 2007 was naturally much changed from that lanky young groom. Now 52, Colin was a big man, tall and overweight, with a fat face; his short, sandy hair was thin and greying. He wore silver spectacles and a conservative blue suit and tie, the image of a middle-ranking, over-eating bank executive.

As he gave evidence Colin spoke calmly, with hardly any emotion, even when describing the moment he was threatened with guns. 'I was scared,' as he said, without much feeling. 'Threats had been made. I didn't know what was going on. I didn't know whether the gun I had seen was going to be used. I was concerned that [the tall officer], who had pulled the gun, was agitated. I didn't know how calm he was. If I had moved my hands there could have been an accident and I could have been shot . . . It was the most scared, I think, I had ever been in my life.'

As his story unfolded it became apparent how remarkably co-operative Colin had been with his abductors. 'I felt I had no choice,' he explained. 'I was sitting there with my hands cuffed, my feet tied. I had no idea where I was. I had been threatened with a gun on two occasions.' This happened in the car, and again at the farm, when one of the lead robbers lost his temper. 'He seemed to be aggressive,' Colin told the court. 'He seemed to think that I was not telling him everything.'

Colin's overriding concern was that the gang had his wife and child, and that they knew where the family lived. This was why he co-operated. But he had given the gang more help than they asked for: opening the vehicle gate from the Control Room, for instance, even though Policeman, the only robber in the depot at that time, hadn't requested he do so. Sir John asked Colin why he hadn't raised the alarm directly his family and staff had freed themselves at the end of the robbery. 'As the last person went, he said, "Don't be silly, we know where you live." I didn't know whether all the robbers had left at that time or whether one or more of them were left in the centre.'

The court was then shown CCTV of the robbery, still images spliced together to make a film. It was dramatic viewing, especially when the four robbers arrived at the front door, dressed in black, brandishing guns. The court watched the bandits being let in by Colin, and saw how the robbers rounded up his staff, many of whom placed their hands on their heads like prisoners of war. There was then the fascination of watching the bandits ransack the vault. By the way Stopwatch stood, legs apart, shoulders hunched, it was plain that Lee Murray could be the man behind the mask. Lea Rusha watched the film with a smile. Colin watched intently. The most affecting sequence came towards the end of the film when his wife and their child were glimpsed, cowering inside the lorry, Lynn sheltering the youngster with her body. The judge had made an order banning publication of information that may lead to the identification of the child, which includes revealing the name, age and even the gender of the youngster, but this was a child of primary-school age, and when one saw the film it became apparent how very small and vulnerable the victim was, a little kid being bullied by masked men with guns. Most of these men had children themselves.

After the movie, Sir John asked Colin what his feelings had been during the robbery. His voice quavered for the first time with what seemed like real emotion as he replied: 'I was terrified. I was very, very concerned because until, as you saw, very late on, I had no idea where Lynn and [our child] were. I didn't know what was going to happen to them. I didn't know what was going to happen to me and my staff [and] as I said before I felt guilty . . .'

Colin said he'd received training about what to do in the event of such a situation, and there were tricks he might have pulled, if the man in the Control Room had followed correct procedure. For example, Gary Barclay should have asked Colin when he saw him with Policeman: 'Who is that with you?' In which case, Colin might have given a code name to indicate he was under duress. But Barclay didn't ask the question. Barclay hadn't noticed the second man until he was in the lobby. Even if Barclay had been more diligent, Colin admitted he might not have given the coded answer, because he didn't know whether Policeman had a gun.

The first defence barrister to cross-examine Dixon was Graeme Wilson, for Lea Rusha, a large, bearded man who wore tattered old robes and unusual Egyptian bangles. His every question seemed to be asked with a sneer, accompanied by a sidelong glance at the jury. 'It is the prosecution case there was an inside man,' Wilson told the witness. 'It would be fair to say that you

had the best information of all?' Dixon conceded that this was
true. Refraining from accusing Dixon directly of being the inside
man, Wilson sowed the seed of suspicion – a strategy that earned
him the nickname 'Smoky' from the Crown team who thought
Wilson was merely throwing up a smokescreen. But Wilson had
plenty of evidence to draw on.

A month before the robbery, Colin Dixon introduced a new
system at Medway House whereby the two keys to the vault were
placed in twin safes outside his office, with Colin the only
member of staff who knew both combinations. Previously, Colin
had access to one key, and needed a colleague to obtain the
second. 'If this robbery had taken place in January 2006, before
the change you brought in,' said Wilson, 'there may not have
been a robbery at all, because no one person could have had
access to the vault.' Colin said that, previously, when key hold-
ers were off sick, staff couldn't open the vault. He made the
change for convenience.

There was more. Colin had plans of the depot, and photographs of the building and of members of staff, including senior
staff who carried personal attack alarms. Some of these photos
had been found on Colin's home computer, in contravention of
company policy. Colin explained that there were legitimate reasons to take pictures at work, of cash cages, say, to establish they
were damaged when they arrived; there hadn't been an office
camera for a time, and he had a colour printer at home. But it
was surprising to hear that he'd also had such sensitive pictures
printed at Boots. It also seemed curious that, the day before the
robbery, Colin had agreed that CCTV engineers, scheduled to be
on site that night, shouldn't come in until the weekend, which
meant they were fortuitously out of the way when the robbery
took place. Smoky spoke bluntly: 'You [had the] opportunity, if
you wished, to be involved in this robbery.'

'*If* I wished.'

Wilson told the court sneeringly that 'Mister' Dixon had been interviewed 27 times by police. Transcripts ran to 730 pages. Colin admitted he had felt less a victim than a potential suspect at times. One of the actions police asked him about at length was why he moved a camera in the Control Room when the robber branded with the name Policeman was tying up Gary Barclay. Policeman hadn't told him to. Colin's explanation was that he felt the camera pointing directly at the robber was 'too much of a risk', and that it might cause him to become agitated, maybe violent.

'Your actions could also have been interpreted as [if] you were part of the gang, in on the robbery?' suggested Wilson. Colin admitted that it could be looked at that way.

Surely the most suspicious aspect of Colin's behaviour on the night was his decision to wait a quarter of an hour after he and his family and staff had extricated themselves from the cages before raising the alarm. 'I was afraid that [if] the robbers were caught they knew where I lived . . . and we would be at risk.'

'If the robbers had been caught, they would have been in police custody!' Wilson retorted.

'Some of them, maybe.'

Wilson pointed out that as a result of this delay the gang had time to get to the flop. He then told the court that during the police investigation Dixon's duty manager, Alun Thomas, told detectives that '£30 million was missing from Securitas, that you knew about it, and [the company] was operating illegally'.

'That, I believe, was the allegation,' said Colin drily, explaining that the £30 million was a bookkeeping discrepancy for the company as whole rather than money missing from his depot in suspicious circumstances. He had no answer to the specific allegation that Securitas was operating illegally, and apparently Wilson wasn't able to elaborate because he changed tack, reading out a list of people including Christopher Bowles, Sean Lupton, a father and son team named Tevfik who ran a fish and chip shop in Whitstable, Tony Harun and Susan Grosvenor. Did the witness know any of them? Colin said that Sue was a friend of his wife, and had looked after their child.

'Anthony Harun is the brother-in-law of Susan Grosvenor,' Wilson announced portentously. '[Harun] is alleged to be a friend or associate of Sean Lupton.'

'It means nothing to me,' said Colin.

Barristers for other defendants followed Wilson, some insinuating that Colin could have been an inside man. All tried to chip away at his credibility, and sometimes they succeeded. Dixon was obliged to admit, for example, that once the robbers had left the depot they would have no way of getting back in, unless he let them in, which didn't tally with his decision to wait before setting off the alarms. Exploratory questions from defence counsel sometimes had unforeseen results, however, such as when the effervescent Charles Conway, for Bucpapa, ventured to ask Dixon whether his experience on the A249 on the evening of 21 February was consistent with the way one was normally treated when stopped by traffic police. 'I've never been stopped by the police before,' said Colin with pride.

'I thought you'd say that!' Conway groaned. A motorist of 52 who had never been stopped by police appeared to be a remarkably law-abiding person.

Ermir Hysenaj was represented by Michael Boardman, a distinguished barrister with a peculiar oratory style that involved lowering his voice to a whisper, to make people pay attention, then rising to a boom. Despite this disconcerting manner – 'We can't hear you!' heckled an irascible Sir John – Boardman scored points time and again for his client, getting off to a good start when he got Dixon to admit that most of Hysenaj's work at

Medway House was done sitting down, which didn't appear consistent with Hysenaj being the inside man Murray and Rusha talked about on the telephone, the one 'walking about' the depot.

Boardman also revealed to the court how big a problem Securitas had with staff recruitment and retention, the depot losing 140 workers between 1998 and 2006. 'Some had left on good terms and some had left on extremely bad terms.' All had inside knowledge of Medway House. Additionally, a large number of workmen had been in and out of the depot recently. Colin assumed that most of the engineers and contractors who regularly attended the depot had been vetted by Securitas head office, but admitted there were others who came occasionally or at short notice to Medway House – to fix the drinks or fax machine, say – who may not have been checked out by anybody. Sometimes this was unavoidable. In short there were a great number of people who knew about the ins and outs of Medway House, some of whom had a grudge against the company.

Rising to re-examine his witness, Sir John Nutting made it plain to Colin that Graeme Wilson was suggesting 'you were one of the robbers'. Wilson objected strongly to this, saying he had merely *floated the possibility*. Colin was, however, unfazed, saying he behaved with the safety of his family and colleagues in mind. 'If they had said "Load up the van by hand", I would have loaded the van up by hand . . . if that's what it took to get rid of them . . . I wanted my wife and child back.' Yet he reproached himself. 'I could have done something different. I should have been braver, I shouldn't have stopped the car,' he said (meaning perhaps that he shouldn't have got *out* of the car). 'I did feel guilty about what I had done, and I still feel guilty about what I had done, but in the clear light of day I don't think I had any choice.'

'Have you been back to your home?' asked the QC, giving his witness an opportunity to reveal the human cost of the robbery.

Colin seemed to open up as a person in the last moments of his evidence when he told the court that he and his family had not been able to return to 16 Hadleigh Gardens since the heist, other than for a few minutes with police to collect personal belongings. They had been obliged to find a new home. Speaking with feeling, he said: 'Both my wife and myself are suffering from something called post-traumatic stress disorder [for which we are receiving treatment]. We have lost our home. It *was* our home. We'd been there twenty years. The job I had for seven years I [couldn't] go back there and, very importantly, [our child's] schooling has been interrupted, and what [our child] has been through, not only that night, but since then, no child should go through.'

4

Lynn Dixon was next in the witness box. She was a foot shorter than her husband, but similarly plump, and wore her dark hair long, in the style of a woman much younger than 46. When her hair fell back, her face was revealed to be ruddy, even haggard. She spoke in a near-whisper at the start of her evidence, clearly very nervous. She broke down in tears repeatedly, the first time when Sir John asked her what her feelings had been when she and her child were transferred from the kidnap car to the van. 'They said they had guns [and] I didn't think we could survive the evening. I was horrified that they could do that to a [child] . . .' She paused, head down, while Margaret the usher brought a tissue. Then she sobbed: 'They just didn't have any feelings!' The witness next broke down when Sir John invited her to describe her 'worst moment'. This was when she thought the gang were going to execute her and her child, having gained access to the depot. 'I thought that was it.'

It emerged that during the early part of the investigation detectives had shown Lynn a police DVD of an address where they thought she and her family might have been taken on the night of 21–22 February. The film was made in daylight, so she asked to go back after dark. 'When I went back in the dark, it was the same place.' The court was then shown pictures of the location: it was the yard at Elderden Farm, a quadrangle formed by the barn Fowler rented to the software firm, Netbox 5, his double garage and other outbuildings. Lynn said she was '100 per cent' sure these were the buildings she had seen on the night, and she believed the red van she and her child were held in was parked next to a rusty oil tank visible in the photos.

Cross-examined by Graeme Wilson, Lynn agreed that Colin's job made them both potential kidnap targets, yet she had to admit that she didn't telephone his work, or the police, when he failed to come home on 21 February. She said she didn't want to panic. Wilson asked about Susan Grosvenor. Lynn described Sue as a good friend who had looked after her youngest child, and said she had found out since the robbery that Sue was related to Tony Harun, whose DNA Wilson told the court had been found on the rear false number plate of the red van.

Lynn's evidence about where she was held affected John Fowler directly. His QC was Alexander Cameron, elder brother of the Conservative Party leader David Cameron, whom he resembled in looks and speech, with the addition of a slight stutter. The QC suggested to Mrs Dixon that her memory of where she was held on the night might not be entirely reliable.

Lynn said indignantly: 'I'm on oath!'

Momentarily taken aback by the vehemence of her reply, Cameron gathered his thoughts and pushed on, comparing Lynn's statements to police about where she and her child had been held with the physical reality of the yard at Elderden Farm. Before

going to the farm, Mrs Dixon told detectives the yard was overlooked by a 'three-bedroom detached dark brick [house]'. The
yard was in fact flanked by a barn, clad with wood, and converted
into offices. Lynn originally described a silvery iron handle on the
yard gate. Fowler's yard gate had a black iron handle. Cameron
suggested to Mrs Dixon that she had decided before going to the
farm that this was the place she had been held, partly based on
pictures and a DVD police had unwisely already shown her, and
she was giving evidence to support a story she had fixed in her
head, even though the facts didn't fit. 'Do you agree?'

'I do not agree. I *know* that was the place. I know that was the
gate I went through.'

In re-examination, Sir John Nutting spelt out to Lynn that the
effect of Graeme Wilson's cross-examination had been that she
hadn't rung the police when Colin didn't come home because
'you were a party to this criminal enterprise'.

'Was that the impression?'

It had been put to her husband that he may have been
involved, and now the defence seemed to be arguing that she had
failed to ring the police deliberately as part of the conspiracy. This
suggestion caused Lynn to break down again. Between her tears,
she sobbed: 'I wish you could have been there.'

Sir John pressed her to answer the suggestion she was 'in on'
the heist.

'I wouldn't dream of putting my [child], my husband, through
anything like that.'

'That you and your husband were part of this criminal enterprise, to rob the Securitas depot and fake the kidnap. What do
you say to that?'

'People don't know us. I wouldn't even consider doing anything like that,' she said. 'It still horrifies me what these people did
to my [child]. . . At first lying that [Daddy] was in hospital. That

was bad enough. Forcing me to lie to my [child, and] all these people wanted was money. Trying to keep calm, not knowing how that night would end . . . or if you would survive . . . We've lost our home of twenty years. We've been relocated . . . been estranged from family and friends, the consequences are that these people have changed our lives completely.'

The judge thanked Mrs Dixon for her time, and told her she was free to go. Lynn glared around Court 8 as she walked to the door in the manner of an innocent soul departing the Inferno, where she had been unjustly tormented by devils.

Her husband's integrity was brought into question again when his police liaison officer PC Brown was called to give evidence. She conceded under cross-examination that she could only conclude Colin was lying when he told her, a month after the robbery, that he couldn't remember taking photos in Medway House with his personal camera. But having spent seventeen months with the Dixons, she decided that they were 'very fine people', and she didn't think Colin was a crook.

Gary Barclay was the first of a series of witnesses who had been working in the depot on the night. Like several of his colleagues, he was a grey, middle-aged man wearing spectacles. He was not very articulate. His attempts to explain to the court why he assumed the robber known as Policeman was Asian – 'he seemed thick when he spoke' – gave an unfortunate impression. Barclay was more sympathetic when he admitted to feelings of guilt for having let the robbers into the depot, and admitted he hadn't been adequately trained to deal with the situation he found himself in.

The likes of Barclay were complemented by another type of Medway House worker: young, often foreign-born agency staff. These were generally brighter, more endearing people. One such was Anca Deiac, the Romanian overpowered in the ladies toilets.

Despite the fact she had suffered more than most, the only worker to have been injured, in fact, Anca gave an admirably direct, unemotional account of what had evidently been a terrifying experience. There was no self-pity in her voice when she said quietly: 'When we were put in the cage, I thought maybe we would be killed.'

Her colleague Lyn Clifton was being cross-examined when Stuart Royle unexpectedly interrupted proceedings by talking loudly through the dock screen to his lawyer, Cameron Crowe. 'He doesn't work for me,' the car dealer was saying, in reference to Ian Jobling. 'Why is he still here?' Justice Penry-Davey sent the jury out before speaking to Royle, who said he had sacked the barrister before the trial and no longer required his services. The judge adjourned so Jobling could go down to the cells to speak to his difficult client.

By the time the court reconvened, another problem had arisen. It had been discovered that one of the jurors, a heavyset man, had a criminal conviction. He had been given a community order for driving offences and obstructing the police, but had failed to declare his convictions when the jury was selected. The matter had only come to light when the juror told his *probation officer* that he couldn't fulfil his community order because he was serving on a jury. When this excuse was read out, the whole court enjoyed a laugh. When the judge straightened his face, he dismissed the juror, warning him that he might yet face prosecution. With this matter sorted out, and the jury down to eleven, Ian Jobling told His Lordship that Royle had decided to dispense with his services. A crowded courtroom was being gradually depleted.*

---

*Juries are often depleted during criminal trials, with jurors dropping out for reasons such as illness. Trials continue so long as at least nine jurors remain.

5

Stuart Royle began his legal career in the absence of the jury by delivering a speech to the judge, in the manner of a man sounding off in the pub. If he was to represent himself, Royle told His Lordship that there were a large number of 'disclosure' documents he needed from the prosecution; he also required an adjournment to read this material, and prepare his case, which he couldn't be expected to do as a Category-A prisoner. Apart from anything else he didn't have access to a computer at Belmarsh. He was only allowed to bring to court what he could carry each day. He couldn't deal with correspondence, because letters took 21 days to reach him in prison, and his cell was searched regularly, which disrupted his paperwork. He even cited Health and Safety, telling Justice Penry-Davey there was a limit on the amount of paper he could have in his cell due to the risk of fire.

If Royle was expecting the judge to suggest he go home to prepare for the trial, he was disappointed. Changing tack radically, as he often would during speeches from the dock, Royle told His Lordship that the police were investigating gunshots at his 'properties' and claimed threats had been made to his children while he was in Belmarsh. Even if true, what this had to do with representing himself was hard to fathom. Regarding his erstwhile counsel, Royle said that Ian Jobling hadn't asked witnesses the right questions and, as a result, he wanted witnesses recalled. In summary, Royle said he was in an impossible situation. But he suggested a solution. He wanted the judge to remove him from Trial I and put him in the next trial 'with the two chaps currently in Morocco'.

Royle knew he was in a poor position in Trial I. The evidence of his co-defendants, Fowler and Borer, incriminated him. It

would be better to be in Trial II, where Royle wouldn't be at log-
gerheads with his co-defendants. With Royle having shown his
hand in this unsubtle way, the judge made it clear that he wasn't
prepared to accommodate the request. It was a legal principle that
opposing defendants should be tried together whenever possible.
Nor would the judge countenance a lengthy adjournment so
Royle could prepare himself. 'The position Mr Royle finds himself in is one he has created,' pronounced Justice Penry-Davey,
who nevertheless was remarkably tolerant of the defendant. 'Mr
Royle, the situation at this stage is there is a witness in the witness box,* do you require to examine this witness?'

'I have no notes,' said Royle, telling the judge he wanted to
remove himself from the trial and take his grievances to the
European Court of Human Rights 'because you've unduly prej-
udiced my trial'. The judge asked for the jury and the witness to
be brought back. Bucpapa's barrister, Charles Conway, proceeded
to cross-examine Lyn Clifton. When Conway had finished, the
judge asked Royle if he had any questions for the witness. Royle
rose to say he hadn't got his notes with him.

'Where are the notes?'

'In the cell downstairs.'

'Why didn't you bring them up?' asked the judge, turning to
the dock officers: 'Can the notes be brought up?'

Royle interjected in the manner of a man about to do everybody a favour: 'What I was going to do, if it would help . . .'
Then he paused and motioned to the prosecution team. 'What
is your name?'

---

*Figuratively speaking. Lyn Clifton's evidence had been interrupted by Royle the
previous Friday, and the witness was waiting outside Court 8 to be called back to
finish his evidence.

'Who?' asked Sir John Nutting, turning around.

'This guy,' said Royle, pointing at the QC, putting one increasingly in mind of Joe Pesci's incompetent attorney in *My Cousin Vinnie*.

'The prosecutor?' asked the judge. 'Sir John Nutting.'

Having established the identity of the man leading the case against him (hard though it was to believe he didn't know who Nutting was), Royle suggested that the CCTV of the robbery should be played again, and that the witness Lyn Clifton should give a commentary, identifying the characters, such as the one the witness had recently referred to as the 'Boss Man'. Ermir Hysenaj was sniggering now at Royle's cocky manner with the judge. But the judge kept his composure and ordered the film replayed. Cross-examined by Royle at the end of the film, Clifton decided that the robber he thought of as 'Boss Man', the one chiefly responsible for his ordeal, was the robber the police called Driver, which meant Royle himself.

'No further questions,' said Stuart Royle, having shot himself in the foot.

This farce contrasted with the sombre and affecting evidence of Securitas supervisor Melanie Sampson, an attractive woman who evidently strove to control her emotions as she told the court about her ordeal. Describing the moment when a robber cut her cable ties, warning that it might hurt, she said with feeling: 'I didn't care if they cut my hands so long as they took them off.' She also said that she feared the gang would kill her. This was powerful evidence delivered by a sympathetic young woman to a predominantly female jury, who appeared to empathize with all she said. Sir John asked what effect all this had had on Miss Sampson. 'Dreadful effects!' she exclaimed. 'I'm suffering from post-traumatic stress disorder and have been since that time. I am [now] unable to work in a job I loved. I am suspicious of police officers, paranoid about security and [have] feelings of great guilt that I allowed myself to be in that position.'

Further strong but more cerebral evidence was given by forensic scientist Catherine Whitmore who explained the basics of DNA evidence, and the process of comparing the DNA of suspects with samples taken from exhibits. Some matches were better than others. For example, Coutts' DNA had been matched to samples on cable ties found in the depot. The chance of the DNA on one particular cable tie *not* being his, or a member of his family, was one in 16 million; while there was a one in a *billion* chance that DNA on another three cable ties was not from Coutts or a relation of his. The scientist said it was reasonable to suppose Coutts' DNA got on the ties because he touched them with his hands or held them in his mouth, as he may have done while tying up the victims.

Coutts was represented by Graham Blower, a large, bluff Northerner with a walrus moustache. He didn't dispute that his client's DNA was on the cable ties, but he got Catherine Whitmore to agree that there were limitations to DNA evidence. For example, a DNA match didn't necessarily mean that the person concerned had any direct contact with the item; the DNA could have been a 'secondary contact', whereby Coutts had touched something or someone who then came into contact with the cable tie, thus passing his DNA on. Also it was not possible to say when the DNA was deposited. It wasn't necessarily on the night of the robbery. In short, although Coutts' DNA was on items left in the depot during the robbery it didn't automatically follow that he had been inside the building.

There was a lot more DNA evidence. Mrs Whitmore told the jury that DNA on the zip pull of a money bag recovered from the Southborough lock-up was a one in a billion match to Coutts; and DNA on the handle of a suitcase found in the Ashford

International Hotel van was a one in 50 million match to
Bucpapa. Again, counsel had little room to argue with the sci-
ence, but reminded the jury of the limitations of the evidence.
The same was true of Rusha's DNA being found around the
mouth of the balaclava in the Ashford van, though in this case the
scientist concerned, Michael Wheelhouse, said it was very
unlikely to be a secondary transfer. There was more bad news for
Rusha when the court heard his DNA was also on drink cans in
the green car with £30,000 in the boot, and his DNA had been
matched to latex scraps in Hogg's bin.

It wasn't long before Royle was on his feet again, complaining. Although the judge was prepared to make allowances for this
difficult defendant, especially so because he was representing himself, and Penry-Davey evidently strove at times not to become
aggravated by Royle's surly manner, there was a limit to how
much insolence he could take. 'If you treat others with a degree
of respect they will respect [you] in the same way,' the judge
rebuked Royle mildly during one tirade. Penry-Davey assured the
defendant he would have access to all the papers he was entitled
to, but everybody would get along better if Royle refrained from
'throwing your weight about'. Alexander Cameron rose to object
about Royle making wild remarks about Fowler in the presence
of the jury. The judge agreed. 'I will not permit this case to
become any sort of demonstration by you,' he told the defendant.

The next day, when the jury were out, Royle took the judge
to task for what he called his 'outburst' yesterday, going on to list
various grievances and demands. Penry-Davey cut him short. 'In
my judgment you are being deliberately obstructive,' he told the
car dealer. 'Will you sit down, please?' Royle remained on his
feet, complaining about this and that until the judge repeated his
request firmly. The men were evidently heading to a showdown.

There was another clash later that day when Royle said he

wanted the prosecution to give him a copy of some CCTV footage. Sir John didn't know what Royle was referring to. The judge said he didn't understand, and indeed it was hard to follow the sense of what Royle was saying. Maybe there was no sense, for he was now laughing and saying: 'I really don't think I can attend court any more.' It was within Justice Penry-Davey's power to compel Royle to come to court, but he chose to warn him simply that, if he didn't, the case would continue without him.

Starting on Monday, 30 July, Royle declined to get into the prison van each morning, telling staff at HMP Belmarsh that he preferred to work on his case in his cell. His solicitor had a clerk in court, so Royle could keep in touch with proceedings. In the circumstances, the judge decided to carry on, and with Royle out of the way the case picked up speed.

Securitas witness Alun Thomas expanded on why he had told the police, in September 2006, that he understood Securitas was 'operating illegally'. He said Colin Dixon had told him that between twenty and thirty million pounds was missing from the company's accounts nationwide. Asked by Graeme Wilson why he told police this Thomas said, 'I believe it might have been a line of enquiry that perhaps [the police] should look at', adding that it crossed his mind the missing money was connected to the robbery. How wasn't explained, but Wilson remarked with heavy emphasis, and one of his sidelong looks, that it did seem something of a 'coincidence' that £30 million was missing from Securitas books prior to the robbery and the same amount was outstanding from the robbery.

This was not total nonsense. Thomas' evidence came at a time when Securitas was telling the financial markets that its UK cash-management division had been overstating the value of cash in its depots. The company declared lower-than-expected earnings in July 2007, and announced it had had to put money aside after

making 'declarations that did not comply fully with note circulation rules in the UK'. The share price fell. By August, the
financial press was reporting that Securitas would have to repay
the Bank of England £15 million to make up for accounting
irregularities, plus the cost of an inquiry. Not long afterwards the
banks who outsourced their cash-handling business to Securitas
in 2001 took back control of cash depots, including Medway
House. Outsourcing cash counting hadn't been a success.

6

Detective Sergeant Andy Nicoll, the first investigation officer on
the scene on the morning after the heist, explained so-called
'dirty phones' to the court, telling the jury that criminals tend not
to use mobile phones registered in their real name when planning
a crime. Instead they buy pay-as-you-go phones for cash, giving
no name or a false name. For example, Murray and Allen bought
two phones from a shop in Bluewater in 2005, giving the name
and address of a person who had nothing to do with them or the
robbery.

Despite such problems, the police had attributed a dozen
mobile numbers to the defendants and their co-conspirators. In
many cases, defendants disputed the phones had ever been theirs,
or only admitted using them some of the time. It was impossible
to say for sure who made the hundreds of phone calls put into
evidence: 350 calls and texts a week on average between the
attributed phones in the weeks leading up to the robbery, rising
to 566 in the last frenetic week of planning. The jury had to
make up their own minds as to who made these calls based on the
evidence.

It was explained that police had found two dirty phones in Lee

Murray's Ferrari, with detectives further discovering that Murray
had apparently recorded himself talking with Rusha on one
phone, between 3.13 and 3.18 p.m. on 11 January 2006. The
five-minute conversation was now played in court, allowing the
jury to hear the voices of Murray and Rusha for the first time,
talking about 'geezers' and 'fings', 'fuckin'' this and 'fuckin'' that.
The phone evidence showed how active Murray was in the conspiracy, according to the police, as well as revealing the pattern of
communication between Murray and the other suspects. There
were two parts to this gang, the London boys and the men from
Kent. It was principally Lee Murray's calls to Rusha that linked
the London axis with their friends in the country. Within these
groups there were individual, apparently exclusive relationships.
Borer only ever spoke to Royle, for example, while Bucpapa had
a virtually exclusive relationship with Hysenaj.

The court heard more about Ermir Hysenaj when the prosecution showed a compilation film of the Albanian at work at
Medway House on 16 January 2006, the day police believe he
filmed the depot with a spy camera in his belt. DC Stewart Catt
was called to tell the jury that, having studied all the CCTV evidence, he could say that Hysenaj's decision to go straight upstairs
to the staff room upon entering the building on 16 January was
unique to that day; as was the fact he wore a belt, and had his
shirt tucked into his jeans in the first part of the evening shift.
These small sartorial details were a crucial part of the Crown's
case against Hysenaj, but in cross-examination Michael
Boardman for Hysenaj showed the court CCTV film of his client
going directly to the staff room upon coming to work on three
more dates, other than 16 January, which Catt had said was the
only occasion he did so. 'I'm not infallible,' the detective conceded. Then Boardman produced CCTV evidence that showed
Hysenaj wearing belts on several days.

'It may possibly be a belt,' said DC Catt, looking uneasily at a still of Hysenaj at work from 4 January 2006.

'What else could it possibly be?' Boardman asked, in his loud voice. 'It's a belt, Mr Catt!'

The officer's assertion that Hysenaj wearing his shirt tucked in, then untucked, was unique to 16 February, was his most important point. The prosecution case was that Hysenaj had his shirt tucked in on this day so as not to obstruct the camera lens, untucking his shirt as normal after he had taken the spy camera off. But Boardman had film of Hysenaj with his shirt tucked in on other occasions in the depot.

Boardman wasn't finished with the witness. If 16 January was the day chosen for Hysenaj's reconnaissance, why did he waste the first seven minutes of his shift by hanging around upstairs in the staff room? DC Catt admitted there was nothing stopping Hysenaj coming downstairs sooner. Boardman established that his client got to the CDP area at 1.54 p.m. on 16 January, which wasn't especially early. The barrister pointed out that Hysenaj wasn't shown on CCTV loitering near the vault or the Control Room, and indeed he seemed to spend a good part of his shift chatting up female staff. And if he was wearing the spy camera he also had to have the bulky recording device and battery pack secreted about his person, yet there were no 'unusual bulges' visible in his clothing on the CCTV. By the time he sat down, Boardman had effectively rubbished DC Catt's evidence, a blow to the prosecution.

7

The jury lost another member during a two-week August break, when a female juror went on holiday and slipped a disc. When the court reconvened, the remaining ten jurors were plunged into a lengthy period of phone evidence, with Murray's name featuring prominently in analysis of the gang's 'dirty phone calls', as Charles Conway described them.

Apart from the recorded conversation with Rusha, police had retrieved text messages from Murray's phones, including two to his friend Roger Coutts, whom Murray called Gurb. Coutts' numbers were programmed into Murray's mobile under that name. Lee also had Coutts' numbers in his address book, which police had recovered in Morocco. In fact, Lee had programmed many mates' names and numbers into his phones, which helped the prosecution establish links between suspects, but you had to decipher the nicknames. Jet and Rush were self-evident. But as Conway asked DS Nicoll, when he was on the stand, 'Who is Brains?' The detective didn't know. Addressing the suggestion that '[Brains] could be the brains in the case', David Jeremy QC for the prosecution pointed out that Murray also had numbers for characters named Titch, Skid and Big Beard. It wasn't possible to say who all these people were. The court did however get a feeling for the sort of man Murray was.

Telephone evidence was voluminous and dull, causing the judge to yawn and at least one defence barrister to fall asleep. The evidence was no less wearing on the ten remaining jurors, one of whom, a young woman who wore revealing tops and changed her hair colour regularly, seemed to have particular difficulty concentrating. This juror was often late for court and was prone to phoning in sick on Monday mornings, which caused everybody else inconvenience. The judge reminded the whole jury to pay attention. 'I've no doubt nearly all of you are doing your best,' he told them in September, refraining from singling anybody out, but making it nonetheless clear that someone wasn't as conscientious as they should be, 'and all of you have the capacity to do that'. He was warning them now, before it became a problem. He didn't want to go down to nine jurors, the minimum number permissible, this far into such a major trial.

Proceedings always livened up when Graeme 'Smoky' Wilson rose to his feet, even in the midst of phone evidence. He had a deliciously mischievous manner when he cross-examined witnesses. Wilson kept asking Crown witnesses, especially police witnesses, difficult questions about characters such as Sean Lupton and Christopher Bowles, who had not been charged, and had not been produced as witnesses in the case, but had evidently been of interest to the police. Wilson pointed out for example that Royle had been in mobile contact with Lupton before and after the robbery. The builder had been questioned by police, and released on bail, after which he had disappeared, and was still a missing person at the time of the trial. 'Would I be right in [suggesting] police believe Mr Lupton is now residing in Northern Cyprus and money from this robbery has ended up in Northern Cyprus?' Wilson asked DS Nicoll one day, when the sergeant was wading through phone evidence.

'I think that some of the money has gone out of this country, yes,' replied the detective. 'We believe that some of it has gone to Northern Cyprus.' Wilson reminded the court that Lupton was an associate of Tony Harun, brother-in-law of the Dixons' babysitter, and pointed out that phone records showed Lupton and Harun in contact before and after the kidnapping. Wilson also said other people in the Whitstable/Herne Bay area had been spoken to by police, including people with links to Northern Cyprus.

Changing direction, Wilson suggested to DS Nicoll that Lee Murray – 'something of a ladies' man' – may have been having an affair with Katie Philp under Lea Rusha's nose at the time of the heist, and that as a result Katie may have used the so-called dirty phone police attributed to Rusha to speak secretly to her lover, thus explaining the calls. 'I do not believe that,' said Nicoll. Wilson further suggested that a reason why Murray may have had 'RUSH' programmed into one of his phones was that he didn't want his wife to know that when 'RUSH' rang it was Katie calling. This provoked snorts of derision from the police officers in court, but Smoky Wilson was content to float the 'possibility'. The barrister then showed how bold he was prepared to be by asking a series of police witnesses whether they or their colleagues had planted evidence in Rusha's house. Unsurprisingly, they all asserted that they hadn't, and didn't know of anybody else planting evidence at Lambersart Close.

Charles Conway made an interesting admission in cross-examination when he said that two phones Jetmir Bucpapa accepted as his had been used by his client not to plan a robbery but to deal drugs, a business he was in along with 'Lupton and Murray and others'. This would be something the court would hear much more about. While his client was apparently happy to be declared a drug dealer, Conway said that Bucpapa maintained he had never acquired the 'mission phone' police ascribed to him, though he may have borrowed the phone to make the odd call. Bucpapa also said he had loaned his phone to Royle on the day the Dixons were kidnapped. So Bucpapa was now apparently implicating Royle, who wasn't in court, having chosen to stay in his cell at Belmarsh.

Hysenaj's position regarding his alleged mission phone was that it had been bought and maybe used by Ermal Kulic, whom Hysenaj described as a friend in his original police interviews. Michael Boardman now said that Kulic was Hysenaj's kid brother (using a false name). This was confusing and possibly meant to be. One got the impression that Hysenaj and Bucpapa were working on the basis that the British would never be able to untangle the curious names and complex relationships of a couple of Albanians.

8

As the months went by a remarkable variety of prosecution witnesses were paraded through Court 8, ranging from Lithuanian car washers to a real-life equivalent to George Bernard Shaw's Professor Higgins, who analysed the speech patterns of the suspects. The jury were also introduced to Securitas executive Tony Benson, who was asked by Sir John Nutting about allegations of illegal activity at Securitas, and missing millions. Benson said he had no knowledge of anything illegal going on in the company, but said that when Securitas Cash Management was formed an audit of money in the depots revealed a £61 million discrepancy in the books.

'Is it proper to call it a loss?'

'We refer to it as an historic variance,' replied Benson, who said it was declared properly in the company accounts.

'Rather than someone trousering sixty-one million quid?' asked Sir John, which prompted the judge to joke that one would need big trousers. While exchanges of this kind raised a chuckle, it was folderol compared to the bombshell that was about to be exploded in Court 8. For the Crown had a sensational surprise – a new star witness.

Chapter Sixteen

THE TURNCOAT

1

Michelle Hogg and Keith Borer were told by the judge at the start of proceedings that they didn't have to attend court when the evidence didn't affect them directly and, as a result, neither defendant was at the Old Bailey every day. When Hogg did attend, she was accompanied by at least one of her parents, sometimes the family friend John Selley, and a solicitor – the latter called upon regularly to escort Michelle to the loo. Apart from her weak bladder, Hogg seemed calmer than at the start of the trial. She chatted amiably with her co-defendants, passing the water jug and bags of sweets in the dock. On Friday, 10 August 2007, she used Ermir Hysenaj's shoulder as a pillow on which to rest her head.

The following Tuesday, after a long weekend, Michelle's barrister William Clegg QC raised a serious matter with the judge. As the court had seen relatively little of Hogg, William Clegg had attended court sporadically, leaving the day-to-day work to his junior. Hogg was, however, fortunate to be represented by Clegg, acknowledged as a 'master of criminal defence', with a reputation for winning acquittals for difficult clients in high-profile cases, notably when he represented Colin Stagg in his 1994 trial for the murder of Rachel Nickell. 'There are lots of cases where the evidence is flawed,' says the barrister, and he had proved the point many times.

A round, red-faced man, with the easy manner of somebody who knows himself on top of his game, Clegg had tried to get Michelle off the hook before the trial started, arguing for a dismissal at a pre-trial hearing. Clegg told the judge that, while his client admitted making up the men accused of the kidnap and robbery, she didn't have any knowledge of what they were going to do, and it wouldn't be logical for the gang to have told her. There was therefore no basis for a charge of conspiracy. The judge ruled against him, saying what was in Hogg's mind was a matter for a jury, and the hairdresser left the court in tears. It had been a good try, though, and as Trial I got under way Clegg won Hogg several small concessions from a judge mindful that the defendant had suffered a nervous breakdown in custody. As noted, Penry-Davey ruled that Hogg didn't have to attend court every day. Family are usually restricted to the public gallery, but in Hogg's case her parents, and John Selley, were permitted to accompany her into the well of the court when she did appear. The Hogg entourage sat next to the dock, collecting Michelle at the end of each session in the manner of anxious parents picking up a child from school. Hogg came and went from the dock in an almost casual manner during hearings, visiting the loo with extraordinary frequency, and due to a panic attack on day one, she wasn't even in the dock when Sir John commenced his opening speech. She sat with Mum in the press seats.

Clegg now informed the judge, in the absence of the jury, that his client had been threatened by her co-defendants in the dock area the previous week. Penry-Davey called Hogg to the witness box to explain herself. Speaking in a trembling voice at first, she told the court that she had been threatened by two defendants on Thursday, 9 August, while they were waiting to be taken into the dock for the afternoon session. Clegg asked his client who threatened her.

'Do I have to name them?'

'Yes, you do.'

'Jetmir and Lea Rusha,' she said, explaining that she was sitting on the stairs that led down to the cells when Bucpapa spoke to her. 'He asked me if I was going to name anybody. I said I wasn't going to name anybody. He said it would be in my main interest not to . . . I interpreted it as a threat.' She claimed Rusha also had a word, telling her, 'That I was to say that the name on the list wasn't him' (a reference to an exhibit document in which the name 'Lil Lee' appeared).

Having entered the witness box, Hogg was liable to being cross-examined by counsel for Bucpapa and Rusha, who suggested that she was not telling the truth, and pointed out that although these alleged conversations had happened on Thursday, Hogg had chosen not to raise the issue with her counsel until after court on Friday. She admitted she had been talking normally with her co-defendants on the Friday, even sharing her water and sweets. 'I have been brought up [to be] polite,' she explained. She agreed she had even rested her head on Hysenaj's shoulder, but insisted that she still felt 'frightened and scared in the dock'. Charles Conway's junior suggested she had been 'laughing and joking' with these people she said she was scared of.

'I've got nothing to laugh and joke about,' she replied, which didn't quite answer the question. Hogg said she wanted to sit outside the dock from now on. Defence counsel were concerned that this was an attempt to distance herself in the eyes of the jury from her co-defendants, even more than she already was. Penry-Davey ruled that Hogg would have to stay in the dock when she attended court, but he wanted the dock officers to separate her from the others.

Not long after this episode William Clegg made an application for further disclosure about three girls who had worked alongside Michelle at Hair Hectik, but were not being called as prosecution witnesses. The application was rejected by Penry-Davey under Public Interest Immunity (PII), the system that allows the Crown to withhold sensitive information from the defence in the public interest. Typically, PII is used to protect informants who give the police vital information on the understanding they will not be identified. Police are extremely reluctant to *burn* informants, in the jargon. If they did reveal their names, others would be less likely to come forward in future. It is for the judge to decide each PII application on its merits and in turning down Clegg's request for more information about Hogg's co-workers Penry-Davey was ruling that aspects of the police investigation should remain secret. It is, however, clear that the police had been tipped off about Hogg by at least one informant. In fact, detectives seem to have benefited from excellent information about the conspiracy, from more than one source, from day one. But the identity of the informants was being kept secret.

Despite the judge's ruling about where Hogg should sit, when court resumed on Wednesday, 3 October 2007, Michelle was sitting outside the dock, in the press seats, with her mother and John Selley, all looking unusually cheerful. William Clegg was also beaming. Something extraordinary had happened. Sir John explained. 'On Friday of last week Mr Clegg [asked] the prosecution as to whether at this late stage the Crown would consider calling Miss Hogg as a prosecution witness and [drop] the case against her,' Sir John told the court. He had discussed the matter with Kent Police, and on Monday he and DCI Judge had gone round the corner to the CPS office in Ludgate Hill to see the Director of Public Prosecutions, who said Hogg could turn Queen's Evidence if she named names, identifying not only the men behind the masks, but others not yet before the court. This was a deal the Crown thought worth doing, with a significant caveat about Miss Hogg, which Sir John gave to the court: 'I emphasize that although she will not face further prosecution, she remains in the eyes of the prosecution an accomplice to these crimes.'

Penry-Davey called the jury in to tell them that, although he could not explain the reason at this stage, he was going to ask them to return not guilty verdicts in Hogg's case 'in the interests of justice'. The hairdresser was asked to stand, as was a member of the jury, who duly pronounced Hogg not guilty of conspiracy to kidnap, rob and possess a firearm. Mick Judge then escorted Hogg from court to give a new statement, which took ten hours.

'Well, that's set the cat among the pigeons!' Sir John remarked outside the court, evidently pleased with his surprise. 'New chapter?' William Clegg asked me with a twinkle. It was a very good result for the defence wizard who'd first approached the prosecution with a view to doing this deal in December 2006, after failing to have the charges against Hogg dropped at the pre-trial hearing. The Crown hadn't taken him up on his offer then, but they had evidently come to the conclusion they needed Hogg to ensure convictions in Trial I, as well as thinking ahead to Trial II. Hogg's evidence against Murray and Allen would be very useful additional ammunition for Nutting.

Hogg's decision to turn QE wasn't good news for the remaining defendants, of course. But there wasn't much reaction from the dock of Court 8; it was as if the boys had been waiting for Hogg to do this. Down in Morocco, Murray and Allen were also sanguine. 'Lee wasn't surprised,' Ben told me on the phone. 'He said he kind of expected it . . . This is part of the corruption of the British system. Paul says he isn't bothered. "She saw me at some meetings. So what?"' In a letter to me some time later, Lee said any jury would have to be brainless to believe Hogg. But the lads were putting a brave face on things. Hogg's decision to change sides had serious consequences for them.

There was also the prospect of Hogg identifying other suspects, who might be charged on the strength of her new statement, and indeed this happened immediately. Michael Demetris was re-arrested at 6.00 p.m. that very afternoon, by DC David Ecuyer. Having been the first suspect arrested at the start of Operation Deliver, way back in February 2006, then released without charge, Demetris was very surprised to have his collar felt again 18 months later. He appeared in court in Maidstone on the Friday charged with conspiracy to rob, kidnap and possess a firearm, and was remanded in custody, later released on bail, with the expectation he would be in Trial II.

While the police obviously wanted to round up more gang members, and Hogg's decision to turn QE helped them, the propriety of a jury being ordered to acquit a defendant against whom they had heard a wealth of evidence, and who the prosecution maintained was an accomplice, was questionable. Some onlookers were left wondering what sort of justice this was.

2

Before Hogg returned to the Old Bailey to give her evidence, Stuart Royle made his first appearance in Court 8 in over two months. In recent weeks the former car dealer had had no legal representation in court, having succeeded in not only sacking his barrister, but also having fallen out with his solicitor. As a result he was hopelessly out of touch with proceedings. This became apparent when he addressed the judge in the absence of the jury on 5 October.

Although he had come to court ostensibly to discuss transcripts of his police interviews, Royle started off by telling His Lordship that he hadn't read the evidence. 'I've not had the time,' he told Penry-Davey.

'You've had a very long time,' replied the judge.

There were other matters Royle wanted to raise, though little he said seemed to have a direct bearing on the case. He made several wild allegations, including telling the judge that John Fowler had once taken a hostage at gunpoint from Wateringbury Car Sales. Royle also made admissions about himself, saying he had been questioned about a robbery on a One Stop shop, and arrested in connection with a stolen Mercedes. He said Sean Lupton was also arrested in connection with this stolen car. When the judge asked Royle why he was raising these issues, the relevance and veracity of which were uncertain, Royle stated that what he was saying was 'exceptionally relevant'. Pressed to explain, he exploded: 'It's quite ridiculous what's going on!' The judge tried to help by asking Royle on what date he claimed to have been arrested about the stolen car. Royle said he didn't know. Nor could he name the arresting officer. In fact, he admitted that when he had raised this matter with his lawyers they told him there was no record of the incident. It was, as he said, as if he was making it all up.

In the midst of this rambling and confusing address, Royle turned to consult Lea Rusha, sitting beside him in the dock, and Rusha told the judge he'd also been arrested regarding a Mercedes, which the police 'took off of me'. Evidently surprised to hear from his client in this way, Graeme Wilson rose hurriedly and told the judge that Rusha appeared to be referring to an

VAULT 2 DOOR - Feb 22 '06 02:01:27

Three robbers are seen in the vault, breaking open cash cages.
Note the different coloured packaging: £10 notes are bundled
up in blue plastic, twenties in red. There was approximately
£200 million in this room.

L BAY 2 VAN - Feb 22 '06 02:05:58

Supermarket sweep: robbers use Sainsbury's shopping trolleys to
wheel money into the lorry.

S&S 1   - Feb 22 '06 02:31:06

At the end of the robbery, the Dixons and depot workers were locked in empty cash cages. Many feared the gang would murder them next.

SERCH BACK - Feb 22 '06 02:42:52

Policeman watches his fellow bandits exit the depot past the wall safes (obscured area) where Colin Dixon stored the keys to the vault. Colin's office is on the right. The toilets are on the left.

Top left: In the first of a series of still images of the robbers in action we see Driver (Royle), with a pump-action shotgun.

Top right: Hi Viz (Bucpapa) guarded Lynn Dixon and her child in the lorry.

Bottom left: The robber police code-named Hoodie is seen carrying a torch.

Bottom right: Mr Average (Coutts) tied up the hostages. He seems to have a cable tie in his right hand.

The only robber not dressed in black was Policeman (top left), whom the real police believe was Keyinde 'Kane' Patterson. Shorty (Rusha) is top right, with an automatic weapon in hand. Left is Stopwatch, whom police believe was Lee Murray, timing the heist with a watch hanging round his neck.

Despite the slickness of the kidnap and robbery, the police soon recovered vital evidence including the red Post Office van, seen here in the car park of the Hook & Hatchet pub at Hucking, Kent. They found the van the day after the robbery, 23 February 2006.

Empty cash cages were found dumped here in a car yard on Friningham Farm, Kent, on the evening of Friday 24 February, 2006.

The day after the robbery Lea Rusha's silver Fiat coupé was caught on CCTV, along with another vehicle, visiting a lock-up garage near Rusha's home in Southborough, Kent. Police found £8.6 million in the garage.

Displayed here is part of the vast haul of Securitas cash Kent Police recovered from the Southborough lock-up associated with Lea Rusha.

12 LAMBERSART CLOSE - SOUTHBOROUGH

LEA RUSHA

Police found masses of evidence at 'Little' Lea Rusha's house in Southborough (pictured). Foolishly, he had left plans to the cash depot in his bedroom. The hapless bank robber is seen here in his custody photo.

33 SHAFTESBURY DRIVE - MAIDSTONE

STUART ROYLE

Looking like he might burst into tears, his dreams of being a millionaire at an end, Stuart 'Slippery' Royle is seen here in his custody photo, after being arrested on Sunday 26 February, 2006. Also shown is his mother's bungalow, which the gang used before the kidnapping and robbery.

Above: Jetmir 'Jet' Bucpapa was arrested with Lea Rusha in London on Monday 27 February, 2006. Jet is seen here in the police station, where he made no comment.

Left: The inside man Ermir Hysenaj was arrested twice before being charged. Here he is in police custody.

This aerial shot of Elderden Farm shows the location of the tree where police found £105,600, also John Fowler's L-shaped house (centre of picture), its swimming pool, tennis court, and outbuildings, including the car yard and the black barn. Hop Engineering operates out of the large sheds in the bottom left hand corner of the picture.

Cash found under a dead tree in Fowler's orchard, packaged in an unusual way.

Detective Chief Inspector Mick Judge, the cheerful officer who led Operation Deliver for Kent Police with mixed results.

EXHIBIT EMF/2

The heist gang were heavily armed, with weapons including this fearsome Skorpian machine pistol, which was found along with £1.3 million in cash in a van at Ashford International Hotel on 24 February, 2006.

The biggest hoard of stolen cash was recovered from a ship container rented by ENR Cars in Welling, south-east London. There was £9.6 million in the container, much of it in bags like this, filled with bundles of £20 notes.

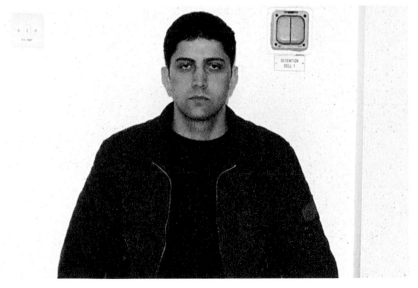

Roger Coutts was in business with the owner of ENR Cars, and parked his boat next to the ship container. Coutts is seen here in custody after his arrest, looking somewhat down in the mouth.

This is the villa Lee Murray bought in Rabat, Morocco, after the robbery. *Inset:* Murray commissioned a mural of his Las Vegas UFC win to decorate his new home.

The living room of Murray's Rabat villa. He spent a small fortune on the house and its décor, including such furnishings as an elephant tusk lamp and harp-shaped bookshelf, but never actually lived here.

Three days after their arrest in Morocco on Sunday 25 June, 2006, Paul Allen (left) and Lee Murray (right), were brought in handcuffs to court in Salé. The court house is adjacent to Salé Prison, the high walls of which are in the background. Allen and Murray were incarcerated in this jail.

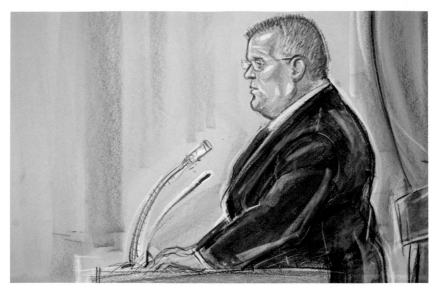

The first major Securitas robbery trial – Trial I – began at the Old Bailey in London in June 2007. Colin Dixon is seen here in an artist's impression giving evidence to the jury. He was a calm and composed witness.

In contrast to her husband, Lynn Dixon was a very emotional witness, breaking down frequently as she gave evidence against the heist gang in Trial I and II.

Royle became more obstreperous as the days passed. On 10 October, he called the judge a 'crook'. Penry-Davey turned a deaf ear. A few days later in the absence of the jury, Royle announced that he believed £2 million of the stolen money had been paid to 'pykeys', and voiced concerns that 'my family is seriously at risk from Mr Fowler and others'. Royle seemed to enjoy himself at times like this, as the star of a show, which he was in a way, but in mid-October he had to relinquish the limelight to another eccentric personality.

Sir John Nutting informed the jury that having been directed by the judge to acquit Michelle Hogg they were about to meet her again as a prosecution witness, even though, in the eyes of the Crown, she 'remains an accomplice'. The jurors smiled. They'd guessed something like this was afoot.

3

Wearing the same ill-fitting black suit she'd had on throughout the trial, and looking as nervous as ever, Michelle took the oath in a shaky, jittery manner on 17 October 2007, before being led through her evidence by Sir John Nutting. She explained that she had been asked by the police to be a prosecution witness when she was first arrested, but hadn't done so on legal advice. Then she had a nervous breakdown. 'Mentally I feel better than I did. I feel stronger and it's the right thing to do.' Sir John asked if she was willing to name the men she'd disguised, and she duly did so saying that, at the invitation of Michael Demetris, she had worked on disguises for Murray, Royle, Rusha and a black man she knew only as Kane, but whom Sir John suggested was Keyinde Patterson. She also named Allen, Coutts, Bucpapa and Philp as accomplices. She said that she hadn't met Shackelton, Millen or Borer.

During this part of her evidence, the court encountered Chelle Hogg, the childlike woman from Shooters Hill of whom so many were fond. She exuded a likeable naïveté. Trying to explain wig-making to the court, she used tissues from the Kleenex box on the stand as a prop, asking the jury timidly, 'Do you know what I mean?' which caused the judge to rebuke her, for witnesses mustn't ask the jury questions. When Penry-Davey admonished Hogg for giving rambling answers, she resorted to one-word replies, in the manner of a child who has taken a telling off to heart. But, just like a child, she soon forgot the admonishment and began prattling away again.

There were chuckles in court as Michelle described her first encounters with Lee Murray, whom she tried to befriend by offering him some of her Hoola-Hoops. She also told the court how she had taken her 'peacock's nose' to his home. When Sir John asked her to explain, Michelle replied artlessly, 'It's just a peacock nose', as if everybody had one. When she said she'd cut up baby bottle teats and her bra to help disguise Kane, Sir John asked in astonishment: 'You used what?'

'I used the straps from my bra . . .'

'What did you do with them?' asked the judge, equally surprised.

'I attached it to Kane, his scalp. It made his eyes slanted.' Everybody in court, save Michelle, laughed. The fact Michelle alone didn't see the joke — she never did — made the moment even funnier, and made her strangely endearing.

When she told the court about a make-up session at her flat on 14 February 2006, Sir John asked if she did anything special on Valentine's Day. 'Nuffink,' she answered sadly. 'I didn't have a Valentine.' Now the court felt sorry for this odd little woman.

Likeable though Hogg was at times like this, she failed to give a plausible answer as to what she thought the disguises she was making were for, and generally seemed only semi-credible as a witness. Defence counsel would surely tear her to pieces, and the formidable Graeme Wilson was first. He made a tactical mistake, however, by asking Hogg if she needed a break before he began. The court was highly amused by her reply. 'I just need a quick wee,' she confided in His Lordship, in the manner of an eight-year-old addressing teacher. '[But] I can hold it a bit longer if you want.'

As it turned out there was a long weekend coming and Wilson had to wait until the following Monday to question the witness properly. When he did so, he made sure the atmosphere in court was less jovial. Warning Hogg to think carefully before she answered, Wilson asked if she maintained she was 'innocent of the crimes that are alleged against you?' Although she had been acquitted, Sir John had made it clear that in the eyes of the Crown Hogg had been an accomplice to kidnap and armed robbery. If she stated that she was innocent Hogg was in danger of committing perjury. 'You can answer, but you don't have to,' the judge advised her. She chose to say she was innocent.

'Do you mean you never knew what you were doing was for the prosecution of crime?'

'I never knew.'

'[But] Sir John told the jury last week that the prosecution [stands] by what they said about you when this case opened . . . Did you know that?'

'I remember Sir John saying I would always be known as an associate. But if I didn't work for Michael Demetris, if I wasn't in his employment, I wouldn't be here now.'

'They are saying you are guilty, in fact.'

'No, I'm not.' Wilson suggested that she was essentially an accomplice who had managed to get off scot-free. She said: 'I was duped by my boss. I didn't know.'

The police had asked her to be a prosecution witness when she was first arrested. Hogg explained her refusal saying she was in shock. 'I had had my whole world turned upside down and inside out because I was employed by Michael Demetris,' she said, beginning to sound less like childlike Chelle, and more like devious Miche, casting all blame onto another. 'That's the sole reason I'm in this disgusting mess.' Wilson suggested she had done a deal, 'because you were desperate to be out of this trial, desperate to avoid conviction . . . and the only way you could guarantee that was by giving evidence for the prosecution'. Hogg said she would have named names in her evidence anyway. Wilson wondered whether that was a truthful remark.

Then he turned to the matter of who 'grassed you up'. Wilson said there were people working at Hair Hectik named Eva, Nina and Maggie; also Demetris' sister Barbara, his cousin Mike and his sister Maria. Hogg mentioned another name, a person called Vasos Kestar. Wilson asked Hogg if these salon workers hadn't been curious as to what she was doing at home for ten days, and wondered whether she had told her colleagues at the salon she was making disguises for 'an inside job'.

'No,' said Hogg.

Wilson asked whether she'd told any of these colleagues that she'd been paid £50,000 for her role in the heist. 'No. I'm in fact still owed seven days' wages off of Michael Demetris.'

The jury was sent out so Wilson could address the judge in less guarded language about the informant who may have 'fingered' Hogg. Wilson and colleagues representing other defendants were particularly interested in a Hair Hectik worker named Nina Francis, who had spoken to detectives. Graeme Blower read an extract from what Francis told the police: 'She [Hogg] told me she was working on masks. She would not give me too much detail, did not trust me fully . . . She was making people look like different people . . . Towards the end she told me less as it got more serious.' This statement seemed to contradict Hogg's account that she 'knew nothing', and defence barristers Blower, Conway and Wilson all wanted Nina Francis called as a witness or, failing that, further disclosure about what she said to police about Michelle Hogg. But Sir John said Nina Francis didn't want to give evidence in court. 'Nina is very scared of the people involved and does not wish to be involved.' Justice Penry-Davey ruled that there would be no further disclosure about this matter.

When the jury returned, Graeme Wilson went through Hogg's police interviews, pointing out discrepancies and inconsistencies in her story. For example, she told police she first realized she had been involved with the gang when she saw reports of the robbery on the BBC News on 22 February 2006, with reference to the gang wearing masks and false facial hair. Wilson asked Hogg if that was correct. She said it was. He pointed out that the media were unaware of the fact the gang wore disguises until the next day, 23 February.

'You are trying to say I'm lying and I'm not.'

'I *am* saying you're lying.'

Wilson reminded Hogg that she told police on 13 July 2006, that 'eight or ten' people came to her flat, whereas she was now saying seven people visited her to do with the disguises. Hogg accused Wilson of nit-picking. 'I'm not a computer, I'm a human being that's suffered a nervous breakdown.' As to what she thought she had been making these masks for, Hogg had told the police and the court different stories at different times: that she knew nothing at all about the purpose of the make-up job; that she thought it was for a party; or a martial-arts video Lee Murray was making; or something to do with a photo shoot. Her story did indeed seem changeable and muddled. When she told Graeme Wilson she had no idea what Demetris and his mates were up to, because 'I was never included in any conversation', one struggled to believe her. After all she had spent many hours, over the course of weeks, with these men in her small flat, in the hair salon, and at Cynthia Royle's bungalow. It was hard to credit that she had not been privy to their scheming.

As to his client, Graeme Wilson suggested to Hogg that she had never met Lea Rusha before this trial. 'That's ridiculous,' retorted Hogg, enjoying her chance to be scornful. 'He must have a twin then, or a complete double.' Wilson asked Hogg what drugs she was on. With a flicker of unease, she admitted using cannabis three times a week at the time of the robbery, sometimes for breakfast, but she didn't smoke dope now. She was on a different drug, anti-depressants. Wilson asked whether Lee Murray supplied her with cannabis.

'No.'

'Are you aware Lee Murray was a drug dealer?'

'No.'

Wilson's relationship with Hogg deteriorated as he went into a second day of cross-examination, and accused her again of lying. Hogg retorted: 'You are just a bully with a wig on!' Wilson *did* come across as a bully, but Hogg seemed to be lying when it suited her. As the barrister continued to put pressure on the witness, Hogg blurted out this excuse for her inability to give a coherent account of events: 'I was in a fragile state of mind [at the time she gave her police interviews] as I am now. You don't like the fact I have told the truth. You are just a bully. Do you get some kind of kick as well? I have been put in this situation because I have worked for Michael Demetris . . . I was not a willing partner in this.' Hogg's voice became louder as she delivered her tirade, and she was almost hysterical at the end, her body trembling, her nose running. Asked by the judge if she would like a break, even though she had only been giving evidence for fifteen minutes, Hogg wailed: 'I just want to get this over and done with.' Then she fled to the loo.

When she returned, Wilson's cross-examination became bogged down in Hogg's reliance on stock answers, invariably throwing the blame onto Demetris, 'an evil man'. Miche accused Wilson of twisting her answers and interrupted him before he could come to the point of questions. When the judge asked her not to do this, she interrupted the judge. She asked to go to the toilet approximately every 45 minutes, made further self-pitying references to her recent nervous breakdown and, without being invited to do so, issued what amounted to positive character references for herself: 'I'm just a normal, law-abiding, creative person,' she told the court, a questionable statement in every respect. Chelle Hogg, who appeared so endearing when examined by Sir John Nutting, was now showing herself up as a most lamentable witness, that is unless she was deliberately trying to hamper cross-examination and confuse the court, in which case Miche was very devious indeed, as Graeme Wilson concluded: 'One thing you certainly are, Miss Hogg, is a liar.'

'How dare you say that!'

It was Stuart Royle's turn to cross-examine Hogg next, at which stage the trial became truly comical. Royle had been attending court regularly over the past week or so, and had calmed down. He seemed to want to deport himself more like a lawyer than a man having a row in the pub. He started his cross-examination of Miss Hogg – as he called her, because, as he explained, they didn't know each other well – by assuring her that he was going to be nice.

'Bless you,' replied Michelle.

The problem was that a lawyer as inexperienced as Royle had difficulty formulating questions the judge would allow, and Hogg could comprehend. 'Can you explain it in Ladybird language, please?' she asked her interrogator. Other questions from the dock were met with a baffled: 'Eh?' Hogg also paid Royle an unexpected and perhaps unwelcome compliment when she told him that the way he had his hair tinted before the robbery suited him. 'It made your eyes look bluer,' she said, 'because you've got young skin.'

'Thank you,' replied Royle, uneasily. This sort of chit-chat didn't do him any good, serving to show how well he and Miss Hogg knew each other. Indeed, he soon lapsed into calling the witness Michelle. That isn't to say theirs was an entirely friendly exchange. In fact, it soon became very nasty. Stuart suggested that Michelle had never been to his mum's house, pointing out that there were many bungalows in Maidstone that looked exactly like 33 Shaftesbury Drive, and she hadn't met him there. 'Bless you, Stuart, but it was that bungalow,' Michelle told him. She remembered clearly that Stuart was there, too. He offered her pizza and a drink. When Royle *insisted* it was not his mum's house, and he hadn't been present, Hogg lost her temper. 'You are absolutely lying, and you are lying by saying the make-up wasn't done at your mum's bungalow.'

The judge urged her to keep cool: 'It is important you just try and remain calm.'

But Hogg was now highly excited. 'The lies that come out of his mouth is just ridiculous!' she said, turning to Royle: 'You must have gremlins talking to you.'

Defendant and witness fell into an argument, talking over each other so much it was virtually impossible to follow what was said. 'I will not have both of you speaking at the same time!' warned the judge.

'I am sorry, My Lord,' said Hogg, 'but he is just talking absolute rubbish. He might as well talk out of his bum!'

'Just behave yourself,' the judge rebuked her.

Royle suggested that Hogg and Murray knew each other very well, so well that Murray's DNA had been found in her bed, as had that of Siobhan Murray. 'What, are you telling me that I have had his wife in my bed as well?' she asked incredulously. (Royle's assertion was based on a misprint in a disclosure document; so-called 'travel DNA' attributed to Lee and Siobhan Lamrani-Murray had been found in Hogg's *bin*, not her bed – in Siobhan's case it was on make-up sponges.) Red in the face now, Royle wound up his cross-examination by telling Hogg that she was a 'drama queen' who was 'involved in this robbery up to your ear'ole [sic]'.

After this squabble, Charles Conway went out of his way to question the witness in a calm, gentlemanly fashion. One of his best points was to ask Hogg why, having a retired policeman as a father, she hadn't gone to the police when she first became suspicious about what she was involved in. 'I was in absolute shock,' was her explanation.

'You weren't too shocked to tear up [and] get rid of evidence.'

Graham Blower took a more direct approach, calling Hogg a liar and asking what she had done with the £50,000 the gang paid her. 'That's absolutely ridiculous,' Miche replied. Another difficult exchange followed between Hogg and Wilson, whom she again accused of being a bully. The exasperated judge banged his hand on his desk, to make her stop interrupting her questioner, causing his clerk to glance up in surprise. Thankfully Hogg was all but finished. Penry-Davey told her she was free to go. 'I'm sorry to be a pain, and keep going to the toilet,' she replied, like a kid again, before walking out of Court 8 into anonymity. Hogg was in the Witness Protection Scheme now, with a new name and a secret address. The police needed to keep her safe and sound until she was called to give evidence in Trial II, against Allen and Murray.

4

With Hogg gone, Royle resumed his grandstanding, complaining about his situation and making all sorts of allegations. He told the court for example that the 'foundation' of the robbery was Lupton's attempt to recover a debt from Terry Lynch. The debt related to the Swiss real-estate scam, which apparently involved a priest. Royle also said there was a £50,000 contract on his life. The judge told him he had no idea what any of this had to do with the case.

More to the point, Royle told the judge that he wanted the Dixons recalled so he could ask them more questions. It was a mark of how far Penry-Davey was prepared to go to accommodate this difficult, unrepresented defendant that he acceded to the recall of Colin Dixon. The cash-depot manager found himself back in Court 8 four months after he had given his evidence just so Royle could ask him whether he was stopped by policemen in a Vauxhall or a Volvo on 21 February 2006. 'I can't remember, but to me, looking back, it does appear to be a Volvo,' said Dixon. This was a small point in Royle's favour, highlighting a disagreement between Dixon and the police who believe the witness was mistaken, and the fake policemen who stopped him were in the Vectra.

Royle's cross-examinations were usually less successful than this. He talked a lot, but much of what he said didn't make sense, partly because he mumbled, apart from when he became angry, when he shouted. He could also be extremely unpleasant, as when he accused a witness of having a prostitute for a sister; the poor woman was in the public gallery at the time. Cross-examining DC Jane Murray, one of the officers who originally interviewed him, Royle asked her whether Lupton and Lynch were police informants. The judge told him he was not permitted to ask such questions. Royle said he believed Lupton was a robber *and* an informant, asking the police witness whether a picture of the robber known as Mr Average was in fact Lupton. The judge told the witness not to answer (which isn't to say anybody seriously thought Lupton was Mr Average, just that the whole area was off limits). Royle complained that if the identities of informants was hidden by Public Interest Immunity his defence was sunk.

The murky subject of PII and police informants came up again when DCI Mick Judge was called as a witness, and Graeme Wilson asked for CCTV from the Ashford International Hotel to be played. The court watched as Christopher Bowles drove his white van into the car park, walked into the lobby of the hotel, paced around, then left by foot, abandoning the vehicle in which the police found £1.3 million and a robbers' kit including a machine gun. Wilson asked DCI Judge: 'It's obvious from the evidence police had information to go to that van?' Penry-Davey intervened to tell Mick Judge not to answer, and reminded Wilson that he had ruled there were some matters that couldn't be gone into in open court. The barrister pushed his luck a little bit further: 'The next question is what was the information?'

'No, don't answer that question,' Penry-Davey told the chief inspector.

DCI Judge was, however, able to confirm that he had 'firm evidence' about money in the van before he sent officers to look in it, and even though they soon linked the van to Bowles it was true that they hadn't raided his home address with armed men. By arrangement with his solicitor, Bowles presented himself at a police station for questioning the next day. He was released that evening without charge. When it emerged that Bowles owned a lock-up, the police took two days to get around to looking in it, eventually searching the judo instructor's house the day after that. All very different to the way the police dealt with Mr Wilson's client, Lea Rusha. The jury were left to work out why.

Regarding the elusive Sean Lupton, Mick Judge said he believed there was a link between Lupton and the white van used to kidnap Colin Dixon, and the Volvo used to kidnap his wife. 'I believe he was involved,' said the detective, agreeing with Graeme Wilson that Lupton may have driven the white kidnap van, and that Lupton's friend Tony Harun was also somebody of interest to them.

Although Lupton was officially still a missing person (with his wife telling journalists she feared he'd been murdered), Mick Judge indicated in court that he believed Lupton was alive and well working as a builder in Northern Cyprus, where it seems some of the proceeds from the robbery had been sent. Several other suspects had links to Cyprus, including two men living in Whitstable: a fish and chip shop owner called Ernie Tevfik and a man named Ersin Katasari. A friend of Lee Murray named Darren Richardson, 'a criminal of some repute', also had links to Cyprus. Richardson was drinking in Tonbridge on the night of the robbery, and he was in Cyprus three days later. Then there was another person of interest on the island named Viv Fonsetta. Kent Police had not enjoyed much success with their enquiries in Cyprus, however, and over the course of the investigation the police had looked at a great many people, the majority of whom hadn't been charged. The detective revealed there were a total of 29 official suspects, including a man named Robert Harriss, who had links to Herne Bay, and who was arrested and questioned about laundering the proceeds of the robbery. 'I suspect he may have been involved,' said DCI Judge, but Harriss had been released without charge, as had several others.

Graham Blower used the opportunity of cross-examining DCI Judge to say that when police searched the home of Derek 'Del Boy' Evans, Nigel Reeve's mechanic at ENR Cars, they'd found £2,000 in consecutive notes which could be traced to the Securitas depot. But before Blower could develop this subject, Sir John Nutting objected on the grounds of the judge's PII ruling, seeming to give a clue that Del Boy might be yet another police informant. As this fascinating subject was ruled off limits, the truth may never be told.

Stuart Royle was also given the opportunity to cross-examine DCI Judge, as well as DS Andy Nicoll, who was called back to answer some final questions on 1 November 2007, having presented masses of phone evidence earlier in the trial. Although Royle had been better behaved during his recent appearances in Court 8, he was particularly boorish this Thursday afternoon, and seemed determined to pick an argument with DS Nicoll, asking belligerently why he had lied in the witness box regarding a phone attributed to Royle, an allegation the officer chose to ignore. As Royle continued to fling accusations about, the judge felt compelled to intervene: 'Mr Royle, this is not the way to adduce evidence.'

'What is evidence?' asked Royle, revealing the depth of his ignorance. 'The law or whatever you call it' was evidently a closed book to him. Rather than try to learn, he again called DS Nicoll a liar. Andy Nicoll was dealing with questions from David Jeremy QC when Royle lost his composure altogether. He stood up in the dock, pointed at the witness, and yelled: 'He's got to stop talking bollocks now!' The judge told him to be quiet. Royle growled back in a threatening manner: 'You are such a crooked judge, I'm telling you, you are getting on my nerves.'

'Mr Royle, if you continue like this, I will have you removed from court.'

'Do that!' snarled the defendant.

In losing his temper Royle showed himself to be an aggressive, menacing, quick-tempered thug, and he stupidly allowed this very unattractive side of himself to slip out while the jury was present, right at the end of the prosecution case. Sir John Nutting rose a few minutes later and told the judge smoothly: 'I must say there were moments in the past four months when I wondered if I would ever say this, but that, My Lord, is the case for the prosecution.'

Chapter Seventeen

GUILTY OR NOT GUILTY?

1

It was time to hear the case for the defence. First up was Lea Rusha, who swaggered to the witness stand like a Kentish Al Capone on 5 November 2007. After 21 months in custody, Rusha's skin was prison-pale, but he was slimmer than the flabby boozer who fought at the Circus Tavern all that time ago and, more recently, posed for police mug shots. He was also smartly dressed in a grey suit and open-neck shirt, his hair short and greased back. He looked sharp. Still, Rusha was hardly a gentleman, as his barrister made clear.

'It's right to say you are not a person of good character, are you?' Graeme Wilson asked his witness.

'That's correct.'

Leaving aside matters Wilson considered too petty to bother the court with, he informed the jury that Rusha had convictions for GBH, shoplifting, common assault, drink-driving and affray. He had been in prison several times. Rusha picked up the story, telling the court that during one of these custodial sentences he'd resolved to channel his aggression into martial arts, claiming that, in his prime, he was one of the top three fighters in his weight in the country. He'd met Lee Murray and Paul Allen through martial arts. 'Any other activity you became involved in with Murray and Allen?' asked Wilson.

'Yes, cannabis dealing, [with] Mr Bucpapa.'

This was a central plank of the defence of both Rusha and Bucpapa. The friends claimed to be involved with Murray, Allen and others in dealing 'weed' or 'puff' as Lea called cannabis. This was their explanation for the network of calls between their mobile phones. In short, Rusha was admitting to being a professional criminal, but seeking to persuade the jury that he was a crook who drew the line at kidnap and robbery. He certainly deported himself like a professional criminal in the dock, exhibiting the *sang-froid* of a man who breaks the law for a living and is prepared for the consequences.

Rusha said he became involved in dealing cannabis with Murray eight months before the robbery. He'd quit his roofing job to spend more time training, and decided to supplement his income dealing weed, as well as doing driving work for Stuart Royle. He shared these little driving jobs with Bucpapa. That's how Lea and Jet knew Royle. As to the other defendants and suspects, Rusha had met Fowler half a dozen times in connection with the car lot, and had been to Elderden Farm. (The jury had heard that Rusha's DNA had been found on Red Bull drink cans at the farm.) Prior to the case, the former roofer said he'd never met Coutts, Hysenaj, Hogg, Borer or Keyinde Patterson. He knew Raluca Millen as Jet's girlfriend.

Regarding Katie Philp, Lea said they'd had a good relationship for several years, but were going through a rough patch prior to February 2006. 'We wasn't getting on. We was rowing.' Since being arrested, Kate had ignored his letters and telephone calls. He now believed she'd been conducting affairs behind his back with two men, one of whom was Lee Murray. This was another plank of Rusha's defence: he asserted that the dirty phone attributed to him could have been Katie's phone, used by her to arrange her affair with Murray. He was turning on Kate to save himself. His explanation for his DNA being on latex scraps in Michelle Hogg's bin was that he'd been in contact with Katie's make-up, thus implying she might have been involved in the conspiracy.

Rusha had no compunction about turning on Lee Murray either. He portrayed Lee as a notorious drug dealer. 'How did you find out Mr Murray was involved in cannabis dealing?' Wilson asked his client.

'I think it was general knowledge. Everybody knew.'

Rusha said he bought his puff from Murray, who, along with his right-hand man Allen, had three or four delivery guys working for him. Rusha said one of these drug mules was Michael Demetris. The weed was delivered to Rusha by runners at a wholesale rate of £800-per-kilo. Rusha met his customers in pubs and at a golf course in the Maidstone area. He sold the weed at a 100 per cent mark-up, earning £800-a-week in the process. He said that £1,500 in cash police found at his house was money he'd earned from drug dealing.

Rusha admitted visiting Herne Bay on 31 January 2006, with Raluca Millen. He said the trip was to do with money Royle claimed he was owed by Terry Lynch. Royle and Lupton were trying to find Lynch, and had information he was staying in a house in Tyne Park, Herne Bay, owned by a man named Paul Smith. Rusha told the court that Lupton asked him to go down to see if Lynch or his wife were at the address. Rusha told Lupton he didn't know what Lynch's wife looked like, so Lupton gave him a shoulder bag with a spy camera in it to film whoever came to the door. 'It was explained to me that it was a "man bag", but

I didn't feel very comfortable carrying a bag. I thought it was a bit poofy.' Before setting off for the coast Lea met Jet and Raluca in a coffee shop and asked if Raluca would come with him to knock on the door. She agreed and they drove down in Jet's VW. Rusha's Fiat was playing up.

Lea said he knew the address they were going to was supposed to be a cul-de-sac, but there was no close in Herne Bay called Tyne Park. There was a Tyndale Park, a regular through road, next to which was a dead end called Hadleigh Gardens. Figuring this was the place, Rusha parked up and Millen knocked at number 16 with the spy bag. When there was no answer (the court had of course seen the film) she came back to the car. Rusha kept the bag and the spy equipment thinking he might try again later. The equipment had been found at his home.

Rusha said Lupton asked him if he knew of a lock-up in the Tonbridge area. Rusha's cousin, Jason, had just such a place in Castle Street, Southborough, and Lea had the key. 'I met a couple of [Lupton's] associates. Took them to the garage complex. They said the garage would be just what they wanted.' This was the garage in which police found £8.6 million.

Rusha said the person speaking on the phone with Murray about 'geezers' and 'tools' wasn't him. Something else he had to explain was his DNA being in the white van found at Ashford International Hotel. Rusha claimed his judo coach Christopher Bowles was involved in cannabis dealing. He said Bowles called him to ask a favour. The Olympian wanted Rusha and Bucpapa to come with him as back-up to the Bishop's Oak pub in Tonbridge to see a man who'd 'started on' his daughter. When Bowles had given this man a talking to, he brought up the subject of cannabis. 'He said in the next few days he'd be getting a delivery of weed and, if I wanted some, to contact him . . . he had a sample in his van.' Bowles, Rusha and Bucpapa all went to inspect the weed. 'Me and Bucpapa and him got in the back of the van . . . We was looking at weed. Didn't want to arouse suspicion.'

Lea said his problems with Kate came to a head on the eve of the robbery. She didn't come home on the night of 19 February 2006, and when she did roll in at eight o'clock the next morning they had a row. 'I told her to pack her things and get out.' Having thrown his girlfriend out, Rusha went to the pub and got drunk. He had a hangover on 21 February, and may have gone back to the pub for a hair of the dog. Katie returned home at 6.30. 'We tried to talk things through. Wasn't really going too well. We started rowing again.' They ordered a take-away from the La Lipu Cuisine restaurant: chicken vindaloo with Bombay potatoes for Lea, chicken biriyani for Kate. After the meal, Katie went upstairs and Lea watched a DVD of *Big Momma's House*.* He went to bed at midnight, waking the next morning at eight. This was his alibi for the night of the kidnap and robbery.

Rusha admitted he had visited his cousin's lock-up the day after the robbery. He said Lupton's friends wanted to store some things and he was helping them, even though he didn't know their names. Graeme Wilson then invited his client to explain the plans to Medway House which police had found in his bedroom. Lea said that he used to drive the cars on Stuart Royle's lot, one of which was a Mercedes. When he opened the boot of the Mercedes there was a black bag inside with a roll of paper. Under the bag were two smaller pieces of paper with drawings on. 'I thought they was just building plans.' Lea wanted to clear out the boot to make room for his sports bag. So he removed the black

---

*Was Rusha having a joke with the court? The plot of *Big Momma's House* involves an FBI agent who uses a prosthetic disguise to go undercover.

bag, put the pieces of paper in his jeans pocket, and stored the roll of paper in his shed. He didn't notice that this was a roll of vinyl printed with the word 'POLICE'.

Wilson asked how the smaller pieces of paper got from Lea's pocket to behind the chair in his bedroom. 'My only explanation is when I took off my jeans [and put them] on the chair, they fell out of my pocket and went behind the chair.' As to who had use of the Mercedes before him, he said it could have included Royle and Lupton. Rusha said the handwriting on the plans wasn't his, and he denied making cable ties into handcuffs, as had been found at Lambersart Close. Indeed, police had found several items at Lea's address which he denied knowledge of, including shotgun cartridges and an air pistol. He also claimed to know nothing about the shotguns in the Castle Street lock-up. As for the balaclavas police had found, Lea said he wore them for motorcycling. He explained away the Post Office gear in his shed saying he used a postman's sack to store fishing tackle.

Dealing with the aftermath of the robbery, Rusha said he and Bucpapa drove to Barking in Essex on 25 February 2006, to collect drug money, then went to a car auction in Deptford. Afterwards they drove down to Kent, where they picked up a VW Beetle from Royle's yard, before returning to London. When Bucpapa tried to ring his wife he couldn't reach her, so he phoned a friend named Eddie who went round to the Hadlow Road flat to see whether Rebecca was home. Eddie reported that Rebecca's car was outside the flat, but the place was swarming with police. 'Automatic thought was he'd been raided for cannabis.' So Rusha asked Eddie to check his house. It was the same story. Deciding it wasn't safe to go home, Lea and Jet booked into the Premier Lodge in Barking. The next day they visited Jet's sister in Deptford. 'She told us she had received a phone call from Rebecca and she said the police had come to the house about the Tonbridge robbery.'

'What was your reaction?' asked Wilson.

'Surprise. Shock,' said Rusha, without feeling. 'Didn't know what to think really.'

They decided to book back into the Premier Lodge. Monday morning they met a solicitor, after which they drove to Deptford to tell Jet's sister they were going to the police. As they approached her flat, they were arrested. Lea had been in custody ever since, a Category-A prisoner, as Wilson told the jury, apparently hoping for sympathy.

'I think I'm Double Category-A,' Rusha piped up with pride.

2

Stuart Royle should have cross-examined Rusha at this stage, but when he failed to show up in court, Justice Penry-Davey invited Sir John Nutting to carry on. It would be hard to imagine two such different characters as the aristocratic Queen's Counsel and the young roofer. Rusha was apparently one of the weakest links in the gang, stupidly leaving evidence for the police to find. The expectation was that the barrister would make short work of the witness. That wasn't how it turned out.

'Let me see if I understand your case correctly,' Sir John began, with a slightly sarcastic tone. Rusha maintained that Michelle Hogg was lying in her evidence; he had no idea his partner Katie Philp was buying prosthetic materials; and he argued that the billion to one match of his DNA to the latex at Hogg's flat implicating him in the heist was 'a cruel twist of bad luck'. There were more such twists. 'Quite accidentally you pocketed plans of the depot.' The plans just happened to fall out of his jeans, lodging themselves behind a chair in his bedroom where the police found them. The fact his DNA was on a balaclava in the white van along with the robbers' kit and stolen money was yet another piece of bad luck, but not the last. 'By a different and terrible coincidence you visited an address on 31 January in Herne Bay on a debt-collecting errand . . . nearby which chanced to be the house belonging to the people you would find yourself later charged with kidnapping . . . That's your case?'

'Yes,' replied Rusha, patiently.

Not only was Rusha saying he had nothing to do with the heist, but others were framing him for the job, and were willing to sacrifice large sums of the stolen cash to incriminate him. 'Some mischievous individual left behind in a lock-up garage, to which you had access, £8.6 million to provide a link between you and this robbery?'

'It's a possibility, yes.'

Pausing for dramatic effect, Sir John asked the witness, 'Do you, as a human being, normally suffer from bad luck?'

'I think in this case, if it wasn't for bad luck, I wouldn't have any!' returned Rusha brightly, bearing up well. As his inquisitor became excited, and tended towards theatricality in his rhetoric and body language, Rusha remained calm, standing still with his hands folded, regarding Sir John with mild amusement. When the sexagenarian, in one of his senior moments – getting 'more senior every day' as he joked – addressed the witness as 'Mr Murray', Rusha smiled indulgently. Sir John made this gaffe more than once, betraying a subconscious desire, perhaps, to have Murray on trial rather than his alleged lieutenant.

Sir John's mind was also on another missing suspect. 'There is a bucket of evidence Paul Allen is also involved in the Securitas robbery, isn't there?' he asked Rusha rhetorically. The witness muttered a noncommittal reply.

The QC went over the evidence the police had against Rusha, including for example the media centre from the spying trip to

Herne Bay recovered from his bedroom. When Nutting suggested he hadn't used it on a debt-collecting errand, but in order to spy on the Dixons, Rusha said: 'You would have to be the most stupid person in the world to do that.'

Sir John pointed out that this wasn't the end of Rusha's stupidity. 'You had the plans in your house!' he cried, hugging his sides with glee. 'You had the plans!'

'Sir John, with all due respect, why would I be leaving things around my house if I was part of the robbery? I would have to be off my nut.'

Cutting to the chase Sir John asked, 'You, Mr Rusha, were one of the policemen, weren't you?'

'You're wrong.'

While one had to admire Rusha's composure under fire, as the hours ticked by it became increasingly apparent that this wasn't the performance of an innocent man unjustly accused of serious crimes. It was the stoicism of a professional crook who didn't want to lose face in front of his mates. At the same time, Rusha had no scruples about betraying some suspects, notably Lee Murray. 'I believe he's conspired with Lupton and others to do this robbery,' Rusha told the court, 'not only to pull off a robbery, but implicate other people to make good his getaway.' The ex-roofer suggested that evidence had been planted on him to give Murray time to make his escape to the continent. He also repeatedly blackened the name of Christopher Bowles, whom he suggested was the robber known as 'Shorty', remarking bitterly that Bowles was 'the one with one and a half million pounds [in his van] who isn't even here'.

Because Graeme Wilson didn't call any witnesses in Rusha's defence, the time soon came to hear evidence from the next defendant on the indictments, Stuart Royle. But Royle wasn't in court. Justice Penry-Davey wrote to Belmarsh to warn Royle that unless he came to the Old Bailey he would lose the right to give evidence or call witnesses. When Royle didn't show his face, the trial moved to its conclusion without him.

3

Jetmir Bucpapa said virtually nothing in his police interviews, so when he came to give evidence in his defence it was the first time anybody in court save his legal team had heard his story in his own words. Like Rusha, Bucpapa was prison-pale, with short, slicked-back hair, wearing an open-neck shirt and blue suit. Bucpapa evidently felt women liked him, and he simpered and smirked at the ladies of the jury as if they would fall for his charms.

The Albanian was a man without previous convictions in the UK or Albania, as Charles Conway told the court, but his defence rested on the argument that he had been dealing drugs with Rusha, Murray and others. It also served Bucpapa's purposes to say that he had worked with Rusha doing driving jobs for Royle. He claimed to have met Ermir Hysenaj early in 2005 when Ermal Kulic introduced them as fellow Albanians in Costa's coffee shop. Bucpapa told the court he dealt cannabis with Kulic and Hysenaj. He never asked where the latter worked. Another chance meeting in Costa's led to his girlfriend Raluca going with Lea Rusha to Herne Bay on a debt-collecting errand. 'I didn't think nothing of it,' said Bucpapa, who lent them his car.

Jet admitted to driving to Sheffield for Lee Murray on 6 February, 2006; the Crown's suggestion was that he was picking up a police scanner from a firm called Radio Swap. Bucpapa said he didn't know what exactly the errand was about. Lee had asked him to lend a car to a mate Bucpapa now knew to be Scott

Needham (an alias for Mark Scott, as the court had heard). He said he met the man at 'Paul Allen's pub', the Forester's Arms in Welling. Bucpapa knew the pub because he dealt cannabis locally. When he smelt alcohol on Needham's breath he decided not to let him drive the car, but chauffeured him to Sheffield. He waited while Needham picked up whatever it was Murray wanted, and they brought the package back to London. Jet said he'd also undertaken an errand to Herne Bay at Murray's request, in the early hours of 19 February, or thereabouts, to pick up another mysterious parcel.

Obliging fellow that he was, Jet had gone with Lea Rusha to back up Christopher Bowles when Bowles' daughter got into an altercation in a pub. Afterwards, Rusha and Bucpapa went with the judo instructor to his van to look at cannabis. This was the same story Rusha had told the court in his evidence, as an explanation of why his DNA was in the van, but their stories weren't consistent. Rusha said they all got *inside* the van; Bucpapa said Rusha 'sat on the side of it [and] I sat on the side next to the passenger seat'.

Getting onto the events of the evening of 21 February 2006, the kidnap day, Bucpapa's alibi involved a motoring tour of London and Kent, via two car washes, a car auction, a pub and a car repair garage. He didn't remember the full names of most of the people he met. When he got home about 10.30 that night, his wife Rebecca was asleep. He claimed he went to bed, waking up at 7.30 a.m. on 22 February. The prosecution case was that Bucpapa was up all night robbing Medway House, as Hi Viz. Part of the evidence against him was that a reflective tabard had been found at Rusha's house with the name 'JET' printed on it. 'Who in their right mind would wear a vest with their name on it in a robbery?' the Albanian asked the court. 'I played no part in this alleged conspiracy in any way, shape or form.'

David Jeremy cross-examined Bucpapa for the prosecution and the QC soon got the better of the Albanian. 'Have you ever been to South Africa?' was his first question, to which the answer was no, but the jury was reminded of Mrs Dixon's evidence that one of the robbers had a South African-sounding accent. Bucpapa's accent could be thought of in that way. The prosecutor then suggested that Bucpapa provided the heist gang with its inside man, his friend Ermir Hysenaj. 'That is absolute rubbish,' said Bucpapa, who unlike Rusha became easily excited when accused.

'Like the rest of the case?'

'You just answered your own question,' sneered Bucpapa, launching into a resentful speech about how the case against him was 'an absolute joke'; he complained that he had spent months in prison 'for a crime I didn't commit'; his wife had been dragged from her bed by police, and had been in and out of hospital 'because of this'; while his mistress had been charged simply for knocking on someone's door; whereas Bowles, whom he believed was part of the conspiracy, hadn't been charged. It was a joke!

'Do you really believe what you are saying or are you just acting?' asked David Jeremy quietly.

'That's the truth . . . I am telling the truth!'

The QC made full use of Bucpapa's admission that he was a drug dealer. 'Your case is you are a criminal, isn't it?'

'I'm not a criminal.'

'You keep forgetting your defence,' said Jeremy. 'You *are* a criminal.' The QC pointed out that the amount of drugs the Albanian admitted to dealing was substantial. 'You are not about the social end of the joint market . . . You are dealing with criminals. This is your world.'

'I sold cannabis, yes, but I'm not an armed robber.'

'When you are drug dealing, you avoid using phones that are traceable to you?'

'Yes, of course,' replied Bucpapa, blithely admitting using dirty phones in the exact way the Crown said the heist gang had.

As Bucpapa fenced ineptly with Jeremy, he became increasingly bad-tempered and tried to deflect attention away from himself, onto the likes of Bowles and Lupton, complaining, 'I've been stitched up in this case.' David Jeremy asked: 'Are you prepared to turn on each other to save your own skins?' When Bucpapa complained again about the effects of all this on his family, Jeremy begged the Albanian to spare the court his hypocrisy, and issued a sobering reminder that the Crown's case was that *he* was the robber Lynn Dixon feared was going to shoot her and her child dead.

Towards the end of cross-examination, the QC returned to Bucpapa's alibi for the evening of 21 February, which involved meeting a cousin named Esmir Demaliaj at a car wash in Aylesford, Kent, and a Kosovan called Xhevdet Bajrami at a car wash in Deptford. The second man, who went by the English name Brian, was listed as a defence witness. Jeremy asked Bucpapa if he had been in contact with Brian since his arrest, or whether he'd asked Rebecca to contact Brian. Jet said he'd written to Brian to ask him to speak to his solicitor, but not the police. He couldn't remember what he'd said to his wife on the subject. Jeremy then played the court a tape recording of a phone call Jet had made from prison to his wife. Rebecca was heard telling Jet that police had been to see Esmir and, when Esmir refused to open the door to them, they shouted through his letter box that they would offer him £1 million for information (possibly a mangled version of the £2 million reward for information). 'They are desperate, the coppers, they haven't got fuck all,' Jet told her on the phone. 'You really need to speak to Brian as well . . . They are playing dirty now.' Rebecca assured her husband that she'd told Brian not to speak to the police. Showing herself to be a loyal wife in the mould of Siobhan Lamrani-Murray, she told Jet: 'You are there for other people's mistakes.'

'Pricks. Fuckin' wankers,' he cursed. 'Just ignore them completely. Don't tell them nothing.'

'Nothing can be in a good way, can it, so they are going to put it in a bad way.'

'They can't fuckin' tie me up for this, you know what I mean.'

'No, of course they can't.'

'They don't like losing,' concluded Jet, before bidding his wife goodnight: 'I will ring you tomorrow, Princess.'

When the tape was over, and Bucpapa had confirmed he and his wife were talking about Brian Bajrami, David Jeremy told the defendant that his alibi was false and he now had three options: one, he could call Brian and Rebecca to give evidence, but that would mean them perjuring themselves 'to save your neck'; two, he wouldn't call either witness, and the court would know why; while option three was to change his plea to guilty. An indignant Bucpapa accused Jeremy in reply of ruining his life and his marriage. That was the end of his evidence. 'Bunch of fuckin' wankers!' he cursed under his breath as he walked past me back to the dock.

Charles Conway called Esmir Demaliaj whom Bucpapa claimed to have seen at the Aylesford car wash on 21 February 2006. Esmir complained to the court about the police hounding him for information, saying that a detective had indeed offered him a million pounds, 'if I told them all they wanted [about Jet]'. The detective came to court and denied this. Be that as it may, when David Jeremy asked Demaliaj the key question: 'Do you remember seeing Jetmir [at the car wash] on the evening of 21 February?' the witness replied, 'No.' So he was useless as an alibi.

Rebecca Bucpapa was an attractive, articulate and admirably calm witness. Indeed, one wondered why she remained married to Jetmir. Despite having discovered that her husband was a drug

dealer and an adulterer, one accused of kidnap and armed robbery, she was standing by him. But she didn't give Jet an alibi.
The best she could say in her husband's defence was that she went
to bed alone about 10.00 p.m. on 21 February 2006, and Jet was
next to her when she woke up the next morning. She said they
spent the following night together. They ate pizza and she
watched *Desperate Housewives*. Thursday they went out for a drink
with Lea Rusha and Katie Philp. Rebecca remembered telling Jet
it was about time he got a proper job. Friday night she cooked
chilli con carne. The last time she had seen her husband before
his arrest was when she got up for work on Saturday, 25 February.
David Jeremy said this wasn't what Rebecca told the police in her
two witness statements. In her 25 February statement she said the
last time she saw Jet was Thursday morning; in her second statement she said she'd last seen him Thursday night. Now she
claimed they last laid eyes on each other Saturday morning.
Jeremy suggested she was adapting her evidence to fit what Jet
wanted her to say. 'You are being a loyal wife to your husband,
is that correct?'

'I consider myself a loyal wife.'

'To the extent you would improve on your memory to have him
staying with you if necessary [when you knew he was on the run]?'

'Not that loyal.'

Rebecca complained about the way she was treated by the
police who raided her house on the Saturday, and gave a weak
explanation for why she didn't telephone Jet right away to ask
him why armed police were at their flat. She claimed she was too
upset to find his phone number until the Sunday. When she did
talk to Jet, she agreed he should stay away from home until he
had taken legal advice (rather than coming straight home and
talking to police, as Jeremy suggested an innocent person would).

When Brian Bajrami was called to the stand, he at least gave

Jetmir an alibi. He said he'd been with Jet in London at about
7.00 p.m. on 21 February. But unlike Mrs Bucpapa, Brian was an
unattractive witness: a tetchy little man who, as the court heard,
had collected convictions for shoplifting and criminal damage
during the short time he had been in the UK.

4

Slim and fresh-faced, Roger Coutts projected a youthful, even
innocent appearance on the stand. But his barrister Graham
Blower began by coming clean with the jury regarding his client's
previous convictions, relatively minor matters in Roger's case, but
a record that showed him to be, like many of the men in the case,
someone who couldn't stay out of trouble. He'd even managed to
pick up a conviction for affray while on bail for the robbery.

Roger denied knowing any of his co-defendants prior to the
case, though he admitted having seen Michelle Hogg when he
went to Hair Hectik to get his hair cut; and, yes, he'd grown up
with Lee Murray. Naturally he also knew Paul Allen. Shortly
before the heist, Murray brought the red van to him to check
over at Northfleet Transit, after apparently taking possession of it
in exchange for money he was owed. This explained why Coutts'
DNA was in the kidnap vehicle. Asked by his brief whether he
had touched or made the cable-tie handcuffs recovered from
Medway House, and whether he left £9.6 million at ENR Cars,
Coutts said: 'No, I never.'

'Who do you think could have put the money there?'

'I think Mr Evans* put the money there,' answered Coutts,

---

*Nigel Reeve's employee at ENR.

who in common with his co-defendants tried to cast the blame onto others whenever possible. He said for instance that prior to the robbery his business partner, Nigel Reeve, had debts he couldn't pay. Since the heist, Reeve had bought two new properties in Spain, and a Mercedes.

Roger couldn't explain why his DNA was on a money bag found in the Southborough lock-up. He said he had a balaclava for paintballing. He'd never been to Michelle Hogg's apartment, and an explanation for him being cell-sited at or near her address could be that his Mum, Nan, and several friends lived in the area.

He said he had a mobile phone with a number ending 812 until January 2006 when he and an employee named Kevin Robinson went to Cyprus to look at property. Despite owing the taxman more than £5,000, Coutts was looking for a holiday home. He said he could afford one. He had £29,000 in the bank when he was arrested. For reasons that were hard to understand, when he returned from Cyprus, Coutts put his 812 sim card in the phone of another Northfleet Transit employee, Hussein Basar (brother of Mus), who Coutts said worked for Lee Murray as a drug runner. 'Mr Basar holds thousands of pounds' worth of drugs for [Murray],' he said, adding that Basar used the 812 phone as 'a drug line'.

Coutts said he had gone with Hussein Basar to Herne Bay on 7 February 2006, to pick up an illicit consignment of cigarettes, thus explaining why the 812 phone was cell-sited in the vicinity of Colin Dixon's home. He also went to Herne Bay with Basar in order to sell the *Shakey Jakey*. Furthermore, Basar was with Coutts when they drove a van down to Kent to pick up stolen gym equipment for Murray, thus explaining why the 812 phone was cell-sited near Redpits in January 2006. Coutts' explanation for being cell-sited in Tonbridge on the kidnap day stretched credibility: he said he was shopping for a ski jacket for his forthcoming holiday. Again, Hussein Basar was with him.

David Jeremy QC asked Coutts in cross-examination where
Hussein Basar was now. He hadn't been called as a witness. 'Mr
Basar fled to Northern Cyprus, because he knew he was wanted,'
replied the garage owner, 'and his brother's been released from
Morocco and he's fled there with him.' (The background to this
was that Mus Basar and Gary Armitage, who had been lan-
guishing in Morocco since serving their prison sentences
alongside Murray and Allen, had finally been given their passports
back and, although their fines had still not been paid, their
Moroccan lawyer, Ben, obtained permission for them to leave the
country. On 27 October 2007, Gary flew to Paris, where friends
picked him up and drove him into the UK. He was arrested at
Dover on warrants for unrelated matters. Mus flew to Turkey,
crossing to Northern Cyprus shortly thereafter, where Kent
Police believed Sean Lupton was hiding out. Now Coutts was
saying Hussein Basar was there, too.)

'I've been caught up in this because of who I know,' Coutts
told David Jeremy QC, referring to Lee Murray who, he
believed, was behind the Tonbridge robbery. He said that,
although he had grown up with Lee, he hated him now. By
asking him to service the red van, Lee had incriminated him. 'He
ain't used his brain. He isn't the cleverest person you will meet,'
said Roger, adding that Lee 'had his bad side'. The prosecutor
invited Coutts to elaborate. 'He is a well-known drug dealer
around that area. The police know him. He drives all the flash
cars around there. That's Mr Murray. He shows off.'

'He's a gangster, isn't he?' asked David Jeremy.

'You could say that, yes.'

Coutts said he and Lee had been on holiday together before
the robbery, and he had wanted to buy Lee's house. That was the
reason for all the calls between them. There were structural
problems with the house, however. 'His 'ouse was falling down.'

One got the impression that Roger thought his old friend an idiot, and wished he'd never met him. 'All he knows about is fighting,' he said. 'He *was* my friend. [But] no friend puts you in that situation,' adding that an armed man had recently threatened Nicholas Coutts with the words: 'Tell your brother to keep his mouth shut.' The implication was that Murray was behind the threat. (Murray's reaction to Roger talking about him in court in this way was surprising: in correspondence with me he raged against those who turned on him in their evidence, calling them rats, except Coutts, whom he forgave, telling me that Roger was 'an exception').

Regarding Michelle Hogg's evidence, Roger Coutts said she had told lies throughout her evidence, noting philosophically: 'The gewl done what she had to do to get off.' Finally, David Jeremy said that Coutts had been undone by a 'simple little mistake': handling the cable ties with his bare hands before putting on his gloves for the robbery. Coutts agreed that his DNA was on the cable ties, but said that he hadn't touched them.

5

John Fowler chose not to go into the witness box. He remained sitting in the dock, dressed smartly in suit and tie as he was every day, as Alexander Cameron QC produced a series of witnesses to attest that they had been in or around Elderden Farm on 21 February 2006, but hadn't seen anything unusual.

These witnesses included Brian Thompson who'd come to the house around 7.00 p.m. to fix a computer, and had seen Mr and Mrs Fowler and their children in the kitchen. Another man called at 9.15 p.m. regarding cars. Neither saw anything odd. Nor had Miles Redding, Finance Director of Netbox5, who told the court he had been working until 10.00 o'clock in his office in Elderden Barn, adjacent to Fowler's yard. His office window overlooked Fowler's yard, yet he heard 'nothing out of the ordinary'. Nor had he seen anything untoward. It emerged during cross-examination that his office window was glazed with frosted glass, his blinds would have been closed and Redding's desk faced away from the window. Nevertheless this was the strongest part of Fowler's defence, which was dealt with in half a day.

6

Michael Boardman called Ermir Hysenaj to the stand. The Albanian made a good first impression. Smartly dressed, he spoke clearly and confidently with occasional idiomatic mistakes which were endearing, such as his comment to David Jeremy: 'you say the whole point of the dirty phones is to do with the dirty talking'. He said he had liked his colleagues at Medway House, but made it plain that he didn't think highly of the company Securitas. They paid 'rubbish' money to agency staff such as himself, then 'very kindly took the lunch hour away'.

He told the court about the life young Albanians live in the UK, most of them entering Britain illegally under false names, typically posing as Kosovan refugees, then finding low-paid jobs and rented flats in such homely places as Gravesend, Hastings and Tunbridge Wells. This was Ermir's story, as it was the experience of his cousin, Elvis Hysenai (as his surname was taken down by immigration officials), who also worked at Medway House prior to the robbery.

Ermir explained his network of friends, few of whom seemed to be the people they presented themselves as. They included Ermal Kulic, whom Ermir first described to police as a friend and now said was his brother. Kulic was a false name. Ermal Hysenaj as he was properly called arrived in the UK illegally aged fifteen, lying to the authorities that he was a 14-year-old Kosovan refugee. Due to his tender years Ermal was first accommodated with a foster family. Ermir said that he and his brother had an Albanian friend named Ali Karuci, whose surname was also false. In this case, it was a curious choice of *nom de plume*. Ermir explained 'Karuci means Dickhead' in Albanian. Then there was Jetmir Bucpapa, the most important of Ermir's associates. Ermir told Court 8 that Ermal introduced him to Bucpapa in Café Costa in 2005. As we have seen, this was a lie, but surprisingly the Crown were not armed with the full facts about Hysenaj and Bucpapa growing up together in Albania and this didn't come out in court.

Hysenaj admitted that the telephone recording of Murray and Rusha talking was clearly about getting an inside man into the depot with a spy camera, but he denied that he was that person. 'It's rubbish.' He claimed never to have known Lee Murray, and said that he hadn't met Rusha prior to the case. The only person in the dock he had known previously was Bucpapa.

Brother Ermal was a cannabis dealer, and Bucpapa was his wholesaler. Hysenaj explained how he also became drawn into the trade. 'Ermal told me that Bucpapa wasn't prepared to supply Ermal with cannabis any more, because he wasn't paying him the money at the right time [so] I said to Ermal, "I will speak to Mr Bucpapa and see if I can take over . . . being the guarantor [for the payments]."' Henceforth, Ermir took a cut of what his brother made from the cannabis deals. When Ermir was cell-sited calling Bucpapa it was drugs they were talking about, he said, while Ermir suggested that the telephone the Crown called his dirty phone was actually Ermal's drug-dealing phone.

'You are surely not trying to even hint at the possibility your own brother was involved [in the robbery]?' asked David Jeremy, appalled by the lack of sibling loyalty.

'I'm not hinting at anything, Mr Jeremy. I'm just saying it may have been Ermal.'

Asked what Ermal had to say about this, Hysenaj said he had no way of knowing. 'He's fled the country. Last time I knew he's gone to Italy.'

'He's left his own brother to carry the can?'

'I don't know why he's gone to Italy . . .'

'Is he really your brother?' asked David Jeremy, and though Hysenaj assured the court that Ermal was his sibling no records were produced to prove the point. The only evidence Ermal even existed was a log of the police arresting a man of that name in May 2006, for being in possession of a stolen car. He had since disappeared from his address and police hadn't been able to find him.

Ermir emerged from cross-examination as an habitual liar. As he admitted, he had lied about who he was to get into the UK; he gave a false name when he married Sue; and he lied repeatedly to police during his interviews about the Securitas robbery. He told them at first he had never known Jetmir Bucpapa, or been given a lift to work by him. Now he was telling the court the opposite. In his police interviews he said Elvis and Ermal were his friends; now they were apparently members of his family, including a brother who spelt his name differently to Ermir. It didn't make sense.

'You are someone who, I suggest, is capable of repeatedly telling lies,' said David Jeremy.

'I have lied in police interviews,' Hysenaj conceded, 'and I've given my reasons why.'

'There is no one you are not prepared to lie about if you think it will help you.'

Ermir's insistence that it was Ermal using the dirty phone not only showed Hysenaj to be a man willing to finger his own brother for a crime, it was incredible. As Jeremy demonstrated, for Ermal to be the person making all the attributed calls to Bucpapa he would have to have been Ermir's shadow in the weeks preceding the robbery. Hysenaj did his best to explain why they were so often together. Ermal was his brother, he gave him lifts, and they were both in the drug business. But then there was the evening of 20 February 2006, when Ermir had been seen on CCTV at Medway House going into the men's locker room. While he was in the gents a phone attributed to Hysenaj with a number ending 053 called Bucpapa's phone; an expert had given evidence the caller might have been in the locker room at Medway House. Ermir's explanation, that his brother was coincidentally using this phone to deal drugs directly outside the building at the exact time he was in the locker room, gave David Jeremy an opportunity to ask sarcastically whether the pavement in front of a cash depot was really an ideal spot to deal drugs.

Finally it emerged that although Hysenaj didn't have a criminal record as such in the UK, he had accepted a police caution for shoplifting in October 2005. As he walked back to the dock, Ermir may well have wondered whether he had been wise to take the stand at all, having been exposed during his evidence as a thoroughly dishonest person.

The last defendant was the sign-writer Keith Borer, who had managed to keep a remarkably low profile during the trial. Like Hogg, he hadn't always been in court, because he was on bail, and didn't have to be. Unlike Hogg, he never drew attention to himself. This was the way he planned to continue. His barrister, Ged O'Connor, informed the court that his client would not be giving evidence in his own defence, and they weren't going to call any witnesses.

7

'It's been a long and somewhat eventful trial,' Sir John Nutting
told the jury in his closing speech, which he delivered nearly six
months after Trial I began in mid-summer 2007. Christmas was
now two weeks away. 'Your numbers have been reduced to ten.'
There was a time when one felt that more might drop away, and
the case might collapse as a result. 'One of the defendants has
played little or no part,' Sir John continued, referring to Royle,
'and another [Hogg] was called as a witness for the Crown three-
quarters of the way through the trial.'

He explained that the prosecution team had spent a lot of time
examining the planning of the kidnap and robbery, in order to
show the jury that *all* the defendants played a part in this conspiracy, whatever they did or didn't do individually on the night
of 21/22 February 2006. Describing Rusha, Royle, Bucpapa and
Coutts as the 'four main conspirators' in the dock, Sir John said
that the Crown considered the absent Lee Murray 'the primary
and principal conspirator'. Murray was also the leader of what Sir
John termed the 'south London axis' of the gang.

In their evidence, Rusha, Bucpapa and Coutts had portrayed
themselves as the victims of a 'wicked and deliberate plot' in
which Michelle Hogg played no small part. After Hogg had
turned Queen's Evidence, Charles Conway questioned whether
such a deal was in the interests of justice. Sir John told the jury
that in a case involving circumstantial evidence a witness who
could give direct testimony was of considerable value to the
Crown, and crucially Hogg could say who she made up. As a
result, Sir John felt confident in saying Murray and Rusha were
the fake policemen who kidnapped the Dixons. 'Miss Hogg is an
accomplice,' he admitted, but it was her involvement that allowed

her to give this invaluable evidence and, he added in breezy reply to Conway's complaint, 'whether the Crown made a decision which was in the public interest or not is really neither here nor there'. The jury would have to decide whether Hogg was a 'cunning [and] wicked person' or 'a rather simple person with a good memory'. In this matter, and more generally, he urged the remaining three men and seven women of the jury to use their common sense.

It was Graeme Wilson for Rusha had who floated the possibility that Colin Dixon was a conspirator. As a result, Sir John told the jury that a new count was to be added to the indictments. In addition to Count 1, the charge of conspiracy to kidnap Mr and Mrs Dixon and their youngest child, there would be an alternative count of conspiracy to kidnap Lynn Dixon and child only, which the jury could select if they believed Colin was the inside man, though Sir John blustered that no husband would put his wife and child in fear of their life.

Graeme Wilson began his defence speech by commending Sir John on his persuasive words. 'He almost convinced me at times,' said the barrister. 'Then I realized what the wily old fox was about.' He suggested that Sir John had been trying to shift the burden of proof onto the defendants. 'They have to prove everything,' Wilson reminded the jury. 'Mr Rusha has to prove nothing.' His client 'knew nothing' about the kidnap and robbery. He wasn't Shorty, though Bowles or Lupton could be. Wilson tore into the prosecution for doing a deal with Hogg, who Sir John Nutting wanted behind bars at the start of the trial. He did a deal to bolster a failing case. (Sir John sat insouciantly writing his Christmas cards as Wilson made these pointed remarks.) Hogg was 'a proven liar [who] has gone into the witness box and committed perjury', but her lies didn't tally with the evidence of others.

'I don't know whether Mr Dixon was or wasn't involved, but his actions certainly raised suspicions about him with the police,' said Wilson, going on to list the many peculiar things the depot manager did leading up to the heist, during it, and directly afterwards, that might lead one to think he could be the inside man.

Wilson said 'DNA evidence is not what it's cracked up to be' while he brushed aside the fact that police had found plans of the depot in his client's house by commenting that 'only an innocent man or a fool would leave such plans in their bedroom'. Rusha wasn't a fool, but he was a cuckold. Wilson asserted that Philp and Murray 'were at it' behind Lea's back, this allegation providing flimsy support for Wilson's other contention that the dirty phone calls between Murray and Rusha's disputed phone had in fact been Murray and Philp making love.

In characteristically excitable style – thumping his papers, raising his voice, almost hopping up and down at times – Charles Conway reminded the jury that much of the evidence against Jetmir Bucpapa was circumstantial. Admittedly there was a DNA match to the handle of a money bag, but it was 'low-copy DNA', with a mere one in 50 million chance of error (instead of one in a billion). Mrs Dixon said one of the robbers had what might have been a South African accent, but she had failed to positively identify this man as Hi Viz. Conway laid into Hogg, 'this perjurer . . . this accomplice' who had done an unseemly deal with the Crown for a 'get out of jail free card'. Having exhausted himself, Conway dashed to Heathrow to catch his Christmas holiday flight to Miami.

Graham Blower told the jury that his client, Roger Coutts, was an 'incredibly stupid' young man with some unsavoury friends, notably a 'tasty geezer' named Lee Murray, for whom he had unfortunately serviced a red van prior to the robbery. It didn't mean he was guilty, though.

After the Christmas break, Alexander Cameron QC reminded
the jury that in order to convict his client they had to be certain
that John Fowler had *prior knowledge* of the plot to kidnap and rob,
not that he came to think, after the event, that he may have been
conned into helping the gang, which is what Cameron suggested
happened. John Fowler had been 'slipperyed' into hiring the lorry
by Stuart 'Slippery' Royle. It was inconceivable John would have
done so in his own name had he known what Royle was planning. Furthermore, KTS records showed the lorry had travelled
233 miles during its hire period, approximately 100 miles short of
the mileage it would have done had it made the journeys the prosecution said with Elderden Farm as its base. Cameron concluded
that some other farm, apparently nearer the depot, had been used.
It was in fact ludicrous to suggest that 'a well-to-do, well-respected
[family man] coming up for retirement' would allow the gang to
use his £1.5 million property to hold kidnap victims, and as the
flop to divvy up the spoils, on an evening when John's wife and
kids were home.

He reminded the jury of the discrepancies between Mrs
Dixon's description of the place she and her family were held and
the Fowler property, saying her 'mind was polluted' by police
showing her pictures of the farm before taking her there.
Telephone evidence placing gang members at Elderden Farm was
'laughable', because 'best server coverage' for phones at the
Fowler property covered 38 square miles, in which there were
countless similar buildings. As to the disposal of the cash cages at
Friningham Farm, not all the cages were found there, which
demonstrated that 'some of the spoils of the robbery had been
divided up somewhere other than Elderden Farm . . . yet another
indication that the theory Elderden Farm was the flop is the
wrong one'.

Michael Boardman told the jury that Ermir Hysenaj was not

the inside man, couldn't be, according to Colin Dixon, who said in his evidence that Hysenaj's job in the cash depot was largely desk-bound. In the recorded phone conversation between Murray and Rusha, their inside man had been 'walking about . . . pushing cages'. Also, if Ermir had been the inside man, he would have provided the gang with better drawings of the depot than those found in Rusha's house. If he had worn the spy camera into the depot, why didn't anybody notice the bulky battery pack and recording device that went with it? There were no suspicious bulges under his clothing on the CCTV, and the police officer who gave evidence about the CCTV had been 'almost completely wrong in every respect'.

The final defence speech came from Ged O'Connor for Borer. 'Rumour has it [that] when this case is over they are going to make a film about it: the biggest cash heist in history,' the young barrister told the jury. 'We hear the process of casting the film is well-advanced and we have been able to [get hold of] a cast list. Sir John, we hear, is to be played by Sir Ian McKellen. As to Mr Wilson, the big bully in the wig, we understand Vinnie Jones will be starring.' There was much laughter in court about this, and at the rest of the casting of the trial characters, including the ambitious hope that Tom Cruise might play the diminutive Michael Boardman (with Ronnie Corbett as stand-in). 'At the risk of being accused of currying favour, His Lordship will be played by Brad Pitt,' ventured O'Connor, which made the old judge laugh. There would be no need to cast any actor as Mr O'Connor himself, however, or indeed for his client, because Keith Borer's role in the whole affair had been so minor, and indeed entirely innocent.

In order to convict Borer, the jury had to be sure that the sign-writer received £6,100 of Securitas' money knowing it to be stolen, and that in doing so that he was acting dishonestly. The truth was that Borer only realized what he was involved in when he saw the news on TV. He hadn't gone to the police, as O'Connor conceded he ought, because he was scared. 'So at the end of this film we are going to make there won't be anybody playing Mr Borer', a 'simple and honest man' whose primary fault was his naïveté.

In his closing remarks, Justice Penry-Davey warned the jury about Michelle Hogg. 'You should approach the evidence of Miss Hogg with great care and considerable caution,' the judge told them. 'You should see what if any independent support there is for her evidence.' As to Stuart Royle, the jury shouldn't hold his absence from court against him, but taken together with other evidence they might 'draw the conclusion [Royle] has not given evidence because he has no answer to the prosecution case'. The same went for Fowler and Borer, who had chosen not to give evidence. On the afternoon of Thursday, 17 January 2008, the judge sent the jury out to deliberate. He requested a unanimous verdict.

8

Margaret the usher led the ten jurors from the court to an adjacent conference room with a long table, tea- and coffee-making facilities and en suite toilets. The jury would be locked in here during court hours until they reached a verdict, with Margaret bringing them food and relaying messages to the judge.

The first job was to choose a foreman. Juror Nine and one of the women volunteered, the latter being selected because she had previously served on a jury. They then sat down to talk, discussing the case as a group for the first time, and referring to the copious notes they had taken over the past seven months. One juror had filled thirty notebooks. The discussions that took place in the jury room cannot be divulged, but Juror Number Nine says they took their job very seriously. Personally, he didn't allow himself to be 'sucked into the theatre' of the trial, but focused on the evidence of the 220-plus witnesses who had passed through Court 8, including those giving difficult scientific and telephone evidence. He also wanted to weigh the prosecution and defence arguments dispassionately. 'The police are telling the truth, or you are telling the truth? Somewhere in the middle is probably the actual truth.' There was a lot for the jury to talk about, and they didn't hurry. When they hadn't reached a verdict by Friday afternoon, the judge sent them home for the weekend.

On Monday the female juror who had repeatedly been late for court failed to show up on time, apparently due to a doctor's appointment, and as a result the jury didn't resume their deliberations until lunchtime. In the afternoon they asked to see the CCTV film again, which took up most of the rest of the day. They still hadn't got verdicts when the judge called them into court at the end of the day. Before sending the jury home, Penry-Davey reminded them of the inconvenience caused when jurors were not punctual. Unusually, he did so in the form of a short verse which he had apparently composed especially:

> *We've all got a date with Court 8,*
> *When you are late, others have to wait.*

'I didn't think anything of it,' says Juror Nine. But the following day a rumour swept the Old Bailey that some of the jurors were unhappy that the judge had addressed his rhyme to them all, whereas only one juror was late repeatedly. As a result they dictated a three-page note of complaint to Margaret, who handed it to the judge, who made no response, in verse or otherwise.

For the journalists, police and barristers awaiting the outcome of the trial, little incidents such as this were fascinating. There was a general feeling that the jury had been flaky from the start, and the rumoured note seemed to bear this out. The fear was that the judge had managed to upset them with his rhyme, with goodness knows what consequences. We watched keenly when the jury was brought into court each day, looking for signs of how they were thinking. One morning several were wearing black. It seemed to me like a guilty colour. But there was no verdict that day. There was also comment that Juror Number Nine, whom I came to know after the trial, was smiling at the defendants as if he wanted to acquit them. When I later told him this he shook his head and laughed, 'My God, the mind games that go on!'

The jury deliberated for the rest of that week, and were sent home on Friday without reaching a verdict. Juror Nine says they felt no need to be quick. 'For God's sake, it was seven months, what's an extra week or two at the end?' Then, just before lunch on Monday, 28 January 2008, having deliberated for 36 hours over seven working days, the jury sent a note into court to say they had verdicts. The timing was unexpected. Monday verdicts in long trials are rare. The public gallery was empty as the defendants (save Royle, who hadn't been attending court for some time) were assembled in the dock, then asked to stand.

Going through the defendants in indictment order the foreman of the jury was asked if they found the men 'guilty or not guilty'. The reply was that they unanimously found Rusha, Royle, Bucpapa, Coutts and Hysenaj guilty on all three of the original counts. That is they found them guilty of conspiracy to kidnap the Dixons (Colin included), guilty of conspiracy to commit robbery and guilty of conspiracy to possess a firearm. Coutts shook his head. Rusha buttoned up his jacket, and smiled. The surprise came when the jury pronounced John Fowler *not* guilty. Dressed smartly in a suit and tie, as he always was, Fowler listened as he was acquitted on counts one, two and three. He dropped his head with relief on the last 'not guilty'. His heart thumped. His knees felt weak.

The judge adjourned the court until after lunch, sending the jury back to deliberate further on Keith Borer, about whom they had not yet reached a decision. Jetmir Bucpapa was smiling as he went back down to the cells. 'Your man's very cheerful,' I remarked with surprise to a member of his legal team as the court emptied. After all, Jet had just been found guilty on all charges.

'He's very thick, too,' came the reply.

Detective Superintendent Paul Gladstone said he was 'over the moon' with the verdicts which seemed a little strong. His junior officers admitted more candidly that they were 'disappointed' about Fowler. There had, however, always been a question mark over the charges against Fowler. The fact he acted as he did after the event, disposing of the cash cages, and telling lies in police interviews, and the fact that large sums of cash were found on his premises, wasn't enough. As Alexander Cameron QC explained skilfully in his summing up, Kent Police never had the evidence to prove beyond a reasonable doubt that the car dealer had *prior knowledge* of the conspiracy. Fowler may have found more difficulty beating a charge of accessory. Police had considered adding such a charge as belt and braces. But they decided it would be 'a cheap way' to proceed against Fowler. It would be an abuse of process to bring accessory charges against him now.

Upstairs in the canteen I had a cup of coffee with Keith Borer who was nervous as a cat as he awaited his verdict, deriving little comfort from the fact that the jury hadn't felt able to convict him yet, and desperate for it all to be over one way or another. As we waited, Keith assured me he was innocent. 'At the end of the day,

Howard,' he said, 'I had nothing to do with it.' He didn't look me in the eye as he said so, but it was hard not to feel sympathy with the sign-writer, who had always been one of the more likeable defendants in the case.

John Fowler walked into the canteen like a man in shock. We shook hands. 'It was a shame that Kent Police didn't do their homework beforehand,' he told me, already resentful. 'They wouldn't have wrecked my life and my family's life. It's going to be extremely difficult [to get back to normality, but] my plan is to get home in the bosom of my family and give them all a big cuddle.'

The call soon came for the final verdict. We left Fowler, now a free man, and hurried back into court. When everybody was assembled, the jury foreman announced that they now had their last verdict. They found Keith Borer *not* guilty of handling stolen goods. Keith lost no time in putting on his coat and asking to be let out of the dock. 'Cheers, Howard,' he said as he hurried away. 'Fuckin' hell!' In his absence, Justice Penry-Davey dismissed a request from Keith's legal team for a small amount of compensation for the business he had lost and his expenses in attending court. 'His conduct is such that, to an extent, he brought these matters on himself.'

Penry-Davey then thanked the jury for their work and told them that in light of the amount of time they had served they were excused jury duty for life, unless they wanted to do it again. Surprisingly Juror Nine said he would. 'I think the verdict that was reached isn't the verdict that we thought it was going to be at the start of the trial,' he later reflected. 'When we started the trial it was a case of *how the hell can these guys not be guilty*, you know? You do have to throw that from your mind completely [and concentrate on the evidence].

'The judge said if you are not sure you must acquit. He made it quite clear . . . You can't go on emotion. If we'd gone on emotion it would have been a very quick deliberation . . . I would have been glad to have been tried by the jury that did that case . . . Guys' lives are at stake here and there's a massive decision to make . . . We all knew, if we had said "Let them go, they are not guilty," they all walked. It's up to us. The system works.'

9

Despite having only attended one full day of the seven-month trial, Ermir Hysenaj's partner, Sue, believed a miscarriage of justice had taken place. 'I totally trust in him and believe in him. He's been telling me that he's innocent for the whole time, nonstop, and I've never wavered on that. I've never for one second doubted him, so I am absolutely horrified, totally and utterly horrified at the whole thing. It's a travesty of justice really. It's unbelievable. So I'm really, really angry with the jury. But I'm especially angry with the police,' she told me, adding that she *knew* Ermir was innocent. Sue knew Ermir was innocent because he told her that he was.

In an interview with the *Sunday Express*, Rebecca Bucpapa described the guilty verdicts as 'scandalous', and similarly vowed to stand by her man. 'I know deep down he cannot live without me. That's what drives me on.'

Linda Fowler had been reunited with John outside his barrister's chambers shortly after the verdicts. They returned to Elderden Farm to celebrate with the rest of the family, then sold their story, with the help of the agent Max Clifford, to the *Daily Mirror* and ITN. John was back, earning money. 'I know people will always think, "He got away with it," but I know, and my family know, I was not involved in any way,' John told the *Mirror*.

Linda remarked in their interview for News at Ten that John had
served two years on remand for his 'stupidity'.

There was a real sense of occasion when Court 8 reconvened
for sentencing on 29 January 2008, standing room only in the
big, ugly courtroom, still with its water-stained ceiling. When
everybody was settled, the defendants trooped in. Of the eight
who started the trial, only four were left to face the music. Hogg
had done her deal, and was nowhere to be seen; Fowler and
Borer had been acquitted; and Royle was boycotting the trial.
The word was that he had been making such a nuisance of himself in Belmarsh he'd been put in solitary confinement. The four
men who remained glanced up at the gallery to see that they had
a few friends and family members in, for once. Rebecca Bucpapa
sat prominently in the front row smiling down at her husband, as
if they might be going to the pictures together later. Ermir's wife
was absent. When Sue asked Ermir on the phone the night
before if he wanted her in court he said it was up to her, and she
chose not to come. 'I thought it would be upsetting.'

After listening to mitigating speeches, Justice Penry-Davey told
the men that they had kidnapped and held a family at gunpoint,
'under the threat of lethal violence [in order] to get access to that
depot and unimaginable quantities of cash'. This was 'organized
banditry for uniquely high stakes'. The depot workers on the
night shift had been terrified and 'some of them continue to
suffer long-term [and life-changing] effects'. The Dixons had lost
their home, their jobs, and been estranged from family and
friends: 'because of your conduct [they] are having to start their
lives again'. The judge sentenced Rusha, Royle, Bucpapa and
Coutts to thirty years each. They would serve at least half, minus
time served. After this it would be up to the Home Secretary
whether they were set free. None were looking to get out of
prison before 2022, at which time the younger men would be

middle-aged, and Stuart Royle would be old. Rusha shrugged and strutted from the dock. Bucpapa followed with a resigned look. Coutts was impassive.

Penry-Davey was slightly more lenient with Ermir Hysenaj, whom he dealt with last. He said the Albanian clerk was 'not a physical part of the gang that went into the depot', and didn't pose a significant risk to the public. He had nonetheless played a crucial role in the conspiracy. He was sentenced to twenty years. Again, he would serve at least half, less time served, which meant he could be out in just over nine years. The judge recommended that, at the end of their sentences, both Albanians should be deported. Ermir seemed on the verge of tears.

10

After sentencing, the national press ran sensational stories, based on little evidence, about Michelle Hogg having a multi-million-pound bounty on her head from gang members who had not yet come to trial. The insinuation on the front page of the *Daily Mirror* was that Murray himself wanted her bumped off.

Journalists also got excited about the whereabouts of Sean Lupton. His wife told two Sunday newspapers (for a fee) that she now had firm information Sean had been murdered on the night he went missing. Therese said her husband was killed by an underworld hitman, whom she referred to as Mr X, over a £2.5 million share of the stolen money Sean had been given to launder.

It was hard to know what the truth was about Lupton, but his whereabouts were not uppermost in the mind of the man who led Operation Deliver. It was noted that although DCI Mick Judge had attended most days of Trial I, he was absent from the

Old Bailey when the verdicts were delivered. He wasn't in Cyprus looking for the boss-eyed builder either, though he would go and have a look for him later. Mick was in Rabat where, on Wednesday, 30 January 2008, the Moroccan Supreme Court finally ruled on the criminal appeals of Lee Murray, Paul Allen and their erstwhile host. Aït Assou's sentence was reduced from three years to eighteen months and he was released. Sentences against the Englishmen were upheld.

Murray had recently won his nationality case, establishing to the satisfaction of the Family Court in Rabat that he was Moroccan, but the Moroccan crown prosecutor had appealed. So what would happen to him was still unresolved. The truth was that the Moroccans didn't know what to do with Murray. They couldn't send a Moroccan back to the UK. But if he stayed in their country they had to live up to their promise to the British and try him for the robbery. They didn't want to do this. Such a trial would be a long and expensive legal circus, with witnesses and press flying out from Britain. The task of translating all the written evidence into Arabic was enough to put everybody off. Murray was a problem for Britain and Morocco. As his lawyer Ben said: 'They wish they could have him disappear.'

For the time being, Lee stayed in Salé Prison. He kept in touch with his mates in London by mobile phone, he watched TV, he read a lot and amused himself by compiling his IQ puzzle book. He hoped to publish his memoirs, and wondered who would play him in the putative heist movie. Lee fancied the idea of Robert De Niro, but knew the actor was far too old for the role. Lee was making new friends in jail, including a Dutchman wanted in Holland for multiple murder. It was good that Lee had somebody to talk to because the really significant result of this new Supreme Court hearing was that Paul Allen's Moroccan vacation was at an end. Almost two years after he and Lee fled the

UK, and twenty months after they were arrested in the Megamall, Paul was handed over to DCI Mick Judge. No commercial airline would let Mick bring a prisoner onboard under arms. So Kent Police hired a private Lear jet to fly Paul home at a cost to the taxpayer of approximately £100,000, on top of the £5 million cost of the police investigation to date, and anything up to £10 million in court costs.

Upon landing at Biggin Hill aerodrome in England, Paul Allen remarked: 'I'm just glad to be home.' He was then transferred under the tightest security in a military Chinook helicopter to Maidstone where he spent a night in police cells before appearing in the adjacent magistrates' court in the morning to be charged with conspiracy to kidnap, rob and possess a firearm. Paul laughed as he was charged, looking forward to his starring role in the second great Securitas trial.

Chapter Eighteen

AT THE END OF THE DAY

1

Charges against the three girlfriends – Kim Shackelton, Katie Philp and Raluca Millen – were dropped in March 2008, when David Jeremy QC came before Justice Penry-Davey at the High Court to explain that, in light of mixed verdicts in Trial I, the Crown didn't believe it was in the public interest to proceed against the women. Recapping, he explained that the case against Philp was that she helped Michelle Hogg with the make-up, that Shackelton helped John Fowler get rid of the cash cages, while Millen took part in the Herne Bay reconnaissance. 'Each one of them would say I did these things for my boyfriend,' said the prosecutor, 'but did not knowingly participate in kidnappings or robbery.' While Hogg had told the Old Bailey that Philp was present at the make-up sessions, she didn't say Katie knew what was going on; the fact that Fowler had been acquitted made the chance of a jury convicting Shackelton less likely, while the evidence against Millen was very different to that against the two men due to appear in Trial II.

Philp and Millen were formally recorded as being not guilty of conspiracy to kidnap, rob and possess a firearm; Shackelton not guilty of assisting an offender. 'It's a public interest thing,' Detective Chief Inspector Mick Judge commented afterwards. 'It's a case of who do you really want to convict in this? It's the people involved in the robbery and planning.'

The chief inspector then led a police expedition to Northern Cyprus to search for the boss-eyed builder Sean Lupton and, of course, the missing money. Unfortunately the press pack got to Cyprus before the police and scared Lupton away. Mick and his men didn't so much as lay eyes on him, though they established that he was alive and well and had been living quietly on the island, working as a builder. Mick wasn't much bothered, figuring that Lupton had only ever played a support role at best, probably helping Royle get his money out of the country, for which he may well have got a modest cut. The feeling was that Lupton would turn up eventually. Mick remained far more interested in Lee Murray, whom he estimated could have got away with as much as £10 million.

It was a long time since Lee had enjoyed the benefit of his money. Although he had won his all-important nationality case in the Family and Appeal courts, the Moroccan authorities had referred the matter to the nation's Supreme Court. Hearings were scheduled and adjourned without apparent rhyme or reason, leaving the former cage fighter in limbo in Salé Prison. Still, he would rather be there than face extradition to the UK, where he had little doubt he would be convicted if tried for the robbery.

What of the other characters? The five convicted men all now faced further legal action for the recovery of the missing £32 million. Under the Proceeds of Crime Act, they each were liable for an equal share and the judge could order the seizure of whatever assets they had if they didn't produce the money. This would take time. Meanwhile, Rusha and Bucpapa alone among the convicted men attempted to launch appeals against their sentences, but were refused by the High Court. Stuart Royle fell uncharacteristically silent, having disappeared into the maze of the prison system. John Fowler, acquitted in the first trial, was grumbling about damage done to his property during the police search of Elderden Farm, notably holes they had drilled in his walls looking for stolen money, and asking, cheekily in the view of the police, for the return of the £105,600 found in his orchard. So far he has been unsuccessful.

2

Paul Allen and the hairdresser Michael Demetris came to trial at the Old Bailey, in the middle of an international financial crisis, on 8 October, 2008, pleading not guilty to the same three counts of conspiracy to kidnap, commit robbery and possess a firearm. Demetris was on bail, so at liberty to leave the dock for lunch and to go home in the evenings, while Allen had the distinction of being the highest security remand prisoner in all England.

After being flown back to the UK, Allen had been sent initially to HMP Woodhill, a Category-A prison near Milton Keynes. When prison plans were found in his possession, he was moved to Strangeways in Manchester, where he was obliged to wear yellow stripes identifying a potential escapee. Shortly before Trial II, Allen was moved south to HMP Belmarsh, the most secure prison in the country, in his home patch of Woolwich. He was kept here in extraordinary conditions and denied family visits. His legal team were subject to body searches when they came to talk to him, having to remove their shoes before being driven to a self-contained prison block where 'AA' prisoners, including terrorist suspects, are held. Remarkably, Allen was deemed to

warrant a still higher level of security, kept in isolation in a special wing of the block, watched by ten officers, strip-searched
several times a day, and classified 'AA/ Exceptional' because of
police intelligence that he might try to escape.

The police put on a massive show of strength on day one of
the second Securitas trial, with armed officers on parade at
Belmarsh as Allen's van left the prison for the City of London,
while a police helicopter followed, as it would for every day of
the trial, adding to a cost to the taxpayer of approximately
£30,000 a day for additional security. Police paranoia was height-
ened on two occasions during the trial when known villains were
observed taking a close interest in the convoy, cutting into it in
traffic on one occasion and taking pictures on another.

In the unlikely event that Paul's mates might try to storm the
court room, plainclothes officers stood sentry outside Court 12 –
another big, ugly room in the new part of the Central Criminal
Court, directly above Court 8 where Trial I had been held.
Demetris and Allen sat behind a Perspex screen in a high-security
dock, accompanied by at least five dock officers. Demetris, 32,
small and saturnine, wore a shirt and tie, his hair shaved to stubble. Allen, now 30, who had let his thick black hair grow
fractionally longer, was a handsome giant who favoured casual,
open-neck shirts. The men chatted together before hearings but
ignored each other when the jury was present. Behind the scenes,
Paul was reunited with his Moroccan lawyer, Ben, who had
flown in from Rabat to consult with his defence QC, Ian Glen,
a plump, self-satisfied-looking silk with a plan up his sleeve.

Sir David Penry-Davey was once again the judge in the case,
DCI Mick Judge leading the team from Kent Police, while Sir
John Nutting was prosecuting in what would be his last case
before retirement. The distinguished old QC outlined the evidence for the jury in his opening speech, not resiling from the

contention that John Fowler's farm had been used as the flop, and that Shackelton, Philp and Millen had helped the gang in various ways, though like Fowler they had been found not guilty as charged. Turning to the men in the dock, he said that Allen played 'an important part throughout, and he assisted Lee Murray who was arguably the leading light in the conspiracies.' (A court order banning identification of Murray had been lifted, so the press was at last free to report Murray's alleged part in the heist, and did so with alacrity, the *Sun* telling its readers Lee was the 'kingpin'.) 'It is not the Crown's case that the defendant Demetris was one of the kidnappers or one of the robbers; but he did help, so the Crown say, to plan both the kidnappings and robbery,' the QC told the jury. 'So he, too, is charged with the conspiracies.'

The first witness was again Colin Dixon, who seemed slightly more relaxed about giving evidence than he had in Trial I though being, paradoxically, more emotional in his answers. He almost broke down in tears while describing the ordeal his wife and child had been put through, explaining again that he had only cooperated with the gang with the safety of his family in mind. In contrast to Trial I, there was no attempt by the defence to float the suggestion that Colin might have been an inside man. That gambit had failed, and if there had ever been any doubts about Colin Dixon's integrity those doubts were now gone. Barristers for Allen and Demetris had no questions for Mr Dixon who, having explained himself convincingly in two trials, left the witness box an innocent man.

Just as barristers for Allen and Demetris didn't ask Dixon a single question, much of the Crown evidence against their clients was admitted. It was agreed that Allen and Demetris were friends of Lee Murray; Allen had accompanied Mark Scott to buy the Vauxhall Vectra used in the robbery; he had travelled to the Midlands to buy and repair the spy camera, and fled to Morocco with Murray. There was no argument about DNA evidence that matched Allen and Demetris to items found at Michelle Hogg's flat, and little dispute about the bulk of the telephone evidence. Joel Bennathan QC, representing Demetris, didn't deny that gang members including Murray had popped into Hair Hectik the day after the heist to get their hair cut by his client, even though this meant in effect that Demetris had changed their appearance after the robbery.

Although he was not of course in court, Lee Murray was mentioned constantly in the evidence, and the court gained new insight into the cage fighter when a police witness named Inspector John Duffy was called to give evidence. Duffy had known Murray well while serving in Plumstead, and had identified Murray from the Kent Police e-fit after the robbery. He told the jury that between 1999 and 2004 Murray had been of particular interest to the Metropolitan Police regarding drug dealing and firearms in south-east London, describing Lee as 'a violent criminal' whose volatile temper was attributed to the use of steroids. When police wanted to question him, they did so with armed back-up. So concerned were the Met about Murray that they placed him under surveillance and, when he started cage-fighting in the United States, Scotland Yard passed intelligence about him to the US authorities, which was why he was unable to obtain a US visa after 2004. Duffy believed Murray saw cage-fighting as a way to cover up and explain away the money he earned from crime.

3

Before the trial progressed further, Ian Glen revealed his plan to win Paul Allen freedom. The barrister believed that Kent Police had conspired with the Moroccan authorities in an unlawful arrest of Allen at a time when Mick Judge and his men didn't have an international arrest warrant for the suspect. Glen's case was that the Megamall fracas was essentially a put-up job, engineered by the Kent detectives in cahoots with their Moroccan counterparts, in order to get Allen into custody, after which Mick Judge could figure out a way to bring him home. If Glen could prove an 'abuse of process' had taken place, Allen might walk free from the Old Bailey without the jury ever having to decide whether he was guilty as charged. To investigate this matter further there would be a trial within a trial, without the jury present, what is known as a *voir dire* (French for 'to speak the truth') the first witness in which was Allen himself.

Having made his way to the witness box, Allen told the judge how, in June 2006, he was living with Lee Murray in the Villa Samira in Rabat, where they had been joined by Gary Armitage and Mus Basar. The friends spent the morning of Sunday 25 June at home, then drove to the Megamall to watch the football. When they arrived, they found the car park swarming with men in casual, sports-type clothing. 'I thought they were a football team or something,' said Paul. 'When we got out of the car they kept looking [at us and] when we looked at them, they looked away.' The doors of the vans opened, and men with guns and batons got out. 'We run into the Megamall,' said Paul, though he claimed not to know for sure who these men were. 'After a couple of minutes or so I stopped. I said to Lee Murray, "Let's just stop."' They got down on the floor, with hands and legs outstretched. 'All of a sudden these guys just all landed on top of us. Jumped on us, screaming in Arabic.'

'You mean literally jumped?' asked Ian Glen.

'Literally jumped. I was getting all sorts of blows . . .'

'Did you fight back at all?'

'Of course not.'

'Why not?'

'You'd have to be out of your mind to fight [fifty] guys with guns. I didn't know these guys were police. There was nothing to say police.' Paul was handcuffed, hands behind his back, and had his feet bound, after which the Moroccans ran him out of the mall 'battering ram position'. The prisoners were put into the white vehicles, face down, with pillow case-type hoods over their heads. 'We still didn't have no indication this was police. We were trying to communicate with each other, "Who are these guys?"' They were then driven, via the Villa Samira, to a police station where they were tied together on the ground before being inter-rogated individually. 'First of all he said, "Where's the guns, and all the money?" And things like that. I said, "What guns? We have no guns." He was asking questions about the guy Adnane, the guy who was injured in the villa.'

'The man who was accused of stealing some of Lee's money?'

'That's correct.'

In between interrogations Lee and Paul were given putrid water to drink and obliged to go to the toilet in a bucket, still tied together. More questions followed. 'They asked me about the big robbery that happened in England, and about Adnane [and] some cocaine [which] was found in the villa.' Paul admitted to Ian Glen that he used cocaine. They all did, except Lee. Picking up the story, Paul said they were moved to holding cells, segregated from other prisoners, and kept there for two or three days. During this time they were asked further questions, including questions about a house Paul had bought via 'one of Lee's companies'. Finally they were handed copies of what purported to be their state-ments. 'There was loads of documents and they said, "Sign!" It was all in Arabic. I didn't know what I was signing,' Paul told the Old Bailey. 'Basically, "You sign or else", and I did.'

The Englishmen were then transferred to Salé Prison, 'the worst place you could possibly imagine,' said Paul (neglecting to mention the TVs, DVD players, pizza delivery and mobile phones the boys had access to). The *chefs*, as prison officers were called, placed them in single cells in 'the Hole', where they were obliged to stoop under low, dank, vaulted ceilings, the only light coming from a dingy window overlooking the exercise yard. Paul slept on the floor with rats crawling about until the British Vice-Consul helped get him moved to a cell with a bed. His new accommodation was also alive with vermin. Using the loo at night was particularly unpleasant. 'In the pitch black, you could feel a rat on your leg,' Paul told the judge, recalling how he'd kick out and hear the rat squeal as it was shaken off.*

Sir John delegated cross-examination in the *voir dire* to his junior, Julian Evans, an unassuming barrister who'd assisted Sir John and David Jeremy throughout Trial I. It was a big moment for Mr Evans to find himself face to face with a man he'd been reading about and talking about for over two years, largely based on documentary evidence. Suddenly here was the man alleged to be 'Hoodie', an apparently polite, even shy young man who mumbled his answers in a manner that betrayed a basic lack of confidence. The barrister began by asking about Lee Murray. Paul said Lee had a bad temper. 'Was he someone who took steroids?' asked Evans, his question based on information from the Moroccan authorities that Paul and Lee were high when they were arrested.

'Yes.'

'Did you both take steroids?'

'Yes. [But] it's a load of rubbish [to say] they make you aggressive.'

---

*A police officer listening remarked that his sympathy was with the rat.

Evans said the Moroccan police had found 18.5 grams of cocaine at the Villa Samira, and in his statement Allen admitted to being a drug addict who used drugs daily. Furthermore, he said in his statement he'd used hashish that morning and admitted that he and Lee resisted arrest with violence at the Megamall. Paul denied all this, expressing incredulity that Lee would also admit in his statement − as Evans suggested − to being a drug addict.

The next witness in the *voir dire* was Mick Judge, who revealed new details about how Kent Police dealt with Allen and Murray in Morocco, explaining as background that the men were first named as suspects in Operation Deliver three days after the robbery, on 25 February 2006. Murray and Allen left the UK the next day. Kent Police discovered the fugitives were in Morocco in late March, and went out to liaise with the local authorities on 10 April, after which Mick kept a team of detectives in Rabat. The DCI explained that dealing with the Moroccan authorities meant going through diplomatic channels, writing letters of request for intelligence about the movements of Murray and Allen, and the visits of their partners Siobhan and Stacie-Lee.

Other lady friends visited when their partners weren't around. By example Paul entertained Stacie-Lee at the Rabat Hilton, then went on a spree with her and Lee and Siobhan Lamrani-Murray to Marrakesh, where they spent £14,000 in hotels and casinos. When Stacie-Lee returned to England, Paul's girlfriend Jade Bovingdon came out to see him. Mick and his officers watched from the shadows, 'very much wanting to be invisible' for fear Murray might flee before they were able to arrest him. As of mid-June, Mick had an international arrest warrant for Murray, but insufficient evidence to obtain one for Allen. (This was the crux of Ian Glen's argument). The plan therefore was to arrest Murray alone. If Paul was with him, the Moroccan police should let Allen go. Mick was not particularly concerned about Allen, knowing his tourist visa expired on the 24th of the month, at which point the Moroccans would deport him.

Mick flew to Rabat on Friday 23 June 2006 to observe the arrest of Murray, meeting his Moroccan counterparts on the Saturday. He and DC Ecuyer were told the plan was to nick Murray at the Villa Samira on Tuesday. Murray had been behaving out of character in recent days, including making calls from telephone kiosks, presumably so the calls couldn't be traced. There was also evidence that he had slipped briefly in and out of the country via Tangier. It looked like he was planning a move.

Saturday evening the chief inspector received a call at his hotel to return to the office of the Moroccan police chief, who told him there was new information. Murray was flying to Paris with Armitage in the morning. When he didn't show, Mick and Dave went for lunch at the Megamall. 'At this point I believed the arrest [date] was going back to Tuesday 27th,' Mick told the court. After getting a bite to eat, the policemen stepped outside the mall to bask in the sun, which is when the Keystone Kops rushed in. Cross-examined by Ian Glen, DCI Judge denied that he or his men connived with the Moroccans to have Allen arrested. It was only because the Megamall operation turned into a brawl, and police found drugs at the villa, that Allen was arrested.

During cross-examination it emerged that prior to the Megamall operation, DCI Judge handed the Moroccans a dossier on Allen and Murray – so they knew who they were dealing with. Allen's file contained his criminal record, which didn't amount to much. Over and above driving offences, Allen had a conviction and a caution for possessing an offensive weapon (a baseball bat and Stanley knife); a conviction for offering to supply cannabis; and, most seriously, in 2001 he was sentenced to six months for affray (a drunken brawl outside a club). In addition, however, Kent Police supplied the Moroccans with 'intelligence' reports which painted a darker picture. Allen was described as a dangerous man with a 'bad cocaine habit' who carried a hand-gun 'and will use it'. Kent Police likewise considered Murray a gun-toting cokehead. Both had little fear of the police, as illus-trated by a story in the dossier about officers trying to enter Allen's home in England on one occasion. He taunted them, saying they'd need SO19 backup (a Metropolitan Police firearms unit) to get past his door. There was another story about him threatening a police officer, plus numerous references to crack-dealing and guns. A few days before Christmas 2002, he and Murray apparently set upon a man at the Rat & Parrot in Bexleyheath, an incident which culminated in Allen shooting their victim twice in the chest. Fortunately, he was wearing a bullet-proof vest. A couple of years later, Allen was suspected of firing a gun at the Lord Raglan pub in Plumstead as an enforce-ment tactic to control drug dealing in the area.

Ian Glen was outraged by this 'intelligence' file, pointing out that his client hadn't been convicted of any offence in relation to these allegations which were no more than a 'series of libels'. Yet Kent Police had seen fit to present this disgraceful dossier to the Moroccans, which caused them to send fifty armed men to arrest Murray and his pals with the result that Allen was cast into a Moroccan dungeon. 'You had no regard for Paul Allen's Human Rights, did you?' the QC asked DCI Judge, with lofty indigna-tion. Mick Judge replied quietly that he had no jurisdiction in Morocco. Glen retorted sarcastically that it was a 'helluva coin-cidence' that the chief inspector and his deputy just happened to be having lunch at the Megamall when this sting operation took place.

'Mr Glen, I'm on oath,' Mick replied. 'I had no idea.'

At this point the *voir dire* was adjourned to allow Mr Glen time to get access to new disclosure documents, and to accommodate the next witness in the main trial – the turncoat Michelle Hogg.

4

A year since her bizarre appearance in Trial I, Michelle returned to the Old Bailey as a protected witness, living at a secret address under a new identity. For her further protection, Justice Penry-Davey banned publication of photographs of the make-up artist, including press pictures taken outside the Old Bailey during Trial I, when Michelle was a homely little woman with shoulder-length blonde hair. The character who walked into court on 27 October, 2008 was radically changed, wearing most obviously a large black wig that all but hid her face. She also appeared to be wearing joke shop spectacles – Hogg did not wear glasses in Trial I – and a false nose. What little one could see of the rest of her face was mortician-yellow, as if the make-up artist had embalmed herself, which was appropriate in what was Halloween week.

Evidently terrified, even more than last time it seemed, Hogg spoke in a nervous, jittery way, soon rambling off the point. Sir John had to tell his witness to 'pause' so the judge and stenographer could make notes, barking: 'Pause!' when she prattled on regardless. Often apparently on the verge of tears, keeping her face turned from the dock, the witness stumbled through her story in this sorry manner, telling the jury she only realized what she had been mixed up in when she saw news of 'a terrible robbery' on television. 'I just felt sick. I just thought to myself, *Please don't let that be what they've done.*' She panicked and cut up things she had been using on the make-up project, like a 'lunatic', chucking everything in the bin. Pictures of Hogg's flat and wheelie bin were displayed on court screens to illustrate her evidence. When she saw these reminders of her old life, Hogg began to cry. 'It's just sad to see my old home.'

Although Joel Bennathan was gentler with Hogg than Graeme Wilson in Trial I – 'the bully with the wig' – Michelle soon reverted to talking over her examiner, avoiding difficult questions, and telling the jury what a good person she was. Conversely she rarely passed an opportunity to blacken the name of her former boss, the defendant Michael Demetris who watched her impassively from the dock.

'You clearly hate Michael Demetris, don't you?' asked Bennathan.

'No, I don't have any feeling towards him whatsoever. I just feel numb and betrayed,' Michelle answered, though she agreed that even before the Lee Murray affair she had 'issues' with Michael. She considered her boss a bully, and felt that he hadn't given her the training he had promised when he hired her, what she referred to as 'a golden carrot' dangled before her. When she spoke like this, 'Chelle seemed a touch simple. At the same time she had a strange ability to dominate the court and dictate its progress. Court proceeded at her pace, often on her terms, as it had in Trial I. Michelle would not be hurried by barristers or His Lordship the judge. She requested, and was granted, frequent toilet breaks, even when it meant everybody else sitting in silence as she went for 'a wee'. The simplest question could plunge her into a profound silence, as if she was thinking deeply, or perhaps not thinking at all, while she would go off on a tangent about almost any matter that popped into her head.

Michelle seemed to possess a remarkably good memory for some things, yet she told the court she had many mental blind spots, so it was no good asking her about such 'pacific' (sic) details as times of when things happened (she wasn't good with time). She was terrible with directions. 'I get lost very easily,' she said, claiming to not know, even vaguely, where Maidstone was. As she was a stranger to geography, she was baffled by technology; she made a virtue of her ignorance of the law, claiming, for example, not to understand that the Crown believed her a guilty conspirator at the start of Trial I, and had trouble with even basic English. When Joel Bennathan asked her a question that included the verb *infer*, she asked: 'What's infer?' The QC explained. She suggested he use easier words in future. 'Ladybird language would be good.' The word *recapitulate* then cropped up. Seeing the problem, the judge interjected with the 'Ladybird' equivalent, for which she was grateful.

The defence barrister pushed on with this difficult witness nonetheless, and in questioning her Joel Bennathan made surprising admissions about his client. While he was careful throughout the trial to separate his client from Paul Allen, Bennathan agreed that Demetris introduced Michelle to Lee Murray, and brought the cage fighter and his friends round to her flat for make-up sessions. Based on what Michelle had told the police in her original statements, the sessions were to do with an MMA video or computer game. (It was never exactly clear what it was.) Demetris agreed that he and Michelle would do the hair and make-up for Lee, and friends of his who had roles in this project, and so began a series of meetings at Hogg's flat.

Michelle had told the police in interviews that these were social, even light-hearted evenings. (One night Murray pranced about her flat doing an impression of Basil Fawlty, shouting: 'Don't mention the war!') It was true that there had been an all-night session at Hair Hectik on Sunday 20 February, but Bennathan suggested that his client had only played a supporting role, and he never asked Hogg to go to Kent to touch up the disguises as she alleged. The barrister further suggested Hogg was lying when she said Michael told her on the evening of 23 February that he had just been with the boys who were 'lying low' after the robbery.

'I'm not lying,' said Hogg, who then fell into an argument with Bennathan, talking over his questions. What with the builders drilling again next door, it was impossible to hear what was being said.

'Stop!' implored the judge.

During another exchange Bennathan suggested Hogg had been covering up for her friend Katie Philp in her police interviews. Michelle denied this, saying Katie had worked out what the boys had done around the same time she had: after the robbery. 'She was absolutely shocked as well.'

'Did she say anything about Lea Rusha?'

'All I can remember her saying is she didn't want Lea to go back to prison.'

Ian Glen began his cross-examination by asking Michelle about her weird appearance. 'You wear your hair on the left-hand side so you can't be seen from the body of the court?'

'So the defendants can't see me,' replied Michelle, declining an invitation to look squarely at the QC. Glen asked the usher to pull the curtain so the witness, screened from the dock, would feel able to look at him directly. Hogg turned reluctantly and in doing so revealed a face of sheer terror, as strange and ghastly a sight as might be found anywhere in London that Halloween afternoon. 'You are wearing a wig?' the QC asked, peering closely.

'Yes.'

'Have you changed your appearance in any other way?'

'I don't think that's very fair . . .' Sir John rose to protest, reminding the judge that the witness had 'protected status'.

'I want to know is she wearing any prosthetics,' said Glen.

'Oh!' groaned Michelle as if a knife had been plunged in her chest.

'Why?' asked the judge. 'I can't see the relevance.' The jury and the witness were sent out so Glen could explain. 'If she has altered her face by sticking on a false nose, that affects her credibility,' he said, adding that 'she must be barmy, frankly, to come to court wearing a false nose.' The judge said such witnesses did alter their appearance as 'a matter of common sense', but he would allow the question. Hogg re-emerged behind the curtain, at which she plucked to ensure Demetris couldn't glimpse her. 'Miss Hogg, are you not reassured you can't be seen by the dock?'

'You're not going to tell them what I look like?' Hogg asked pitifully.

'You have decided since [Trial I] to lead a new life, to change your appearance?'

'I wouldn't say I'm "leading a life".'

'Have you put on a prosthetic nose?'

'Would you like to come up here and have a look?' she asked, as if daring him to come over and pull it.

'Have you or not?'

'Of course not!'

'Good.'

'I haven't got any make-up on, like prosthetic [make up],' she added, though she had obviously done something to change her appearance above and beyond putting on a wig. But enough was enough and Ian Glen moved on. 'I suggest Paul Allen was never involved in you disguising anybody, was he?'

'No, [but] he was present at my flat, at the salon and in Kent.'

'He was never there when a nose or chin was put on?'

'Yes, he was,' said Hogg firmly. Having been on the verge of a breakdown moments earlier, she now regained her composure

and recalled dates with surprising accuracy. In fact, she gained
confidence as Glen accused her of telling stories to fit the prosecution case. His final question related to the cigarette end found
at her flat with Paul's DNA on it. 'He never smoked in your flat,
did he?' asked the silk, which was a strange argument to pick, as
he had already admitted the DNA evidence and his client didn't
dispute going to Hogg's flat. 'Yes, he did,' replied Hogg hotly,
continuing after Glen had resumed his seat. 'So did Michael
Demetris,' she said, adding, in the peevish manner of the smoker,
that Michael preferred to smoke other people's cigarettes.

It was Friday afternoon. Everybody was tired. In re-examination, Sir John Nutting snapped at his witness, who never seemed
to know which exhibit file she should be looking at. 'The silver
bundle!' the baronet roared when she picked up the wrong one
for the umpteenth time, but there was no point being hard on
Miss Hogg. She would do things her way.

'After this, can I have a wee please?'

5

The *voir dire* continued in fits and starts when the jury were
absent. Ian Glen requested disclosure of diplomatic files relating
to Allen from the British Embassy in Rabat and the Foreign and
Commonwealth Office. The judge ruled in his favour and when
the files were obtained Glen argued that he found evidence here
to support his contention that Allen had been unlawfully arrested
in Morocco, such as a reference to Kent Police's presence in
Rabat needing to be kept quiet, and officers viewing the
detainees surreptitiously in jail – both points denied by DCI
Judge.

There was no love lost between Mick Judge and Ian Glen at

this stage, the QC asserting baldly that Kent Police were lying when they said they didn't want Allen arrested with Murray. They had connived in back rooms with the secret policemen of a 'dreadful regime with a history of arbitrary detention' to trick Allen into custody. DCI Judge was 'guilty of bad faith' in his lack of note-taking about what he did (the officer said he left note-taking to his deputy). As a result, Glen didn't have a paper trail of what he believed had passed between the Kent and Moroccan police, which was 'calculated because DCI Judge knows Mr Allen was incorrectly arrested in Morocco.' In conclusion Glen told His Lordship: 'It's in fact a set-up. That's the truth of it. There was no assault on police [at the Megamall]. There couldn't be [because] they were arrested by armed men, and the confessions were manifestly false . . . The only reason for the arrests was for the benefit of Kent Police while other evidence could be gathered.' This was all part of the 'general corruption of which the Moroccan proceedings are redolent.' Ian Glen asked for a stay of proceedings. The judge said he'd give his ruling later.

6

When the jury were invited back to court – ignorant of this legal drama – they were told that three of Paul Allen's fingerprints had been found on cellophane wrapping discovered near the dumped cash cages at Friningham Farm. An expert witness said the plastic was the same as that which had been used to wrap holdalls the gang stored money in. Fingerprint evidence was even more compelling than DNA evidence. The jury heard that each of Allen's fingerprints were individual and different to every other fingerprint in the world.

The jury also heard how Paul left the UK with Lee Murray

after the heist. The friends were driven to Dover in Lee's Mercedes by their mate Bradley Fitzgerald on the night of Sunday 26 February 2006. The three men sailed for the continent at one minute to midnight, on return tickets booked in Lee's name. Four days later they were in Holland where Dutch police received a call from an Amsterdam jeweller worried about men loitering around his shop. 'He said that two men had been in the shop and he had a bad feeling about them,' Amsterdam policeman Wieger Van Dijk said in a statement. While the officer was talking to the jeweller the suspects walked past laden with carrier bags. The policeman stopped the men and asked for ID, which Murray and Allen didn't have, an offence in Holland that caused them to be arrested. At this point a third man stepped forward identifying himself as Marc De Werd, their 'manager'. When the Englishmen were searched they were each found to be carrying wads of cash, in bundles more than an inch thick. 'I'm sure one of them had four piles.' The cash was confiscated, but returned to the men once their identities had been verified at the station, and a check on the police computer showed that they were not wanted. After this, Paul and Lee travelled to Morocco.

The Crown wanted to present financial evidence about Allen's free-spending lifestyle in Morocco, the evidence outlined for the judge in the absence at the jury. His Lordship heard that when the Moroccan police searched the Villa Samira they found bank statements, bank cards and foreign exchange slips that revealed Murray and Allen had access to a great deal of money. Both had set up businesses in Rabat, with business and personal bank accounts, notably with the Attijariwafa Bank. Statements showed Allen paid €485,000 into one account alone. There was evidence that Paul and Lee regularly exchanged large sums of euros for local dirham, moved money between their accounts, and bought themselves expensive cars and villas. Ian Glen argued that this evidence was inadmissible. There were rules, under the Banking Act, about how financial evidence should be adduced. In this case, the documents were not originals, as they should be, but photocopies; some of the paperwork was in Arabic, other parts in French, and the Crown weren't tendering bank staff as witnesses. Penry-Davey agreed the evidence was not in order. As a result, absurdly one might think, the jury would hear nothing of Allen's millionaire lifestyle in Rabat. Paul looked pleased. DCI Judge and his officers were crestfallen, grumbling about the invocation of the old-fashioned Banking Act. In truth they should have lined up Moroccan bank witnesses.

Ian Glen's victory on the Moroccan evidence was counterbalanced the following day when the judge ruled against him on his application to stay the trial on the grounds that Allen's Moroccan arrest was unlawful, the matter discussed in the *voir dire*. Allen, who'd had a faint hope until now that he might simply walk free from the Old Bailey, shrugged. It had been a long shot, and now it was his turn to give evidence.

Having taken his seat in the witness box, Paul began by telling the jury about his early life in Woolwich where he had grown up with Lee Murray, got into scrapes with the law, spent some time in jail, and conducted a long-term relationship with Stacie-Lee Dudley, with whom he had three children. 'My youngest son he doesn't even really know me,' he said of Kane Allen, who was two when Paul was arrested. Dad had been in prison ever since. 'Terrible really.' Things had gone from bad to worse for the family since the robbery, with their Chatham home repossessed by the mortgage company. Paul had bought the house from Lee Murray, whom he worked for as a driver/minder. Lee had a propensity to get into fights when he was out and about. 'He was [a] bit of a loony sometimes.' Paul described the two Funky Buddha brawls as an example. Dismissing the suggestion

Lee had been attacked by rival gangsters outside the Mayfair club, Paul said he believed the fights were over girls, and described how the blood gushed out of his friend 'like somebody had turned on a tap.'

Asked how Lee earned his living, Paul said that apart from cage fighting his boss had 'a lot of real estate' including a street of rental properties. 'Also, I'm not going to lie to the jury, he did some illegal things,' Paul added. 'Bits of drugs and stuff like that.' Asked why he and Lee went to Amsterdam after the robbery, Paul said it was a good place for Lee to train. They then drove down through Spain to Morocco with Marc De Werd. Morocco was also good for training, and Lee wanted to buy property there. 'It was like a road trip,' said Paul. 'Quite an experience.' Ian Glen passed over what Lee and Paul had done in Morocco.

On a different topic, Paul said Lee often bought mobile phones for him and they changed their phones regularly as part of what Ian Glen characterised as a 'criminal lifestyle', which is to say getting up to such pranks as dealing in stolen fitness equipment. That was how Allen met Stuart Royle, whom he never liked. He knew Roger Coutts better, as an old friend of Lee's; he met Rusha and Bucpapa through Lee, and knew Michael Demetris as a barber. Paul agreed that he had gone to Chesterfield with Lee to buy a spy camera before the robbery, and went back to get the camera fixed with Kane Patterson. 'Lee was talking about filming inside a training camp, spying on some of the fighters.' Murray may also have wanted to spy on his wife.

'Did you have anything to do with this robbery at all?' asked Ian Glen.

'No, of course not,' replied Allen, smirking.

As he admitted to buying the spy camera, Allen agreed that he had gone with Mark Scott to buy the Vauxhall Vectra used in the robbery. 'I didn't know it was going to be used as a police car,'

said Allen who, in common with defendants in Trial I, was happy
to heap blame on Murray, saying he had been one of those whom
Lee duped. Allen also admitted going to Hogg's flat to meet Lee,
saying he knew Hogg had been disguising a scar on Lee's forehead. 'He was very vain, Lee Murray, always looking in the
mirror.' Paul was at Vicarage Park the night the bald caps were
damaged. Hogg had gone 'off her head' and Roger left in a snit
after Lee told him off. Yet Paul claimed never to have worked out
what was really going on.

As to why he was cell-sited in Herne Bay, often late at night,
Paul said he may have been on his way to see a bouncer mate
named Big Marcus who lived in Margate. 'Maybe I was dropping
some steroids for him, because I also sold steroids.' He denied that
there had been gang meetings or make-up sessions at his home
in Chatham. When Lee was cell-sited in the vicinity, Allen suggested Lee might have been drinking in the nearby Hungry
Horse pub. Paul explained away his fingerprints on cellophane
found with the dumped cash cages at Friningham Farm by saying
he might have touched items in the boot of Lee's car. 'The
bottom line is, members of the jury, I had nothing to do with
this,' Allen told the jury with all the sincerity he could muster.
'Do I really deserve twenty-five years or the rest of my life in jail
for buying a car and a camera? That's what you've got to ask
yourself, ladies and gentlemen of the jury. Have I really got to be
away from my family?'

Under a long and relentless cross-examination by Sir John
Nutting, Allen failed to explain away the evidence against him,
including the cell-site evidence, saying repeatedly in a dull, bored
manner: 'I have no explanation', 'I can't remember' or 'I dunno.'
By the third day he'd rather agree with Sir John than even try
and answer his questions, yawning, stretching, rolling his eyes,
saying simply 'whatever'. After a brief re-examination by Ian

Glen, that was the case for the defence. No further witnesses were called and no alibi was offered for the night of the heist. Allen's case seemed hopeless.

7

In contrast, Michael Demetris' defence was impressive. Brisk and well-prepared, Joel Bennathan told the jury that his client admitted doing a hair and make-up job for Murray and his associates, but never suspected he was getting mixed up in a conspiracy to kidnap and commit armed robbery, and denied telling Hogg after the raid that he had just been with the boys and they were 'lying low'. The QC told the jury his client had no previous convictions and, while he hadn't done well at school, he had successfully taken over the family hairdressing salon from his mother, with whom he still lived, and made a go of it. The 'blue rinse brigade' of female senior citizens was the backbone of Hair Hectik, but Michael was ambitious. He had styled the hair of TV presenter Sarah Beeny for a Channel 4 programme and was keen to do more media and celebrity work. Indeed, he saw Lee Murray as a celebrity client, and was eager to get involved in Lee's video game project.

The barber appeared to be nervous and distracted as he stepped into the witness box, but he got off to a good start when the judge asked him genially: 'Do people still have blue rinses?'

'Yes, they do!' replied the barber, and the jury laughed.

Demetris said Lee Murray became a Hair Hectik client around 2004–05, when he asked Michael to straighten his naturally frizzy hair. 'He was extremely vain about every aspect of his appearance,' said Demetris, speaking in a flat south London accent. 'He told me he'd had plastic surgery.' Michael straightened Lee's hair,

and tried out various styles on the fighter. Soon Lee was bringing his friends and family to the salon to get their hair done. At
the weekend Lee and Michael went clubbing together and visited
casinos in the West End. During the summer of 2005 Murray visited Demetris in Cyprus, where the barber was on holiday, and
Demetris helped Murray buy a home on the island. It was around
this time that Hogg came to work at Hair Hectik. Michael found
Michelle to be a very slow worker – 'quite moany [and] always
late.'

After the Funky Buddha stabbing in September 2005, Murray
developed alopecia, which is to say his hair started falling out.
Michael did his best to disguise the bald patches, while Hogg
touched up the scar on Lee's forehead. So far the evidence of
Demetris and Hogg was more or less in accord. In January 2006
Murray told Michael he had been offered a part in a 'play station
game'. The idea was that Murray and his mates would act out
fights against a blue screen. There was a meeting about this game
at the salon, with Murray, Rusha and Philp, who Lee wanted to
do the make-up. 'I pulled Lee Murray aside and asked him if she
was any good. He said he didn't know. I said, "Why don't you use
Michelle? She's done it before."'

Michael agreed that Michelle could work from home for
Murray on the project, not for money, but for the prestige the
salon would get by being credited on the game. Lee would cover
Miche's wages and pay for any special products she required.
Everybody arranged to meet at Michelle's flat on Monday 6
February for the first session. There was a drama beforehand
when Lee came to Hair Hectik to undergo his regular hair-
straightening procedure. This involved Michael's cousin, Little
Mike, essentially ironing Lee's hair. In the process, he burnt the
cage fighter so badly that a piece of his ear came off on the iron.
'He didn't feel it,' said Demetris. 'He's got cauliflower ears.'

Leaving part of his ear behind, Murray went to Hogg's flat in
Vicarage Park, meeting up with Rusha, Bucpapa, Coutts, Royle
and Allen. Demetris was there, too. He said he discussed with
Hogg making up the likes of Royle as characters in the game, but
denied he suggested Royle should be made up like a Sikh. That
was Hogg's department. In the days that followed, Michael
popped in to see Hogg occasionally to check on how she was
getting on.

After a while Michelle demanded more information about the
project. 'To get Michelle off my back' Demetris asked Murray,
who told him they were making a game called *Hit Man*. The
barber denied having a conversation with Hogg whereby she told
him 'If anything dodgy is going on I don't want to be part of it',
but he admitted organizing the now-famous all-night hair and
make-up session at the salon on Sunday 19 December, in the
belief that Murray's game was being shot on the Monday. His
main job that night was applying hair extensions to Kane
Patterson, but he also dyed Rusha's brown hair red and tinted
Royle's white hair brown.

Michael knew Hogg was going down to Kent to work with
the boys on the Monday. 'Lea Rusha told her to go to Kent.'
Michael kept in touch with his stylist by phone because he
wanted her back at work as soon as possible. A plumbing problem at the salon kept Michael busy that morning, after which he
received a call from Murray asking for spirit gum, which might
be used to attach false hair. Michael got the impression that Lee
was at Paul's house in Chatham. The jury had heard that
Demetris had written Allen's address in the salon diary, but the
barber denied taking the spirit gum down to Chatham himself,
as the prosecution claimed. He passed the errand to Hogg, who
was already down in Kent. Michael maintained that he'd never
been to Allen's house, and disputed phone evidence that put

Murray at or in the vicinity of his own home at various times leading up to the heist, suggesting Lee might have been visiting Little Mike, who lived nearby, or even a local brothel.

Demetris also had to explain the return visit to the salon by Murray, Rusha and Bucpapa on Wednesday 22 February. From Michael's point of view, the boys had just completed Murray's *Hit Man* game, rather than a robbery. 'They said [the shoot] went well,' said Demetris, who shaved Rusha's hair, cut and bleached Bucpapa's hair, also shaving a pattern into it, then gave the oh-so-vain Lee Murray his usual treatment.

'Did you ask them lots of questions about [the shoot]?' Bennathan asked.

'No. I was fairly busy that day. I didn't get much time to speak.'

That evening Demetris went to Plumstead to look at a flat he was thinking of buying, and called in on Hogg. 'She was really quiet,' he said. 'I felt there was someone else in the flat [because] all the internal doors were shut.' The news of the Tonbridge robbery was on television. Michelle made a remark about having just been down that way. Michael said he'd seen Murray earlier. Lee had paid him £400 for the all-nighter. 'I told her I would give her £100 . . . She said she could do with the money.'

'Is she telling the truth when she said you were smiling like a Cheshire Cat?'

'Absolutely not.'

'Did you say to her, "How does it feel to be part of history?"'

'No.'

'Did you tell her you'd seen the boys and they were "lying low"?'

'No.'

Defendants who had given evidence thus far in Trials I and II fared badly in cross-examination, appearing sullen, smarmy, stupid and argumentative. In contrast, Demetris remained calm and polite while he was questioned by Sir John Nutting. Moreover, the barber gave the impression of a man trying his best to answer the barrister fully, though he frequently asked Sir John to repeat his questions. Still, it is no crime to be slow-witted, which was the impression one got. In the main, Demetris didn't dispute the story put to him. He *had* got Hogg involved with Murray and his gang. Their stories diverged when Hogg said Michael knew what Murray was up to. 'Looking back now, the way I worked, I should have asked more questions,' the barber admitted, disarmingly. 'It's completely obvious now Lee Murray had other plans from what he was telling us.'

8

In his closing speech Sir John reminded the jury that the men in the dock played different roles in the heist. Allen was at the heart of the conspiracy along with Murray, 'the principal architect and mainspring of this criminal enterprise', while Demetris 'organised and recruited a willing tool in the shape of Miss Hogg whose expertise was important.' It was true that Hogg had changed sides in Trial I, and had charges dropped against her as a result. She had to be viewed as 'an accomplice', but telephone evidence corroborated her story. He urged the jury not to be taken in by Demetris, who was 'not a young *ingénue* who Lee Murray and his followers could have fooled for one moment.' The barber joined in the conspiracy with his eyes open, and was obviously trusted by Murray, so much so that the cage fighter didn't flee the country when Demetris was arrested promptly on Thursday 23 February. It was only when 'Old Slippery', that unreliable rogue Stuart Royle, was arrested on the Sunday that Murray and Allen thought it prudent to skip the country. The fact they fled together was evidence contrary to Allen merely being Murray's 'chauffeur', as Ian Glen suggested.

In a woolly closing speech, stuffed with mixed metaphors, Glen argued that Allen could not be a kidnapper or robber, being simply too tall to be one of the robbers on the CCTV film, based on height estimates given by an expert witness. On another point he asked the jury: 'Where is Paul Allen's money?' If he was a robber, he'd have a share of the proceeds. 'There's no evidence he's linked to any money.' This was brazen. Allen was linked to masses of money in Morocco, but Glen had succeeded in keeping this evidence out of the trial. Ultimately this notional join-the-dots puzzle of police evidence didn't make a tiger's head, as Mr Glen put it, concluding his speech with his final and favourite metaphor; it made a butterfly, and this butterfly deserved to be set free.

Joel Bennathan was much more specific in his closing speech. 'It's all about Michelle Hogg,' he told the jury. Most specifically, it was about the alleged conversation between Hogg and Demetris on the night of 23 February when she said the barber came round to her flat grinning like the Cheshire Cat and said the boys were 'lying low'. Hogg was a 'deeply strange and dishonest witness' and without her evidence – in particular the 'lying low' conversation – there was no case against his client. In this Bennathan was surely correct, but he found more to be said in Michael Demetris's defence. The barrister was able to list an additional ten good reasons why the jury could be sure his client was innocent, including his clear and truthful evidence in the dock: the fact he had not been linked to any of the stolen money, which conspirators had 'coming out of their ears';* Michael didn't dump

---

*Police found £3,200 in cash at Demetris' home, but this was nothing to do with the robbery.

his mobile phone after the robbery as the gangsters did; and he made no attempt to erase the record of Allen's address in the Hair Hectik diary for the day of the robbery. Last and perhaps not least Michael was unlike the other robbers and kidnappers in character. They were men with 'time on their hands' who turned to crime to make a living. Demetris was a successful businessman. Bennathan urged the jury to end what had been a 'two-and-a-half year nightmare for Michael Demetris with three, swift, unanimous verdicts of "not guilty".'

The judge sent the jury out to consider their verdicts before lunch on Thursday 18 December, with a warning to approach Michelle Hogg's evidence with 'great care and considerable caution', reminding them that she had given evidence in exchange for having charges against her dropped. 'You will have to consider whether she is lying about Demetris and others to save her own skin.' Due to seasonal illness, the jury didn't deliberate on Friday, but all twelve jurors managed to get to court on Monday when, after a short conflab, they passed a note to say they had reached a verdict for one of the defendants.

Paul Allen and Michael Demetris were told to stand. The jury foreman announced that they unanimously found Demetris *not* guilty on all three counts. There were gasps in the gallery; the barber sank down below the bar of the dock with relief. Minutes later he was let out, fetched his coat, and hurried away. Kent Police were downcast. 'It's clear that [the jury] didn't believe Michelle Hogg,' concluded DS Andy Nicoll. 'I'm very disappointed.' Since she had turned QE, the police held to the view that Hogg was telling the solemn truth about what she did, and what words were exchanged between her and Demetris. To a dispassionate observer, it seemed that the police placed too much faith in Hogg. One wondered whether this was because she was herself a policeman's daughter. While much of what she said in evidence may have been true, she didn't seem to be telling the whole truth, and came across in both trials as an unreliable lynch-pin upon which to hang a case. If she hadn't changed sides from defendant to prosecution witness, Demetris never would have faced a jury, and if one doubted Hogg when she told her story about Michael coming round to the flat with the Cheshire Cat grin, there was no choice other than to acquit the barber.

The case against Paul Allen did not rely on the evidence of the ditzy make-up artist, and the expectation was that the Enforcer would now be found guilty. By the end of Monday the jury had not come to a decision, however, so the judge sent them home for the long Christmas/ New Year break. Court reconvened on Monday 5 January 2009, when it started to become clear that the jury were struggling. The judge told them he would accept a majority verdict on which at least ten of them were agreed. On Thursday, the jury foreman admitted they couldn't even do that. They were a hung jury, which came as a surprise to most people in court who thought the case against Allen conclusive. Penry-Davey had no choice but to discharge the jury and order a retrial, to be held at Woolwich Crown Court in September 2009. In the meantime, Allen would remain in custody in adjacent Belmarsh prison.

9

During the long wait for Paul's retrial news came from Morocco, in June 2009, that Lee Murray had finally, definitively, won his nationality case and was pronounced a Moroccan citizen. There was no further question of him being extradited to face trial in the UK. Instead, the Moroccan authorities began the process of examining the evidence to see if they were able to try him in

Rabat for the Tonbridge heist. In the meantime, Lee remained in Salé Prison.

When Paul Allen came before Justice Penry-Davey again at Woolwich Crown Court on 28 September 2009, Allen turned his case on its head by entering a guilty plea to all three charges – conspiracy to kidnap, commit robbery and possess a firearm – which he had pleaded not guilty to at the Old Bailey. Ian Glen QC entered the guilty pleas, in agreement with the Crown Prosecution Service, on the basis that his client had not been an active robber or kidnapper on that distant February night, that he hadn't *handled* any firearms, had only been brought into the conspiracy by Murray after the inside man, Hysenaj, had been recruited, after which he had essentially acted as Murray's errand boy, his financial benefit not exceeding £1 million worth of property in Morocco. At the same time Glen accepted Allen was part of the planning and preparation for the kidnap and robbery. The background to this dramatic turnaround was that, having exhausted all stratagems in Trial II, and facing the prospect of a shorter, more focused retrial, without the distraction of a co-defendant, Allen saw guilty verdicts staring him in the face. At the same time Kent Police had struggled to prove in Trial II that Allen had been a robber in the depot, the robber called Hoodie. With a guilty plea, on the agreed terms, the defence hoped Justice Penry-Davey would give Paul a slightly lighter sentence in what was essentially a plea bargain, while the prosecution would be happy to get a guilty verdict.

Paul's partner, Stacie-Lee Dudley, led a dozen or so friends and family to court to see her lover sentenced on 5 October 2009, smiling and waving from the glazed-in gallery. Paul sat behind an additional 15-ft reinforced glass screen, flanked by dock officers with armed police standing guard outside the court room. He smiled up at the gallery, and across at me, as he listened to the closing remarks. Though the Crown now accepted that Allen wasn't an active robber and kidnapper, the prosecution repeated that Allen was 'at the heart' of the conspiracy, doing important work for Murray, who was 'the brains' behind the job, while reminding the judge of the human cost of the heist. The Dixons had been so upset by the experience of giving evidence last time, that they had been off work sick afterwards, and hadn't wanted to go through a third trial, while other witnesses, Securitas workers on the night, continued to suffer a range of psychological problems.

In his closing remarks, Ian Glen said that his client had been Lee Murray's loyal, docile companion and helper for many years. They went to school together, they worked together in the cage-fighting world, and when it came to the heist Lee had assigned his mate a 'menial role', after which they fled together. 'The only gain he made were those few months living high on the hog in Morocco,' said the QC, who explained that property Allen had acquired in Rabat would be forfeited, while his home in England had long since been repossessed. 'He now has nothing to his name. His wife and children are living on benefits.' At the end of the day, sitting in the dock of Woolwich Crown Court, Paul had wound up back within the purlieus of the patch of south-east London in which he had been born and raised, with even less to show for himself than when he started out on his criminal adventure with Lee Murray.

In sentencing, Justice-Penry Davey told Allen: 'Your pleas are very late, but I think it right you have some limited credit for saving a further long expensive trial and putting witnesses through the evidence again.' He handed down three concurrent terms of 18 years, of which Allen would serve at least half. The 1,068 days he had spent in custody since the issue of a British extradition warrant would be subtracted from the sentence, which meant in effect he could be out in seven and a half years. Allen was pleased, smiling and nodding as he left the dock. 'I'm 'appy,' said his girl-friend Stacie-Lee outside court.

Mick Judge and his detectives felt Paul might have got a few more years, but their chief constable, Michael Fuller, was on hand to proclaim the conviction and wider Securitas investigation a resounding success for him, his team and Kent Police. 'I was always very confident we would solve the case,' said the chief, reminding me of the part he personally had played in organizing the investigation team, citing the number of men they had put behind bars and the money recovered. 'The key people are now convicted and the victims haven't had to suffer the trauma of going through another trial – they've suffered enough.'

Of the £52.9 million stolen, Kent Police had in fact found less than half, as I reminded him. 'Still a lot of money missing,' Fuller conceded, but he was hopeful that more money would turn up. Indeed, bits and pieces did on a fairly regular basis, most recently £100,000 had been found under the floorboards of friends of Roger Coutts. It was however impossible to link this and other small finds directly to the robbery, and the truth was that the bulk of the missing millions had almost certainly long since been dis-persed among the criminal fraternity, in Britain and abroad. In the final analysis, Mick Judge guessed that Royle's three missing cash cages, containing as much as £9 million, were smuggled out to Northern Cyprus; another big lump went to Morocco, some via Dubai; while Kane Patterson was probably sitting on another large chunk down in the West Indies, in a bar with a drink in his hand, and a big smile on his face.

Lee Murray had also outfoxed the British authorities, slipping away to Morocco before Kent Police could lay hands on him, then fighting successfully against extradition. It was anybody's guess what might happen next to Lightning Lee in a country with such a strange and unpredictable legal system; also, a place where convicted criminals can lessen their sentence by paying fines. The feeling was that one day quite soon Lee might be walking around in the sunshine again. The comfort Kent Police took was that for the meantime at least the former cage fighter was, as he had been for three long years now, locked up in prison. 'The main thing is Lee Murray hasn't got his freedom, and hasn't benefited from the robbery,' the chief constable told me with a smile, before stepping outside, on a misty autumn afternoon, to do his television interviews.

SOURCE NOTES

Some shorthand terms are used in the source notes:

- Ben is the nickname of Abdellah Benlamhidi El Aissaoui, the Moroccan lawyer representing Lee Murray and others.

- Trial I refers to the trial of Rusha, Royle, Bucpapa, Coutts, Fowler, Hysenaj, Hogg and Borer at the Old Bailey, June 2007–January 2008.

- Trial II refers to the trial of Allen and Demetris at the Old Bailey, October 2008–January 2009.

- FPA stands for the Ferrari Press Agency.

- Police titles are abbreviated. PC stands for Police Constable, of course; DC for Detective Constable; DS for Detective Sergeant; DCI for Detective Chief Inspector; D. Supt. for Detective Superintendent; and ACC for Assistant Chief Constable.

- When I cannot identify a source, I have used the phrase 'confidential source' or 'police source', the latter meaning I was given guidance by a police officer.

The epigraph is taken from *The Engineer's Thumb*, first published in *The Adventures of Sherlock Holmes* in 1892. I referred to the Oxford Sherlock Holmes (Oxford, Oxford University Press, 1993).

INTRODUCTION: ONE IN 53 MILLION

Lee Murray is quoted from a letter to the author, dated 19/6/08. Lee told me in a separate communication, via his Moroccan extradition lawyer, Abdellah Benlamhidi El Aissoui, hereafter referred to by his

English nickname of Ben, that the letter was intended as an introduction to my book.

Justice Penry-Davey lifted the court order banning identification of Murray at the Old Bailey on 2 October 2008, after the prosecutor Sir John Nutting read out a letter from the author arguing that the order had become 'artificial'. The judge agreed.

CHAPTER ONE: NO HOLDS BARRED

Lea Rusha's fight at the Circus Tavern: I referred to my interviews with promoter Lee Johnstone, Lee Banda (quoted) and the MC Phil 'Boo' Walker; also a DVD of the event: *Extreme Fighters: Slugfest* (UKMMAC, 2003).

Lea Rusha's background and criminal history: author's interviews, local enquiries, family records and evidence in Trial I. All quotes are from the author's interviews unless otherwise indicated.

Barred from the Imperial Hotel: Mike Stanley of the Imperial Hotel, Southborough.

Barred from Da Vinci's: Dee Hamid of Da Vinci's.

Works for SD Samuels: thanks to managing director Fred Mills.

Expensive cars: Robert Neve and other interviewees in Southborough.

Jetmir Bucpapa's background: family records, correspondence with David Conquest (quoted); Rebecca Bucpapa's interview with the *Sunday Express*, 3/2/08 (quoted); and evidence in Trial I. I am grateful to a confidential source for help with Bucpapa's early life in Albania; thanks also to Muhamed Veliu of Top-Channel TV. Background reading: *Let's Go Eastern Europe* (New York, St. Martin's Press, 2005).

Inside 34 Hadlow Road: Trial I evidence and local enquiries.

Friendship with Rebecca Weale: her statement in Trial I.

Rusha and Bucpapa train at the Angel Centre: Banda to author.

Rusha's association with Murray: Trial I. (Rusha and Bucpapa claimed in court that they dealt drugs with Murray, who was named by the prosecution as a gangster who played a leading role in the conspiracy).

'Balls the size of coconuts': Lee Murray's 19/6/08 letter to the author.

CHAPTER TWO: LIGHTNING LEE

Lee Murray's background: author's enquiries, interviews, family records.

Brahim 'Brian' Lamrani background and quotes: my meetings and discussions with Mr Lamrani. Also birth and marriage records, and discussions with his friends and neighbours (his 'dress', etc.).

Friendships made at Foxfield Primary School: thanks to school staff; I also spoke to Siobhan Lamrani-Murray (*née* Rowlings); and referred to Murray's comments in *Paris Match*, 16/5/07.

Gurb nickname: Trial I.

Buttmarsh Boys: I am grateful to Mark Hollands (quoted). Thanks also to local residents, including Kelly Bradbury.

Brahim Lamrani beats his son and is cautioned by police: author's interview with Mr Lamrani (quoted).

Gary Armitage background: author's interview with Gary and Kelly Armitage (quoted).

Eaglesfield School: thanks to staff, including Will Walton.

Murray on his intelligence: quoted from his 19/6/08 letter to the author. Also his reference to being a bully.

Paul Allen background: family records.

Basars: birth records, interview with neighbours and Doreen Basar. Evidence in court in Trial I, during Roger Coutts' defence.

Stealing sim cards: Mark Hollands.

Murray and drugs: author's interviews with friends, neighbours and local police; Murray was convicted of drugs offences in Rabat in 2007 and named as a drug dealer in Trials I and II. Allen was named as his right-hand man, and Hussein Basar as his driver.

Mark Epstein on crack-dealing and Murray's custodial sentences: interview with the author.

Murray and Armitage with a stolen television: police source; also author's interview with Armitage who described his further problems with the police, and said he had been in Feltham with Murray. Murray's British lawyer Derek Parker confirmed that Murray had several juvenile convictions, and had spent some time in youth custody. Also police sources.

Heights of Murray and Allen: Trial I.

Use of steroids and black panther tattoo: Trial II.

Murray's dealings with local police as a young man: author's interviews with two detectives who didn't wish to be named (quoted).

Murray's daughter born: birth certificate.

Epstein on the 1999 arrests: quoted from interview with the author.

Lee Murray's fight record: I referred to my interviews with his promoters, interviews he has given about his fight career and www.sherdog.com.

Peacock's Gym: author's interview with Martin Bowers (quoted). For the criminal exploits of Martin and his brothers, I consulted various news reports including BBC News Online, 'Brothers Jailed for Airport Raid', published 16/10/04; and the *Sunday Mirror*, 24/10/04.

Murray marries: wedding certificate.

Murray's tattoo: thanks to Gary Armitage.

All Dave Courtney quotes: author's interview.

Leicester Square fight: thanks to Remco Pardoel (quoted).

For the Royal Albert Hall street brawl I referred to my interviews with friends of Murray and an interview he gave to SFUK Articles & Interviews, 17/9/02, from which I quote: 'Paul got into a . . .', etc. Also the *Sun* (3/3/08) and Pat Miletich's comments on ESPN, August 2008.

Murray claims to be a millionaire: quoted from 19/6/08 correspondence with the author.

Top One Security: Companies House records; and author's discussions with company accountant Anthony Creed and company secretary Josephine Montila.

Murray moves to Onslow Drive and purchase price: property records.

Background reading on the suburbs: *Semi-Detached London* by Alan A. Jackson (London, Wild Swan Publications, 1991).

The 2003 'road rage' incident: I interviewed the Meyer family (quoted) and residents on the Abbey Wood Estate, including Roy and Maureen Price and a female witness whom I quote ('I thought he'd killed him'), but who did not wish to be named. I also referred to police sources; Woolwich Crown Court records; the Crown Prosecution Service;

Murray's UK lawyer Derek Parker; and the *Daily Mirror*, 30/9/05.

Births of Lee Brahim Lamrani-Murray and Lenie Brahim Lamrani-Murray: birth records. Murray is named as the father on both birth certificates.

UFC 46: DVD of the event, which includes backstage footage of Murray and his team, from which I quote conversation; I also spoke with Terry Coulter and referred to www.ufc.com.

Fees paid to Murray and other fighters: Nevada State Athletic Commission.

Murray's visa problems: UFC statement dated 24/5/04; Metropolitan Police sources and Murray's own comments in interviews, including an interview with Jeff Cain posted at www.lockflow.com, from which I quote: 'What it was . . .'

US Immigration footnote: Trial II.

David Meyer's caller: author's interview with Meyer (quoted).

Witness is approached: author's interview with the witness, and a police source.

Cage Rage 8: DVD of fight and author's interview with Andy Geer (quoted).

Road Rage case: police source, Woolwich Crown Court, author's interview with the Meyers and Murray's lawyer.

Murray drives down to Kent: Trial I.

CHAPTER THREE: THE CASH DEPOT AND THE GANG

Murray stopped by police in Strawberry Vale: Trial I.

Description of Medway House and work done there: evidence given by Colin Dixon and others during Trial I; building plans and related correspondence lodged with Tonbridge and Malling Borough Council; my local enquiries; correspondence with Paul Fullicks, Security Director of Securitas Cash Handling Services Europe; and interviews with security industry workers and former Medway House staff.

Jim Easton quoted from author's interviews.

Note Circulation Scheme: thanks to the Bank of England, where I was briefed by a senior official, whom I quote but was asked not to name. I also referred to www.bankofengland.com.

Police quote 'easily protected . . .' from the 1980 planning application for the depot.

Securitas background: thanks to Paul Fullicks, and other interviewees.

The 1983 Curtain Road robbery: the *Guardian*, 18/2/02; *Time*, 5/12/83.

Previous robberies; thanks to Paul Fullicks, Erle Gardner and DCI Nikki Holland of Merseyside Police.

Steve Morris quoted from author's interview.

Fred Mills quote: author's interview.

Lee Banda quote: to the author.

Rusha worked for Royle during summer 2005: Trial I.

Stuart Royle background: family records; author's interviews with family members, including Cynthia Royle (quoted), Diane Turner (formerly Royle) and Vicky Davis (*née* Royle) who is quoted. Thanks also to Cynthia Royle's neighbours and friends in Maidstone. NB: Royle refused to speak with or correspond with the author.

Physical description of Royle: author's observations, enquiries and what Royle said in police interviews in 2006. His criminal history: police sources.

Royle seen to hit his wife: author's interview with neighbours Terry and Sabine Green, confirmed by Diane Turner (formerly Royle), who also confirmed her daughter's account of mistreatment by Stuart Royle.

Kim Shackelton description and background: author's observations, interviews, enquiries and family records.

Stuart Royle's businesses in Union Street: interviews with local shopkeepers.

Vicky Royle's confrontation with her father: author's interview with Vicky (quoted).

Royle leaves Union Street: author's local enquiries, also *Kent Messenger's* interview with the landlord, published 1/2/08.

Royle at Cudham Close: author's interview with neighbours (quoted), who did not wish to be named.

John Fowler background: family records and author's discussions with Linda Fowler (quoted); Derek Horne (quoted); Tom Ryan and other friends, neighbours, business associates and tenants. Also evidence in Trial I, and the Fowlers' interviews with the *Daily Mirror* and *Kent Messenger*, 1/2/08.

Helen 'Nell' Fowler background: thanks to June and Snowy Underdown.

Dave Payne quote: to author.

Fowler's fraud conviction: thank you to Stuart Hill, Court Manager at Snaresbrook Crown Court. Also Trial I.

Rental portfolio: I spoke to tenants of the Fowlers.

Motor dealing at Elderden Farm: various sources including the evidence of Norman Underdown in Trial I.

'Slippery' nickname: Trial I.

Royle owed Fowler money: Linda Fowler to the author (quoted); and Trial I.

Martin Bloe's story was related to me by Sue Broughton of Pelican Court (quoted), and touched on in evidence in Trial I.

Tony Gaskin quoted from author's interviews.

Redpits: thanks to Starnes plc and David Page of Page & Wells, Clamper Craig and Langley neighbours. I referred to Maidstone County Court documents in the case of Redpit Ltd vs Kim Shackelton, Stuart Royle and Christina Royle. Judgment given 20 October 2005. Claim # 5MS03047. Also evidence in Trial I, re the Feb 2005 sales agreement between Royle, Shackelton and Rusha.

Terry Lynch/Swiss real-estate scam: evidence in Trial I, including Lynch's statement to police, and police sources.

Cynthia Royle in retirement: author's interviews with Mrs Royle (quoted) and her neighbours including Ray and Ann Berry. I met Andrew Royle. Former neighbour Terry Green told me he had been asked to witness a loan from Mrs Royle to her son.

Royle to neighbours: author's interviews.

Royle wanted to buy the second house at Redpits: Page & Wells.

Christening party: Vicky Royle, who provided the wording of the text message.

Terry Lynch quoted from evidence in Trial I.

Sean Lupton background: author's enquiries, including an interview with Mrs Therese Lupton (quoted), and her interview with the *Mail on Sunday*, 3/2/08 (quoted).

Rusha and Bucpapa claimed in their evidence in Trial 1 to be involved in dealing marijuana with Murray.

Rusha is arrested re the stolen Mercedes: Royle's letter to Kent Police, dated 27/9/05, read in evidence in Trial I; Royle and Rusha addressed the court in October on this subject in the absence of the jury.

Barbados holiday: Trial I.

Coutts' background: his evidence in Trial I and author's enquiries. Coutts was said in court to have had an affair with the barmaid, but in evidence he said they were just friends.

Siobhan Lamrani-Murray found out about Lee's other family: thanks to Graham Blower and Remco Pardoel. Mrs Lamrani-Murray refused to discuss the subject with the author.

Murray and the tracking device: Trial I.

CHAPTER FOUR: STABBED IN THE HEART

First Funky Buddha fight: as described by Murray in an interview with Jeff Cain of *MMA Weekly*, 28/11/05. The manager of Funky Buddha confirmed two incidents involving Murray outside the club.

Murray double-crossed others: author's sources.

Dave Courtney quoted from author's interviews.

Barbara Murray almost had a fit: according to Murray in his interview with Cain.

The 28 September 2005 stabbing: Murray has given two accounts of the fight, one to Jeff Cain (as above); and one to the *News of the World* (2/7/06). Murray is quoted from the Cain interview, unless otherwise stated. I spoke to the Metropolitan Police about the incident, interviewed witnesses, security and door staff in the area, and viewed CCTV footage of the fight. I also consulted press reports in the (London) *Evening Standard*, *Sun* and *Daily Mirror* (all 29/9/05), and spoke to the owner and the manager of Funky Buddha.

Lee Murray – 'Take me to the hospital' – *News of the World*, 2/7/05. Also 'I lay down . . .'

Murray's condition and condition of the other two victims: Metropolitan Police.

Discussions with Andy Jardine: author's interview with Jardine (quoted).

The *News of the World* interview: thanks to Matthew Bell at the Ferrari Press Agency (FPA). The *News of the World* ran the pictures after the robbery on 2/7/06.

Murray goes back into training: www.teammurray.co.uk, later posted on YouTube.

Murray too badly injured to fight again: author's interview with various associates including Andy Geer (quoted).

Attempted sale of 32 Onslow Drive: Trial I.

Murray's association with Michael Demetris: Trial I. Background: family records, author's enquiries and interviews (one confidential) and www.channel4.com. Also Trial II.

Hogg meets Murray: her evidence in Trial I (quoted).

Hogg background: her evidence in Trial I, family records, local enquiries including author's interviews with Purnell and neighbours who did not wish to be named (all quoted). Hogg's CV, as read in Trial I, and employer statements. Also Trial II.

CHAPTER FIVE: THE INSIDE MAN

Ermir Hysenaj background: court evidence, including his own evidence in Trial I; author's local enquiries in Crowborough; interviews with his partner Sue Lee (quoted); his co-worker Jackie Howse and neighbour Hilda Stiller (quoted). Thanks to Hysenaj's legal team, Hilda Stiller, Muhamed Veliu of Top-Channel TV, Tirana, FPA and confidential sources. Also the evidence of Richard Leslie in Trial I.

Rusha and Bucpapa dealt in cannabis together: both admitted as much in Trial I.

Turnstile gate: author's enquiries, interviews and correspondence with Tonbridge and Malling Borough Council.

Hysenaj's work inside the depot and description of the depot: the evidence of Hysenaj and others in Trial I; author's enquiries and interviews, including interviews with Paul Fullicks (quoted) and former Securitas staff and executives who had worked with the company came forward after the trial to talk about security lapses at the depot. Thanks to Steve Morris, Jim Easton and Erle Gardner (all quoted). For technical details I referred to building plans of Medway House lodged with the local council, and the websites of Securitas, Loomis and Giesecke & Devrient.

Matthew Harmer exchange with Hysenaj quoted from Harmer's evidence in Trial I.

Colin Dixon background: evidence in Trial I; family records, author's interviews; local enquiries in Herne Bay and Littlebourne; interviews with former Securitas executive Erle Gardner (quoted). Colin Dixon's height, which was an issue in Trial I, is taken from evidence at the Old Bailey, 4/12/07.

Further identification of the Dixons' child prohibited by a court order issued by the Honourable Mr Justice Penry-Davey at the Old Bailey, 26/6/07.

Colin Boddington quoted from author's interview. Thanks also to Hadleigh Gardens residents: Steve Hutton and John and Shirley Wenman.

Northern Bank Raid/Tiger Kidnapping: background press cuttings.

Redpits litigation: Maidstone County Court records. Also a confidential source (quoted).

Martin Bloe: thanks to Sue Broughton who is quoted from my interview.

Promise Finance: evidence of Alexander White in Trial I (quoted).

Royle and Lynch: Trial I. Quotes are from Lynch's statement to police about the investment fraud.

CHAPTER SIX: MOTORS, MASKS AND MAKE-UP

Colin Dixon's secret address and 46 ways home: Trial II.

Dixon's training: author's interviews with Paul Fullicks of Securitas and others.

Stuart Royle had his ex-wife followed: author's interview with Vicky Royle.

Tracesmart: evidence in Trial I.

Lupton link: Trial I evidence; police sources; author's interview with Therese Lupton. Also her interview with the *Mail on Sunday* (3/2/08). The author additionally spoke to Tony Harun.

The Spy Shop: Trial I, including the evidence of Mandy and Philip Stevens (quoted).

Allen with Murray at the Spy Shop: Trial II.

Gang meeting on 6 January 2006: deduced from Trial I cell-site evidence.

Conversation between Murray and Rusha: Trial I, including expert evidence of Dr John French.

Rusha's tenuous connection to the depot: police source.

Keyinde Patterson: Trial I and II evidence. For background, I referred to press cuttings and police sources.

Allen and Patterson at the Spy Shop: Trial I.

Allen and Patterson stopped on the motorway: officer's statement read in Trial I. Also Trial II.

The meetings and phone calls between Murray and others were revealed in Trial I.

Hysenaj's behaviour at work on 16/1/06: CCTV evidence shown in Trial I.

Movements of the gang members on 16 January: based on cell-site evidence, heard in Trial I.

Further contact between Murray's phone and the Spy Shop regarding tracking devices: Trial I, including the evidence of Philip Stevens.

Murray linked to JJN, Try & Lilly and Smart Parts: Trial I.

One Stop robbery: police source.

Coutts goes to Cyprus: his evidence in Trial I.

Vehicles obtained: Trial I.

Items purchased from Screenface on 25/1/06: Trial I.

Details about the purchase of equipment from Charles H. Fox Ltd of Covent Garden: Trials I and II. The author visited the shop and spoke with staff, who explained the history of the store, and the process of making prosthetic masks.

Hogg and Demetris: Hogg's evidence in Trial I (her comments and dialogue are quoted from her evidence and statements throughout this chapter, unless otherwise indicated).

The cock-and-bull story Murray told Demetris: Demetris' defence in Trial II, in which he was found not guilty.

Hogg thought the 'pieces' were for a party or 'video or theatrical event': Hogg in police interviews, read by Justice Penry-Davey at a preliminary hearing at the Old Bailey, 15/12/06. Also Trial I evidence.

Murray online: Trial I evidence.

Purchase of the Vauxhall Vectra: Trial I.

Purchase of the LDV van: Trial I; including the witness statement of Thomas Wilkin (quoted) and DCI Judge.

Raluca Millen background: author's discussions with her sister Gianina (quoted) and other enquiries. Millen was named as a pole dancer in Trial I. Regarding the escort agency, thanks to a police source.

What Rusha says he and Millen were doing in Herne Bay: his evidence in Trial I.

Millen at Herne Bay: Trial I and II evidence, when the film of the reconnaissance was played, with a soundtrack recording from which the conversation between Millen and Rusha is taken.

Mrs Dixon's decision not to come to the door: her evidence in Trial I.

Hogg and Demetris: quoted from her evidence in Trial I.

Volvo stolen: Trial I evidence, statement of Mr Lindsey read in evidence; and Kent Police press conference 25/2/06. Thanks to FPA.

Royle and Promise Finance: evidence of Alexander White in Trial I (quoted).

Activity at 33 Shaftesbury Drive: author's interviews with next-door neighbours including Ann and Ray Berry (quoted and recalled dialogue with Mrs Royle). Also Mr Berry's evidence in Trial I.

The red van at Wateringbury Car Sales and Jimmy Royle cleaning it: the evidence of Harish Norda, owner of the Shell service station, in Trial I.

Murray at Hair Hectik: recalled by Hogg in her evidence in Trial I and Trial II.

Sally Davison: evidence heard in Trial I and II.

The making of the masks: based on Trial I and II evidence, evidence of expert witness John Cormican in Trial I and II, and author's discussions with Charles H. Fox staff.

Murray's texts to Gurb: Trial I.

Murray and Rusha and Philp at Charles H. Fox: phone evidence in Trial I.

'Your bird . . .' recalled by Hogg in Trial I.

Murray crashes his Ferrari: Trial II evidence. Thanks also to a police source.

Mission phones: Trial I.

Keith Borer: Trial I evidence, and author's discussions with Borer.

Man seen taking photographs of Medway House: Trial I.

CBA Law and Lawrence: Trial I evidence of Lucy Smith.

Run-up to the robbery: Trial I.

Hogg to Demetris: 'If anything dodgy is going on . . .', etc.: her evidence in Trial I and Trial II. His denial: Trial II.

Tough-looking men at Onslow Drive, Sidcup: author's interviews with neighbours.

Kidnap planned for Monday: although the kidnap was not carried out until Tuesday, 21 February 2007, there is evidence the gang meant to move 24 hours earlier.

Fitting of the disguises at Hair Hectik: Trial I evidence, including Michelle Hogg's evidence (quoted) and cell-site evidence. Looked like Dracula: Trial II.

CHAPTER SEVEN: KIDNAP

Fluctuations in use of money: Bank of England.

Activities of the gang members leading up to the kidnap taken principally from evidence given at Trial I, including cell-site analysis which allows one to plot the likely movements of the gang and other suspects. All timings are from police evidence.

In Trial I, David Jeremy QC said the Crown believed the robbery was initially planned for Sunday night.

Rental of the white lorry: Trial I. The fact that Fowler intended to hire the lorry for 24 hours, from 20–21 February, became clear in the evidence of KTS employees including Sean Hughes (quoted).

Fowler had helped Royle with his credit card before: Fowler's police interviews.

Lorry seen near Elderden Farm on 20/2/06: Hop Engineering witnesses, Trial I.

Fowler's finances: Trial I evidence and author's enquiries including a County Court Judgment against Fowler issued in Hastings in January 2006 (Case No: 5HS02752).

Linda Fowler quoted from discussion with author.

Keith Borer at the farm: Trial I evidence, including his police statements.

'It's massive': John Fowler's police interviews.

Michelle Hogg's movements: Trial I and Trial II. She is quoted from her evidence for the prosecution unless otherwise indicated.

Directions: Exhibit CM/5/96, Trial I.

The use of 33 Shaftesbury Drive was revealed in Trial I. The author interviewed Cynthia Royle and her neighbours including Ray and Ann Berry (quoted and recalled dialogue).

The gang may have originally planned to use Redpits, changing to Elderden Farm at the last minute: police source.

Weather on 20/21 February 2006: Meteorological Office.

Lee Ray: his evidence in Trial I.

Fowler calls KTS on 21/2/06: Trial I evidence of Michael Young, managing director of KTS.

Bucpapa watching Medway House: his defence counsel said in Trial I that this was the Crown's case vis-à-vis his phone use on the morning of the kidnap.

Diane Rowbotham quoted from Trial I evidence.

Mrs Linfoot watches Royle: her evidence in Trial I (quoted) and that of her mother.

Cynthia Royle dialogue: recalled by the Berrys to the author.

Preparations for the kidnap and robbery at Shaftesbury Drive: Trial I.

Colin Dixon's route home on 21/2/06: Trial I evidence, including CCTV footage of Dixon leaving work. I also retraced Dixon's journey on the first anniversary of the kidnap.

Description of the kidnapping: Trial I and Trial II evidence and police sources.

Andrea Rowe saw a man in Thurnham Lane: her statement to police read in evidence in Trial I.

Rusha had reconnoitred the Three Squirrels: revealed in cross-examination in Trial I.

Dialogue with kidnappers/robbers is from Colin Dixon's evidence in Trial I. Mr Dixon is quoted throughout from his evidence in court.

Correct procedure: thanks to Paul Fullicks of Securitas, former Securitas staff Steve Morris, Erle Gardner, and Jim Easton.

The Fowlers at home: Trial I evidence and author's discussion with Linda Fowler (quoted).

Layout of Elderden Farm: local enquiries, also film, maps and photos shown in Trial I.

Directors of Hop Engineering were disturbed by noise: the evidence of David Deacon, Andrew Sisley and others in Trial I.

The kidnap of Lynn Dixon and her child: principally Mrs Dixon's evidence in Trial I (including her quotes and recalled dialogue with the kidnappers).

What the child wore: evidence in Trial I.

Shirley Wenman goes for a walk: author's interview. Thanks also to John Wenman.

Interrogation: Colin Dixon's police statements and evidence in Trial I.

CHAPTER EIGHT: ROBBERY

The description of the robbery is based primarily on police witness statements and evidence given during Trial I and II, principally by Colin Dixon, Lynn Dixon and Medway House staff Gary Barclay, Lyn Clifton, Anca Deiac, Mark Garrott, Michael Laughton-Zimmerman, Ndumiso Mnisi, Melanie Sampson and Alun Thomas. (All quoted and recalled dialogue is from their evidence, unless otherwise indicated.) I also referred to the CCTV footage of the robbery; to my own interviews, including discussions with police and Bank of England sources; to former Securitas Security Inspector Steve Morris; and press coverage of the robbery. Again, cell-site evidence was important. All timings are from police evidence.

Keyinde Patterson was named as a likely candidate to be Policeman by the prosecution in Trial I and Trial II.

'Tonight it's Control Room Surprise!' recalled by Lyn Clifton in his evidence at Trial I.

Tilting the camera should have triggered the alarm: Steve Morris to author.

Colin Dixon – 'You better move his feet' – Colin Dixon police interview, 27/3/06.

Alun Thomas' experience, apart from his evidence in court I referred to his comments in the *Sun*, 28/2/06, in which he recalls conversation between the Dixons at the end of the raid.

Mark Garrott: his evidence in Trial I, including what he remembered the robbers saying: 'We need to get them all together,' 'When I call your name . . .' and 'Just move them. . .'

Lyn Clifton's ordeal: his evidence, and my discussion with Mr Clifton.

Erle Gardner quoted: author's interviews.

Tony Mason's quotes: his interview with the *Sun*, 29/1/08.

Ndumiso Mnisi's ordeal and quotes: apart from his statement, read to the court in Trial I, I referred to his comments in the *Sun*, 27/2/06.

Nobody watched the live feed: author's interviews with Paul Fullicks and Steve Morris.

Gang members use their phones as they exit: cell-site analysis revealed in Trial I.

'Come on, let's rock 'n' roll!' recalled by Mel Sampson in her evidence in Trial I.

CHAPTER NINE: THE FLOP

The aftermath of the robbery in the depot: evidence given by Colin Dixon and Securitas staff witnesses in Trial I, from which they are quoted unless otherwise indicated. As per previous notes, Trial I cell-site evidence was an important source. I also refer to Trial II evidence.

Alun Thomas quoted from his interview with the *Sun*, 28/2/06: 'When they didn't come back . . .'

Colin Dixon said they should 'wait a while', according to Anca Deiac in her evidence in Trial I.

Observations of staff members: Trial I.

First police on the scene: Trial I.

The flop: The Crown case in Trial I and Trial II was that the gang used Elderden Farm as the flop. Fowler always denied any knowledge of this in police interviews, and indeed he was acquitted of all charges.

DS Andy Nicoll quoted from author's interviews. Thanks also to Securitas staff such as Steve Morris who came forward after Trial I.

Paul Fullicks quoted from author's interview.

Sarah Hudson's diary: Trial I.

The bonfire: evidence of Maurice Donnelly and others in Trial I.

It was debated and never conclusively established in Trial I whether any of the items found in the fire had belonged to the Dixons.

Phones go dead/call traffic decreases: Trial I.

Activity at Friningham Farm: Trial I, including the evidence of Ann Day and Paul Burden; also the author's interview with Mr Burden (quoted).

In his police interviews, Fowler said he was assisted by Kim Shackelton at Friningham Farm. She was charged with assisting an offender, the charges later dropped by the CPS, at which time it was made clear by the prosecution that while she may have been asked to do certain things by her boyfriend (Royle) her position was that she had acted innocently throughout. Shackelton was nevertheless identified in Trial II as the woman who helped Fowler dispose of the cash cages. Kim Shackelton declined to speak to the author.

CHAPTER TEN: OPERATION DELIVER

Dumping the cages: Fowler admitted in interviews disposing of the cages at the farm; Kim Shackelton was picked out of an identity parade by Ann Day as the woman she had seen with Fowler dumping the cages

(Trial I). Shackelton was charged with assisting an offender, but later acquitted.

The police investigation: Trial I; with thanks to D. Supt. Paul Gladstone and DCI Mick Judge. As per previous notes, cell-site evidence from Trial I was an important source in plotting the movements of the conspirators.

'This is far bigger . . .' recalled by D. Supt. Paul Gladstone in conversation with the author.

Forensic samples from the Dixons: Trial I.

Inside the Bank of England: author's enquiries at the Bank of England. I quote a senior Bank of England official who did not want to be identified and referred to www.bankofengland.co.uk. The insurance claim: thanks to D. Supt. Gladstone and Paul Fullicks.

Initial audit of missing money: Tony Benson's evidence in Trial I (quoted) 'no less than £51.5 million'.

DC Catt's work: Trial I.

Jean Wilkins quote: to the author.

Lynn Dixon calls her mother: author's conversation with Pamela Parker; also Dominic Dixon's comments to the *Sun*, 25/2/06.

Care of the Dixons in the aftermath of the robbery: evidence in Trial I, during which Colin Dixon conceded he felt like a suspect.

'Line of enquiry': police source.

Paul Fullicks and Steve Morris on Colin Dixon's behaviour: author's interviews (quoted).

Jackie Howse quote: to the author.

Lyn Clifton – 'They wouldn't have got in . . .' – to the author.

All Colin Dixon's quotes in this chapter are from his police interviews, read in evidence in Trial I.

Movements of the suspects after the robbery: Trial I evidence.

Michelle Hogg quoted from her evidence for the prosecution in Trial I.

Rebecca Weale quoted from her statement, read in Trial I.

Royle and the scrap dealers: the evidence of Roger Sugden (quoted) and others in Trial I.

Royle pays Borer, etc.: Trial I. Thanks also to Keith Borer.

Ferrari Press Agency: thanks to Matthew Bell and Adam Gillham (both quoted).

Fowler at the Seat garage: evidence of John Davis in Trial I (recalled dialogue from his evidence and statement). Thanks also to Alexander Cameron QC.

Paul Gladstone quoted from an FPA report of the 22/2/06 news conference.

Hysenaj's evening: his police interviews.

Demetris comes round to see Hogg: her evidence in Trial I and Trial II (quoted dialogue). Demetris' version: Trial II.

PC Brown's notes – 'He doesn't appear to be concerned . . .' – read in Trial I.

Daily Mail and *Sun* front pages; editions of 22/2/06.

Ricky Clark: author's interviews with Ricky and his mother Sue; also evidence in Trial I.

Code name chosen: DS Nicoll.

Chief Constable Michael Fuller is quoted from an interview with the author.

Plan to merge police forces: author's interviews and sources, various press reports and the Home Office website.

Political dimension and relations with the Flying Squad: author's sources.

Murray's name provided by the Met: author's interviews with Chief Constable Fuller and DCI Judge.

Setting up Operation Deliver: thanks to D. Supt. Gladstone and DS Nicoll (quoted).

Fowler and the lorry: Trial I.

Friends in the traveller community: Royle and Brunning in court, 10/10/07.

Burem quoted from Trial I evidence.

Hogg arrested: evidence in Trial I, including that of DC Ecuyer. Also the author's discussion with police sources. Hogg's QC, William Clegg, gave the first names of the other salon workers in Trial I, and requested further information about what use they had been to the police, but after an *ex parte* hearing in chambers this was denied under Public Interest Immunity. I also refer to legal argument on 12/10/07 and 16/10/07, and Trial II evidence.

Martin Brunt quoted from author's interview.

Securitas' dealings with media and reward: thanks to Carl Courtney (quoted) and Paul Fullicks. The reward was described as the biggest ever offered in the UK on Sky News, for example, 25 February 2006.

Paul Fullicks quote – 'Managing people . . .' – FPA report of the 23/2/06 press conference.

Hogg statement to police: Trial I.

Recovery of items at 14 Vicarage Park: first revealed at the Old Bailey 15/12/06; also Trial I.

Sheik/Sikh: Trial I.

Identification of handwritten notes: expert witness in Trial I.

Discovery of Colin Dixon's car at the Cock, Detling: author's interview with landlord Colin Howarth. Also *Kent Messenger*, 3/3/06.

Vehicles found in Burberry Lane: evidence in court, Trial I; author's enquiries and press reports.

CHAPTER ELEVEN: BANG! BANG! BANG!

Hogg released on bail: Trial I.

Secret meeting: revealed in legal argument in Trial I, 12/10/07.

Demetris released: Trial I.

The Dixons in the safe house: evidence of PC Brown in Trial I.

Press at Hadleigh Gardens: author's interviews with neighbours Colin Boddington, Steven Hutton and John Wenman (last two quoted).

Dominic Dixon's comments to the *Sun*, published 25/2/06.

Purchase of the disc cutters: Trial I.

Fowler pays Johnson in cash on Friday: Trial I.

Siobhan Lamrani-Murray stores a bag of money at the home of Ria and Myra Anderson: author's interview with Myra Anderson (quoted); the money was later seized by police, and forfeited at a court hearing in Maidstone, on 6/3/07, under the Proceeds of Crime Act, case reported in the *Kent Messenger*, 9/3/07. I also referred to evidence in Trial I.

Rusha gave bags of money to Christopher Bowles: Trial I. The jury in Trial I was shown CCTV footage of a man identified as Bowles at the Ashford International Hotel. The author spoke to Mr Bowles, who said he coached Lea Rusha. The 1993 ecstasy case: Trial I.

Discovery of the van at the Ashford International Hotel and what was in it: Trial I, including the evidence of forensic scientists, Bowles' statements to police; local enquiries and press coverage.

Adrian Leppard – 'This is the face . . .' – 24/2/06 press conference.

Friningham Farm: evidence of Paul Burden in Trial I and the author's interview with Burden (quoted, and dialogue recalled by).

Mercer arrested and released: police source.

DCI Judge joins the investigation: author's interviews (quoted).

Colin Dixon's statement released by Kent Police on 25/2/06. Thanks also to Paul Fullicks.

Mrs Linfoot: Trial I evidence.

Bowles' explanation 'I just panicked': heard in legal argument in Trial I.

The Bucpapa home raided: Mrs Bucpapa is quoted from her evidence in Trial I; also police evidence; and thanks to David Conquest.

Robert Neve on the raid on Rusha's home: author's interview (quoted).

What police found at Lambersart Close: Trial I.

Tankerton arrest: statements of arresting officers read in Trial I; author's interviews with eyewitnesses Douglas Gilbert and Gala Jackson-Coombs (both quoted); author's discussions with a police source; and the *Sun*, 27/2/06.

Raid on Cynthia Royle's home: thanks to neighbours in Shaftesbury Drive.

What police found at Royle's addresses: Trial I.

Fowler's arrest: Trial I, including his police interviews; the author also spoke to Linda Fowler (quoted).

Fowler and Royle's police interviews: quotes are from interviews read in evidence in Trial I. Thanks also to DCI Judge.

Murray on the other suspects, 'the wallies': note to the author, read to me by his lawyer, 9/3/07.

Theories as to how suspects left the country: author's sources, and press reports.

Murray and Allen become suspects: Trial II.

Murray and Allen leave the country: Trial I; also police sources.

CHAPTER TWELVE: FINDING THE MONEY

Raid on Elderden Farm: evidence in Trial I; press reports; and author's interviews with neighbours, including Kenneth Salmon.

Linda Fowler arrested: Alexander Cameron QC in legal argument at the Old Bailey, 11/10/07. Also, *Kent Messenger*, 1/2/08.

What Norman Underdown told police: his evidence in Trial I.

What police saw and smelled: DS Bartlett's evidence in Trial I.

John Fowler is quoted throughout from his police interviews.

Deptford arrest: statements of arresting officers read in Trial I; also an eyewitness quoted in the *Sun*, 28/2/06; and the author's correspondence with David Conquest.

What police found at Rusha's address and Bucpapa's address: Trial I evidence.

Royle is quoted from his police interviews.

Final audit of the missing money: Trial I. (Footnote: higher figure released by Kent Police, 27/2/06.)

Background on other historic crimes: *Guinness Book of World Records* (various editions); *Bullion: The Story of Britain's Biggest Gold Robbery*, by Andrew Hogg, Jim McDougall and Robin Morgan (Harmondsworth, Penguin, 1988); and various press cuttings.

Martin Brunt and DCI Judge quoted from author's interviews.

What was found at Elderden Farm: Trial I evidence; press reports and thanks to Martin Brunt and Steve Morris.

John Fowler and Stuart Royle are quoted throughout this chapter from their police interviews, read in Trial I.

Lynn Dixon exchange quoted from evidence in Trial I.

Linda Fowler's reaction to raid: to the author.

Press coverage of the raid on Elderden Farm: *Daily Mail* and the *Sun*, both 1/3/06.

Shackelton and CBA Law: the evidence of Lucy Smith in Trial I (quoted).

Agency folders blank: author's interview with Steve Morris (quoted).

Ermir Hysenaj arrest and interviews: Trial I, press reports; author's interviews with Hilda Stiller (quoted), and a police source.

Ermal Kulic used a false name: Hysenaj's evidence in Trial I.

Maidstone Magistrates, 2/3/06: thanks to FPA.

Shackelton picked out of identity parade: Trial I.

Redpits saga: author's interview with David Page and evidence in Trial I from Lucy Smith and others. Thanks also to Starnes plc.

Raid on ENR Cars: author's local enquiries and interviews with Nigel Reeve, Minnie Graves, Peter Chute and Ian Jackaman; with thanks to other workers on the estate.

Money found at Welling: Trial I.

Evans arrest: thanks to DCI Judge.

Nigel Reeve quoted from author's interviews.

The white van found at Friningham Farm: author's interview with Paul Burden (recalled dialogue) and Trial I evidence.

Norman Underdown did some work on the van: his evidence in Trial I.

Bucpapa and Rusha do not answer police questions: Trial I.

Bucpapa and Rusha in court 3/3/06: thanks to FPA.

Raid on Peggy Stapley's lock-up: Trial I evidence; author's interview with Mrs Stapley (quoted). Thanks also to William Fuller and James Hughes (quoted) who explained how he had sublet the lock-up to Lea Rusha's cousin, Jason Hodge, who declined to discuss the matter with the author, but was linked to the garage during Trial I. Ben and a police source were also helpful.

Vehicles at the lock-up: CCTV played to the court in Trial I.

Arrest of Coutts and raid on his home in Harding Drive, Bexleyheath: Trial I; thanks to neighbours including Jacqueline Wall and Pat Mitchell (quoted). Thanks also to DCI Judge.

Michael Fuller quoted from 6/3/06 Kent Police press conference: FPA copy.

CHAPTER THIRTEEN: THE ROAD TO MOROCCO

Murray leaves the UK: Trial I, and police sources.

Money laundering in general: police sources. Background reading: *The Laundrymen: Inside the World's Third Largest Business* by Jeffrey Robinson (London, Pocket Books, 1998).

Moroccan nationality: thanks to Murray's Moroccan lawyer.

Murray's links to Morocco: author's interviews with Ben and Murray's father, Brahim Lamrani; also a report by Majdoulein El Atouabi in *Maroc Hebdo*, 30/6/06; and *Paris Match*, 16/5/07.

Brahim Lamrani told the author he travelled to Morocco on 21/2/06.

Murray and Allen arrested in Amsterdam: Amsterdam Police. Thanks also to Remco Pardoel, and UK police sources. Also Trial II.

Murray and Allen leave Amsterdam/Basar picks up Mercedes: police source.

Mus Basar background: author's discussions with Doreen Basar.

Kent Police not looking for Murray at this stage: DCI Judge.

Tonbridge Hotel: FPA 12/3/06.

Murray's reaction to Southborough find: Ben.

Evidence linking Murray to kidnap and robbery: Trial I.

Arrest of Stacie-Lee Dudley: police source and Trial II.

Police call on Murray's parents: *Paris Match* 16/5/07; and talk to his 'manager', the *Sun*, 17/3/06.

Search of the Murray home: Trial I evidence; author's interviews.

British authorities liaise with Morocco: author's discussions with DCI Judge and reference to an article in *Maroc Hebdo*, 30/6/06.

Murray first named in connection with the heist: author's interview with Martin Brunt (quoted); with reference to his 16/3/06 broadcast; I also referred to the *Daily Mail* and *Sun*: editions of 17/3/06.

Arrest of Siobhan Murray and search of Onslow Drive: Trial I, and police source. Also Trial II (money in handbag).

Fitness equipment and recovery of dirty phones: Trial I.

Thamesmead raid/cash seizure: author's interview with Myra Anderson (quoted); a court hearing at Maidstone magistrates on 27/3/07, reported in the *Kent Messenger* on 6/4/07; the author also referred to the *Sun*, 25/3/06; and police sources.

Murray and Allen enter Morocco: author's interviews with Adnane Ghannam, and police sources.

Morocco impressions: the author visited Morocco, guided by Reda Fakhar of Moroccan News Network. Background reading: the *Rough Guide to Morocco*, by Mark Ellingham, Shaun McVeigh, Daniel Jacobs and Hamish Brown (London, Rough Guides, 2004).

Murray and Islam: Murray's friend Mark Epstein told the author in July 2008 that Murray had converted to Islam.

Villa Samira: author's visit to the house and interview with the caretaker, Mousaffia Abrik, who explained the rendezvous at the water tower.

Money box: author's interviews with household staff, also with reference to court hearings in Rabat.

Dixon child returns to school: author's interview with the child's headmaster.

It was reported in the (London) *Evening Standard*, 14/10/06, that the Dixons might relocate to Australia. Author's enquiries indicate otherwise.

Sale of house: author's enquiries.

Colin Dixon is given another job within Securitas: Trial I.

Questioned regarding his camera and photographs on his home computer: Trial I, during which PC Lorraine Brown's notes were read (quoted).

Ermir Hysenaj rearrested, questioned and charged: Trial I (quotes from interviews); press cuttings, Kent Police and author's local enquiries.

Sue Lee's quotes: author's interview, apart from 'This has left me . . .': FPA.

Hysenaj and Bucpapa famous at home: author's interview with Albanian journalist Muhamed Veliu.

Bag found at Millen's flat: Trial I.

Gianina McLaughlin on her sister's arrest: author's interview.

Raluca Millen's first court appearance and quotes: FPA.

Tony Gaskin's story and quotes: author's interviews.

James Royle's prison visits: author's interviews with Clamper Craig and Tony Gaskin.

Cynthia Royle loses her home: author's interviews with Mrs Royle and her neighbours, including Ann Berry (quoted). Thanks also to Richard Luckhurst who bought Mrs Royle's bungalow, neighbour Trevor Inkpin, and a police source.

James Royle threatened: Trial I.

Linda Fowler attacked: FPA.

Linda Fowler – 'I don't answer . . .' – to author.

Forester's Arms fire: author's interview with neighbours Marjorie and Charlie Hagon (quoted); also Bexley Council (details of the licencees), London Fire Brigade, and the Metropolitan Police who confirmed the fire was treated as 'a suspect arson'. No arrests were made.

Borer first arrested and interviewed: Trial I, quotes from his police interviews; the evidence of police officers and a computer expert; also author's local enquiries.

Murray and Allen's lifestyle in Morocco: author's local enquiries and interviews, including interviews with Adnane Ghannam and Mousaffia Abrik (both quoted). Thanks also to Ben.

Agdal flat: author's local enquiries.

Money: police source. Also Trial II.

Murray buys his villa: author's interviews and local enquiries in Rabat, including a visit to the villa; also press coverage, including the *Sun*, 1/7/07, from which the Moulay Yousef quotes are taken. Also *Paris Match*, 16/5/07.

Paul Allen's villa: author's interviews and local enquiries in Rabat, including a visit to the villa.

Membership of Moving: author's local enquiries.

Shopping habits: author's interviews with Ghannam, and shopkeepers in the Megamall, including staff at Tommy Hilfiger, Gabbana and the Café Armando. Also *Paris Match*, 16/5/07.

Plastic surgery: police sources. Also referred to in Trial II.

Female visitors: author's interviews with household staff Ghannam and Abrik, and special sources.

Michael Fuller – 'unfortunate' – author's interview.

Police surveillance operation in Rabat: an interview with police chief Mustapha Mouzouni quoted in *Maroc Hebdo*, 30/6/06. Also Trial II evidence.

Eurostar story: confidential sources.

Murray asks for his DVD to be shown in nightclubs: author's enquiries in Rabat.

Allen bought cocaine locally: Allen admitted possession and use of cocaine in court in Rabat, 7/2/07.

Discovery of the missing money: author's interviews with Ghannam and Abrik (quoted); also court testimony and evidence in Rabat, notably on 7 and 21/2/07, when Murray and his associates stood trial on various offences relating to this incident. It was established that the three policemen were bogus. Assou claimed he didn't know this, but admitted paying them 3,000 dirham.

Adnane Ghannam's ordeal was described to the author by Ghannam, who also recalled dialogue spoken by Allen and Murray during the assault. I referred to my interviews with Abrik, who was a witness, and to court proceedings in Rabat described in the next chapter.

CHAPTER FOURTEEN: *BOSH!*

Extradition warrant: DCI Judge.

Murray invites Basar and Armitage to Rabat: author's interviews and discussions with Gary Armitage, Kelly Armitage (quoted), Doreen Basar (quoted) and Lisa Guidotti; also evidence in court in Rabat, February 2007.

Mus Basar arrest: Trial II. Police found £14,000 in his flat: police source.

Mus Basar background: Doreen Basar.

Armitage family background: author's interviews with Gary and Kelly Armitage.

Drugs at the villa: established in court in Morocco, 21/2/07.

Arrests in the UK to do with money laundering: at the time of writing this matter has still not come to trial, so I have not gone into the details.

Saturday-night supper: author's interview with the proprietor of Pueblo's Café.

The Megamall arrest is reconstructed from various sources including author's interviews with Gary Armitage (quoted); DCI Mick Judge, DC David Ecuyer; the doorman Said (quoted), the proprietor of Armando's Café, Abdelali Berouayel, and other mall workers and shop staff; also court evidence in Rabat, February 2007; and press reports, notably in *Maroc Hebdo*, 30/6/06; and *La Gazette du Maroc*, 3/7/06. Also Trial II evidence. DCI Judge quote 'I thought . . .' to the author.

The British ask the Moroccans to arrest Murray: evidence in court in Rabat, February 2007; local press coverage and author's discussions with Ben and DCI Judge.

Taken in convoy back to the house: thanks to eyewitness Patrick Bernard.

Police search of the house: author's interview with Mousaffia Abrik (quoted) and Gary Armitage (quoted); also evidence in court in Rabat, February 2007.

Derek Parker hears the news: author's interview (quoted).

Daily Mail report of arrest: edition of 26/6/06.

D. Supt. Paul Gladstone quoted: uk.news.yahoo.com.

Duncan Campbell writing in the *Guardian*: edition of 3/7/06.

Salé Prison: I visited the prison and spoke to Gary Armitage and others about conditions. I also refer to Lee Murray's 19/6/08 letter to me from the prison. Additional background: *Paris Match* 16/5/07.

Background on Abdellah Benlamhidi El Aissaoui, aka Ben, and his relationship with his clients: author's interviews with Ben, as he is referred to throughout these notes.

Speech patterns: based on author's discussions with Armitage, Basar and their relatives.

Boys lose weight, and don't take food supplements: Ben, Trial II.

Armitage refers to Murray as 'the Boss', *Paris Match*, 16/5/07.

Kelly Armitage on why she wouldn't visit: author's interview.

Doreen Basar on visiting her son: to the author.

Prisoners buy privileges: author's interviews with Ben (quoted).

Coutts interviews and evidence: Trial I.

Coutts' court appearance at Maidstone: FPA.

Philp goes to work at Harrods: Diane Rowbotham's evidence in Trial I. Also home searched.

Keith Borer interviews and charge: Trial I.

Michelle Hogg's second arrest: author's notes at the Old Bailey, 15/12/06 and 24/10/07. Her comments to police are from Sir John Nutting's opening in Trial I, quoting from her 13/7/06 police interviews; except 'My boss asked me to do him a favour . . .' and 'working holiday' which were read out at the Old Bailey on 15/12/06; and 'I have now lost complete faith . . .': Trial I. Also Hogg's evidence in Trial II.

Secret meetings: legal argument in Trial I.

Hogg's prison time and nervous breakdown: author's discussion with Jeffrey Hogg, and trial evidence.

Aït Assou arrested in Tangier: interview with his father-in-law, conducted in Morocco on my behalf by Reda Fakhar. Charges against Assou: court hearings in Rabat, February 2007.

Adnane Ghannam bribe claim: author's interview with Ghannam (quoted).

Six police raids in Kent on 9/11/06: Trial I evidence; DCI Judge; and author's discussions with Therese Lupton and Tony Harun (both quoted). I also quote from Mrs Lupton's 3/2/08 interview with the *Mail on Sunday* ('He just said they asked . . .') and her interview with the *Sunday Mirror* of the same date: 'He told me he was going to see a very hard man . . .'

Sports hall next to Herne Bay Railway Station: author's interviews with Tony Gaskin (quoted); Kent Police and local press reports.

Money seized and forfeited from Sean Lupton: court hearing at Maidstone Magistrates 6/3/07, reported in the *Kent Messenger*, 9/3/07. Also author's interview with Therese Lupton (quotes and recalled conversation).

Letter: Trial I.

Harun arrested/money seized/DNA matched the red van number plate: Trial I, and police sources. I also spoke to Mr Harun (quoted).

Sean Lupton's continued disappearance: author's interview with Therese Lupton (quoted), DCI Judge and other police sources.

Ben gave interviews and photos to the press (*Maroc Hebdo*, for example, 27/10/07): author's interviews with Ben.

€3 m in the bank: *Paris Match*, 16/5/07.

Ben on Murray and Allen's nationality: quoted from author's interviews.

Murray on the Moroccan authorities: quoted from his 19/6/08 letter to the author.

London meeting between British and Moroccan authorities: reported in *Al Massae* and the *Assabah* newspapers (editions of 27/1/07).

Salé court hearings, 7 and 21 February 2007: covered for the author by Reda Fakhar; thanks also to Ben. Also Trial II evidence.

Gary and Mus walk free: author's local enquiries and interviews with Ben.

The British intervene to stop Murray being freed: author's discussions with Ben (quoted, and recalled conversation with Murray).

Lupton seizure case: *Kent Messenger*, 9/3/07.

The Murray/Anderson seizure: Maidstone Magistrates Court, 27/3/07, reported in the *Kent Messenger* 6/4/07. Thanks also to Myra Anderson.

Author's discussion with Siobhan Lamrani-Murray: by telephone 24/3/07. Her interview with *Al-Ayyam*, published 31/3/07.

£14,000 in Basar's flat: police source.

Basar and Armitage quoted from conversations with the author.

Murray and Allen at the Supreme Court in Morocco, 2/5/07: author's sources within the court. Thanks also to Ben (quoted).

Seizure of assets and frustration: DCI Mick Judge.

Negotiations with the *News of the World*: author's sources.

CHAPTER FIFTEEN: THE OLD BAILEY

The author attended all the pre-trial hearings at the Old Bailey during 2006–07, and every day of Trial I. All the material in Chapters Fifteen, Sixteen and Seventeen, including all quotes, are drawn from these notes (unless indicated otherwise). My thanks to court staff, the barristers in the case and Kent Police.

Court costs: author's discussions with legal teams. The cost of the Crown case was revealed at a CPS briefing in December 2007.

Juror Number Nine: author's interviews (quoted). NB: This juror approached the author voluntarily after the trial, after checking with the judge whether he could do so, and agreed to be quoted.

Securitas' problems: financial reports at www.Forbes.com (8/7/07); Reuters (26/7/07), *Guardian* (7/8/07) and BBC News Online (7/8/07).

CHAPTER SIXTEEN: THE TURNCOAT

As with the introductory note to the previous chapter, the author attended every day of Trial I and the material in this chapter, including all quotes, are drawn from the author's notes (unless indicated otherwise).

William Clegg QC was described in the *Lawyer* magazine (22/9/03) as 'that master of criminal defence'. I also quote him from this article: 'There are lots of cases . . .'

Clegg's application to dismiss charges against Hogg: Old Bailey, 15/12/06. Author's notes.

Sir John Nutting comment – 'Well, that's set . . .' – to the author.

William Clegg comment – 'New chapter?' – to the author.

Ben's quotes: author's interviews.

Murray to author: letter of 19/6/08.

Juror Nine quoted from author's interviews.

CHAPTER SEVENTEEN: GUILTY OR NOT GUILTY?

As with the previous two chapters, the author attended every day of Trial I and the material in this chapter, including quotes, are drawn from the author's notes, unless indicated otherwise.

Gary Armitage and Mus Basar leave Morocco: my discussions with Ben and DCI Judge.

Murray's reaction to defendants turning on him in court: Murray letter to the author, 19/6/08.

The Crown didn't know Hysenaj and Bucpapa grew up together: confidential sources.

Juror Number Nine quotes: author's interviews.

Verdict reaction quotes are from the author's discussions and interviews, unless otherwise indicated.

Rebecca Bucpapa – 'scandalous', etc. – *Sunday Express*, 3/2/08.

John Fowler – 'I know people will . . .' – *Daily Mirror*, 1/2/08. Also reference to the ITN interview (Mrs Fowler quoted); and *Kent Messenger*, 1/2/08.

Bounty on Hogg's head: newspapers including the *Daily Mirror*, 29/1/08, and *Daily Star*, 30/1/08.

Therese Lupton talked to the *Sunday Mirror* and *Mail on Sunday*, 3/2/08.

Lee Murray's life in jail: author's correspondence with Murray, and discussions with Ben.

Paul Allen's extradition: thanks to DCI Judge. Also Trial II (Allen quote).

Paul laughs in court: the *Sun*, 2/2/08.

CHAPTER EIGHTEEN: AT THE END OF THE DAY

The girlfriends acquitted: author's notes at the High Court, 17/3/08.

DCI Judge reaction: to the author. Also the search for Lupton.

Lee Murray in Morocco: thanks to Ben; also my correspondence with Murray.

John Fowler and the money in the orchard: police source.

Lea Rusha's leave to appeal: denied at the High Court on 29/10/08.

Paul Allen moved: author's attendance at a pre-trial hearing in which Allen wore yellow stripes, and discussions with his legal team. The exceptional circumstances of Allen's custody were raised in Trial II by Ian Glen QC, who discussed Allen's security status with the author, as did police sources.

£30,000-a-day: thanks to a member of Allen's legal team.

Murray the "kingpin": the *Sun*, 8/10/06.

Trial II. The author attended virtually every day of Trial II at the Old Bailey (October 2008–January 2009). Trial evidence is reported from the author's notes, with thanks to the police, court staff and barristers.

DS Nicoll quoted from a discussion with the author.

Murray wins his nationality case: author's police and legal sources.

Allen's guilty plea, and sentencing at Woolwich Crown Court, 5 October 2009: author's notes. Chief Constable Fuller and Stacie-Lee Dudley quoted from discussions with the author. Thanks also to Mick Judge.

AUTHOR'S NOTE AND
ACKNOWLEDGEMENTS

The story of the Tonbridge robbery caught my eye in February 2006 for three reasons. First, the amount of money stolen was a world record. Second, it appeared to be a classic caper, a type of crime story which attracted me; and, third, it happened in a part of England I know well. As arrests were made and money was recovered, I realized just how familiar I was with the landscape of the robbery.

My family are from Woolwich and Plumstead, in south-east London, where Lee Murray was born and raised. I was born in the nearby suburb of Welling, where police found £9.6 million in a lock-up garage. I knew the surrounding London suburbs where Lee Murray, Paul Allen and Roger Coutts came to live intimately. This part of London was my home until I was twenty. It is where I went to school, and started work as a journalist. The suburbs of south-east London merge into Kent, the county where the heist took place, and where the other significant characters are from, and Kent is very familiar to me, too.

Personal connections gave me a foreknowledge and feeling for the place and the characters of the story. What I mean is I felt I knew these sort of people, how they talked and lived. But that didn't mean researching the book was easy. Criminals are often show-offs, but they are also secretive. To delve into their affairs in order to write an investigative, as opposed to a hagiographic, book is, in a sense, to cross them. The process of researching and writing *Heist* was difficult. Dealing with these characters, one sometimes felt uncomfortable.

Work on this book also went on far longer than I originally expected, with numerous delays in bringing the defendants to trial. I felt encouraged at the start of the police investigation to see how many suspects Kent Police rounded up, and what quick work they made of it. Then came the decision to divide those who had been charged into two groups, with Trial I starting belatedly in the summer of 2007. It ran months over schedule, eventually finishing in January 2008, which pushed the start date for Trial II back to October 2008, two and a half years after the heist. During this time several people who had originally been charged were acquitted. Others whom the police wanted to bring to trial remained, for various reasons, beyond their reach. The fact that two of the main suspects, Murray and Allen, travelled to Morocco after the robbery, then resisted extradition, made everything far more complicated. Kent Police struggled long and hard to get these men to trial, and so long as their legal situation was unresolved, I didn't have a publishable book.

Despite all these problems, I continued working on *Heist*. I wrote it concurrently with events, so the book could be brought out as expeditiously as possible once the legal issues had been settled. The fact that the book can be published now is only because of all the work that went into the project beforehand. *Heist* wasn't written quickly. On the contrary, I have worked on it steadily for three years. The amount of time it took was unforeseen, and inconvenient, but as the years passed, and I stuck with it, I found that my knowledge of the story widened and deepened. Trial I lasted seven months. I was in court every day. Inevitably, one gets to know a story well in those circumstances, and forges relationships with many of the characters involved.

Aside from the gangsters, and the police officers, I probably now know the story of the heist as well as anybody. That isn't to say I know everything about it. As I have already mentioned, crime is a secretive business, and even when you study a caper as closely as I have studied this one mysteries remain. The reader will notice that in the book I occasionally suggest something may have happened in a certain way, with caveat words such as 'maybe', 'possibly', or 'probably'. My experience is that some readers are put off by this kind of writing, but they shouldn't be. The intention is to suggest a solution where there is doubt, based on everything one knows, rather than asserting fact where there are only possible answers. My knowledge of these events is not universal or complete. The police don't know all the answers either. Ultimately it is up to you, the reader, to make your mind up about the grey areas of the story, based on the evidence. I invite you to do so. Solving mysteries is part of the fun of reading about crime.

In using the word fun in the previous paragraph I am reminded that, of course, this robbery was a terrifying experience for the Dixon family, who were kidnapped by the gang, and for the cash-depot staff who were held hostage in the early hours of 22 February 2006. It is true to say that the heist gang behaved as cowards and bullies, and that the way they treated the Dixon child, in particular, is despicable. Doubly so because many of these gangsters are fathers themselves, with young children, so they were terrorizing a kid of an age with their kids, for money. That is the level of these men. But it is also true that nobody was killed in the heist, or even seriously injured, and the story of what happened *is* full of interest, drama and, yes, fun. I smiled and laughed many times at these hopeless crooks, this bunch of misfits who pulled off the world's biggest cash robbery, but didn't seem to know what to do next.

Researching *Heist* was a journalistic exercise in many ways and I am grateful to several colleagues in the press who helped me. I was a newspaperman for the first thirteen years of my career, becoming a full-time author in 1997, and I encountered several old friends and acquaintances working on this book. My thanks to Geoff Garvey, who gave me my first job in journalism, hiring me in the early 1980s to work at the Ferrari Press Agency, in Sidcup, just down the road from where Lee Murray came to live. Geoff is a fine fellow, full of useful information and good, cheerful advice. He is also an experienced crime reporter, formerly crime correspondent for the *Evening Standard*. So I thought it appropriate to dedicate this book to him, dealing as it does with a crime in his own back yard.

The Ferrari Press Agency continues to provide stories to the national press from south-east London and Kent, and the Tonbridge robbery happened on Ferrari's patch in 2006. I am grateful to the current owners, Matthew Bell and Adam Gillham; and to Martin Brunt of Sky News, whom I worked with at the agency as a young man. More widely, I would like to mention the following colleagues in the media: Rajy Abdellah of *Maroc Hebdo* in Casablanca; Jeremy Britton and Chris Summers of the BBC; Duncan Campbell of the *Guardian*; Reda Fakhar and Said Benomar of Moroccan Press Network in Rabat; John-Paul Ford Rojas at the Press Association; Samana Haq at ITN in London; Chris Hunter, Eve Parish and Helen Wagstaff of the *Kent Messenger*; David McGee at the *News of the World*; David St George, doyen of the Old Bailey press room; and Muhamed Veliu of Top-Channel TV in Tirana.

I am unable to identify all my sources. But the following individuals were helpful in different ways, some at great length over a long period of time, others with the odd word: Moussaffia Abrik, Mrs Houssein Al Fadiani, Myra and Raina Anderson, Gary and Kelly Armitage, Andrew Bailey, Lee Banda, Nicola Barnes, Doreen Basar, Basil Beach, Joel Bennathan QC, Patrick Bernard, Abdelai Berouayel, Ray and Ann Berry, Kelly Betts, Graham Blower, Michael Boardman, Colin Boddington, Keith Borer, Martin Bowers, Christopher Bowles, Kelly Bradbury, Sue Broughton, Jetmir Bucpapa, Paul Burden, Alexander Cameron QC, Dexter Casey, Paul Chamberlain, Terry Charles, Peter Chute, Sue and Ricky Clark, Chris Clarke and Liz Bailey, William Clegg QC, Geoff Crabtree (and the staff at Starnes plc), 'Clamper' Craig, Lyn Clifton, David Conquest, Charles Conway, Terry Coulter, Carl Courtney, Dave Courtney, Brenda Coutts, DS Mark Cowens, Anthony Creed, James Curtis, Vicky Davis (*née* Royle), Ian Dean, Stacie-Lee Dudley, Jim Easton, DC David Ecuyer, Abdellah Benlamhidi 'Ben' El Aissaoui, Mark 'the Beast' Epstein, Julian Evans, Simon Evenden, Michael Fermor, David Ferris, John and Linda Fowler, Chief Constable Michael Fuller, William Fuller, Paul Fullicks, Erle Gardner, Tony Gaskin, Andy Geer, Remco Gerretsen (and colleagues with the Amsterdam Police), Adnane Ghannam, Douglas Gilbert, Robert Girling, D. Supt. Paul Gladstone, Ian Glen QC, Wendy Gordon, Minnie Graves, Terry and Sabine Green, Lisa Guidotti, Charlie and Marjorie Hagon, Dee Hamid, Mary Harris, Tony Harun, Stuart Hill at Snaresbrook Crown Court, Steve Hobbs, Jeff Hogg, Peter and Jenny Hollamby, DCI Nikki Holland, Paul Hollands, Derek Horne, Colin Howarth, Jackie Howse, James Hughes, Steve Hutton, Ermir Hysenaj, Jonathan Ingram, Trevor Inkpin, Ian Jackaman, Gala Jackson-Coombes, Andy Jardine, Lee Johstone, Jean and Pat Jones, DCI Mick Judge, DC Bob Kelly, DCI Nicky Kiell, Greg Krieger, Brahim Lamrani, Lee and Siobhan Lamrani-Murray, Ann Lee at Charles H. Fox Ltd., Sue Lee (Hysenaj), DC

Clive Llewellyn, Richard Luckhurst, Therese Lupton, Babobahai Master, Gianina and Paul McLaughlin, Jimmy Man, David Meyer and family, Mick Milgate, Fred Mills, Guy Mitchell, Pat Mitchell, Josephine Montila, DC Mick Morrell, Pete Morris at the Crown Prosecution Service, Steve Morris, Robert Neve, Darren Nicholls, DS Andy Nicoll, Karen Noble, Sir John Nutting QC, Ged O'Connor, Sharon Owen, David Page, Jon Parker, Remco Pardoel, Derek Parker (Murray's British lawyer), Pamela and Derek Parker (Lynn Dixon's mother and step-father), Dave Payne, Roy Price, Sylvia Purnell, Nigel Reeve, Cynthia Royle, Louise Ryan, Tom Ryan, Lea Rusha, Kenneth Salmon, Jatinder Sokhol, Shoel Stadler, Mike Stanley, Peggy Stapley, Hilda Stiller, Kate Stone, Dougie Truman, Diane Turner (formerly Royle), June and Snowy Underdown, Jacqueline Wall, Will Walton, Grant 'the Ref' Waterman, Jacqueline Weller and Jim Watts, Nigel and Karen at Wickham Tools, John and Shirley Wenman, Jean Wilkins, Leslee Williams, Graeme Wilson, Patrick Withall and DC Alastair Worton.

Thank you to Kent Police and the staff at the Old Bailey; to Andrew Gordon who commissioned this book for Simon & Schuster, and to Kerri Sharp who took over and edited it after Andrew moved on. Rory Scarfe helped with the pictures and Martin Soames was our legal guide. Finally thank you to my agents, Gordon Wise and Tally Garner, at Curtis Brown.

INDEX